Trust Management and Information Security

Trust Management and Information Security

Edited by **Stephen Mason**

WILLFORD PRESS
New York

Published by Willford Press,
118-35 Queens Blvd., Suite 400,
Forest Hills, NY 11375, USA
www.willfordpress.com

Trust Management and Information Security
Edited by Stephen Mason

International Standard Book Number: 978-1-68285-275-0 (Hardback)

Printed in the United States of America.

Contents

Preface   VII

Chapter 1   **Efficient semi-automated assessment of annotations trustworthiness**   1
            Davide Ceolin, Archana Nottamkandath and Wan Fokkink

Chapter 2   **A trust-based framework for vehicular travel with non-binary reports and its**
            validation via an extensive simulation testbed   32
            Robin Cohen, Jie Zhang, John Finnson, Thomas Tran and Umar F Minhas

Chapter 3   **Trust-based Decision-making for the Adaptation of Public Displays in**
            Changing Social Contexts   63
            Michael Wißner, Stephan Hammer, Ekatarina Kurdyukova and Elisabeth André

Chapter 4   **Reusable components for online reputation systems**   86
            Johannes Sänger, Christian Richthammer and Günther Pernul

Chapter 5   **Two sides of the coin: measuring and communicating the trustworthiness of**
            online information   107
            Jason RC Nurse, Ioannis Agrafiotis, Michael Goldsmith, Sadie Creese and Koen
            Lamberts

Chapter 6   **A decentralized trustworthiness estimation model for open, multiagent systems**
            (DTMAS)   127
            Abdullah M Aref and Thomas T Tran

Chapter 7   **Understanding user perceptions of transparent authentication on a**
            mobile device   147
            Heather Crawford and Karen Renaud

Chapter 8   **How buyers perceive the credibility of advisors in online marketplace: review**
            balance, review count and misattribution   175
            Kewen Wu, Zeinab Noorian, Julita Vassileva and Ifeoma Adaji

Chapter 9   **Local user-centric identity management**   193
            Audun Jøsang, Christophe Rosenberger, Laurent Miralabé, Henning Klevjer,
            Kent A Varmedal, Jérôme Daveau, Knut Eilif Husa and Petter Taugbøl

Chapter 10 **Detecting Sybil attacks in vehicular networks**   221
            Muhammad Al-Mutaz, Levi Malott and Sriram Chellappan

Chapter 11   **Efficient private multi-party computations of trust in the presence of curious and malicious users**   **240**
Shlomi Dolev, Niv Gilboa and Marina Kopeetsky

Permissions

List of Contributors

Preface

As the internet grows and connects the world in new ways, information security has become significant. The book combines perspectives of the leading researchers in the field of trust management and information security and discusses important theories and practical methods. It presents a holistic view of security management, risk management and the formulation of security policies. The text also presents various security models, information management and security technologies. The legal and privacy issues associated with information management and security are also addressed. This is an essential read for students, experts and professionals alike.

This book has been the outcome of endless efforts put in by authors and researchers on various issues and topics within the field. The book is a comprehensive collection of significant researches that are addressed in a variety of chapters. It will surely enhance the knowledge of the field among readers across the globe.

It gives us an immense pleasure to thank our researchers and authors for their efforts to submit their piece of writing before the deadlines. Finally in the end, I would like to thank my family and colleagues who have been a great source of inspiration and support.

Editor

Efficient semi-automated assessment of annotations trustworthiness

Davide Ceolin[*], Archana Nottamkandath[*] and Wan Fokkink

*Correspondence: d.ceolin@vu.nl;
a.nottamkandath@vu.nl
The Network Institute, VU University
Amsterdam, de Boelelaan, 1081a,
1081HV Amsterdam, The
Netherlands

Abstract

Crowdsourcing provides a valuable means for accomplishing large amounts of work which may require a high level of expertise. We present an algorithm for computing the trustworthiness of user-contributed tags of artifacts, based on the reputation of the user, represented as a probability distribution, and on provenance of the tag. The algorithm only requires a small number of manually assessed tags, and computes two trust values for each tag, based on reputation and provenance. We moreover present a computationally cheaper adaptation of the algorithm, which clusters semantically similar tags in the training set, and builds an opinion on a new tag based on its semantic relatedness with respect to the medoids of the clusters. Also, we introduce an adaptation of the algorithm based on the use of provenance stereotypes as an alternative basis for the estimation. Two case studies from the cultural heritage domain show that the algorithms produce satisfactory results.

Keywords: Trust; Annotations; Semantic similarity; Subjective logic; Clustering; Cultural heritage; Tagging; Crowdsourcing; Provenance

Introduction

Through the Web, cultural heritage institutions can reach large masses of people, with intentions varying from increasing visibility (and hence visitors) to acquiring user-generated content. Crowdsourcing is an effective way to handle tasks which are highly demanding in terms of the amount of work needed to complete and required level of expertise [1], such as annotating artifacts in large cultural heritage collections. For this reason, many cultural heritage institutions have opened up their archives to ask the masses to help them in tagging or annotating their artifacts. In earlier years it was feasible for employees at the cultural heritage institutions to manually assess the quality of the tags entered by external users, since there were relatively few contributions from Web users. However, with the growth of the Web, the amount of data has become too large to be accurately dealt with by experts at the disposal of these institutions within a reasonable time. Nevertheless a high quality of annotations is vital for their business. The cultural heritage institutions need the annotations to be trustworthy in order to maintain their authoritative reputation. This calls for mechanisms to automate the annotation evaluation process in order to assist the cultural heritage institutions to obtain quality content from the Web. Annotations from external users can be either in the form of tags or free text, describing entities in the crowdsourced systems. Here, we focus on tags in the cultural heritage domain, which describe mainly the content, context and facts about an artifact by associating words to it.

The goal of this paper is to propose an algorithm for computing the trustworthiness of annotations in a fast and reliable manner. We focus on three main evaluation aspects for our algorithm. First, the trust values produced by our algorithm are meant as indicators of the trustworthiness of annotations, and therefore they must be accurate enough to warrant their usefulness. Accuracy of trust values is achieved by carefully handling the information at our disposal and by utilizing the existence of a relationship between the features considered (e.g., the annotation creator) and the trust values themselves. If the information is handled correctly and the relationship holds, then the trust values are accurate enough and form a basis to automatically decide whether or not to use the annotations. We evaluate this first research question by applying our algorithm on two different datasets, one from a SEALINC Media project experiment and the other from the Steve.Museum dataset. In both cases we divide the dataset into two parts, training set and test set, so as to build a model based on subjective logic and semantic similarity in the training set, and then evaluate the accuracy of such a model on the test set.

The goal of the work described in this paper is to automate the process of evaluation of tags obtained through crowdsourcing in an effective way, by means of an algorithm. In fact, crowsourcing provides massive amounts of annotations, but these are not always trustworthy enough. So we aim at automating the process of deciding whether these are satisfactorily correct and of high quality, i.e. of evaluating them. This is done by first collecting manual evaluations about the quality of a small part of the tags contributed by a user, and then learning a statistical model from them. Throughout the paper we refer to this set as "training set". On the basis of such a model, that assumes the existence of a relation between the user reputation and his overall performance, the system automatically evaluates the tags further added by the same user or user stereotype (i.e. set of users behaving similarly, e.g., users that always provide their tags on Sunday morning). We refer to this set of "new" tags as "test set". Suppose that a user, Alex, provides annotations to the Fictitious National Museum. We propose a method that automatically evaluates these annotations, based on a small set of annotations that the museum previously evaluated from which we derive Alex' reputation, or the reputation of the users whose annotation behaviour is similar to Alex'. We will return on this example more in detail in the following sections.

We employ Semantic Web technologies to represent and store the annotations and the corresponding reviews. We use subjective logic to build a reputation for users that contribute to the system, and moreover semantic similarity measures to generate assessments on the tags entered by the same users at a later point in time. By reputation, we mean a value indicating the estimated probability that the annotations provided by a given author (or, later in the paper, by a given user stereotype) are positively evaluated. In subjective logic, we use the expected value of an opinion about an author as the value of the reputation. The opinion is based on a set of previously evaluated tags. In order to reduce the computation time, we cluster evaluated tags to reduce the number of comparisons. Our experiments show that this preprocessing does not seriously affect the accuracy of the predictions, while significantly reducing the computation time. The proposed algorithms are evaluated on two datasets from the cultural heritage domain. These case studies show that it is possible to semi-automatically evaluate the tags entered by users in crowdsourcing systems into binomial categories (good, bad) with an accuracy above 80%.

Apart from using subjective logic and semantic similarity, we also use provenance mechanisms to evaluate the quality of user-contributed tags. Provenance is represented by means of a data record per tag, containing information on its creation such as time of day, day of the week, typing speed, etc., obtained by tracking user behavior. We use provenance information to group annotations according to the "stereotype" or "behavior" (or "provenance group") that produced them. In other words, we group them depending on whether they are produced by, for instance, early-morning or late-night users. Once the annotations have been grouped per stereotype, we compute a reputation for each stereotype, based on a sample of evaluations provided by an authority: we learn the policy adopted by the authority in evaluating the annotations and we apply the learnt model on further annotations. The fact that we take into account provenance and not rely solely on user identities makes our approach suitable for situations where users are anonymous and only their behavior is tracked. By "policy" we mean a set of rules that the institution adopts to evaluate tags. The fact that we do not have an explicit definition of such rules (nor we could ask for it) determines the need to learn a probabilistic model that aims at mimicking their evaluation strategy. For instance, we do not know a priori if one of two conflicting tags about the same image is wrong, both because we do not know the image (these could refer to two distinct image parts) and the museum policies (which may prohibit their coexistence, in principle). So, we rely only on the museum evaluations and we do not consider the possible impact of conflicting tags.

We propose three algorithms for estimating the trustworthiness of tags. The first learns a reputation for each user based on a set of evaluated tags. Then it predicts the evaluations of the rest of the tags provided by the same user by ranking them according to the user performance in each specific domain (using semantic similarity measures) and then accepting a number of tags proportional to the user reputation. The second algorithm reduces the computational complexity by clustering the tags in the training set, and the third algorithm computes the same prediction on the basis of the user stereotype rather than on the basis of each single user identity. The novelty of this research lies in the automation of tag evaluations on crowdsourcing systems by coupling subjective logic opinions with measures of semantic similarity along with provenance metrics. The only variable parameter that we require is the size of the set of manual evaluations that are needed to build a useful and reliable reputation. Moreover, in the experiments that we performed, varying this parameter did not substantially affect the performance (resulting in about 1% precision variation per five new observations considered in a user reputation). We will further investigate in the future about the impact of this parameter. Using our algorithms, we show how it is possible to avoid asking the curators responsible for the quality of the annotations to set a threshold in order to make assessments about a tag trustworthiness (e.g., accept only tags which have a trust value above a given threshold).

Background and literature review

Trust has been studied extensively in Computer Science. We refer the reader to Sabater and Sierra [2], Gil and Artz [3] and Golbeck [4] for a comprehensive review of trust in computer science, Semantic Web, and Web respectively. The work presented in this paper focuses on trust in crowdsourced information from the Web, using an adapted version of the definition of Castelfranchi and Falcone [5], reported by Sabater and Sierra [2], so we decide to trust or not trust tags based on a set of beliefs and assumptions about who produced the tags and how these were produced. We quantify these beliefs, for instance, though reputations.

Crowdsourcing techniques are widely used by cultural heritage and multimedia institutions for enhancing the available information about their collections. Examples include the Tag Your Paintings project [6], the Steve.Museum project [7] and the Waisda? video tagging platform [8]. The Socially Enriched Access to Linked Cultural (SEALINC) Media project investigates also in this direction. In this project, Rijksmuseum [9] in Amsterdam is using crowdsourcing on a Web platform selecting experts of various domains to enrich information about their collection. One of the case studies analyzed in this paper is provided by the SEALINC Media project.

Trust management in crowdsourced systems often employs wisdom of crowds approaches [10]. In our scenarios we cannot make use of those approaches because the level of expertise needed to annotate cultural heritage artifacts restricts the potential set of users, thus making this kind of approach inapplicable or less effective. Gamification, that consists of using game mechanisms for involving users in non-game tasks, is another approach that leads to an improvement of the quality of tags gathered from crowds, as shown, for instance, in von Ahn et al. [1]. The work presented here is orthogonal to a gamified environment, as it allows us to semi-automatically evaluate the user-contributed annotations and hence to semi-automatically incentivize them. By combining the two, museums could increase the user incentiviazion (showing his reputation may be enough to incentivize a user) while curating the quality of annotations. Users that participated in the experiments that provided the datasets for our analyses did not receive monetary incentives, so leveraging incentives related to gamification and personal satisfaction (by means of reputation tracking) may reveal to be an important factor in increasing the accuracy of the tags collected. In folksonomy systems such as the Steve.Museum project, tag evaluation techniques such as comparing the presence of the tags in standard vocabularies and thesauri, determining their frequency and their popularity or agreement with other tags (see, for instance, Van Damme et al. [11]) have been employed to determine the quality of tags entered by users. Such mechanisms focus mainly on the contributed content with little or no reference to the user who authored it. Also, in folksonomy systems the crowd often manages the tags, while in our scenarios, the crowd only provides the tags, that are managed by museums or other institutions, according to specific policies. Medeylan et al. [12] present algorithms to determine the quality of tags entered by users in a collaboratively created folksonomy, and apply them to the dataset CiteULike [13], which consists of text documents. They evaluate the relevance of user-provided tags by means of text document-based metrics. In our work, since we evaluate tags, we cannot apply document-based metrics, and since we do not have at our disposal large amounts of tags per subject, we cannot check for consistency among users tagging the same image. Similarly, we cannot compute semantic similarity based on the available annotations (like in Cattuto et al. [14]). In fact, since we do not have at our disposal image analysis software nor explicit museum policies, we can not know if possible conflicts between tags regarding the same image are due to the fact that some are correct and some not, or to the fact that they refer to different aspects (or parts) of a complex picture. Therefore, instead of assuming one of the two cases a priori, we determine the trustworthiness of the tags on the basis of the reputation of their user or provenance stereotype. As future direction, we plan to consider also inputs from image recognition software that will help us dealing with conflicting or dubious tags. In open collaborative sites such as Wikipedia [15], where information is contributed by Web users, automated quality evaluation mechanisms have been investigated (see, for instance, De La Calzada et al. [16]). Most of these mechanisms involve computing trust from article revision histories and user groups (see Zeng et al. [17] and Wang et al. [18]). These algorithms track the changes that a particular article or piece of text has undergone over time, along with details of the users performing the changes. In our case study, tags do not have a revision history.

Another approach to obtain trustworthy data is to find experts amongst Web users with a good intention (see De Martini et al. [19]). This mechanism assumes that users who are experts tend to provide more trustworthy annotations. It aims at identifying such experts, by analyzing the profiles built by tracking user performance. In our model, we build profiles based on user performance in the system. So the profile is only behavior-based, and rather than looking for expert and trustworthy users, we build a model which helps in evaluating the tag quality based on the estimated reputation of the tag author. However there is a clear relation between highly reputed users and experts, although these two classes do not always overlap. Modeling of reputation and user behavior on the Web is a widely studied domain. Javanmardi et al. [20] propose three computational models for user reputation by extracting detailed user edit patterns and statistics which are particularly tailored for wikis, while we focus on the annotations domain. Ceolin et al. [21] build a reputation- and provenance-based model for predicting the trustworthiness of Web users in Waisda? over time. We optimize the reputation management and the decision strategies described in that paper.

We use subjective logic to represent user reputations, in combination with semantic relatedness measures. This work extends Ceolin et al. [21,22]. Similarity measures have been combined with subjective logic in Tavakolifard et al. [23], who infer new trust connections between entities (e.g., users) given a set of trust connections known a priori. In our paper, we also start from a graphical representation of relations between the various participating entities (annotators, tags, reviewers, etc.), but: (1) trust relationships are learnt from a sample of museum evaluations, and (2) new trust connections are inferred based on the relative position of the tags in another graph, WordNet. We also use semantic similarity measures to cluster related tags to optimize the computations. In Cilibrasi et al. [24], hierarchical clustering is used for grouping related topics, while Ushioda et al. [25] experiment on clustering words in a hierarchical manner. Begelman et al. [26] present an algorithm for the automated clustering of tags on the basis of tag co-occurrences in order to facilitate more effective retrieval. A similar approach is used by Hassan-Montero and Herrero-Solana [27]. They compute tag similarities using the Jaccard similarity coefficient and then cluster the tags hierarchically using the k-means algorithm. In our work, to build user reputations, we cluster the tags along with their respective evaluations (e.g., accept or reject). Each cluster is represented by a medoid (that is, the element of the cluster which is the closest to its center), and in order to evaluate a newly entered tag by the same user, we consider clusters which are most semantically relevant to the new tag. This helps in selectively weighing only the relevant evidence about a user for evaluating a new tag.

In general, different cultural heritage institutions employ different values and metrics of varying scales to represent the trustworthiness of user-contributed information. The accuracy of various scales has been studied earlier. Certain cases use a binary (boolean) scale for trust values, as in Golbeck et al. [28], while binomial values (i.e., the probabilities of two mutually exclusive values zero and one, that we use in our work) are used in Guha et al. [29] and Kamvar et al. [30].

Relevant for the work presented in this paper is the link between provenance and trust. Bizer and Cyganiak [31], Hartig and Zhao [32] and Zaihrayeu et al. [33] use provenance and background information expressed as annotated or named graphs to produce trust values. We use the same class of information to make our estimates, but we do not use named graphs to represent provenance information. We represent provenance by means of the W3C recommendation PROV-O, the PROV Ontology [34,35]. Provenance is employed for determining trustworthiness of user-contributed information in crowdsourced environments in Ceolin et al. [21], where provenance information is used in combination with user reputation to make binomial assessments of annotations. Also, they employ support vector machines for making the provenance-based estimates, while we employ a subjective logic-based approach. Provenance is used for data verification in crowdsourced environments by Ebden et al. [36]. In their work, they introduced provenance tracking into their online CollabMap application (used to crowdsource evacuation maps), and in this way they collect approximately 5,000 provenance graphs, generated using the Open Provenance Model [37] (which has now been superseded by the PROV Data Model and Ontology). In their work they have at their disposal large provenance graphs and can learn useful features about the artifact trustworthiness from the graphs topologies. Here, the graphs at our disposal are much more limited, so we cannot rely on the graph topology, but we can easily group graphs in stereotypes. Provenance mechanisms have also been used to understand and study workflows in collaborative environments as discussed in Altintas et al. [38]. We share the same context with that work, but we do not focus on the workflow of artifact creation.

The rest of the paper is structured as follows: first we describe the research questions tackled and we connect the datasets used with them. Then we explain our research work in detail and present and discuss the obtained results. Lastly, we provide some final conclusions.

Research design and methodology

The goal of this paper is to propose an algorithm for computing the trustworthiness of annotations in a fast and reliable manner. We focus on three main evaluation aspects for our algorithm. First, the trust values produced by our algorithm are meant as indicators of the trustworthiness of annotations, and therefore they must be accurate enough to warrant their usefulness. Accuracy of trust values is achieved by carefully handling the information at our disposal and by utilizing the existence of a relationship between the features considered (e.g., the annotation creator) and the trust values themselves. If the information is handled correctly and the relationship holds, then the trust values are accurate enough and form a basis to automatically decide whether or not to use the annotations. We evaluate this first research question by applying our algorithm on two different datasets, one from a SEALINC Media project experiment and the other from the Steve.Museum dataset. In both cases we divide the dataset into two parts, training set and test set, so as to build a model based on subjective logic and semantic similarity in the training set, and then evaluate the accuracy of such a model on the test set.

The second evaluation we make regards the possibility to perform trust estimations in a relatively fast manner, by properly clustering the training set on a semantic similarity basis. Here the goal of the contribution is to reduce the computational overhead due to avoidable comparisons between evaluated annotations and new annotations. We evaluate this contribution by applying clustering mechanisms in the training set data of the aforementioned datasets and by running our algorithm for computing trust values on the clustered training sets. The evaluation will check whether clustering reduces the computation time (and in case it does, up to which magnitude) and whether it affects the accuracy of the predictions.

Finally, we show that the algorithm we propose is dependable and not solely dependent on the availability of information about the author of an annotation. Our assumption is that when the identity of the author is not known or when a reliable reputation about the author is not available, we can base our estimates on provenance information, that is, on a range of information about how the tag has been created (e.g., the timestamp of the annotation). By properly gathering and grouping such information to make it utilizable, we can use it as a "stereotypical description" of a user's behavior. Users are often constrained in their behavior by the environment and other factors; for instance, they produce tags within certain periodic intervals, such as the time of the day or day of the week. Being able to recognize such stereotypes, we can compute a reputation per stereotype rather than per user. While on the one hand this approach guarantees the availability of evidence, as typically multiple users belong to the same stereotype, on the other hand this approach compensates on the lack of evidence about specific users. We evaluate our hypothesis over the two datasets mentioned before by splitting them into two parts, one to build a provenance-based model and the other to evaluate it.

Methods
Here we describe the methods adopted and implemented in our algorithm. We start describing the tools that were already available and that we incorporated in our framework, and then we continue with the framework description.

Preliminaries
The system that we propose aims at estimating the trustworthiness of new annotations based on a set of evaluated ones (per user or per provenance stereotype, as we will see). In order to make the estimates, we need to make use of a probabilistic logic that allows us to model and reason about the evidence at our disposal while accounting for uncertainty due to the limited information available. For this reason we employ subjective logic, which fits our needs. Moreover, since the evidence at our disposal consists of textual annotations, we use semantic similarity measures to understand the relevance of each piece of evidence when analyzing each different annotation.

Subjective logic
Subjective logic is a probabilistic logic that we extensively use in our system in order to reason about the trustworthiness of the annotations and the reputations of their authors, based on limited samples. In subjective logic, so-called "subjective opinions" (represented

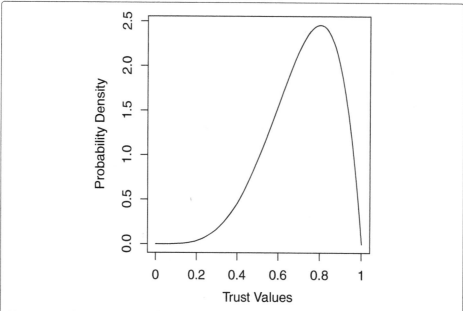

Figure 1 Beta distribution of the user trustworthiness. We use a Beta distribution to describe the probability for each value in the [0 . . . 1] interval to be the right reputation for a given user or the right trust value for a given tag.

as ω) express the belief that source x owns with respect to the value of assertion y (for instance, a user's reputation). When y can assume only two values (e.g., true or false), the opinion is called "binomial"; when y ranges over more than two values, the opinion is called "multinomial". Opinions are computed as follows, where the positive and negative evidence are represented as p and n, respectively, and b, d, u and a represent the belief, disbelief, uncertainty and prior probability, respectively. A binomial opinion is represented as:

$$\omega_y^x(b, d, u) \tag{1}$$

where:

$$b = \frac{p}{p+n+2} \quad d = \frac{n}{p+n+2} \quad u = \frac{2}{p+n+2} \quad a = \frac{1}{2} \tag{2}$$

Such an opinion is equivalent to a Beta probability distribution (see Figure 1), which describes the likelihood for each possible trust value to be the right trust value for a given subject. An expected probability for a possible value of an opinion is computed as:

$$E = b + a \cdot u \tag{3}$$

The belief b of the opinion represents how much we believe that the y statement is true (where y is, for instance, the fact that an annotation is correct), based on the evidence at our disposal. However, the evidence at our disposal is limited (and since the evidence is obtained by asking an authority, such as a museum, to evaluate an annotation, we aim at keeping it limited in order to avoid overloading the museum with such requests), so we must take into account the fact that other observations about the same fact might, in principle, disagree with those currently at our disposal. This leads to uncertainty, which is represented by the corresponding element of the opinion, u. The disbelief d represents, instead, the disbelief that we have about the statement y based on actual negative evidence at our disposal. Disbelief is the counterpart of belief, and the sum of belief, disbelief and uncertainty is always one ($b + d + u = 1$).

Whereas belief, disbelief and uncertainty are based on the actual evidence observed, the base rate a encodes the prior knowledge about the truth of y according to x (before observing any evidence). The final opinion about the correctness of y is then obtained by aggregating a and b in a weighted manner, so as to make b count more if it is based on more evidence than a (and thus its uncertainty is lower). This explains the meaning of E, which represents exactly such an aggregation. One last consideration regards the fact that E represents both the expected value of the opinion and of the Beta distribution equivalent to it. u is tightly connected to the variance of the Beta distribution, as they both represent the uncertainty about the belief to be significant.

These elements make subjective opinions ideal tools for representing the fact that the probabilities that we estimate about the trustworthiness of annotations, authors and provenance stereotypes (that are defined later in this section) are based on evidence provided by a museum (that consist of evaluations based on the museum's policy), and that the estimates we make carry some uncertainty due to the fact that they are based on a limited set of observations.

Semantic similarity

The target of our trust assessments are annotations (that is, words associated to images, in order to describe them), and our evidence consists of evaluated annotations. In our system we collect evidence about an author or a provenance stereotype (which is defined later in this section) that consist of annotations evaluated by the museum, and we compare each new annotation that needs to be evaluated against the evidence at our disposal. If, for instance, we based our estimates only on the ratio between positive and negative evidence of a given author, then all his annotations would be rated equally. If, instead, we compared every new annotation only against the evidence at our disposal of matching words, we would have a more tailored, but more limited estimate, as we cannot expect that the same author always uses the same words (and so that there is evidence for every word he uses in an annotation).

In order to increase the availability of evidence for our estimate and to let the more relevant evidence have a higher impact on those calculations, we employ semantic relatedness measures as a weighing factor. These measures quantify the likeness between the meaning of two given terms. Whenever we evaluate a tag, we take the evidence at our disposal, and tags that are more semantically similar to the one we focus on are weighed more heavily. There exist many techniques for measuring semantic relatedness, which can be divided into two groups. First, we have so-called "topological" semantic similarity measures, which are deterministic measures based on the graph distance between the two words examined, based on a word graphs (e.g. WordNet [39]). Second, there is the family of statistical semantic similarity measures, which include, for instance, the Normalized Google Distance [40], that measures statistically the similarity between two words on the basis of the number of times that these occur and co-occur in documents indexed by Google. These measures are characterized by the fact that the similarity of two words is estimated on a statistical basis from their occurrence and co-occurrence in large sets of documents.

We focus on deterministic semantic relatedness measures based on WordNet or its Dutch counterpart Cornetto [41]. In particular, we use the Wu and Palmer [42] and the Lin [43] measure for computing semantic relatedness between tags, because both provide us with values in the range $[0, 1]$, but other measures are possible as well. WordNet is a directed and acyclic graph where each vertex v, w is an integer that represents a synset (set of word synonyms), and each directed edge from v to w implies that w is a hypernym of v. In other words w shares a "type-of" relation with v. For instance, if v is the word "winter" (hyponym), w can be the word "season" (hypernym). The Wu and Palmer measure calculates semantic relatedness between two words by considering the depths between two synsets in WordNet, along with the depth of the Least Common Subsumer, as follows:

$$score(s1, s2) = 2 * \frac{depth(lcs(s1, s2))}{depth(s1) + depth(s2)}$$

where $s1$ is a synset of the first word and $s2$ of the second. WordNet is an acyclic graph where nodes are represented by synsets and edges represent hypernym/hyponym relations. If a synset is a generalization of another one, we can measure the depth, that is the distance between the two. The first ancestor shared by two nodes is the Least Common Subsumer. We compute the similarity of all synsets combinations and pick the maximum value, as we adopt the upper bound of the similarity between the two words. The Lin measure considers the information content of the Least Common Subsumer and the two compared synsets, as follows:

$$2 * \frac{IC(lcs(s1, s2))}{IC(s1) + IC(s2)}$$

where IC is the information context, that is the probability of finding the concept in a given corpus, and is defined as:

$$IC(s) = -log\left(\frac{freq(s)}{freq(root)}\right)$$

and *freq* is the frequency of the synset. So the Wu and Palmer measure derives the similarity of two concepts from their distance from a common ancestor, while the Lin similarity derives it from the information content of the two concepts and their lowest ancestor. The Wu and Palmer similarity measure is more recent and has shown to be effectively combinable with subjective logic in Ceolin et al. [44], so when we deal with datasets of tags in English (Steve.Museum dataset), we use its implementation provided by the python nltk library [45]. Instead, when we work on datasets composed of Dutch tags (e.g., the dataset from the SEALINC Media project experiment), we rely on pyCornetto [46], an interface to Cornetto, the Dutch WordNet. pyCornetto does not provide a means to compute the Wu and Palmer similarity measure, but it provides the Lin similarity measure, and given the relatedness of the two measures, in this case we adopt the Lin measure.

For more details about how to combine semantic relatedness measures and subjective logic, see the work of Ceolin et al. [44]. By choosing to use these measures we limit ourself in the possibility to evaluate only single-word tags and only common words, because these are the kinds of words that are present in WordNet. However, we choose these measures because almost all the tags we evaluate fall into the mentioned categories and because the use of these similarity measures together with subjective logic has already been theoretically validated. Moreover, almost all the words used in the annotations that form the dataset we used in our evaluations are single-word tags and common words, hence this limitation does not affect our evaluation significantly. The algorithm proposed is designed so that any other relatedness measure could be used in place of the chosen ones, without the need of any additional intervention. The choice of the semantic similarity and how the semantic similarity is used both affect the uncertainty of the expected results of the algorithms that we propose. In fact, these algorithms use semantic similarity to weigh the importance of evidence when evaluating tags, i.e. words associated with cultural heritage artifacts. We use a deterministic semantic similarity measure which, although it constitutes a heuristics, is based on a trustworthy data source (WordNet) and this implies that the measure is less uncertain than a probabilistic measure based on a limited document corpus. Still, the semantic similarity measure represents an approximation and part of the uncertainty these imply is due to their use: semantic similarity measures represent the similarity between synsets, but we have at our disposal only words without an indication of their intended synset (a word may have more meanings, represented by synsets). Since we are situated in a well-defined domain (cultural heritage), and since words are all used to tag cultural heritage artifacts, we assume that words are semantically related, and hence, when computing the semantic similarity between two words, we make use of the maximum of the similarity between all their synsets. Despite the fact that this introduces an approximation, we will show in Section Results that the method is effective.

Datasets adopted

We validate the algorithms we propose over two datasets of annotations of images. The annotations contained in these datasets consist of content descriptions and the datasets contain also the evaluations from the institutions that collected them. For each annotation, the datasets contain information about its author and a timestamp. Since each institution adopts a different policy for evaluating annotations, we try to learn such a policy from a sample of annotations per dataset, and find a relationship between the identity of the author or other information about the annotation and its evaluation.

SEALINC media project experiment

As part of SEALINC Media project, the Rijksmuseum in Amsterdam [9] is crowdsourcing annotations of artifacts in its collection using Web users. An initial experiment was conducted to study the effect of presenting pre-set tags on the quality of annotations on crowdsourced data [47]. In the experiment, the external annotators were presented with pictures from the Web and prints from the Rijksmuseum collection along with a pre-set annotations about the picture or print, and they were asked to insert new annotations, or remove the pre-set ones which they did not agree with (the pre-set tags are either correct or not). A total of 2,650 annotations resulted from the experiment, and these were manually evaluated by trusted personnel for their quality and relevance using the following scale:

- 1 : Irrelevant
- 2 : Incorrect
- 3 : Subjective
- 4 : Correct and possibly relevant
- 5 : Correct and highly relevant
- typo : Spelling mistake

These tags, along with their evaluations, were used to validate our model. For each tag, the SEALINC Media dataset presents the following elements: author identifier, artifact identifier, timestamp, evaluation. We do not focus on the goals of the experiment from which this dataset is obtained, that is, we do not analyze the relation between the kind of tag that was proposed to the user, and the tag that the user provided. We focus on the tag that the user actually proposes and its evaluation and we try to predict the evaluation of the tags provided by each user, given a small training set of sample evaluations about each of them.

We neglect the tags evaluated as "Typo" because our focus is on the semantic correctness of the tags, so we assume that such a category of mistakes would be properly avoided or treated (e.g., by using autocompletion and checking the presence of the tags in dictionaries) before the tags reach our evaluation framework. We build our training set using a fixed amount of evaluated annotations for each of the users, and form the test set using the remaining annotations. The number of annotations used to build the reputation and the percentage of the dataset covered is presented in Table 1: in the first column "# annotation per reputation" we report the number of evaluated annotations we use to build each reputation, while in the second column, "% training set covered" we report the percentage of annotation used as training set compared to the whole dataset.

Steve.Museum project dataset

Steve.Museum [7] is a project involving several museum professionals in the cultural heritage domain. Part of the project focuses on understanding the various effects of crowdsourcing cultural heritage artifact annotations. Their experiments involved external annotators annotating museum collections, and a subset of the data collected from the crowd was evaluated for trustworthiness. In total, 4,588 users tagged the 89,671 artifacts using 480,617 tags from 21 participating museums. Part of these annotations consisting of 45,860 tags were manually evaluated by professionals at these museums and were used as a basis for our second case study. In this project, the annotations were classified in a more refined way, compared to the previous case study, namely as: {Todo, Judgement-negative, Judgement-positive, Problematic-foreign, Problematic-huh, Problematic-misperception, Problematic-misspelling, Problematic-no_consensus, Problematic-personal, Usefulness-not_useful, Usefulness-useful}. There are three main categories: judgement (a personal judgement by the annotator about the picture), problematic (for several, different reasons) and usefulness (stating whether the annotation is useful or not). We consider only "usefulness-useful" as a positive judgement, all the others are considered as negative evaluations. The tags classified as "todo" are discarded, since their evaluation has not been

Table 1 Results of the evaluation of Algorithm 1 over the SEALINC Media dataset

# Tags per reputation	% Training set covered	Accuracy	Precision	Recall	F-measure	Time (sec.)
5	8%	0.73	0.88	0.81	0.84	87
10	19%	0.76	0.87	0.84	0.86	139
15	31%	0.76	0.86	0.86	0.86	221
20	41%	0.84	0.87	0.96	0.86	225

Results of the evaluation of Algorithm 1 over the SEALINC Media dataset for training sets formed by aggregating 5, 10, 15 and 20 reputations per user. We report the percentage of dataset actually covered by the training set, the accuracy, the precision, the recall and the F-measure of our prediction.

performed yet. The Steve.Museum dataset is provided as a MySQL database and consists of several tables. Those most important for us are: "steve_term", that contains information like the identifiers for the artifact annotated and the words associated with them (tags); "steve_session" that reports information about when the tags are provided and by whom, and "steve_term_review" that contain information about the tag evaluations. We join these tables and we select the information that is relevant for us: the tags, their authors, their timestamps (i.e. date and time of creation) and their evaluation. We partition this dataset thus obtained into a training and a test set, as shown in Table 2, along with their percentage coverage of the whole dataset and the obtained results (in the second column, "% of training set covered"). We use the training set to learn a model for evaluating user provided tags, and we consider the tags in the test set as tags newly introduced by the authors for which we build a model.

System description

After having introduced the methods that we make use of, and the datasets that we analyze, we provide here a description of the system that we propose.

High-level system overview

The system that we propose aims at relieving the institution personnel (reviewers in particular) from the burden of controlling and evaluating all the annotations inserted by users. The system asks for some interaction with the reviewers, but tries to minimize it. Figure 2 shows a high-level view of the model.

For each user, the system asks the reviewers to review a fixed number of annotations, and on the basis of these reviews it builds user reputations. A reputation is meant to express a global measure of trustworthiness and accountability of the corresponding user. The reviews are also used to assess the trustworthiness of each tag inserted afterwards by a user: given a tag, the system evaluates it by looking at the evaluations already available. The evaluations of the tags semantically closer to the one that we evaluate have a higher impact. So we have two distinct phases: a first training step where we collect samples of manual reviews, and a second step where we make automatic assessments of tags trustworthiness (possibly after having clustered the evaluated tags, to improve the computation time). The more reviews there are, the more reliable the reputation is, but this number depends also on the workforce at the disposal of the institution. On the other hand, as we will see in the following section, this parameter does not affect significantly the accuracy obtained. Moreover, we do not need to set an "acceptance threshold"

Table 2 Results of the evaluation of Algorithm 1 over the Steve.Museum dataset

# Tags per reputation	% Training set covered	Accuracy	Precision	Recall	F-measure	Time (sec.)
5	18%	0.68	0.79	0.80	0.80	1254
10	27%	0.70	0.79	0.83	0.81	1957
15	33%	0.71	0.80	0.84	0.82	2659
20	39%	0.70	0.79	0.84	0.81	2986
25	43%	0.71	0.79	0.85	0.82	3350
30	47%	0.72	0.81	0.85	0.83	7598

Results of the evaluation of Algorithm 1 over the Steve.Museum dataset for training sets formed by aggregating 5, 10, 15, 20, 25 and 30 reputations per user. We report the percentage of dataset actually covered by the training set, the accuracy, the precision, the recall and the F-measure of our prediction.

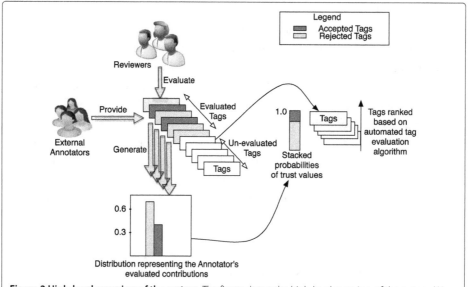

Figure 2 High-level overview of the system. The figure shows the high-level overview of the system. We evaluate a subset of user-contributed tags and use it to build the annotator reputation model. We evaluate the remaining set of the tags based on semantic similarity measures and subjective logic. The unevaluated tags are then ranked based on the annotator reputation model and the model serves as a basis to accept or reject the unevaluated tags from the users.

(e.g., accept only annotations with a trust value of say at least 0.9, for trust values ranging from zero to one), in contrast to the work of Ceolin et al. [21]. This is important since such a threshold is arbitrary, and it is not trivial to find a balance between the risk to accept wrong annotations and to reject good ones.

We introduce here a running example that accompanies the description of the system in the rest of this section. Suppose that a user, Alex (whose profile already contains three tags which were evaluated by the museum), newly contributes to the collection of the Fictitious National Museum by tagging five artifacts. Alex tags one artifact with "Chinese". If the museum immediately uses the tag for classifying the artifact, it might be risky because the tag might be wrong (maliciously or not). On the other hand, had the museum enough internal employees to check the external contributed tag, then it would not have needed to crowdsource it. The system that we propose here relies on few evaluations of Alex's tags by the Museum. Based on these evaluations, the system: (1) computes Alex's reputation; (2) computes a trust value for the new tag; and (3) decides whether to accept it or not. We describe the system implementation in the following sections.

Annotation representation

We adopt the Open Annotation model [48] as a standard model for describing annotations, together with the most relevant related metadata (like the author and the time of creation). The Open Annotation model allows to reify the annotation itself, and by treating it as an object, we can easily link to it properties like the annotator URI or the time of creation. Moreover, the review of an annotation can be represented as an annotation which target is an annotation and which body contains a value of the review about the annotation.

To continue with our example, Figure 3 and Listing 1 show an example of an annotation and a corresponding review, both represented as "annotations" from the Open Annotation model.

Listing 1 Example of an annotation and respective evaluation. The annotation is represented using the Annotation class from the Open Annotation model. The evaluation is represented as an annotation of the annotation.

```
@prefix rdf: <http://www.w3.org/1999/02/22-rdf-syntax-ns#> .
@prefix oac: <http://www.w3.org/ns/openannotation/core/> .
@prefix foaf: <http://xmlns.com/foaf/0.1/> .

ex:user_1 oac:annotator Annotation; foaf:givenName "Alex" .
ex:annotation_1 oac:hasBody tag:Chinese;
                oac:annotator ex:user_1;
                oac:hasTarget ex:img_231;
                rdf:type oac:annotation .
ex:review oac:hasBody ex:ann_accepted;
          oac:annotator ex:reviewer_1;
          oac:hasTarget ex:annotation_1;
          rdf:type oac:annotation .
ex:annotation_accepted oac:annotates ex:annotation_1 .
```

Trust management

We employ subjective logic [49] for representing, computing and reasoning on trust assessments. There are several reasons why we use this logic. First, it allows to quantify the truth of statements regarding different subjects (e.g. user reputation and tag trust value) by aggregating the evidence at our disposal in a simple and clear way that accounts both for the distribution of the observed evidence and the size of it, hence quantifying the uncertainty of our assessment. Second, each statement in subjective logic is equivalent to a Beta or Dirichlet probability distribution, and hence we can tackle the problem from a statistical point of view without the need to change our data representation. Third, the logic offers several operators to combine the assessments made over the statements of our interest. We made a limited use of operators so far, but we aim at expanding this in the near future. Lastly, we use subjective logic because it allows us to represent formally the fact that the evidence we collect is linked to a given subject (user, tag), and is based on a specific point of view (reviewers for a museum) that is the source of the evaluations.

Trust is context-dependent, since different users or tags (or, more in general, agents and artifacts) might receive different trust evaluations, depending on the context from which they situate, and the reviewer. In our scenarios we do not have at our disposal an explicit description of trust policies by the museums. Also, we do not aim at determining a generic tag (or user) trust level. Our goal is to learn a model that evaluates tags as closely as

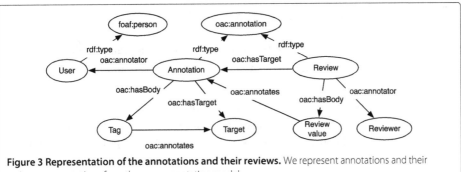

Figure 3 Representation of the annotations and their reviews. We represent annotations and their reviews as annotations from the open annotation model.

possible to what that museum would do, based on a small sample of evaluations produced by the museum itself.

User reputation computation and representation We define a user reputation as a global value representing the user's ability to tag according to the museum policy. With global we mean that the user reputation is not related to a specific context, because this value should represent an overall trust level about the user production: a highly reputed user is believed to have the ability to produce high-quality tags and to choose tags/artifacts related to his/her domain of expertise. Also, the possible number of topics is so high that defining the reputation to be topic-dependent would bring manageability issues. Expertise will be considered when evaluating a single tag, as we will see in the next paragraph.

We require that a fixed number of user-contributed tags are evaluated by the museum. Based on those evaluations we compute the user reputation using subjective opinions, as in Equation 4.

$$\omega_u^m \left(\frac{p_u^m}{p_u^m + n_u^m + 2}, \frac{n_u^m}{p_u^m + n_u^m + 2}, \frac{2}{p_u^m + n_u^m + 2}, \frac{1}{2} \right) \tag{4}$$

where m and u represent the museum and the user respectively and p and n the count of positive and negative pieces of evidence respectively. So, for instance, p_u^m is the count of positive pieces of evidence that the museum m collected about user u, and n_u^m the negative ones.

The algorithm that we will describe makes use of a single value representing the user reputation, so in place of the values computed as in Equation 4, the algorithm makes use of the expected value of that opinion, as shown in Equation 5.

$$E(\omega_u^m) = \frac{p_u^m}{p_u^m + n_u^m + 2} + \frac{1}{2} \cdot \frac{2}{p_u^m + n_u^m + 2} \tag{5}$$

To continue with the running example, suppose that Alex contributed three tags: {Indian, Buddhist} were evaluated as accepted and {tulip} as rejected. His reputation is:

$$\omega_{Alex}^{museum} = \left(\frac{2}{5}, \frac{1}{5}, \frac{2}{5}, \frac{1}{2} \right) \quad E(\omega_{Alex}^{museum}) = 0.6 \tag{6}$$

Tag trust value computation and representation Tag trust values are represented by means of subjective opinions, as in Equation 7.

$$\omega_t^m \left(\frac{p_t^m}{p_t^m + n_t^m + 2}, \frac{n_t^m}{p_t^m + n_t^m + 2}, \frac{2}{p_t^m + n_t^m + 2}, \frac{1}{2} \right) \tag{7}$$

Here, we still use the tags created by the user and the corresponding evaluations to compute the trust value, but despite the computation of the user reputation, evidence is weighed with respect to the similarity to the tag to be evaluated. This means, that we do not consider each piece of evidence as equally contributing to the computation of the reputation, i.e. evidence is weighed according to the semantic similarity with respect to the tag that we are evaluating. So p and n are determined as in Equation 8, where sim is a semantic relatedness measure and t is a tag to be evaluated and so, despite Equation 4 where each piece of evidence counted as one, here each piece of evidence counts as a real number between zero and one corresponding to the value of the semantic similarity.

$$p_t^m = \Sigma_{t_i \in train} sim(t, t_i) \; if \; evaluation(t_i) = true$$
$$n_t^m = \Sigma_{t_i \in train} sim(t, t_i) \; if \; evaluation(t_i) = false \qquad (8)$$

The tag "Chinese" inserted by Alex is evaluated as:

$$p_{Chinese}^m = sim(\text{Chinese, Indian}) + sim(\text{Chinese, Buddhist}) = 1.05$$

$$n_{Chinese}^m = sim(\text{Chinese, tulip}) = 0.1$$

$$\omega_{Chinese}^m \left(\frac{1.05}{1.05 + 0.1 + 2}, \frac{0.1}{1.05 + 0.1 + 2}, \frac{2}{1.05 + 0.1 + 2}, \frac{1}{2} \right)$$

$$E(\omega_{Chinese}^m) = 0.95$$

Tag evaluation In order to evaluate tags (i.e. decide to accept or reject them), we define an ordering function on the set of tags based on their trust values (see Equation 9). The ordered set of tags is represented as $\{t\}_1^{|tags|}$, where $|tags|$ is the cardinality of the set of tags. For tags t_1 and t_2,

$$t_1 \leq t_2 \iff E(\omega_{t_1}^m) \leq E(\omega_{t_2}^m) \qquad (9)$$

Recall that $E(\omega_u^m)$ is the user reputation, being the expected percentage of correct tags created by the user. Hence, we accept the last $E(\omega_u^m) \cdot |tags|$ tags in $\{t\}_1^{|tags|}$ (see Equation 10) as $\{t\}_1^{|tags|}$ is in ascending order, so we accept the tags having higher trust value.

$$evaluation(tag) = \begin{cases} rejected & if \; t \in \{t\}_{E(\omega_u^m) \cdot |tags|}^1 \\ accepted & otherwise \end{cases} \qquad (10)$$

We saw how the reputation of Alex was 0.6. He inserted five new tags, so $0.6 \cdot 5 = 3$ will be accepted. The tag "Chinese" had a trust value of 0.95, which ranks it as first in the ordered list of tags. Therefore the tag "Chinese" is *accepted*.

Algorithm

We provide here a pseudocode representation of the algorithm that implements the tag evaluation procedures, and we explain it in detail.

Input The algorithm takes as input two vectors. The first vector, i.e. the training set, is composed of tuples formed by tags, their evaluation (e.g., "useful") and the user identifier (which consists of a URI, since we use the Semantic Web representation described above). The second vector (test set) is composed of tuples formed by tags and the identifier of the user that provided them.

Output The intended output consists of a vector of tuples formed by the tags in the test set and their estimated evaluation.

build_user_reputation Builds a reputation for each user in the training set, following Equation 4. A reputation is represented as a vector of probabilities for possible tag evaluations.

trust_values Trust values are represented as vectors of probabilities of possible tag evaluations, following Equation 7.

Algorithm 1: Algorithm to compute trust values of tags base on user reputation.

Input: A finite set of elements in $Training\_set = \{\langle tag, evaluation, UserID\rangle\}$ and
$Test\_set = \{\langle tag, UserID\rangle\}$

Output: A finite set of evaluated tags $Result\_Test\_set = \{\langle tag, trust\_values\rangle\}$

1 **for** $UserID \leftarrow UserID_1$ **to** $UserID_n$ **do**
2   ▷ for *all tags* in *Training_set*
3      $rep[UserID] \leftarrow$ build_reputation $(Training\_set)$
4 **for** $UserID \leftarrow UserID_1$ **to** $UserID_n$ **do**
5   ▷ for *all users* in *Test_set*
6   **for** $Tag \leftarrow tag_1$ **to** tag_n **do**
7   ▷ for *all tags* in *Test_set*
8           $trust\_values[Tag] =$ comp_tv $(Training\_set)$
9      $s\_tags \leftarrow$ sort $(tags(trust\_values)$
10     $Result \leftarrow$ assess $(s\_tags, rep[UserID])$

11 **return** *Result*

---

comp_tv Implements Equation 7 using Equation 8. The value actually stored is the expected value of the opinion, that is $E(\omega_t^m) = \frac{p_t^m}{p_t^m + n_t^m + 2} + \frac{1}{2} \cdot \frac{2}{p_t^m + n_t^m + 2}$.

sort_tags The tags are sorted according to their trust value, following the ordering function in Equation 9.

assess The assess function assigns an evaluation to the tag, by implementing Equation 10.

Clustering semantically related tags

Reputations built using large training sets are likely to be more accurate than those built using smaller ones. On the other hand, the larger the set of tags used for building the reputation, the higher the number of comparisons we will have to make to evaluate a new tag. In order to reduce this tension, we cluster the tags in the training set of a user based on semantic similarity, for each resulting cluster we compute the medoid (that is, the element of the cluster which is, on average, the closest to the other elements), and we record the evidence counts. Clustering is performed on a semantic basis, that is, tags are clustered in order to create subsets of tags having similar meanings. After having clustered the tags, we adapt the algorithm so that we compute a subjective opinion per cluster, but we weigh it only on the semantic distance between the new tag and the cluster medoid. In this way we reduce the number of comparisons (we do not measure the distance between the new tag and each element of the cluster), but we still account for the size of the training set, as we record the evidence counts of it. We use hierarchical clustering [50] for semantically clustering the words, although it is computationally expensive, because: (1) we know only the relative distances between words, and not their position in a simplex (the semantic distance is computed as $1 - similarity(word_1, word_2)$), and this is one of the algorithms that requires such kind of input; and (2) it requires only one input argument, a real number "cut", that determines the number of clusters of the input set S of words. If cut $= 0$, then there is only one cluster; if cut $= 1$, then there are n clusters, where n is the cardinality of S. Clustering is performed offline, before any tag is evaluated, and here we focus on the improvement of the performance of the newly introduced tags. Algorithm 2 incorporates these optimizations. As Algorithm 1, Algorithm 2 takes as input the training set (composed of tuples formed by a tag, its evaluation and its author identifier) and a test set (composed of tuples formed by tags and their author identifier) and outputs a set of tuples formed by the tags in the test set and their estimated evaluations.

To continue with the running example, the museum can cluster the tags inserted by Alex before making any estimate. We have only three tags in the training set, which result in two clusters, {Indian, Buddhist} and {tulip}.

$$p_{Chinese}^m = sim(\text{Chinese, Indian}) \cdot 2 = 1.75$$

$$n_{Chinese}^m = sim(\text{Chinese, tulip}) = 0.1$$

$$\omega_{Chinese}^m \left(\frac{1.75}{1.75 + 0.1 + 2}, \frac{0.1}{1.75 + 0.1 + 2}, \frac{2}{1.75 + 0.1 + 2}, \frac{1}{2} \right)$$

$$E(\omega_{Chinese}^m) = 0.72$$

This result is different from the previous trust value computed in a non-clustered manner (0.95). However, this variation affects all the computed trust values, and the overall performance of the algorithm even benefits from it, as a consequence of a better distribution of the evidence weights.

Provenance-based trust values

The algorithms described so far are based on the fact that there exists a relationship between the identity of an author and the trustworthiness of his annotations, or that the user reputation is a meaningful estimate. However, there might be cases when the user reputation is not available, for instance if there is not enough evidence about his trustworthiness or in case his identity is not known. We show that the algorithm is not firmly

---

Algorithm 2: Algorithm to compute trust values of tags based on user reputation, with clustering of the evaluated tags in the training set.

Input: A finite set of elements in *Training_set* = {⟨*tag,evaluation, UserID*⟩} and
  Test_set = {⟨*tag,UserID*⟩}

Output: A finite set of evaluated tags *Result_Test_set* = {⟨*tag,trust_values*⟩}

1 **for** *UserID* ← *UserID$_1$* **to** *UserID$_n$* **do**
2   ▷ for all tags in *Training_set*
3 *rep[UserID]* ← build_reputation (*training_set*)
4 *clusters[UserID]* ← build_clust (*training_set*)
5 *medoids[UserID]* ← get_med (*clusters,UserID*)

6 **for** *UserID* ← *UserID$_1$* **to** *UserID$_n$* **do**
7   ▷ for *all users* in *Test_set*
8 **for** *Tag* ← *tag$_1$* **to** *tag$_n$* **do**
9   ▷ for *all tags* in *Test_set*
10   *trust_values[Tag]* = comp_tv (*medoids[UserID],rep[UserID]*)
11 *sort_tags* ← sort (*trust_values*)
12 *Result* ← assess (*sort_tags,rep[UserID]*)

13 **return** *Result*

---

dependent on the user reputation and, in case this is not available, other classes of information can be used as well. This class of information is so-called provenance information about how an artifact (in this case, an annotation) has been produced, and represents, therefore, an extension of the information about the sole author of the annotation.

We follow a reasoning similar to a previous work of Ceolin et al. [21], as we use "provenance stereotypes" to group annotations. By stereotype we mean a class of provenance traces classified according to the user behavior they hint at. For instance, we could have "Monday early morning users" or "Saturday night users". We suppose that a given behavior should be associated with a particular reputation and hence with a given degree of trustworthiness of the annotations created in that manner, for two reasons:

- The trustworthiness of a given annotation might be affected by when it is created. For instance, late at night, users may on average be more tired and hence less precise than on other moments of the day.
- Users tend to follow a regular pattern in their behavior, because, for instance, their availability for annotating is constrained by their working time. Therefore, by considering their behavior, we implicitly consider their identity as well, even when they act as anonymous users, as shown in Ceolin et al. [21].

In order to apply this kind of reasoning, we need to refer to the provenance information at our disposal about the annotations. In particular, these include only the day of the week and the time of creation for the dataset considered, but other information, when available, might be used as well (e.g., the typing duration for a given annotation). Since annotations are hardly created at the same time, in general do not coincide, we need to group them in order to be able to identify patterns in the data that allow us to link specific provenance information to the trustworthiness of the tags. In fact, the creation time of a tag may be recorded as a timestamp, but since tags are probably created at different times, we need to increase the granularity of this piece of information and analyze the part of the day or the day of the week when the tag was created, rather than the exact moment (tracked by the timestamp). Of course, this grouping introduces some uncertainty in the calculations because it introduces an approximation and because, in principle there are several possible groupings that we can apply, with different granularity and semantics (e.g., the days can be distinguished in weekdays and weekends, or simply be kept as single days of the week). In the next section, we report the results we obtained and we provide a possible explanation of why the grouping we propose allowed us to obtain the results we achieved, in the case studies we analyzed. Lastly, from the modeling point of view, each group or stereotype can be thought of as a **prov:bundle** from the PROV Ontology [35], that is a "named set of provenance descriptions", where each set groups provenance traces according to the day of the week and the part of the day they belong to.

Despite the mentioned previous work, we do not apply support vector machines to learn the trustworthiness of the annotations created with a given stereotype. Rather, we collect a predefined amount of evidence (i.e. of evaluated annotations) per group, and we evaluate the remaining annotations of the same group based on the reputation estimated using the evidence collected, so as to exploit the provenance semantics instead of using it only as a statistical feature.

For representing provenance information we adopt the W3C Recommendation PROV-O Ontology [35], which provides founding types and relations for representing this specific kind of information, like entities and activities, which coincide with tags and tag creation processes respectively.

Computing the reputation of a provenance stereotype Once we have decided how to group the provenance traces, we start collecting evidence per group. We fix a limit to the amount of evidence needed to create the opinion representing the stereotype's reputation. (In the experiment described in the next section we vary this limit to evaluate the impact it has on the accuracy of the reputation itself.). The reputation is computed as in the **build_reputation()** procedure described in Algorithm 3. First we determine which stereotype the annotation belongs to. Then we increment the evidence count for the evaluation of the current tag until we reach the limit per stereotype. Lastly, we convert the list of evidence counts in subjective opinions.

Algorithm 3: Algorithm to compute trust values of tags using provenance stereotypes. First we present the procedure for computing the reputation of the provenance stereotypes and then we predict the trustworthiness of tags based on their provenance group.

---

1 **procedure** build_reputation()

    Input: A finite set of elements in *Training_set* = {⟨*tag,evaluation, ProvenanceID*⟩}

    Output: A set of provenance group reputations

        Result_Test_set = {⟨*ProvenanceID, reputation_values*⟩}

2   **for** *tag **in** training_set_tags* **do**

3   *i* ← *tag.get_stereotype_id()*

4   **if** length (*trainingset[stereotypes[i])]*) <*n* **then**

5   *trainingset*[length (*trainingset[stereotypes[i]]*) + 1] ← get_eval (*tag*)

6   **else**

7   *testset*[length (*testset[stereotypes[i]]*) + 1] ← get_eval (*tag*)

8   **for** *s **in** stereotypes* **do**

9   *rep*[*s*] ← compute_reputations (*s*)

10   **return** *s*

    Input: A finite set of elements in *Training_set* = {⟨*tag,evaluation, ProvenanceID*⟩}

        and *Test_set* = {⟨*tag, ProvenanceID*⟩}

    Output: A finite set of evaluated tags *Result_Test_set* = {⟨*tag,trust_values*⟩}

1 **for** *s **in** trainingset[stereotypes]* **do**

2   *rep*[*s*] ← build_reputation (*Training_set*)

3 **for** *s **in** testset[stereotypes]* **do**

4   **for** *Tag* ← *tag_1* **to** *tag_n* **do**

5   *trust_values*[*Tag*] ← compute_tv (*Training_set*)

6   *s_tags* ← sort_tags (*trust_values*)

7   *Result* ← assess (*s_tags,rep[s]*)

8 **return** *Result*

In a previous work, Ceolin et al. [51] estimated the trustworthiness of the tags in a test set by weighing them based on semantic similarity with all the tags by the same user from the training set. Another work, Ceolin et al. [52], demonstrated how the user expertise in a specific topic can be estimated from evidence from semantically close areas. Here we follow a similar approach, but we differ in that the works mentioned evaluate the annotations on a user basis, while we use provenance stereotypes instead.

Once the training set has been built, we evaluate the trustworthiness of the annotations in the test set for each group. We compare each annotation to be evaluated against each piece of evidence in the training set, and we use the semantic similarity emerging from that comparison to weigh the evidence and compute an opinion per annotation.

Once we have obtained one trust value per tag, we have to decide whether or not to accept the tag itself. To be more precise, for each tag we compute an entire opinion, representing the probabilities for each tag to be correctly evaluated with one of the possible evaluations. Now we must decide which evaluation to assign to the annotation. One strategy would use, for each annotation, the evaluation having the higher probability. We do not adopt this strategy because by doing so we will most likely tend to evaluate all tags of a given stereotype with the same dominant evaluation. For instance, if 95% of the training set annotations of one stereotype are useful, we will most likely evaluate all its annotations in the test set as useful. In turn, this implies that we do not take into account that we estimated that 5% of the annotations are not useful.

So we use an approach that combines the stereotype reputation with the trust values of the annotations, because we want to take fully into account the probabilities that are estimated by means of the reputation, and trust values estimate the trustworthiness of annotations.

Algorithm 3 presents the algorithm for annotation evaluation. First, it provides a procedure for computing the reputation of provenance stereotypes that takes as input a training set composed of tuples formed by tags, their evaluation and the identifier of the provenance stereotype they belong to. This procedure returns a set of pairs consisting of provenance stereotype identifiers and their reputation. Then the algorithm evaluates the new annotations, i.e. the annotations in the test set. This second procedure takes as input the training set (formed by tuples composed of tags, their evaluations and the identifier of the provenance stereotype they belong to) and the test set (formed by tags and their provenance stereotype identifier) and outputs a series of pairs consisting of the list of tags in the test set and the corresponding predicted evaluations.

To continue with the running example, suppose that Alex created his tag ("Chinese") on Monday at 13.00. Suppose, further, that in the cluster Monday-afternoon already the tags {Japanese, Christian} have been evaluated as useful, while {rose} has been evaluated as not useful. Now the trust value of the tag Chinese is evaluated as before, with as only difference that the evaluation is made on the basis of the provenance group it belongs to, and not of the author:

$$p_{Chinese}^{m} = sim(\text{Chinese, Japanese}) + sim(\text{Chinese, Christian}) = 0.9 + 0.63 = 1.53$$

$$n_{Chinese}^{m} = sim(\text{Chinese, rose}) = 0.57$$

$$\omega_{Chinese}^{m} \left(\frac{1.53}{1.53 + 0.57 + 2}, \frac{0.9}{1.53 + 0.57 + 2}, \frac{2}{1.53 + 0.57 + 2}, \frac{1}{2} \right)$$

$$E(\omega_{Chinese}^{m}) = 0.62$$

The reputation of the cluster is:

$$\omega_{Cluster}^{m} \left(\frac{2}{5}, \frac{1}{5}, \frac{2}{5}, \frac{1}{2} \right)$$

$$E(\omega_{Cluster}^{m}) = 0.6$$

So the tag inserted by Alex will be accepted only if it is one of the 60% best tags belonging to that cluster.

Implementation

The code for the representation and assessment of the annotations with the Open Annotation model has been developed using SWI-Prolog Semantic Web Library [53] and the Python libraries rdflib [54] and hcluster [55], and is available on the Web [56].

Results and discussion

We evaluated the algorithms that we proposed by running them on Steve.Museum and SEALINC Media experiment datasets. As described before, we split each dataset into a training and a test set, learn a model based on the training set, and evaluate it on the test set. There is a tradeoff between complexity and performance. On the one hand, a larger training set in general produces a more accurate model. On the other hand, an increased size of the training set induces a larger number of comparisons for each estimate, and hence an increased computation cost. To determine an optimal size for the training set in each case study, we have run the algorithm with different training set sizes, expressed in terms of annotations per user reputation, and tracked their performance.

Some errors can be due to intrinsic limitations of the experiment rather than imprecision of the algorithms. For instance, since training and test set are part of the same dataset, a larger training set means a smaller test set, and vice versa. Since our prediction is probabilistic, a small training set forces us to discretize our predictions, and this increases our error rate. Also, while an increase of the number of annotations used for building a reputation produces an increase of the reliability of the reputation itself, such an increase has the downside to reduce our test set size, since often only few annotators produce a large number of annotations. Nonetheless, we are bound to this limitation because we can only rely on learning reputations and trust values from museum evaluations since we do not have any possibility to decide if the internal inconsistency of the tags regarding a given image implies low trustworthiness of one or more of them.

Both the Steve.Museum dataset and the SEALINC Media dataset present an unbalanced distribution of tags, since about 76% of tags is evaluated as "useful" in the first, and 74% of the tags is evaluated as "4" or "5" in the second. In other words, in each of the datasets, about three quarters of the tags are positively evaluated. So, in principle, if we predict that all the tags are correct, then our accuracy would be 74% and 76% respectively, but that can hardly happen. In fact, our algorithm is made in such a manner that, even if an annotator has a very high reputation (e.g., 95%), still we do not accept all his tags, rather we accept only the 95% of them. New tags are all classified as trustworthy only if the user reputation is 100% or if it is very high (e.g., 99%) and because of discretization, the amount of untrustworthy tags is so small (e.g., 2%) that it is neglected. So, it may happen that all the tags provided by a given user are predicted to be trustworthy, but since users are treated as "silos", i.e. they are evaluated independently of each other in our system, then this means that there are other users in the dataset for which some tags are predicted to be untrustworthy, so to justify an overall percentage of trustworthy tags of 76% or 74%. Another important fact is that we cannot evaluate our system on a test set that is artificially balanced in terms of amount of positive and negative evidence. Indeed the basic assumption of our system is that the annotator reputation is representative enough of his performance. So, if a user has 80% reputation, our system will accept about 80% of his new tags. If we build the test set so that it is balanced, then our system will not be able to properly classify all the tags. Instead, we prefer to work with real data, so to be able to test if the annotator reputation is really representative of his performance. Since all the users in our system have high reputation, then necessarily our test set is unbalanced. Lastly, we must add that, since our system hardly evaluates all the tags as trustworthy, if the system was not able to predict at least some of the real trustworthy tags as trustworthy and some untrustworthy tags as untrustworthy, then the accuracy of the system would be higher than 74% or 76%. The fact that this is not the case, as we will see in the remainder of this section, testifies the effectiveness of the algorithms proposed.

Estimation of annotation trustworthiness based on user reputation - Algorithm 1

First, we evaluated the performance of algorithm 1. The results of SEALINC Media experiment are reported in Table 1, where correct tags are considered as a target to be retrieved, so that we can compute metrics such as precision, recall and F-measure. This first case study provided us interesting insights about the model that we propose. The evaluation shows positive results, with an accuracy higher than 80% and a recall higher than 85%.

Then, we applied the same evaluation over the Steve.Museum dataset and we reported the results obtained in Table 2, using the same metrics as before (that is, precision, recall, accuracy and F-measure). Here the performance is less favorable than for the first case study (accuracy around 70% and precision around 80%). This is possibly due to the different size of the Steve.Museum dataset, which may make it more varied than the SEALINC Media dataset. Moreover, the basic assumption of our algorithm is the existence of a correlation between the user identity and his trustworthiness. This might not always be the case, or the correlation might not have always the same strength (e.g. a good user in some situations might not annotate accurately). Also, we aim at learning the museum policies for trusting annotations, but these are not always easy to learn. Lastly, the decrease of accuracy with respect to the previous case is possibly due to the different tag distribution (of positives and negatives) of the dataset and different domains. Different distributions can make it harder to discriminate between trustworthy and untrustworthy tags (as one may encounter mostly one type of observations). Different domains can lead to a different variability of the topics of the tags and this fact affects the reliability of clusters computed on a semantic basis (since clusters will tend to contain less uniform tags, and medoids will be, on average, less representative of their corresponding clusters), and consequently affects the accuracy of the algorithm.

It is important to stress that, on the one hand, the increase of the size of the training set brings an improvement of the performance, while on the other hand, performance is already satisfactory with a small training set (five observations per user). Also, this improvement is small. This is important because: (1) the sole parameter that we did not set (i.e. size of the training set) does not seriously affect our results; and (2) when the size of the training set is small, the performance is relatively high, so the need of manual evaluation is reduced. The results are satisfactory even with a small training set, also thanks to the smoothing factor of subjective logic that allows us to compensate for the possibly limited representativity (with respect to the population) of a distribution estimated from a small sample.

Improving computational efficiency of the estimation of annotation trustworthiness - Algorithm 2

We evaluated the performance of Algorithm 2 on both datasets. Table 3 and Table 4 report the results for the SEALINC Media and the Steve.Museum datasets, respectively. Algorithm 2 is a variant of Algorithm 1 as it attempts to improve the computational efficiency of the first, while trying not to compromise its performance. We ran our evaluation with the same setting as before, with the same training set sizes. Moreover, in one case (Table 3) we also ran the algorithm with two different values for the "cut" parameter, to check its influence on the overall performance.

By comparing Table 3 with Table 1 we can see how the performance of Algorithm 1 is kept, and in some cases even improved, while the execution time is significantly reduced. The same holds for the Steve.Museum case, as we can see by comparing Table 4 and Table 2. Here, in a few limited cases the performance degrades, but in a negligible manner, and the computational time saving is even more evident than in the SEALINC Media case. The "cut" parameter, apparently, does not affect the performance much.

These considerations make us conclude that, at least in these case studies, it is worth clustering the training set on a semantic similarity basis, as this leads to a better computational efficiency, without compromising the performance in terms of precision, accuracy and recall.

Estimation of annotation trustworthiness based on provenance stereotypes - Algorithm 3

We evaluated the performance of Algorithm 3 on both datasets. Table 5 and Table 6 present the results for the SEALINC Media and the Steve.Museum datasets. We ran this evaluation with the same setting as before. Since we were interested only in checking whether the trustworthiness estimations based on provenance stereotypes perform as well as those based on user reputations in terms of precision and recall, we do not report the execution time of the algorithm.

Table 3 Results of the evaluation of Algorithm 2 over the SEALINC Media dataset

# Tags per reputation	% Training set covered	Accuracy	Precision	Recall	F-measure	Time (sec.)
clustered results (cut = 0.6)						
5	8%	0.73	0.88	0.81	0.84	43
10	19%	0.82	0.87	0.93	0.90	24
15	31%	0.83	0.87	0.95	0.91	14
20	41%	0.84	0.87	0.96	0.91	18
clustered results (cut = 0.3)						
5	8%	0.78	0.88	0.88	0.88	43
10	19%	0.82	0.87	0.93	0.90	14
15	31%	0.84	0.87	0.95	0.91	16
20	41%	0.84	0.87	0.96	0.92	21

Results of the evaluation of Algorithm 2 over the SEALINC Media dataset for training sets formed by aggregating 5, 10, 15 and 20 reputations per user. We report the percentage of dataset actually covered by the training set, the accuracy, the precision, the recall and the F-measure of our prediction.

Table 4 Results of the evaluation of Algorithm 2 over the Steve.Museum dataset

# Tags per reputation	% Training set covered	Accuracy	Precision	recall	F-measure	Time (sec.)
		clustered results (cut = 0.3)				
5	18%	0.71	0.80	0.84	0.82	707
10	27%	0.70	0.79	0.83	0.81	1004
15	33%	0.70	0.79	0.84	0.82	1197
20	39%	0.70	0.79	0.84	0.82	1286
25	43%	0.71	0.79	0.85	0.82	3080
30	47%	0.72	0.79	0.86	0.82	3660

Results of the evaluation of Algorithm 2 over the Steve.Museum dataset for training sets formed by aggregating 5, 10, 15, 20, 25 and 30 reputations per user. We report the percentage of dataset actually covered by the training set, the accuracy, the precision, the recall and the F-measure of our prediction.

By looking at the results we see that the performance is very satisfactory, and that the results achieved with this algorithm outperform those reported in the tables before, obtained with Algorithm 1 and Algorithm 2. In Table 5 precision is about 88% and recall ranges between 73% and 88%. The decrease in accuracy for the training set built with 20 annotations per reputation is plausibly due to the fact that many provenance stereotypes do not have 20 or more annotations available, so these cluster cannot contribute to the overall accuracy measurement, while they did with 5, 10 or 15 annotations per reputation.

Moreover, the amount of evidence needed to make these assessments is low, as demonstrated by the percentage covered by the training set over the dataset. In Table 6 the performance is even higher than in Table 5. First, this is due to the existence of a correlation between the provenance group an annotation belongs to and its trustworthiness. Second, the fact that the provenance stereotypes that we considered for this experiment are 21, which is much less than the number of users, together with the unbalance between useful and non-useful annotations in the Steve.Museum dataset (the first are much more plentiful than the latter) compensates a collateral effect of smoothing. In fact, smoothing helps in allocating some probability to unseen events (for instance, possible future mistakes of good users). So, because of smoothing, we predicted the existence of non-useful annotations for users who actually did not produce them (the dataset contains only relatively few non-useful annotations). Since there are many more users than provenance stereotypes, this error is higher with user-based estimates, where there are many more smoothed probability distributions (one per author), which causes many more annotations to be wrongly evaluated as non-useful. On the other hand, with provenance stereotypes, this error was much more limited, because the corresponding smoothed reputations introduced fewer wrong non-useful evaluations. Still, we will continue employing

Table 5 Results of the evaluation of Algorithm 3 over the SEALINC Media dataset

Annotations in each reputation	Accuracy	% of Dataset Covered by the Training set	Precision	Recall	F-measure
5	0.68	1.69%	0.88	0.73	0.80
10	0.71	3.35%	0.87	0.80	0.83
15	0.78	4.97%	0.88	0.88	0.88
20	0.72	6.45%	0.87	0.80	0.83

Results of the evaluation of Algorithm 3 over the SEALINC Media dataset for training sets formed by aggregating 5, 10, 15 and 20 reputations per user. We report the percentage of dataset actually covered by the training set, the accuracy, the precision, the recall and the F-measure of our prediction.

Table 6 Results of the evaluation of Algorithm 3 over the Steve.Museum dataset

Annotations in each reputation	Accuracy	% of Dataset Covered by the Training set	Precision	Recall	F-measure
5	0.84	0.25%	0.84	0.99	0.90
10	0.84	0.45%	0.84	0.99	0.90
15	0.84	0.66%	0.84	0.99	0.90
20	0.84	0.86%	0.84	0.99	0.90
25	0.84	1.04 %	0.84	0.99	0.90
30	0.84	1.22 %	0.84	0.99	0.90

Results of the evaluation of Algorithm 1 over the Steve.Museum dataset for training sets formed by aggregating 5, 10, 15, 20, 25 and 30 reputations per user. We report the percentage of dataset actually covered by the training set, the accuracy, the precision, the recall and the F-measure of our prediction.

smoothing, as these are posterior considerations based on the availability of privileged information about the test set (i.e. its evaluation), and smoothing allows to compensate the lack of this information. On the other hand, the specific Steve.Museum dataset possibly shows a limitation of smoothing.

In the previous section, we hypothesized that the time of creation of an annotation may implicitly affect its trustworthiness and that the users follow approximatively regular patterns in their behaviors. To support these statements, we made the following analyses:

- we computed the average of the user reputations per provenance group. The averages vary from 0.73 to 0.84 in the Steve.Museum case study and from 0.75 to 0.91 in the SEALINC Media case study. Each user that took part in the SEALINC Media experiment, participated only once. Moreover, their contributions are concentrated in the mid part of the weekdays, so we could not make additional checks. In the Steve.Museum dataset, instead, we also run a series of Wilcoxon signed-ranked tests at 95% confidence level (since the data distribution is not always normally distributed, as shown by a Shapiro-Wilk test at 95% confidence level, we prefer not to use a t-student test), and we discovered that:

  - there is no significant difference within user reputations in the morning, afternoon, and night slots respectively across the week. For instance, we took the reputations in the morning slots for Monday, Tuesday, etc. and the Wilcoxon signed-rank test showed no significant difference. The same holds for the afternoon and the night ones;
  - there is a significant difference between the morning and the afternoon slots and the afternoon and night slots. Here we compared the series of reputations per slot across the week;
  - if we compare the averages of the reputations with respect to the days (for instance, considering the three slots of Monday versus the three slots of Tuesday, etc.) we see no significant difference;
  - there is no significant difference between weekends and weekdays.

The first two points support our hypothesis because they show that actually there are some relevant differences between groups and actually these depend on the time of creation of an annotation. The third and the fourth point show that, at least in this case study, it is not useful to keep track of the day of the week when the annotation was created. On the other hand, the fact that we recorded the day of the week allowed us to check if there is any difference both among days and between weekend and weekdays, while if we started directly with this latter distinction, we could not have decreased the granularity.

- as we stated in the previous item, the average number of provenance groups a user contribution belongs to is 1 in the SEALINC Media dataset. In the Steve.Museum dataset, instead, the average number of groups a user contributions belongs to is 1.17, variance 0.56. This means that most of the users' contributions belong to one group. So we can say that, approximatively, there exists a one-to-many relation that links the groups with the users: given a group, we can identify a group of users that provide annotations mostly in that group. This means that, when we analyze the annotations that belong to a given group, then we implicitly analyze the annotations produced by a group of users that annotate mostly in that time interval. So the provenance group acts as a proxy to this group of users, and hence, in practice, we analyze the annotations in that group based on the reputations of the users linked to that group. In principle, there may be a high variance among the users belonging to a given provenance group. However, in the case studies analyzed in this paper, this does not happen to be the case, since the variance of the users reputation belonging to a given group is low.
- in the Steve.Museum case study, the variance of the user reputations ranges between 0.12 and 0.15. This shows that, even if the averages of user reputations per group range between 0.73 and 0.84, the reputations are not sparsely distributed. Rather, within provenance groups users tend to be rather homogeneous in terms of reputation. The same holds for the SEALINC Media case study, where the variance of user reputation per provenance group ranges between 0.004 and 0.01;
- the time that we used in our computation is the server time and the fact that, in principle, the annotations are collected worldwide, this might imply that our calculations are misleading. However, since: (1) as shown before, there is a consistent distinction between morning, afternoon and night reputations (which is determined by user performance, and users tend to contribute at fixed times), (2) the amount of tags annotated as "problematic-foreign" is very small (about 1.9%) and (3) the artifact annotated in the case study belong mainly to U.S. cultural heritage institutions, we assume that the annotations are approximatively provided by users in the same time zone or in the neighboring ones.

When grouping the tags based on time, the choice between coarser and finer granularity is not trivial and, in general, affects the uncertainty of the final result. Grouping the tags at a coarser granularity allows easily collecting evidence for a given group and finding a semantic justification for the differences between groups. If we find a difference between morning and afternoon tags, we can easily suppose (and possibly test) that this is due to the influence that different parts of the day have on the user conditions (tired, sleepy, etc.). If we find a difference between tags made at 8.00 a.m. and at 9.00 a.m., we may need additional information to justify semantically the reasons of such differences. On the other hand, a finer granularity may reveal to be useful to avoid to group together heterogeneous tags. All these are generic considerations, and the choice of the best granularity depends on the peculiarities of the single use case evaluated. In our cases, as is evident from the considerations above, we chose a coarser granularity for the hours of the day and a finer one for the days of the week, because this combination was the most significant and gave us the highest accuracy. Future work will investigate the possibility to automatically determine the best granularity level for this grouping.

Conclusions

We presented an algorithm for automatically evaluating the trustworthiness of user-contributed annotations by using subjective logic and semantic similarity to learn a model from a limited set of annotations evaluated by an institution. Moreover, we introduce two extensions of this algorithm. The first extension makes use of semantic similarity to cluster the set of evaluated annotations at our disposal (training set) and hence improve the computational efficiency of the algorithm. The second extension regards the possibility to adapt the algorithm to use provenance information instead of the user reputation as a basis for the trustworthiness estimations.

We evaluated each algorithm on two different datasets of annotations from the cultural heritage domain. The algorithm based on user reputation satisfactorily allows us to estimate the annotation trustworthiness with an accuracy of about 80% in one case and 70% in the other one. Clustering effectively helps in increasing the efficiency of the first extension, and the use of provenance information actually allow us to compute accurate estimates of annotations trustworthiness.

With the growth of information on the Web and with active contributions from online users, it becomes necessary to devise algorithms to automate the evaluation of the quality of the contributed information. Our methods are been proven to evaluate user contributed tags in cultural heritage domain with relatively high accuracy. We will aim, on the one hand, at reducing even further the need for evaluated annotations to bootstrap our system so to reduce the burden of cultural heritage institutions in this process, and on the other hand, we will investigate methods for further increasing the accuracy of our algorithms and for making effective use of more complex provenance information. This can be vital for the cultural heritage institutions which do not have many resources in terms of labour or finances at their disposal and decide to rely on crowdsourcing platform, as well as for many other institutions in similar situations.

Lastly, one of the research directions we intend to pursue regards the possibility to add analyses about the content of the annotated artifacts. For instance, the output of visual analysis tools in the case of cultural heritage artifacts could help to improve the quality of our estimates by combining the evidential reasoning we adopt with knowledge about the artifacts themselves. Such a direction opens up for applications of our approach in other contexts. In fact, we could apply our algorithm in combination with natural language processing methods in order to obtain tools for automatically reviewing, for instance, wiki articles or restaurant reviews.

Abbreviation
SEALINC Media: Socially enriched access to linked cultural media.

Competing interests
The authors declare that they have no competing interests.

Authors' contributions
DC contributed by designing the research questions, collecting one dataset, by designing the algorithms and implementing them, and by writing the article. AN contributed by collecting the datasets, by assisting the algorithm design and implementation and by writing the article. WF supervised the research carried, helping in defining the research questions, and proofread the article. All authors read and approved the final manuscript.

References

1. von Ahn L, Dabbish L (2004) Labeling images with a computer game In: Proceedings of the 2004 Conference on Human Factors in Computing Systems, CHI '04, Association for Computing Machinery, pp 319–326
2. Sabater J, Sierra C (2005) Review on computational trust and reputation models. Artif Intell Rev 24: 33–60
3. Artz D, Gil Y (2007) A survey of trust in computer science and the Semantic Web. J Web Semantic 5(2): 58–71
4. Golbeck J (2006) Trust on the World Wide Web: a survey. Foundations Trends Web Sci 1(2): 131–197
5. Castelfranchi C, Falcone R (1998) Proceedings of the 4th International Conference on Multi-Agent Systems, ICMAS '98. IEEE Computer Society, pp 72–79
6. Ellis A, Gluckman D, Cooper A, Greg A (2012) Your paintings: a nation's oil paintings go online, tagged by the public In: Proceedings of Museums and the Web 2012, Online
7. US Institute of Museum and Library Service (2013) Steve Social Tagging Project. [Accessed 9 January 2013]
8. Netherlands Institute for Sound and Vision (2012) Waisda? http://waisda.nl. [Accessed 14 August 2012]
9. Rijksmuseum (2013). https://www.rijksmuseum.nl/. [Accessed 23 September 2013]
10. Surowiecki J (2004) The wisdom of crowds: why the many are smarter than the few and how collective wisdom shapes business, economies, societies and nations. Anchor
11. Damme CV, Coenen T (2008) Quality metrics for tags of broad Folksonomies In: Proceedings of the 2008 International Conference on Semantic Systems, I-semantics'08. Journal of University Computer Science
12. Medelyan O, Frank E, Witten IH (2009) Human-competitive tagging using automatic keyphrase extraction In: Proceedings of the 2009 Conference on Empirical Methods in Natural Language Processing, EMNLP '09. Association for Computational Linguistics, pp 1318–1327
13. CiteULike (2012) CiteULike. http://www.citeulike.org/ [Accessed 8 December 2012]
14. Cattuto C, Benz D, Hotho A, Stumme G (2008) Semantic Grounding of Tag Relatedness in Social Bookmarking Systems In: Proceedings of the 7th International Semantic Web Conference, ISWC2008. Springer
15. Wikimedia Foundation (2013) Wikipedia. http://www.wikipedia.org. [Accessed 4 March 2013]
16. De la Calzada G, Dekhtyar A (2010) On measuring the quality of Wikipedia articles In: Proceedings of the 4th Workshop on Information Credibility, WICOW '10. Association for Computing Machinery, pp 11–18
17. Zeng H, Alhossaini MA, Ding L, Fikes R, McGuinness DL (2006) Computing trust from revision history In: Proceedings of the 2006 International Conference on Privacy, Security and Trust: Bridge the Gap Between PST Technologies and Business Services, PST2006. Association for Computing Machinery, p 8
18. Wang S, Iwaihara M (2011) Quality evaluation of wikipedia articles through edit history and editor groups In: Proceedings of the 13th Asia-Pacific Web Conference, APWeb'11. Springer-Verlag, pp 188–199
19. Demartini G (2007) Finding experts using Wikipedia In: Proceedings of the 2nd International ISWC+ASWC Workshop on Finding Experts on the Web with Semantics, FEWS 2007. CEUR-WS.org
20. Javanmardi S, Lopes C, Baldi P (2010) Modeling user reputation in wikis. Stat Anal Data Mining 3(2): 126–139
21. Ceolin D, Groth P, van Hage WR, Nottamkandath A, Fokkink W (2012) Trust evaluation through user reputation and provenance analysis In: Proceedings of the 8th International Workshop on Uncertainty Reasoning for the Semantic Web, URSW 2012, pp 15–26. CEUR-WS.org
22. Ceolin D, Nottamkandath A, Fokkink W (2012) Automated evaluation of annotators for museum collections using subjective logic In: Proceedings of the 6th IFIP WG 11.11 International Conference on Trust Management, IFIPTM. Springer, pp 232–239
23. Tavakolifard M, H P, Knapskog SJ (2009) Inferring trust based on similarity with TILLIT In: Proceedings of the 3rd IFIP WG 11.11 International Conference on Trust Management, IFIPTM, pp 133–148
24. Cilibrasi R, Vitányi PMB (2006) Automatic meaning discovery using Google In: Kolmogorov Complexity and Applications. Dagstuhl Seminar Proceedings
25. Ushioda A (1996) Hierarchical clustering of words and application to NLP tasks In: Proceedings of the 16th International Conference on Computational Linguistics, COLING. Association for Computational Linguistics, pp 28–41
26. G Begelman PK, Smadja F (2006) Automated tag clustering: improving search and exploration in the tag space In: Proceedings of the Collaborative Web Tagging Workshop at the WWW 2006
27. Hassan-Montero Y, Herrero-Solana V (2006) Improving tag-clouds as visual information retrieval interfaces In: Proceedings of Multidisciplinary Information Sciences and Technologies Conference, INSCIT 2006. Association for Computational Linguistics
28. Golbeck J, Hendler J (2004) Accuracy of metrics for inferring trust and reputation in semantic web-based social networks In: Proceedings of the 14th International Conference Engineering Knowledge in the Age of the Semantic Web, EKAW
29. Guha R, Kumar R, Raghavan P, Tomkins A (2004) Propagation of trust and distrust In: Proceedings of the 13th International World Wide Web Conference, WWW2004. Association for Computing Machinery, pp 403–412
30. Kamvar SD, Schlosser MT, Garcia-Molina H (2003) The Eigentrust algorithm for reputation management in P2P networks In: Proceedings of the 12th International World Wide Web Conference, WWW2003. Association for Computing Machinery, pp 640–651
31. Bizer C, Cyganiak R (2009) Quality-driven information filtering using the WIQA policy framework. J Web Semantics 7: 1–10
32. Hartig O, Zhao J (2009) Using web data provenance for quality assessment In: Proceedings of the 1st International Workshop on the role of Semantic Web in Provenance Management, SWPM 2009. CEUR-WS.org
33. Zaihrayeu I, da Silva PP, McGuinness DL (2005) IWTrust: Improving user trust in answers from the Web In: Proceedings of the 3th International Conference on Trust Management, vol 3477 of *iTrust*. Springer, pp 384–392
34. W3C (2013) PROV-DM: The PROV Data Model. http://www.w3.org/TR/2012/CR-prov-dm-20121211/. [Accessed 16 July 2013]
35. W3C (2013) PROV-O: The PROV Ontology. http://www.w3.org/TR/prov-o/. [Accessed 16 July 2013]

36. Ebden M, Huynh TD, Moreau L, Ramchurn S, Roberts S (2012) Network analysis on provenance graphs from a crowdsourcing application In: Proceedings of the 4th International Conference on Provenance and Annotation of Data and Processes, IPAW'12. Springer-Verlag, pp 168–182

37. Moreau L, Clifford B, Freire J, Futrelle J, Gil Y, Groth P, Kwasnikowska N, Miles S, Missier P, Myers J, Plale B, Simmhan Y, Stephan E, den Bussche JV (2011) The open provenance model core specification (v1.1). Future Generations Comput Syst 27(6): 743–756

38. Altintas I, Anand MK, Crawl D, Bowers S, Belloum A, Missier P, Ludäscher B, Goble CA, Sloot PMA (2010) Understanding collaborative studies through interoperable workflow provenance In: Proceedings of the 2nd International Conference on Provenance and Annotation of Data and Processes, IPAW'10. Springer, pp 42–58

39. Miller GA (1995) WordNet: a lexical database for English. Commun ACM 38(11): 39–41

40. Cilibrasi RL, Vitanyi PMB (2007) The Google similarity distance. IEEE Transactions on Knowledge and Data Engineering 19(3): 370–383. http://dx.doi.org/10.1109/TKDE.2007.48.

41. Vossen P, Hofmann K, de Rijke M, Sang ETK, Deschacht K (2007) The Cornetto database: architecture and user-scenarios In: Proceedings of 7th Dutch-Belgian Information Retrieval Workshop, DIR 2007, pp 89–96

42. Wu Z, Palmer M (1994) Verbs semantics and lexical selection In: Proceedings of the 32nd annual meeting on Association for Computational Linguistics, ACL '94. Association for Computational Linguistics, pp 133–138

43. Lin D (1998) An information-theoretic definition of similarity. In: Proceedings of the 15th International Conference on Machine Learning, ICML '98. Morgan Kaufmann Publishers Inc., pp 296–304

44. Ceolin D, Nottamkandath A, Fokkink W (2012) Subjective logic extensions for the semantic web. In: Proceedings of the 8th International Workshop on Uncertainty Reasoning for the Semantic Web, URSW, pp 27–38. CEUR-WS.org

45. Loper E, Bird S (2002) NLTK: The Natural Language Toolkit. In: ETMTNLP '02. Association for Computational Linguistics, Stroudsburg, PA, USA, pp 63–70

46. Marsi E (2013) pyCornetto. https://github.com/emsrc/pycornetto.

47. Leyssen MHR, Traub MC, van Ossenbruggen JR, Hardman L (2012) Is it a bird or is it a crow? The influence of presented tags on image tagging by non- Expert users. CWI Tech. Report INS-1202, CWI

48. Sanderson R, Ciccarese P, de Sompel HV, Clark T, Cole T, Hunter J, Fraistat N (2012) Open annotation core data Model. Tech. rep., W3C Community

49. Jøsang A (2001) A logic for uncertain probabilities. Int J Uncertainty Fuzziness Knowledge-Based Syst 9(3): 279–212

50. Gower JC, Ross GJS (1969) Minimum spanning trees and single linkage cluster analysis. J R Stat Soc 18: 54–64

51. Ceolin D, Nottamkandath A, Fokkink W (2013) Semi-automated assessment of annotation trustworthiness In: Proceedings of the 11th Annual Conference on Privacy, Security and Trust, PST2013. IEEE Computer Society

52. Ceolin D, Nottamkandath A, Fokkink W (2012) Automated evaluation of annotators for museum collections using subjective logic In: Proceedings of the 6th IFIP WG 11.11 International Conference on Trust Management, IFIPTM 2012. Springer, pp 232–239

53. SWI-Prolog Semantic WebLibrary (2013). http://www.swi-prolog.org/pldoc/package/semweb.html. [Accessed 10 April 2013]

54. Python libraries rdflib (2013). http://www.rdflib.net/. [Accessed 10 April 2013]

55. Eads D (2008). http://scipy-cluster.googlecode.com/. [Hcluster: Hierarchical Clustering for SciPy]

56. Code published online (2013). http://trustingwebdata.org/JTM2013. [Accessed 23 September 2013]

A trust-based framework for vehicular travel with non-binary reports and its validation via an extensive simulation testbed

Robin Cohen[1], Jie Zhang[2]*, John Finnson[1], Thomas Tran[3] and Umar F Minhas[1]

*Correspondence:
zhangj@ntu.edu.sg
[2]School of Computer Engineering,
Nanyang Technological University,
Singapore, Singapore
Full list of author information is
available at the end of the article

Abstract

In this paper, we offer an algorithm for intelligent decision making about travel path planning in mobile vehicular ad-hoc networks (VANETs), for scenarios where agents representing vehicles exchange reports about traffic. One challenge that arises is how best to model the trustworthiness of those traffic reports. To this end, we outline an algorithm for effectively soliciting, receiving and analyzing the trustworthiness of these reports, to drive a vehicle?s decision about the path to follow. Distinct from earlier work, we clarify the need for specifying the conditions under which reports are exchanged and for processing non-binary reports, culminating in a proposed algorithm to achieve that processing, as part of the trust modeling and path planning. To validate our approach we then offer a detailed evaluation framework that achieves large scale simulation of traffic, travel and reporting of information, confirming the value of our proposed approach by demonstrating the average speed of vehicles which follow our algorithm (compared to ones that do not). This experimental framework is promoted as a significant contribution towards the goal of evaluating trust algorithms for intelligent decision making in traffic scenarios.

Keywords: Multi-faceted trust modeling; Multiagent systems; VANET; Vehicle routing; Traffic control

Introduction

In this paper, we present a method for exchanging reports between agents in multiagent systems that allows the trustworthiness of peers providing non-binary information to be modeled, as part of an agent?s decision making process. We are motivated by the problem of enabling agents to make travel decisions based on traffic reports received by peers, in a setting of mobile vehicular ad-hoc networks (VANETs). In this environment, maintaining a multi-faceted trust model is of value and our proposal for supporting non-binary reports ultimately integrates each facet of this trust model, in order for an agent to determine which travel path to follow. For example, a non-binary report could indicate a traffic congestion figure, rather than a binary response to a question such as ?Is the traffic heavy?? Our starting point is a model that includes a calculation of the consensus opinion about roads from the majority of agents, but that assumes only binary reports. From here, we sketch algorithms that clarify in greater detail how to support effective communication between the agents in the environment and how this would then dictate the travel decision making of an agent who is receiving traffic reports from peers.

In order to demonstrate the effectiveness of our framework, we introduce a detailed testbed that simulates vehicles traveling in an environment, making path planning decisions based on non-binary traffic reports from peers whose trustworthiness has been modeled. We offer an extensive set of simulations that serve to validate our approach, illustrating how effective the average path time taken by our vehicles is, in comparison with a best case scenario with perfect knowledge and with models that integrate less detailed trust modeling.

The dual contributions are: i) an effective decision making process for intelligent agents in VANET environments where trust is modeled and non-binary reports are exchanged ii) an extensive testbed of use for measuring the value of different trust modeling algorithms, in travel environments where agents exchange reports. We clarify the importance of these contributions in comparison with related work in the field.

Background: multi-faceted trust model

In this section, we outline our original framework for modeling trust in VANET environments ([1-3]). We consider the driver of each vehicle in our VANET environment to be represented by an agent. In order for each vehicle on the road to make effective traffic decisions, information is sought from other vehicles[a] (about the traffic congestion on a particular road). As a result, for each driver an intelligent agent constructs and maintains a model for each of the other vehicles. Travel decisions are then made based on a multi-faceted model of agent[b] trustworthiness. This is necessary because when asked, each agent may report inaccurate traffic congestion, in an effort to deflect other vehicles from certain roads. In particular, we propose a core processing algorithm to be used by each agent that seeks advice (about travel paths, based on traffic) from other vehicles in the environment as summarized below.

Algorithm 1: Computation Steps

---

while *on theroad* **do**

    Send requests and receive responses;

    if *in need of advice* **then**

        Choose n; //number of agents to ask for advice

        //according to roles and experiences

        Prioritize n agents;

        if *response consensus > acceptable ratio* **then**

            Follow advice in response;

        else

            Follow advice of agent with highest role and highest trust value;

    Verify reliability of advice;

    Update agents? trust values;

In order to cope with possible data sparsity, various facets (highlighted in this section in bold) of each agent are taken into consideration when reasoning about travel, including the agent?s role, location and inherent trustworthiness (determined on the basis of past experiences with this particular agent - i.e. whether past advice has proven to be trustworthy). Each of these facets of the agent is stored within the trust model.

We first acknowledge that certain vehicles in the environment may play a particular **role** and, on this basis, merit greater estimates of trustworthiness. For example, there may be vehicles representing the police and other traffic authorities (authority) or ones representing radio stations dedicated to determining accurate traffic reports by maintaining vehicles in the vicinity of the central routes (expert). Or there may be a collection of agents representing a ?commuter pool? routinely traveling the same route, sharing advice (seniority).

Consideration of any past personal **experiences** with agents allows the model to include any learning about particular agents due to previous encounters, specifically modeling trustworthiness each time and adjusting the level of trust to be higher or lower, based on the outcome of the advice that is offered. The equations which adjust experience-based trust are as below:

$$T_A(B) \leftarrow T_A(B) + \alpha(1 \quad T_A(B)) \tag{1}$$

$$T_A(B) \leftarrow T_A(B) + \beta(1 \quad T_A(B)) \tag{2}$$

Experience-based trustworthiness is represented and maintained following the model of [4] where $T_A(B) \in (\quad 1, 1)$ represents A?s trust in B (with -1 for total distrust and 1 for total trust) which is incremented by $0 < \alpha < 1$ using Equation (1) if B?s advice is found to be reliable (positive experience), or decremented by $\quad 1 < \beta < 0$ using Equation (2) if unreliable (negative experience), with $\beta > \alpha$ to reflect that trust is harder to build up but easier to tear down. Distinct from the original model of [4], the values of α and β can be set to be event-specific. For example, when asking about a major accident, these values may be set high, to reflect considerable disappointment with inaccurate advice. We also incorporate a requirement for agents to reveal whether the traffic information they are providing has been directly observed or only indirectly inferred from other reports that agent has received. The critical distinction of direct or indirect reporting then influences the values set for α and β, introducing greater penalties for disappointment with direct advice. In [2] we discuss at greater length the incentives to honesty that are introduced within this framework; for brevity, we omit that discussion in this paper.

A central calculation to influence the travel decision of each agent is the determination of **majority consensus** amongst the agents providing advice about a particular road. The agent maintains, as part of her model of other agents, a list of agents to ask for advice. This list is ordered from higher roles to lower roles with each group G_i of agents of similar roles being ordered from higher experience-based trust ratings to lower ratings. The agent sets a value n and asks the first n agents[c] from her ordered list the question (thus using priority-based trust), receives their responses (reports), and then performs majority-based trust measurement. Suppose that q of these n agents declare that their reports are from direct experience/observation. The requesting agent determines whether there are sufficient direct witnesses such that she can make a decision based solely on their reports.

If $q \geq N_{min}$, then the requesting agent will only consider the reports from the q direct witnesses if a majority consensus on a response can be reached, up to some tolerance set by the requester (e.g. the agent may want at most 30% of the responders to disagree), then the response is taken as the advice and followed. If $q < N_{min}$, then there are insufficient direct witnesses; the agent will consider reports from both direct and indirect witnesses, assigning different weight factors to them, computing and following the majority opinion. (Once the actual road conditions are verified, the requesting agent adjusts the experience-based trust ratings of the reporting agents: It penalizes (rewards) more those agents who reported incorrect (correct) information in the direct experience case than those agents with incorrect (correct) information in the indirect experience case.) If a majority consensus cannot be reached, then instead, the agent relies on role-based trust and experience-based trust (e.g., taking the advice from the agent with highest role and highest experience trust value). Note that in order to eventually admit new agents into consideration, the agent will also ask a certain number of agents beyond the nth one in the list. The responses here will not be considered for decision, but will be verified to update experience-based trust ratings and some of these agents may make it into the top n agents, in this way.

The computation of majority consensus adheres to the set of formulae outlined as follows: Suppose agent A receives a set of m reports $\mathcal{R} = \{R_1, R_2, \ldots, R_m\}$ from a set of n other agents $\mathcal{B} = \{B_1, B_2, \ldots, B_n\}$ regarding an event. Agent A will consider more heavily the reports sent by agents who have higher level roles and larger experience-based trust values. When performing majority-based process, we also take into account the **location** closeness between the reporting agent and the reported event, and the closeness between the **time** when the event has taken place and that of receiving the report. We define C_t (time closeness), C_l (location closeness), T_e (experience-based trust) and T_r (role-based trust). Note that all these parameters belong to the interval $(0, 1)$ except that T_e needs to be scaled to fit within this interval by $(T_e + 1)/2$.

For each agent B_i ($1 \leq i \leq n$) belonging to a subset of agents $\mathcal{B}(R_j) \subseteq \mathcal{B}$ who report the same report $R_j \in \mathcal{R}$ ($1 \leq j \leq m$), we aggregate the effect of its report according to the above factors. The aggregated effect $E(R_j)$ from reports sent by agents in $\mathcal{B}(R_j)$ can be formulated as follows [2]:

$$E(R_j) = \sum_{B_i \in \mathcal{B}(R_j)} \frac{T_e(B_i) T_r(B_i)}{C_t(R_j) C_l(B_i) W(B_i)} \tag{3}$$

$W(B_i)$ is a weight factor set to 1 if agent B_i who sent report R_j is an **indirect** witness, and $W(B_i)$ is set to a value in $(0, 1)$ if user B_i is a direct witness[d].

A majority consensus can be reached if

$$\frac{M(R)}{\sum_{R_j \in \mathcal{R}} E(R_j)} \geq 1 \quad \varepsilon \tag{4}$$

where $\varepsilon \in (0, 1)$ is set by agent A to represent the maximum error rate that A can accept and $M(R) = \max_{R_j \in \mathcal{R}} E(R_j)$. A majority consensus can be reached if the percentage of the opinion (the effect among different reports) over all possible opinions is above the threshold set by agent A.

The trust modeling framework described so far clarifies the algorithms that lead to the calculation of the trustworthiness value which would then be stored in each agent model.

Trip planning decisions of a vehicle would then be made in light of these particular agent models. One element that requires further clarification is detailed agent communication protocols to exchange reports. This is elaborated in the section that follows.

Agent communication protocols to exchange reports

The framework in [3] (see also [1,2]) is designed with a pull based communication protocol, where agents send requests to other agents for information. In addition to this classic pull oriented design, we introduce a push based protocol for broadcasting information. These protocols dictate when communication is initiated and to whom. Either or both of the two protocols can be used for communicating information between agents. Algorithm 2 describes the push and pull based protocol and how a priority road information request is sent by agents. This is part of our proposal for specifying when trust modeling should be integrated into the decision making process of these agents.

We note that this algorithm serves to provide important detail and clarification to advance the earlier proposal of [3]. In that work, the messaging proposed was vague. It was suggested that the message content (congestion information about a road) would be a ?yes? or ?no? response to a question ?Is this road congested?? and that this response would be pulled to the requesting agent. When the pulls would occur was left vague as ?in need of advice? As such, which roads were being investigated was also left unspecified. The concept of a priority road, introduced below, facilitates messaging and serves to provide the clearer specification of communication. Roads are placed into priority for an agent if there is a gap of information about congestion; subsequent to receiving a report about a priority road, that road?s status may be altered to cause it to be removed from the priority list (if sufficient information on that road has accumulated). How agents choose to designate a road as priority can be left as an implementation detail. In the simulations used to validate our model, if road information was empty or was sufficiently old, that road would be added to the priority list.

Algorithm 2: Pull and Push Based Communication

---

while *on the road* **do**

    if *Triggered according to communication frequency* **then**

        //Pull protocol

        //Get road to request advice about and agent to request from

        if *priority road exists* **then**

            Choose highest priority road;

            Get trustworthy agent;

            if *Trustworthy agent exists* **then**

                Send request to trustworthy agent for advice concerning the high priority road;

            else

                Send request to any agent for advice concerning the high priority road;

    //Push protocol

    //Broadcast current location and congestion to agents

    Broadcast current location and congestion;

The pull protocol allows agents (requester) to request information from other agents (requestee). The trustworthiness of the information from the requestee agent is modeled and used to determine what path to follow based on the report produced. On the other hand, the push protocol allows agents to send information to other agents, even if it were not requested. The trustworthiness of the sender agent is still modeled; this may then be employed during decision making about travel paths. Both of these protocols are set to occur according to a certain communication frequency; this is the tactic employed during our simulation of traffic which serves to provide the validation of our proposed framework (see Section ?Simulation results?). Setting the communication to happen fairly frequently allows agents to inquire about any roads for which they lack sufficient guidance and keeps the information flowing between agents, from the push broadcasting.

Three types of messages are supported within our protocol. The three messages are a transmission of an agent?s location and congestion (Location and Congestion Push), a request for congestion information about a specific road (Priority Road Information Pull Request), and a response for congestion information about a specific road (Priority Road Information Pull Response).

We begin with a clarification of how our messaging framework would support trust modeling in the context of Boolean traffic reports. Algorithm 1 theoretically sends requests only to agents in a prioritized list, when advice was needed. Our proposed update to this algorithm, shown in Algorithm 3, would have each agent?s knowledge base continuously updated with periodic messages, from the pull, push or both protocols. When advice is needed, the most relevant and trustworthy reports are chosen and used.

Algorithm 3: New Majority Computation Steps, with Advice Gathering Update

---

while *on the road* **do**
  Send requests and receive responses;
  if *in need of advice* **then**
    Choose n reports R; //number of reports to use for advice
    Check Priority Road(Current Road);//to help update the Priority list
    Prioritize n reports; //according to roles and experiences
    if *response consensus > acceptable ratio* **then**
      Follow advice in response;
    else
      Follow advice of agent with highest role and highest trust value;
  Verify reliability of advice;
  Update agents? trust values;

The work by Minhas et al. mentioned in Section ?Background: multi-faceted trust model? presented a Multi-faceted Trust Management Framework that was described as operational for Boolean values of congestion (Heavy (True), Light (False)). In order to calculate a majority opinion, reports which featured the same Boolean value of congestion were aggregated together. The percentage of reports with same congestion value would be compared against a threshold to determine whether the advice would be followed. The trust modeling itself respects the formulae outlined in Section ?Background: multi-faceted trust model? The use of a new advice gathering protocol (as per Algorithm 2) would not intrinsically alter the majority opinion calculation; it simply clarifies how traffic reports are retrieved. Note that calling *Check Priority Road(Current Road)* within this algorithm has the eventual effect of coping with stale or missing information on roads that are critical to current path planning.

Our proposed numeric trust modeling

In this section we clarify how our framework could support the use of numeric traffic reports, leading to a ?confidence metric? used for trust modeling, in contrast to the Boolean evaluation of traffic in Section ?Background: multi-faceted trust model? Our new proposed confidence metric and use of numeric congestion and trust values serve to allow a more accurate description of traffic and agent information.

The original theory in Section ?Background: multi-faceted trust model? assumed that congestion would be communicated as a simple *true* (Heavy) or *false* (Light), stating either that the road was congested or not. However, direct application may result in an unfair and biased calculation of the majority opinion. This is because determining whether a road is congested or not is a subjective opinion and is prone to inaccuracies. Also, by representing the congestion as a Boolean, this severely limits the system?s ability to compare roads, evaluate agents, and make the best decisions. Our proposed model seeks to alleviate this problem by representing congestion as a number, which will bring a more suitable level of accuracy to the system[e].

Formula (3) shows the calculation for the aggregated effect of a majority opinion. The new way of representing congestion as a numeric value requires a careful recasting of formula (3). (3) aggregates the effect of all agents that sent the same report (i.e. cong = true). This simple aggregation of similar reports is impossible with the new congestion representation because there are no longer only two types of reports (Cong=true or Cong=false). In the new framework, each report must be evaluated for addition into the majority opinion system. This is done by giving the report a confidence and then evaluating it for inclusion into the majority opinion (similar to the aggregated effect calculation).

The following sections will detail how the factors of experience and role based trust, time and location closeness, and whether the advice is direct or indirect are incorporated into our proposed confidence metric and utilized in calculating a majority opinion.

Confidence calculation

Confidence functions as a metric similar to trust, and is calculated by combining many different report and agent factors, which were introduced in Formula (3) and will be described in detail later in this section. These factors include experience and role based trust, time and location closeness, and whether the advice is direct or indirect.

Our proposed equation for calculating confidence must effectively replace Formula (3), while representing a trust-like metric. Modifications to confidence should then be reflected in a manner similar to how trust is increased and decreased in Equations (1) and (2). α and β function in these equations as a standard for increasing and decreasing trust, respectively. For our proposed confidence calculation it did not make sense to atomically increase or decrease the value according to the influencing factor (role, time closeness, etc.). The increase or decrease should reflect the significance of the factor. As a result, our proposed confidence metric replaces Formula (3) with Equation (6), where Equations (1) and (2) are used as the basis for calculating the confidence of report R_j, through a modified summation of a geometric series[f].

The factors of role based trust, time and location closeness, and whether the advice is direct or indirect in Formula (3), are reflected through Variable (G). Each factor is integrated, in turn, yielding an overall *Conf* value. In order to do so, G needs to be calculated, as explained in the subsections that follow[g]. Experience based trust of an agent automatically forms the default value of the confidence metric ($CurrConf(R_j)$). Variable (G) represents the number of times[h] to increase or decrease confidence. G?s calculation is specific to each factor. If G is calculated to a negative value, this indicates that β should be used instead of α. Examples are shown in Section ?Confidence calculation examples? The following sections briefly detail how each factor influences G; however the exact calculations are dependent on how parameter values are chosen, within an implementation.

$$\gamma(G, \alpha, \beta) = \begin{cases} \alpha & \text{if } G \geq 0 \\ \beta & \text{otherwise} \end{cases} \tag{5}$$

$$Conf(R_j) = (CurrConf(R_j) \quad 1)(1 \quad \gamma(G, \alpha, \beta))^G + 1 \tag{6}$$

Majority

Majority based trust is incorporated into our framework as a core algorithm for determining the trustworthiness of an agent, to then dictate whether to believe the congestion value reported about a road, which influences path planning. Section ?Background: multi-faceted trust model? describes majority based trust as a consensus, with a value which has been agreed upon by many agents. For our proposed non-Boolean extension to trust modeling, majority based trust is described as an opinion, where a similar value has been agreed upon by many agents. The rationale for the change from a Boolean based congestion value to a numerical congestion value was described in the beginning of Section ?Our proposed numeric trust modeling?

The advice is used by choosing and prioritizing information from various reports and calculating a majority opinion, which is followed if its confidence is above a threshold, similar to the threshold of Equation 4. The primary advice presented in Section ?Background: multi-faceted trust model? would be road congestion reports, which would be used to help an agent decide what roads to take and which to avoid by considering all the facets of the multidimensional trust model. This continues to hold in our framework. In our calculation, if the confidence is below a threshold, then the advice is used from the report with the highest confidence.

The majority opinion is calculated using Algorithm 4. All relevant advice reports referencing a location are retrieved and prioritized into a list of size n. The majority opinion is then calculated, stored, and reported back to the agent. If a report contains information that is suspicious with respect to other reports that have been observed, such as an extremely high congestion report, the sender is reported as a suspicious agent. Labeling agents as suspicious is helpful in order to remove them from consideration, regardless of their current trustworthiness value. The framework will then process the suspicious agent, profiling it and updating its trust value in the knowledge base.

Algorithm 4: New Majority Computation Steps, with Numerical Congestion Metric

---

while *on the road* **do**

    Send requests and receive responses;

    if *in need of advice* **then**

        Choose *n* reports *R*; //number of reports to use for advice

        Check Priority Road(Current Road);//to help update the Priority list

        Prioritize *n* reports; //according to Confidence (roles, experiences, time, location, and if report is indirect or direct)

        foreach *n reports* **do**

            if R_j *suspicious* **then**

                Report suspicious agent R_j;

            else

                Include report R_j in Majority;

            if *Majority suspicious* **then**

                Decrease Majority confidence;

        if *Majority confidence > acceptable threshold && Number of reports > n threshold* **then**

            Follow advice in response;

        else

            Follow advice of report with highest confidence;

    Verify reliability of reports;

    Update users? trust values;

Majority calculation

Algorithm 4 is a modified algorithm from Algorithm 1, which shows the calculation of a majority opinion in the framework. The algorithm uses suspicious agent detection in helping to avoid the inclusion of congestion advice which is outside a standard deviation from the current majority congestion. The majority opinion is used if there are at least *n* agents to use advice from and the majority confidence is above the majority threshold.

Suspicion calculation

Suspicion detection is important to include to help avoid congestion advice that greatly deviated from the current majority. Only using advice that has similar congestion reports forms our majority opinion, rather than conceiving of majority opinion as just an average congestion of the highest trusted agents (*n*).

    If an agent is deemed suspicious, then they are reported and the agent?s advice is not used in the majority opinion calculation. However, the reverse is possible where if an agent?s advice has higher confidence than the majority and confidence greatly deviates from the majority. If this happens then the majority confidence is decreased proportionally and the agent?s advice is potentially used as the *report with highest confidence*.

Experience

Experience based trust is the most basic type of trust and is applied to every agent in our framework. As detailed in Section ?Background: multi-faceted trust model?, it is trust as a result of direct experiences with the individual agent. This is updated when the model encounters information that it can use in a judgmental nature. An example of such information would be from detecting suspicious information being reported by an agent, encountering definitive information that can be used as a comparison factor against information previously reported by an agent, or processing the opinion of a more trusted agent about the agent in question. Since experience based trust is the most basic type of trust, this forms the basis of the confidence calculation.

This facet of trust management is very simple but powerful. Section ?Simulation results? demonstrates this through *basic* simulations which only use experience and majority based trust.

Role

Experience based trust is a powerful tool for profiling agents; however, it is often challenged in scenarios with data sparsity. Data sparsity is an absence of agents with which the resident agent has had previous experience. This is often the case in the real world where it is rare to encounter a car which you have previously profiled.

Role based trust helps alleviate the issue of data sparsity by assigning roles to agents in our framework. As detailed in Section ?Background: multi-faceted trust model?, predefined roles (e.g. police patrols, traffic reporters or taxi drivers) are assigned to all agents in the system. Different roles may be associated with different levels of trust. The model uses the four different types of roles, motivated by the classification of Minhas et al: *Ordinary*, *Seniority* (e.g. commuter pool), *Expert* (e.g. news station car), *Authority* (e.g. police).

Role based trust is incorporated into a proposition?s confidence calculation by increasing it by a magnitude proportional to the particular role?s rank. Equation 7 shows how G is calculated for Equation 6. *RPenal* is a standard value for weighting roles, and *RoleRank* is the rank of the roles. G is inversely proportional to *RoleRank* so that higher roles (*Authority* has *RoleRank* of 2) warrant greater increases in confidence.

$$G = RPenal/RoleRank \qquad (7)$$

Time/Location

It can often be the case that an agent receives a great deal of reports about a road, with some being more accurate than others. A combination of time and location closeness is used in confidence calculations to determine how accurate reports are. Time closeness is a measure of how old the report is with respect to when the advice is needed. Location closeness is a measure of how how far the agent providing the report is to the road in question.

Time and location closeness helps alleviate the issue of old and inaccurate reports by assigning these metrics to traffic report propositions and using them in confidence calculations in our framework. As detailed in Section ?Background: multi-faceted trust model?, metrics of time and location closeness are used in calculating a majority consensus. Our proposed model similarly uses these metrics in calculating a majority opinion, through modifying the confidence of propositions by a magnitude inversely proportional to these metrics[i].

Equations 8 and 9 show how G is calculated for Equation 6. *TPenal* and *LPenal* are standard values for weighting time and location respectfully. *TimeDifference* and *LocDifference* are time difference and location difference respectively. *MultiplicativeFactor* is a standard multiplicative factor for the calculation (max confidence increase will be *MultiplicativeFactor*, and not 1, if *TimeDifference* or *LocDifference* is 0.). The calculation finds the difference, for example, between *Time Difference* and *TPenal* and then divides the difference by *TPenal*. This achieves the purpose of scaling the values to be within their unit metrics[j].

$$G = (TPenal \quad TimeDifference)/TPenal * MultiplicativeFactor \qquad (8)$$

$$G = (LPenal \quad LocDifference)/LPenal * MultiplicativeFactor \qquad (9)$$

Direct/Indirect

The framework of this paper also incorporates the distinction of direct and indirect reports. Direct reports are reports which have been directly observed and reported by an agent. Indirect reports are direct reports of a third agent which are stored in the knowledge base of the agent the resident agent is communicating with.

For example, when one agent (Ar) communicates with another agent (A2) through a pull request concerning a priority road (R1), A2?s highest confidence traffic report concerning R1 may have been reported by another agent (A3) and not A2. A2 would send Ar the report and indicate that it is an indirect report[k] (A2 did not create the report), which would include A2?s confidence of the report. A2 calculates the confidence using the report?s experience and role based trust, and time closeness[l].

The inclusion of indirect reports, as opposed to only allowing direct reports, is important because it greatly increases the response rate of a pull request concerning a priority road. Indirect reports, however, may be more inaccurate than direct reports. This is taken into consideration through the use of the corresponding agent?s confidence of the report (A2?s confidence of the report) and by modifying the confidence value of a report by a predetermined factor.

Equation 10 shows how G is calculated for Equation 6. *InPenal* is a standard value for penalizing indirect reports, and *IfIndirect* is 1 if the report is indirect and 0 otherwise.

$$G = InPenal * IfIndirect \qquad (10)$$

Confidence calculation examples

This subsection presents two examples which describe how the confidence metric for a report is calculated according to the multidimensional trust factors of experience and role based trust, location and time closeness, and whether the report is indirect or not. The following examples will show iterative modifications to the confidence value of a report according to the various factors.

The following calculation demonstrates how the confidence value for the report was calculated. Note that all the parameter values used in these examples are the ones used in our implementation[m].

Example 1. (illustrating α)

Confidence	$= Agent\_39 : trust\_degree\ (0.6)$
G_{time}	$= (\text{TPenal}(90) - \text{TimeDiff}(18))/\text{TPenal}(90)$ $*\text{MultiplicativeFactor}(1.5)$
G_{time}	$= 1.2$
Confidence(0.6)	$= (\text{Confidence}(0.6) - 1)(1 - \alpha)^{|G_{time}|} + 1$
Confidence	$= 0.6475$
G_{loc}	$= (\text{LPenal}(200) - \text{LocDiff}(100))/\text{LPenal}(200)$ $*\text{MultiplicativeFactor}(1.5)$
G_{loc}	$= 0.75$
Confidence(0.6475)	$= (\text{Confidence}(0.6475) - 1)(1 - \alpha)^{|G_{loc}|} + 1$
Confidence	$= 0.674$

Example 2. (illustrating β)

Confidence	$= Agent\_41 : trust\_degree\ (0.7)$
G_{role}	$= \text{RPenal}(8)/\text{RoleRank}(2)$
G_{role}	$= 4$
Confidence(0.7)	$= (\text{Confidence}(0.7) - 1)(1 - \alpha)^{|G_{role}|} + 1$
Confidence	$= 0.8032$
G_{time}	$= (\text{TPenal}(90) - \text{TimeDiff}(180))/\text{TPenal}(90)$ $*\text{MultiplicativeFactor}(1.5)$
G_{time}	$= -1.5$
Confidence(0.7813)	$= (\text{Confidence}(0.7813) - 1)(1 - \beta)^{|G_{time}|} + 1$
Confidence	$= 0.7413$
G_{loc}	$= (\text{LPenal}(200) - \text{LocDiff}(500))/\text{LPenal}(200)$ $*\text{MultiplicativeFactor}(1.5)$
G_{loc}	$= -2.25$
Confidence(0.7604)	$= (\text{Confidence}(0.7604) - 1)(1 - \beta)^{|G_{loc}|} + 1$
Confidence	$= 0.6100$
$G_{indirect}$	$= \text{InPenal}(-2) * \text{IfIndirect}(1)$
$G_{indirect}$	$= -2$
Confidence(0.6991)	$= (\text{Confidence}(0.6991) - 1)(1 - \beta)^{|G_{indirect}|} + 1$
Confidence	$= 0.4385$

Travel decisions when using numeric trust modeling

Algorithm 4 clarifies whether an agent will choose to take a certain road or not based on consensus about the congestion on the road. If the agent wants to reason about which road to choose (from a set of possible roads), it can run Algorithm 4 for each road. This algorithm is of use in scenarios such as the simulations we present in the following section, where a path planning algorithm is considering specific roads in order to propose the one that is best for the agent?s decision making. This algorithm continues to clarify our proposal for integrating trust modeling into agent decision making, in these travel environments.

Simulation results

This section describes the simulation tests performed to compare and contrast the effectiveness of our model?s implementation against a system that does not use traffic information in routing and a best case scenario. Included in the comparisons displayed in our graphs are less comprehensive trust modeling options. (For example, our proposal with only experience-based and majority-based trust modeling is one comparator; another is an algorithm that takes all reports at face value and does not incorporate trust modeling at all).

We have designed an extensive simulation testbed that can be used to validate our model by modeling traffic flow within an environment, tracking the path times of cars to determine the effectiveness of travel decisions. When vehicles make path planning decisions based on reports from other agents, if the accompanying trust modeling has been effective, the vehicles? completion of travel paths should be timely. The implementation makes use of the following third party software, JiST/SWANS, vans, DUCKS, and Protege^n. JiST stands for Java in Simulation Time; it is a high-performance discrete event simulation engine that runs over a standard Java Virtual Machine (JVM). SWANS stands for Scalable Ad-hoc Network Simulator; it is built on top of the JiST platform and serves as a host of network simulation tools. Vans is a project comprising the geographic routing and the integrated Street Random Waypoint model (STRAW). STRAW utilizes an A* search algorithm to calculate shortest path to a destination. It also allows realworld traffic to be simulated by using real maps with vehicular nodes (briefly illustrated in Appendix D). DUCKS is a simulation execution framework, which allows for a Simulation Parameters file to be provided to define the simulation. Protege is a free, open source ontology editor and knowledge base framework. Note that the simulation constructed here, while inspired by that employed for the original model of [3], goes far beyond, to enable a rich modelling of traffic scenarios with effective measurement of successful travel.

The simulation was set to poll cars every 6?15 seconds; with 100 cars in total, experience with every other car would be gained quickly^o. In order to simulate environments with low experience-based trust, we introduce a variable called sparsity. For example, 80% sparsity resembles having a lack of previous experience with 80% of the agents. In the simulation, this variable effectively ignores updates of trust values, thus hindering experience-based trust.

These graphs chart the performance of simulations that either use trust modeling (i.e. profiling (P), (Hon #) or not^p (no P, Hon #)). Agent honesty represents the percent of honest agents in the simulation (i.e. 0.5 is 50% honesty). Role-based trust (Role #) represents the percent of agents in the simulation that have been assigned a role (i.e. 0.2 will have 20% of agents assigned a role). Sparsity (Spars #) represents the percent sparsity in the simulation (i.e. 0.8 will have 80% sparsity). Dishonest lie percentage (Lie #) represents the percent of the time which a dishonest agent will lie (i.e. 0.8 means dishonest agents will lie 80% of the time)(set at 100% if unspecified).

In Appendix B we display the various parameters set for the experiments and how the values were chosen (while the path planning for the simulation is displayed in Appendix C). Our first set of experiments incorporated experience-based trust and majority-based trust, alone. These were the central elements of the original model of [1-3]. We call this type of simulation Basic. Simulations with all the other additional components added are referred to as Full. The other trust modeling components individually indicated are time closeness (Time), location closeness (Loc), and indirect advice (Indir). (Full) indicates when all multidimensional trust components are being used. The VANET trust modeling results are also compared against two additional simulations: the first is a worst case scenario where traffic is ignored (no traffic)^q, and the other is a best case omnipresent version (omni) which simulates the ability for any car to look up the exact congestion of any road at anytime. All simulation tests results are averaged over 5 runs.

Figure 1 examines the average path time (appropriate due to the ultimate goal of reducing the travel time of users). This figure compares the worst case scenario against the best case scenario and various simulations which use our VANET system with the *Basic* simulation settings, at different degrees of honesty. Greater average path time in the figure indicates lower performance. The *Basic, Hon 0.1* simulation did much worse than the other *Basic* simulations most likely due to the extreme lack of trustworthy agents, but it still performed significantly better than the *Basic, No P, Hon 0.1* simulation. The *Basic* curves that incorporate trust modeling show approximately a 35% decrease in average path time over the worst case scenario. The curves in the scenarios are representative of the simulations approaching a steady state. Another observed trend is the tendency for the profiling-enabled simulations to reach a steady state faster than the other simulations. The curves here are useful for the next experiment described below.

Figure 2 compares the worst case scenario against the best case scenario and various simulations which use our VANET system with the *Full* (all trust multidimensional trust components activated) simulation settings, at different degrees of honesty. As seen in the figure, all of the simulations that used our trust modeling framework (*Full*) or the omnipresent setup averaged close to the same path time at the end of the 10000 second simulation. The other simulations produced a predictably declining performance as the

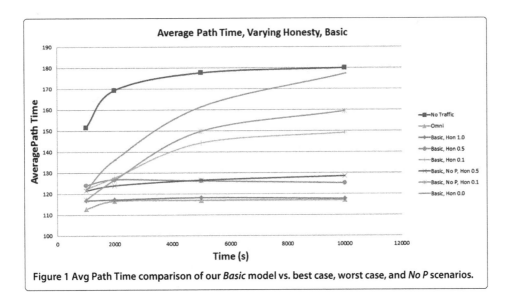

Figure 1 Avg Path Time comparison of our *Basic* model vs. best case, worst case, and *No P* scenarios.

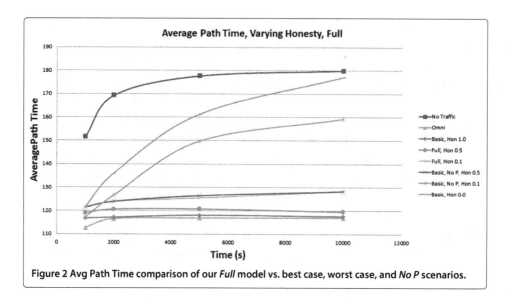

Figure 2 Avg Path Time comparison of our *Full* model vs. best case, worst case, and *No P* scenarios.

honesty percentage approached the worst case scenario. In contrast with Figure 1, *Full* simulations performed significantly better compared to the *Basic* simulations of similar honesty.

Figure 3 compares the average path time, at 10,000 seconds, of the *No Traffic, Omni, Basic, Basic, No P,* and *Full* scenarios, across a range of honesty values. *No Traffic* and

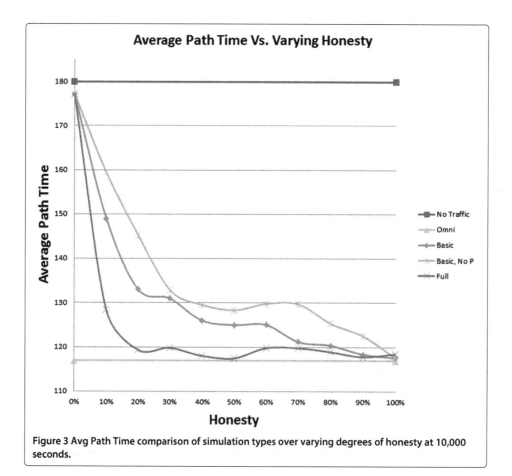

Figure 3 Avg Path Time comparison of simulation types over varying degrees of honesty at 10,000 seconds.

Omni are shown as straight lines because they do not use honesty values, but are useful as comparisons. The figure clearly shows the effectiveness of our framework across the range of honesty values. The *Basic* scenario consistently performs better than the *Basic, No P* scenario. The *Full* scenario also consistently performs better than the *Basic* scenario. All of the framework enabled simulations have a similar average path time at 0% honesty because they have no useful traffic data (and at 100% honesty because there are no untrustworthy agents to deflect through profiling). Figure 3 clearly demonstrates the impact dishonest agents can have on simulations (*Basic, No P*) and the effectiveness our proposed model framework scenarios (*Basic* and *Full*) can have on countering the influence of dishonest agents.

Figure 4 demonstrates the increased effectiveness of each of the multidimensional trust components described in Section ?Our proposed numeric trust modeling? The incremental components demonstrated are the base system (experience and majority based trust), then role based trust (Role 0.2), time and location closeness (Time, Loc), and indirect advice (Indirect). These simulations also simulate honesty at 50%, data sparsity at 50%, and additionally compare them to the best case scenario[r]. As seen in the figure, the incremental addition of trust components demonstrated predictable and substantial increases in performance. The simulation with sparsity enabled showed a predicably worse performance than its counterpart. This reflects the fact that when one has little experience-based trust, one makes poorer decisions. The simulation with role-based trust enabled shows a dramatic increase in performance, which demonstrates the impact roles have in situations with data sparsity. The best case scenario and the simulations with the higher number of trust components averaged close to the same path time at the end of the 10000 second simulation. The curves in the scenarios are representative of the simulations approaching a steady state. Another observed trend is the tendency for the component-enabled simulations to have a steadier state than the other simulations.

Figure 5 explores variations in parameter values to demonstrate the robustness of our proposed framework. We note that, even if there are very few roles assumed or if dishonest agents lie inconsistently, our framework is able to adapt and yield excellent

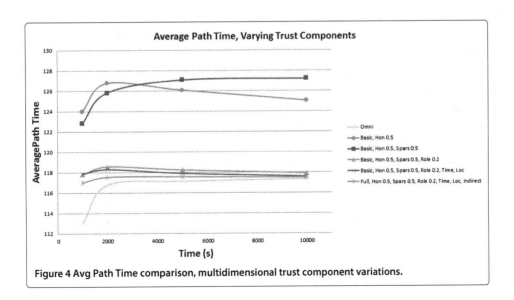

Figure 4 Avg Path Time comparison, multidimensional trust component variations.

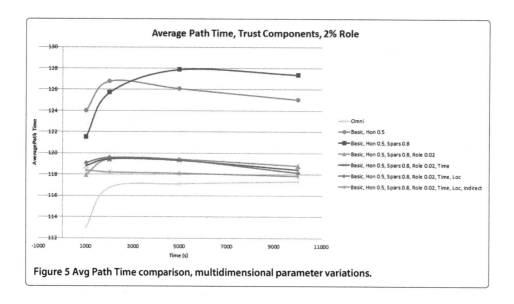

Figure 5 Avg Path Time comparison, multidimensional parameter variations.

performance, approaching that of the *Omni* (omniscient) curve. When using all dimensions (at least some or all of role, time, location, indirect), being more challenged with experienced-based trust (higher sparsity) degrades performance slightly as does having less role-based trust to rely on.

The final set of graphs show the robustness of our simulation framework through experiments that modify simulation-specific variables, such as the number of agents and messaging frequency.

Figure 6 compares the average path time, at 10,000 seconds, of the *No Traffic, Omni, Basic, Basic, No P,* and *Full* scenarios, across a range of values for the number of agents in the environment. The figure clearly shows the robustness of our framework across the span of agent values. The simulations around 50 agents have approximately the same path time because with such a small number of cars there is no real need for using traffic information in path planning. When increasing the number of agents, the *Basic* scenario consistently performs better than the *Basic, No P* scenario. The *Full* scenario also consistently performs better than the *Basic* scenario, when there are more than 50 agents. Figure 6 clearly demonstrates the robustness and scalability of our proposed model framework and implementation across a range of values for the number of agents in the environment.

Figure 7 compares the average path time, at 10,000 seconds, of the *No Traffic, Omni, Basic, Basic, No P,* and *Full* scenarios, across various messaging intervals (where x-y means that messages are sent every x to y seconds)[s]. The purpose of the figure is to demonstrate the robustness of the simulations when there are more or fewer messages. *No Traffic* and *Omni* are shown as straight lines because they do not use communication protocols, but are useful as comparisons. The figure clearly shows the robustness of our framework, especially the *Full* scenario, across various messaging intervals. The *Basic* scenario consistently performs better than the *Basic, No P* scenario until the message interval increases to (12?30 seconds) at which point the two lines are comparable. (This is because Basic is no longer receiving information at a sufficient frequency). The *Full* scenario consistently performs better than the Basic scenario, with a more gradual decrease in performance as the message interval increases[t].

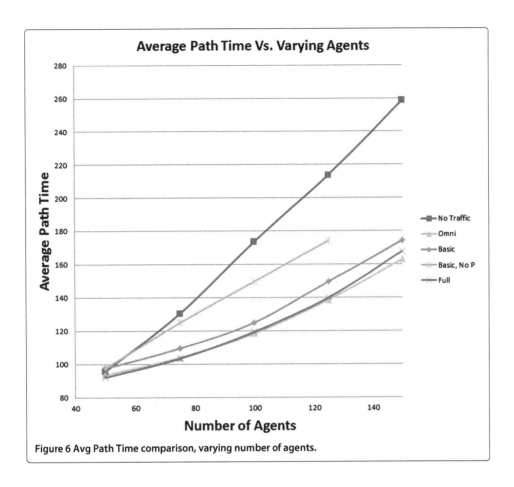

Figure 6 Avg Path Time comparison, varying number of agents.

Figure 8 compares the average path time, at 10,000 seconds, of the *No Traffic*, *Omni*, *Basic*, *Basic, No P*, and *Full* scenarios, with various communication protocols enabled. *No Traffic* and *Omni* are listed under *No Msgs* because they do not use communication protocols, but are useful as a comparison. This figure is important for backing up our claim in Section ?Agent communication protocols to exchange reports? that replacing the pull protocol, for requesting agent location and congestion data, with the push protocol, which more simply sends out the resident agent?s location and congestion data, does not impact performance. Our design rationale for this was to reduce the number of messages sent between agents.

Discussion and related work

The results presented in the previous section offer detailed experimentation incorporating a variety of metrics to validate the effectiveness of our proposed model. The experimental evidence presented serves to provide impressive confirmation of the value of the multi-faceted trust modeling algorithm that is central to the proposed decision making of the vehicles. With our particular trust modeling in place, even in scenarios where there is considerable deception in the environment, our vehicles are able to perform their path planning extremely well, maintaining an effective travel time, without significant compromise from poor path selection. This paper offers a wealth of experimental evidence to examine the proposed new trust model in considerable detail, in a thorough way. All of this is demonstrated due to our significant simulation testbed that can be used

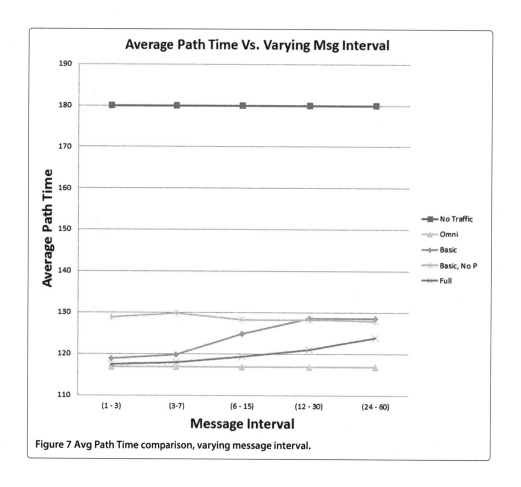

Figure 7 Avg Path Time comparison, varying message interval.

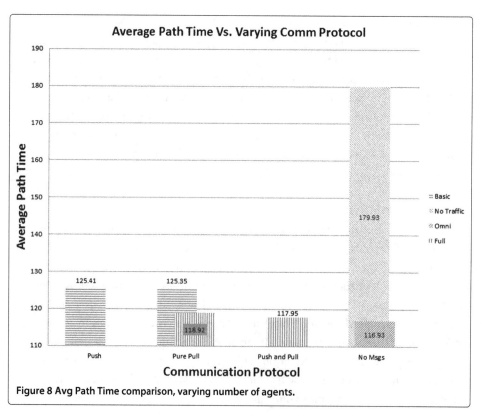

Figure 8 Avg Path Time comparison, varying number of agents.

to simulate actual traffic flow with large numbers of cars in a general mobile vehicular ad-hoc network (and as such constitutes one of the contributions of our work).

The model presented in this paper is one component of a larger framework that we designed, in order to effectively exchange and record reports between vehicles in order to direct travel decision making. In particular, we have developed more detailed proposals for employing ontological representations, for modeling users and for updating parameter values, the details of which have been omitted from this paper. It is important to note, however, that the reasoning component of our overall framework is designed to operate autonomously on a separate thread from all other implementation components. The only interaction with other components comes from other components issuing tasks to the reasoner?s queues. These tasks are either agents of interest or recently updated local road segments. These are subsequently processed and result in an update to one or more agents?t trust variables or no action at all. Agents of interest are agents that have demonstrated either a highly accurate or inaccurate report during a congestion evaluation. Recently updated local road segments are road segments and their congestion value, which have been reported directly from the resident agent. The reasoner can ultimately inspect its knowledge base to evaluate any propositions that were reported in within a specific time of this local report. Additional details are offered in [5].

We note that our simulation is to model a scenario where the actual reports are being exchanged by drivers (in cases where they may be extreme frequency, due to the number of cars on the road). While the car?s speed (as mentioned) can be reported as a stand-in for congestion, certainly GPS readings could form the basis for some automatic vehicle to vehicle reporting. We discuss the potential use of GPS as part of future work, in Section ?Conclusion and future work? Note that indirect reports are simply reports that have been forwarded by other parties and not derived from direct observation.

A focus of the research presented in this paper is our proposal for reasoning with numeric information provided by agents, set in a framework for modeling trustworthiness according to confidence values. How majority consensus can be computed for non-Boolean trust modeling is clarified in detail. This research may be of value to trust modeling researchers considering a variety of possible applications. While we have sketched our proposed formulae and their validation in the context of a specific VANET application, the approach is applicable to any scenario where experience-based trust and majority consensus are to be integrated into the overall determination of user trustworthiness. The formulae in use would simply omit the undesired elements of Equation (3): for instance, time and location may be irrelevant. The remaining calculations would remain the same.

The framework presented in this paper required a calculation of majority consensus in order to guide the decision making of a user. Other researchers have integrated majority opinion into their trust modeling but have instead used this calculation to reflect the general reputation of an agent (e.g. just how trustworthy a user is may be represented as a numeric value calculated as the average of all the scores provided by peers (say 1 for trustworthy and 0 for untrustworthy). For instance, Zhang and Cohen [6] have calculations that integrate a public reputation into the trustworthiness calculation and that also weight the contributions provided by peers according to the estimated trustworthiness of each of the advisors. The Beta Reputation System (BRS) [7] filters out advice about a user that is not in the majority and makes use of the rest of advice to model the reputation of that user. We integrate here important consideration of time and location as well, in order to value more highly the reports from users closer to the destination. In so doing, we are able to weight the combination of majority and experience based considerations more appropriately.

Others have employed a social network for trust modeling (e.g. [8,9] consider trust propagation in a network but this is less relevant in our sparsely populated environment) and others propose the use of stereotypical trust [10] (but in our domain a small set of roles can be used to reflect levels of trust.) Wang and Vassileva [11] also describe trust as multi-faceted; this work is more focused on having trust calculated differently in distinct contexts. In addition, their selection of peer advice is based on similar preferences; for our domain, location of the user and the time of its report are more critical determinants.

Some trust modeling research has introduced Dirichlet distributions in order to represent trustworthiness as something other than a pure binary value, then predicting the values of variables based on past experience. BLADE [12] models the evaluation function of advisor agents in this way, but this research is not focused on how to set decision making afterwards based on this form of trust modeling. The model of Fung et al. [13] is focused more on direct experience decision making, so not on evaluating the trustworthiness of the reports of third parties.

Our work also contrasts with other efforts currently proposed for traffic decision making[u]. Also focusing on the modeling of the trustworthiness of vehicular entities, the sociological trust model proposed by Gerlach in [14] shares some similarities with the multi-faceted trust management framework of Minhas et al. [1-3]. Gerlach has identified various forms of trust including situational, dispositional and system. Additionally, he presents an architecture for securing vehicular communication. However, he does not provide a formalization of the architecture for combining the different types of trust together. Raya et al. [15] propose data-centric trust establishment that deals with evaluating the trustworthiness of the data reported by other entities rather than trust of the entities themselves. One of the shortcomings of their work is that trust relationships in entities can never be formed; only ephemeral trust in data is established. Golle et al. [16] also present a technique that aims to address the problem of detecting and correcting malicious data in VANETs. Their approach maintains a model of every entity which contains all the knowledge that a particular entity has about the VANET. Incoming information can then be evaluated against the entity?s model of the VANET. If all the data received agrees with the model with a high probability, then the entity accepts the validity of the data. However, this approach assumes that each vehicle has global knowledge of the network and solely evaluates the validity of data, which may not be feasible in practice. Dotzer et al. [17] have suggested building a distributed reputation model that exploits a notion called opinion piggybacking where each forwarding entity (of the message regarding an event) appends its own opinion about the trustworthiness of the data. This approach repeatedly makes use of the opinions from different nodes. The nodes that provide opinions about a message earlier will have larger influence than the nodes which generated opinions later, which may be undesirable. Patwardhan et al. [18] propose an approach in which the reputation of an entity is determined by data validation. In this approach, a few entities, which are named as anchor nodes here, are assumed to be pre-authenticated, and thus the data they provide are regarded as trustworthy. Data can be validated by either agreement among peers or direct communication with an anchor node. Malicious nodes can be identified if the data they present is invalidated by the validation algorithm. One problem about this scheme is that it does not make use of reputation of entities when determining the majority consensus.

Compared with the above mentioned trust modeling work, our work also provides a detailed design and implementation for the communication protocols between agents in the VANET environment, clearly specifying how an agent sends a request for location and congestion information and how an agent makes use of requested information as part of its travel decision making. This outlines how agents can effectively operate and interact with each other in order to facilitate traffic flow within their multiagent system. Another contribution offered is a proposal for reasoning with information that has been obtained through frequent broadcasting and polling. This is distinct from simply requesting information just prior to a critical decision, which may be challenging for environments such as ours with dynamic change and real-time decision requirements.

In all, the approach presented in this paper coincides well with several desiderata for designing multiagent systems for vehicular transportation, as expressed by other researchers. For example, our efforts to provide detail on the communication needed in order to support effective travel decision making also coincides well with the arguments made in [19]: that collaboration between vehicles is important and that communication is a necessary component for effectively resolving that coordination. In addition, our paper outlines how a multiagent trust model can assist in directing vehicles with travel decision making, of assistance in the managing of traffic on our roads. The importance of appropriately managing traffic has been discussed at length in [20], which outlines well the potential that techniques from artificial intelligence afford to assist in the management of this important problem. That paper in fact also points out the need for effective frameworks for simulating the network. The testbed that we develop in our research may be of some assistance in helping to resolve this challenge.

Our final reflection on related work discusses additional efforts within the current literature on developing simulations for VANET environments and research that draws out the connection of trust modeling to the messaging networks of MANETs.

At the Agents and Transportation workshop of AAMAS 2014, two papers introduced new proposals for agent-based simulation of traffic and transportation. The work of Taillander [21] is interesting in that it allows the fine tuning of various unusual traffic scenarios as part of the representation (e.g. car accidents). With this kind of focus, very large networks were also supported in the simulation. This effort does not consider messaging and trust modeling (but these may be quite interesting extensions to consider, within this context). The model developed by Huynh et al. [22] is most interested in representing the collective behaviour of drivers through various simulations, but is of interest as it focuses on addressing traffic density and on modeling drivers in the environment as decision makers. within the literature on modeling trust in VANET environments Two recent short papers offer additional suggestions for simulations in VANET environments. Chou and Lan [23] clarify that simulations are critical to properly test VANET communication models. They are interested in modeling the effects on network behaviour of traffic light changes and cars overtaking each other. Their simulations cover 1000 seconds for 300 cars (in comparison to our tracking of up to 10000 seconds for examination of 100-car average path time). Piokorwski et al. [24] emphasize the importance of realistic simulations and highlight the central role of information exchange; they note that the traces of their proposed simulation can be used within the JiST/SWANS environment, to acknowledge its value as a platform. Their exploration of how to play with the mobility of various vehicles is an interesting additional feature that is offered.

MANETs compared to VANETs surfaces as a theme in the survey paper of [25]. VANETs are claimed to have greater issues of mobility of nodes and network fragmentation. The paper in turn introduces us to two papers that also provide relevant comparison to our own work, ones that are more focused on networking characteristics. Shaik and Alzaharani [26] have a concern with trust focused more on the proliferation of false identities; false location and time are both cited as of interest, which coincides well with our proposed model. The TRIP model [27] suggests the combination of direct experience and reputation (elements contained within our model as well) but assume that a history is built up for vehicles, travelling consistently on the same roads. A final paper that helps to clarify the use of trust modeling for MANET environments is that of the TARo project [28]. An anonymous routing protocol is proposed and explained in detail. This work illustrates the important companion problem of managing identities through cryptographic research.

Conclusion and future work

In conclusion, we offer an approach for supporting reasoning about agent trust with advice from peers, whose trustworthiness is then also modeled, when non-numeric reports are provided and have shown the merit of our framework in the context of the VANET application (resulting in effective travel decisions due to the modeling of trustworthiness). As such, we offer a method that supports the exchange of more detailed trustworthiness information, leading to more precise and valuable calculations. We have outlined our method for integrating various reports from peers in full detail. We have also clarified in depth how communication between peers would take place, through a combination of push and pull protocols, in order to assure effective exchange of real-time information and to extend the original model of Minhas et al. [1-3] which left as underspecified the exchange of information between agents, for effective travel decision making. Our overall solution integrates a number of novel modeling elements (priority roads, suspicious reports) which support the final algorithm that is presented. The detailed simulation framework allows for the adjustment of a wide variety of parameters which have been implemented to draw out the benefit of the full combination of our methods for trust modeling for effective transportation decisions that support exchange of traffic information. Included here is a method for simulating a dearth of experience for experience-based trust (our sparsity parameter), which can be varied in the experiments and a variable to model the extent to which agents in the environment have specific roles which may increase their trustworthiness (the role parameter). In all, with our testbed we offer an avenue for measuring the relative benefit of different trust modeling options. Parts of this research were presented at the TRUM workshop at UMAP 2012 [29].

There are a number of avenues for future work. The obvious first direction is to explore a variety of other application domains where agents may need to rely on reports from peers that offer non-binary trust values. It would be interesting, for instance, to examine the possible value of a kind of push and pull-based communication in environments such as peer recommender systems or electronic marketplaces, where rating scales mirror the kind of non-binary reports we have been discussing. Another avenue for future work would be to enhance our current solution for our chosen application of traffic reports and transportation. In earlier work, we discussed the need to distinguish second-hand reports from first-hand reports, applying penalties for incorrect reports declared to be first hand knowledge [2]. Integrating more sophisticated methods for reasoning about the trustworthiness of reports based on whether they were in fact second hand may be of value. In addition, it is quite apparent that the collective travel decision making of the entire set of vehicles on the road is an important consideration. Each agent may be advised to make its final travel decisions by reasoning about the actions likely to be taken by other agents once they have received (perhaps similar) reports. This is another topic that we are currently exploring within our research.

The work of Bazzan et al. [30] may shed some light on how to achieve this particular goal. A form of multiagent reinforcement learning may be effective in coordinating the activities of the collective of cars on the road. The work of [19] also emphasizes the value of machine learning for vehicle coordination, again suggesting this as the most promising first step for our future efforts on this topic. Regardless, the issue of system-wide coordination is one that has been argued as of significant importance for any intelligent approaches to managing traffic, as discussed in [20]. As such, this is certainly a valuable topic for future exploration.

As a final avenue for future work, it would be useful to continue to assess the value and contribution of our simulation testbed. A useful starting point would be to explore how to employ the existing testbed for other trust models that have been developed, in order to demonstrate its robustness. One class of trust models that would be appropriate to examine are ones based on Dirichlet distributions, designed to cope with multi-valued information. Extending one of these kinds of models for decision making of agents and then demonstrating its value with the testbed that we have developed would be an interesting future project. In addition, a paper that has just recently been published [31] provides an excellent survey of agent-based technology for traffic and transportation; comparing our simulation testbed and what it offers to designers against frameworks being explored by other authors, to address other vehicular challenges, would be another very informative path for future research.

As a final comment, we clarify that this research was designed with a realworld implementation in mind as the ultimate application. Reflecting on what might actually be deployed in the future, an implementation as a phone GPS add-on we feel could actually be possible. Implementing the framework in this manner would allow for easy integration into a city?s driving population. The Android operating system and platform is a viable candidate for implementation due to its use of Java as a primary language and the capability to allow applications access to a wide range of phone systems (such as the GPS). Android phones also allow multi-threading. The phones could communicate with each other through minimal Internet access. Once we migrate to the use of GPS, we move to reflecting on the value of reports exchanged mechanically, so into a territory where deliberate misinformation by drivers is less of an issue. In any case, we acknowledge that may certainly be new avenues for the future to enable vehicles to make travel decisions based on coordinated communication with other vehicles on the road.

Endnotes

[a]For now, we are assuming that reports are coming in from vehicles on the road rather than other disassociated entities. As clarified in Section ?Agent communication protocols to exchange reports?, we distinguish those vehicles reporting first hand observation from those that are passing on information acquired indirectly.

[b]For the remainder of the paper, we use the term agent to refer to the intelligent entity that is directing the actions of its vehicle. The word user refers to the driver who will ultimately be deciding where to direct the vehicle.

[c]This integrates task-based trust. For instance, an agent may set n to be fairly small, say $n \leq 10$, if she needs to make a quick driving decision, or set a larger n if she has time to process responses.

[d]For example, setting $W(B_i) = 1/2$ for the case of direct witnesses indicates that the requesting agent values direct evidence two times more than indirect evidence.

[e]Note that a reported congestion value for instance of 23 would ideally be representing the actual number of cars on the road; for our simulation, for example, the actual number of cars is known and can be reported by truthful vehicles. Agents that are not truthful will be providing inaccurate values in their reports. It may also be reasonable for cars to report their speed and for this to be a reflection of the road?s congestion.

[f]A geometric series is necessary because the calculations are capturing atomic increases in trust values but we are reasoning about non-Boolean factors that are therefore not atomic. See Appendix A for a fuller depiction of the geometric series in question.

[g]The order of application used throughout our experiments is the one we follow in this section of the paper.

[h]Note that we use the absolute value of G as the exponent in order to ensure that the number of times is a positive number.

[i]This is consistent with the placement of these factors in the denominator of Equation 3.

[j]This required scaling was not considered in sufficient detail in the model of Minhas et al. and Equation 3.

[k]The trust model described in this paper can be incorporated with a penalty mechanism such as the one presented in [2] to more severely reduce the trust value of an agent who is not a direct witness but claims to be one, resulting in the agent not being responded/helped by other agents in the system.

[l]Location closeness is not incorporated because it is dependent on the agent who is using the report.

[m]However, we use InPenal=-2 in the example here instead for a more effective illustration.

[n]Protege is used due to our knowledge-based representation for storing trust and traffic information; the details of this part of our solution have been omitted in this paper.

[o]Note that packet delivery success for the messaging is 100%. We did not simulate packet failure since this would be too similar to just reducing the volume/frequency of messages.

[p]With no profiling, no trust modeling is done and all reports received are simply assumed to be entirely trustworthy.

[q]Routing without traffic just uses a shortest path calculation.

[r]The worst case (i.e. No Traffic) is not present so that a finer granularity of the presented simulations can be shown.

[s]Messages are sent according to intervals to avoid all agents sending messages at the same time.

[t]This more gradual decrease is likely due in part to the pull protocol requesting information on roads with more immediate priority and use, generating information on roads that will be used in decision making.

[u]A more complete discussion of trust management for VANETs can be found in the recent survey paper [32].

Appendix A Confidence geometric series

This appendix seeks to further clarify and detail the geometric series equation and design rationale for calculating confidence in Section ?Confidence calculation? and to provide examples.

In Section ?Confidence calculation? we proposed Equation 6(11) for calculating the confidence of a report. Equations 1(12) and 2(13) are used as the basis for calculating the confidence of report R_j in Equation 6(11), through a modified summation of a geometric series.

$$Conf(R_j) = (CurrConf(R_j) \quad 1)(1 \quad (\alpha \ or \ \beta))^G + 1 \tag{11}$$

The following will describe why a geometric series was necessary.

Equations 12 and 13 shown below are used to modify the trust of an agent. In the framework it is necessary to attribute a trust value to each report from an agent, which we define as confidence, due to each report having possibly different attributes, such as age and if the report was observed indirectly.

$$T_A(B) \leftarrow \begin{cases} T_A(B) + \alpha(1 \quad T_A(B)) & \text{if } T_A(B) \geq 0, \\ T_A(B) + \alpha(1 + T_A(B)) & \text{if } T_A(B) < 0, \end{cases} \tag{12}$$

$$T_A(B) \leftarrow \begin{cases} T_A(B) + \beta(1 \quad T_A(B)) & \text{if } T_A(B) \geq 0, \\ T_A(B) + \beta(1 + T_A(B)) & \text{if } T_A(B) < 0, \end{cases} \tag{13}$$

A report?s confidence is initially set to the experience-based trust of the agent that provided the report. If Equations 12 and 13 were used to atomically increase a report?s confidence according to various attributes (Time, Loc, Indirect, etc.), then their influence on confidence would be disproportionate to their value and importance. A simple solution to this issue would be to weight or multiply α and β according to the attribute (Time, Loc, Indirect, etc.). However, this can result in the confidence value being above 100% or below 0%. In addition, to solve this by simply placing a bound on the confidence value (So that max is 100% and minimum is 0%) would not be faithful to the founding research.

Equations 12 and 13 implicitly bound $T_A(B)$, and have an effect of decreasing the magnitude by which trust is increased or decreased as the trust value becomes greater or smaller, respectively. Equation 11 is intended to reflect the culmination of several increases or decreases, according to 12 and 13. If you were to graph the trust value over all atomic iterations, the graph would form a Sigmoid function (?S? curve).

Equation 14 for a geometric series is shown below. Equation 15 shows the calculation at n terms in the series. This is the type of calculation we need because we need to calculate confidence after Equation 12 or 13 has been applied n times (Equivalent to G in Equation 11). Equation 15 can not be used because it does not take into consideration the result of the previous calculation, which we need to. Equation 16 describes our calculation, after Equation 12 or 13 has been applied n times, and the series which we need to represent for our calculation. Equation 16 describes the need for each term of n terms to sum the result of all previous terms. This is due to Equation 12 and 13 multiplying α and β by $T_A(B)$ (the previous trust value). The simplification of Equation 16 is equivalent to Equation 6(11).

$$a + ar + ar^2 + \ldots + ar^{n-1} = a\frac{1-r^n}{1-r} \qquad (14)$$

$$a_n = ar^n \qquad (15)$$

$$\begin{aligned} a_n &= a_{n0} + r(1 + / - a_{n0}) + r(1 + / - a_{n1}) \\ &\quad + r(1 + / - a_{n2}) + \ldots + r(1 + / - a_{n_{n-1}}) \\ &= (a-1)(1-r)^n + 1 \end{aligned} \qquad (16)$$

Defining our confidence calculation using Equation 11(6, the simplification of Equation 16) allows us to utilize Equations 12 and 13, their Sigmoid nature and implicit bounding, use of decimal numbers for $G(n)$ (providing a granularity that atomic changes do not allow), and a representation of the calculation in a simple format.

The following example demonstrates the modification of confidence according the time difference attribute.

Example 3. (Modification of Confidence according to Time)

$Confidence_0$ $= Agent\_39 : trust\_degree\,(0.6)$

α $= 0.1$

G_{time} $= (\text{TPenal}(90) - \text{TimeDiff}(45))/\text{TPenal}(90)$
                                 $*\text{MultiplicativeFactor}(4)$

G_{time} $= 2(\text{Increase } Confidence_0 \text{ twice})$

$Confidence_0$ $= 0.6$

$Confidence_1$ $= (0.6) + \alpha(1 - (0.6))$
                                 $= 0.64$

$Confidence_{2(G_{time})}$ $= 0.64 + \alpha(1 - (0.64))$
                                 $= 0.676$

(Again using Equation 6)

$Confidence_2$ $= (Confidence_0 - 1)(1 - \alpha)^{|G_{time}|} + 1$
                                 $= ((0.6) - 1)(1 - \alpha)^2 + 1$
                                 $= 0.676$

Appendix B Simulation curves and parameters

The various curves and parameters used in our simulations are summarized in full in this appendix. Table 1 displays a fuller description of the different curves that are plotted in our figures. Table 2 lists various parameters that can be adjusted in the simulations and displays the default values that we used. Table 3 indicates the variables from our framework?s formulas which are also modeled in the simulation testbed. The ability to set all the values shown in the three tables provides deeper insight into the richness of the simulation testbed that we have designed.

Appendix C Pathing

Agents within the JiST/SWANS simulation software utilize an A* search algorithm that determines the most effective path for a car to take to its destination.

Table 1 Simulation types

Name	Description	Type
No Traffic	Simulation without our framework or any incorporation of traffic data.	Worst case scenario
Omni	Simulation without our framework but incorporations traffic data by querying the road through the JiST/SWANS simulator.	Best case scenario
Basic	Simulation with just Majority and Experience based trust.	Basic scenario
Full	Simulation with all multidimensional trust components.	Full utilization scenario
Full/Basic + (Parameter(s))	Full or Basic simulation with a modification on one or more parameters.	Special case scenario.

The A* search algorithm is the driving force behind when an agent is *in need of advice*. The algorithm is called either when a new destination is set for an agent, and the agent has to find out how to most effectively reach the destination, or if an agent?s path is reassessed during their journey, so that the algorithm can incorporate more recently received traffic information.

The A* algorithm used within our framework operates as follows:

1. It is provided with the agent?s current location and destination.
2. It incrementally assesses potential roads, from the current location to the destination, according to a cost.

   (a) The potential road?s cost is calculated as its length plus congestion (triggers *in need of advice*).

Table 2 Simulation framework variables

Parameter name	Description	Representation	Default value
Honest agents	Percent of honest agents.	Hon # (0.5 is 50% honesty)	0.5
Number of agents	Number of agents and cars simulated in the tests.	Agent # (100 is 100 agents)	100
Message interval	Interval between congestion request messages sent by the agents.	Msgl #-# (6?15 is 6?15 second message intervals)	6-15
Profiling	Use of profiling.	No P indicates no use of profiling (False)	True (Basic, Full)
Role	Use of role based trust.	Role # (0.2 is 20% agents are given a role above *Ordinary*)	0(Basic) 0.2(Full)
Time closeness	Use of time closeness factor.	Time	False(Basic) True(Full)
Location closeness	Use of location closeness factor.	Loc	False(Basic) True(Full)
Indirect messages	Use of indirect messages.	Indirect	False(Basic) True(Full)
Information sparsity	Percent of agent trust updates ignored to simulate data sparsity.	MThresh # (0.6 means 60% of trust updates are ignored)	0
Dishonest Lie Percent	Percent of the time a dishonest agent lies.	Lie # (0.8 is 80% of the time dishonest agents lie)	1

Table 3 Simulation algorithm variables

Parameter name	Description	Representation	Default value
Majority N	Number of agents used in a majority opinion.	MajN # (10 is 10 agents used)	10
Honest trust increase α	Standard increment to an agent?s trust resulting from an honesty evaluation, with a maximum value of 1.0.	α # (0.1 is 10% trust increase)	0.1
Dishonest trust decrease β	Standard decrement to an agent?s trust resulting from an honesty evaluation, with a minimum value of 0.0.	β # (0.2 is 20% trust decrease)	0.2
Advice trust threshold	Threshold where only agents with a trust value above this percent may be considered for advice.	AThresh # (0.41 is 41% trust threshold)	0.41
Majority confidence threshold	Threshold which the majority opinion must be above in order to be considered.	MThresh # (0.51 is 51% majority threshold)	0.51
Role penalization	Standard factor for increasing confidence depending on agent role.	RPenal #	8
Time penalization	Standard comparison factor for time closeness.	TPenal #	90
Location penalization	Standard comparison factor for location closeness.	LPenal #	200
Indirect penalization	Standard factor for modifying confidence if the advice is indirect.	InPenal #	1
Congestion weight	Standard factor for weighting the congestion value when calculating a road?s A* cost.	CongWeight #	20

3. It returns a list of roads which forms a path to the destination that has the least cost (which theoretically takes the shortest amount of time, according to current traffic information).

The algorithm attributes a cost to every road segment. The JiST/SWANS initially calculated this cost as the length of the road segment. In our implementation, cost is calculated as the length of the road segment and its congestion. *RoadCong* is the congestion of the road, which is multiplied by a simulation specific weight *CongWeight*. The retrieval of a road?s congestion signifies an agent being *in need of advice* from Algorithm 4.

To facilitate efficient use of congestion information, and to increase the speed of the A* search algorithm, the implementation post-processes traffic information to form majority opinions so that the information can be immediately retrieved during algorithm execution. This means that majority opinions are calculated every time new information is retrieved, which is then stored in a local hash table for constant time (O(1)) retrieval by the A* algorithm.

Appendix D Pictorial depiction of grid-like maps in simulations

In this appendix, we display one example of the grid-like maps that are used in the third-party software that forms the backdrop for our simulation testbed. Figure 9 shows a snapshot of a simulation run where bold lines are extracted road segments and small rectangles represent vehicles on the streets.

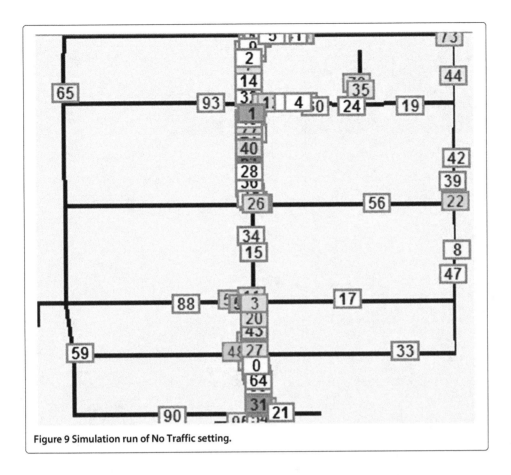

Figure 9 Simulation run of No Traffic setting.

Competing interests
The authors declare that they have no competing interests.

Authors⊠ contributions
JF came up with the formulation of the proposed approach and conducted experiments to evaluate the approach. RC and JZ drafted the paper. TT and UFM proofread the draft and provided comments and suggestions to improve the draft. JZ was also in charge of submitting the paper and corresponding with the editors of the journal and Springer Open Production Team. All authors read and approved the final manuscript.

Acknowledgement
Thanks to Graham Pinhey for his assistance with this paper. Financial support was received from NSERC (the Natural Sciences and Engineering Council of Canada).
Parts of this research were presented at the TRUM workshop at UMAP 2012 [29]. The work is also partially supported by the project of Dr. Jie Zhang funded by the MOE AcRF Tier 1.

Author details
[1] David R. Cheriton School of Computer Science, University of Waterloo, Waterloo, Canada. [2] School of Computer Engineering, Nanyang Technological University, Singapore, Singapore. [3] School of Electrical Engineering and Computer Science, University of Ottawa, Ottawa, Canada.

References
1. Minhas UF, Zhang J, Tran T, Cohen R (2010) Promoting effective exchanges between vehicular agents in traffic through transportation-oriented trust modeling. In: Proceedings of international joint conference on Autonomous Agents and Multi Agent Systems (AAMAS) workshop on Agents in Traffic and Transportation (ATT). ACM. pp 77?86
2. Minhas UF, Zhang J, Tran TT, Cohen R (2010) Intelligent agents in mobile vehicular ad-hoc networks: Leveraging trust modeling based on direct experience with incentives for honesty. In: Proceedings of the IEEE/WIC/ACM international conference on Intelligent Agent Technology (IAT). pp 243?247
3. Minhas UF, Zhang J, Tran TT, Cohen R (2011) A multifaceted approach to modeling agent trust for effective communication in the application of mobile ad hoc vehicular networks. IEEE Trans Syst Man Cybern C Appl Rev 41(3):407?420

4. Tran T, Cohen R (2003) Modelling reputation in agent-based marketplaces to improve the performance of buying agents. In: Proceedings of the ninth international conference on User Modelling (UM). Springer. pp 273?282

5. Finnson J (2012) Modeling trust in multiagent mobile vehicular ad-hoc networks through enhanced knowledge exchange for effective travel decision making. Master?s thesis, School of Computer Science, University of Waterloo. Waterloo, Canada

6. Zhang J, Cohen R (2008) Evaluating the trustworthiness of advice about seller agents in e-marketplaces: a personalized approach. Electron Commerce Res Appl 7(3):330?340

7. Whitby A, J?sang A, Indulska J (2004) Filtering out unfair ratings in bayesian reputation systems. In: Proceedings of the Workshop on Trust in Agent Societies, at the Autonomous Agents and Multi-Agent Systems Conference (AAMAS2004), New York. July 2004

8. Yu B, Singh MP (2003) Detecting deception in reputation management. In: Proceedings of the second international joint conference on Autonomous Agents and Multiagent Systems. AAMAS ?03. ACM, New York. pp 73?80

9. Yolum P, Singh MP (2005) Engineering self-organizing referral networks for trustworthy service selection. IEEE Trans Syst Man Cybern Syst Hum 35(3):396?407

10. Burnett C, Norman T, Sycara K (2011) Sources of stereotypical trust in multi-agent systems. In: Proceedings of the 14th international workshop on trust in agent societies. p 25

11. Wang Y, Vassileva J (2003) Bayesian network-based trust model. In: Proceedings of the IEEE/WIC international conference on Web Intelligence (WI). pp 372?378

12. Regan K, Poupart P, Cohen R (2006) Bayesian reputation modeling in e-marketplaces sensitive to subjectivity, deception and change. In: AAAI. pp 1206?1212

13. Fung CJ, Zhang J, Aib I, Boutaba R (2011) Dirichlet-based trust management for effective collaborative intrusion detection networks. IEEE Trans Netw Serv Manag 8(2):79?91

14. Gerlach M (2007) Trust for vehicular applications. In: Proceedings of the international symposium on autonomous decentralized systems. IEEE. pp 295?304

15. Raya M, Papadimitratos P, Gligor VD, Hubaux J-P (2008) On data-centric trust establishment in ephemeral ad hoc networks. In: Proceedings of the 27th Annual IEEE International Conference on Computer Communications (IEEE INFOCOM). pp 1238?1246

16. Golle P, Greene D, Staddon J (2004) Detecting and correcting malicious data in vanets. In: Proceedings of the 1st ACM international workshop on vehicular ad hoc networks. ACM. pp 29?37

17. Dotzer F, Fischer L, Magiera P (2005) VARS: a vehicle ad-hoc network reputation system. In: Proceedings of the IEEE international symposium on a world of wireless, mobile and multimedia networks. pp 453?456

18. Patwardhan A, Joshi A, Finin T, Yesha Y (2006) A data intensive reputation management scheme for vehicular ad hoc networks. In: Proceedings of the Third Annual International Conference on Mobile and Ubiquitous Systems: Networking & Services. IEEE. pp 1?8

19. Desjardins C, Laum?nier J, Chaib-draa B (2009) Learning agents for collaborative driving. In: Bazzan A, Kl?gl F (eds). Multiagent systems for traffic and transportation engineering. IGI Global, Hershey. pp 240?260

20. Bazzan AL (2007) Traffic as a complex system: Four challenges for computer science and engineering. In: Proceedings of the XXXIV SEMISH. Citeseer. pp 2128?2142

21. Taillandier P (2014) Traffic simulation with the gama platform. In: Klugel F, Bazzan A, Ossowoski S, Chaib-Draa B (eds). Proceedings of the international conference on Autonomous Agents and Multiagent Systems (AAMAS) sixth workshop on Agents in Traffic and Transportation (ATT). pp 77?86

22. Huynh N, Cao VL, Wickramasuriya R, Berryman M, Perez P, Barthelemy J (2014) An agent based model for the simulation of road traffic and transport demand in a Sydney metropolitan area. In: Klugel F, Bazzan A, Ossowoski S, Chaib-Draa B (eds). Proceedings of the International Conference on Autonomous Agents and Multiagent Systems (AAMAS) sixth workshop on Agents in Traffic and Transportation (ATT)

23. Chou C-M, Lan K-c (2009) On the effects of detailed mobility models in vehicular network simulations. In: Proceedings of the ACM MobiCom

24. Piorkowski M, Raya M, Lugo AL, Papadimitratos P, Grossglauser M, Hubaux J-P (2008) TraNS: realistic joint traffic and network simulator for VANETs. ACM SIGMOBILE mobile computing and communications review 12(1):31?33

25. Vidhya S, Mugunthan SR (2014) Trust modeling scheme using cluster aggregation of messages for vehicular ad hoc networks. IOSR J Comput Eng 16(2):16?21

26. Shaihk R, Alzahrani A (2013) Intrusion-aware trust model for vehicular ad hoc networks. Security and Communication Networks. doi:10.1002/sec.862

27. Marmola FG, Pere GM (2012) Trip, a trust and reputation infrastructure-based proposal for vehicular ad hoc networks. J Netw Comput Appl 35(3):934?941

28. Chen J, Boreli R, Sivaraman V (2010) Taro: Trusted anonymous routing for manets. In: Proceedings of the IEEE/IFIP 8th international conference on embedded and ubiquitous computing. pp 756?762

29. Finnson J, Cohen R, Zhang J, Tran T, Minhas UF (2012) Reasoning about user trustworthiness with non-binary advice from peers. Adaptation and Personalization (UMAP) workshop on Trust, Reputation and User Modeling (TRUM). pp 12

30. Bazzan ALC, de Oliveira D, da Silva BC (2010) Learning in groups of traffic signals. Eng Appl Artif Intell 23(4):560?568

31. Bazzan A, Klugl F (2013) A review on agent-based technology for traffic and transportation. Knowl Eng Rev:1?29. doi:10.1017/S0269888913000118

32. Zhang J (2011) A survey on trust management for vanets. In: Proceedings of the 25th international conference on Advanced Information Networking and Applications (AINA). IEEE. pp 105?112

Trust-based Decision-making for the Adaptation of Public Displays in Changing Social Contexts

Michael Wißner[*], Stephan Hammer, Ekatarina Kurdyukova and Elisabeth André

*Correspondence:
wissner@hcm-lab.de
Human Centered Mutimedia,
Augsburg University, Universitätsstr.
6a 86159, Augsburg, Germany

Abstract
Public displays may adapt intelligently to the social context, tailoring information on the screen, for example, to the profiles of spectators, their gender or based on their mutual proximity. However, such adaptation decisions should on the one hand match user preferences and on the other maintain the user's trust in the system. A wrong decision can negatively influence the user's acceptance of a system, cause frustration and, as a result, make users abandon the system. In this paper, we propose a trust-based mechanism for automatic decision-making, which is based on Bayesian Networks. We present the process of network construction, initialization with empirical data, and validation. The validation demonstrates that the mechanism generates accurate decisions on adaptation which match user preferences and support user trust.

Introduction

Recent years have brought about a large variety of interactive displays that are installed in many public places. Apart from simply providing information (e.g. news or weather) to people in public places, such as coffee bars or airports, public displays make it possible for passing individuals to view, edit and exchange specific data between each other. While ubiquitous display technologies offer great benefits to users, they also raise a number of challenges. In particular, they might show a behavior that negatively affects user trust.

First, ubiquitous display environments are characterized by high dynamics. People may approach and leave a display at any time requiring the system to permanently adapt to a new situation. Due to the high complexity of the adaptation process, the user may no longer be able to comprehend the rationale behind the system's decisions which may negatively affect the formation of user trust. This echoes the view put forward by Rothrock et al. [1]. According to them, the sudden changes in an adaptive display's user interface (such as displayed content, layout or the used modality) are not always self-explanatory for the users. If they cannot recognize the reason for a system adaptation or if they do not consider the adaptation as plausible given the current situation, user trust can be impaired, which can lead to disuse of the system in the worst case.

Due to sensor technology that has become available in the recent years, interaction with ubiquitous displays is no longer exclusively based on input explicitly provided by a user, for example, by controlling displays with a mobile phone. Instead, systems exploit information that is implicitly given by the context in which an interaction takes place. A typical form of implicit interaction with public displays is enabled by proxemics behaviors, i.e. the interpretation of human body position, orientation, and movement to proactively initiate system reactions [2]. On the one hand, the use of implicitly provided information facilitates human-computer interaction and contributes to its robustness. On the other hand, it raises trust issues with the user because proactive system actions are frequently not understood by the users and limit their control over the system. Furthermore, deficiencies of the underlying sensor technology might cause a rather obscure system behavior. Similar issues were reported by Müller et al. [3]. In interviews with the users of their adaptive digital signage system, which automatically adapts to the assumed interest of an audience, it was revealed that some users had the feeling that the system was presenting randomized information. This shows that the users were no longer able to understand the rationale behind the system's decisions.

Finally, the social setting with the possibility of viewing personalized information in the presence of other people inevitably raises privacy issues. Since public displays are typically shared by several people, personal information for a particular user has to be protected from unwanted views by others, for example, by migrating it to the user's personal device. Otherwise, there would be the risk that people lose trust in such displays and abandon using them. Röcker and colleagues [4] found that users wish to take advantage of large displays in public settings, however, they are worried about the protection of their data. The problem is aggravated by the fact that user typically interact with ubiquitous display environments on an occasional basis without having the possibility to verify the security of the underlying infrastructure.

To sum up, there is an enormous need for sophisticated trust management in ubiquitous display environments in order to ensure that such environments will find acceptance among users. In this paper, we present a decision-theoretic approach to a trust management system for ubiquitous display environments that assesses the user's trust in a system, monitors it during the interaction and applies appropriate measures to maintain trust in critical situations [5]. Such situations arise inter alia when other people enter the user's private space [4], when the system has to generate presentations based on inaccurate user or context data [6] or when the system's adaptation behavior mismatches the user's expectations [7].

While most work in the area of computational trust models aims to develop trust metrics that determine on the basis of objective criteria whether a system should be trusted or not, the focus of our work is on trust experienced by a user when interacting with a software system. A system may be robust and secure, but nevertheless be perceived as not very trustworthy by a user, for example, because its behavior appears opaque or hard to control to them. Following the terminology by Castelfranchi and Falcone [8], our work focuses on the affective forms of trust that are based on the user's appraisal mechanisms. More specifically, our objective is the development of a computational trust model that captures how a system - in this paper an ubiquitous display environment - is perceived by a user while interacting with it.

As a test bed for our research, we employ four prototype applications that have been developed as part of a university-wide display management system. They run on public displays located in public rooms at Augsburg University. They can be operated and assisted by mobile phones. All four applications require sophisticated mechanisms to adapt to various trust-critical events. Some may disclose private information about users, and thus should be able to intelligently adapt to the surrounding social context in order to avoid possible privacy threats. Possible options include the hiding, masking or migration (to a mobile device) of the critical data. Others might allow multiple users to interact simultaneously and thus should open space for new users as they approach, rearranging the current users' content if necessary.

In the rest of the paper, we first discuss related work on increasing the user's trust in ubiquitous display environments by appropriate interface design. After that, we present our model of a trust management system and mechanism for automatic decision-making based on Bayesian Networks (BN). Relying on empirical data gathered in both an online and a live study, we initialize and validate the networks and demonstrate how they can be used to generate adaptation decisions in changing social contexts.

Background and literature review

While research on computational models of trust has become very popular in the area of agent-based society, approaches that model trust as a user experience are rare. This is unsurprising because the psychological aspects of trust are hard to measure directly. In the following, we will first review work on computational models of trust starting from approaches that have been presented for agent-based societies and social networks before we discuss how the concept of trust has been treated in the context of ubiquitous display environments.

Computational models of trust

Much of the original research on trust comes from the humanities. Psychologists and sociologists have tried for a very long time to get a grasp of the inner workings of trust in interpersonal and interorganisational relationships. Other fields, such as economics and computer science, relied on their findings to come up with dedicated models of trust that are adapted to the specific requirements of their domains and the context they are applied to. Since trust is a social phenomenon, it seems to be a promising approach to exploit models that have been developed to characterize trust in human societies as a basis for computational models of trust.

Especially in the area of multi-agent systems, computational models for trust-based decision support have been researched thoroughly. Pioneering work in this area has been conducted by Marsh [9] who modeled trust between distributed software agents as a basis for the agents' cooperation behavior. Computational mechanisms that have been proposed for trust management in agent-based societies include Bayesian Networks [10], Dempster-Shafer Theory [11], Hidden-Markov Models [12], Belief Models [13], Fuzzy models [8], game-theoretic approaches [14] or decision trees [15]. There is empirical evidence that the performance of agent-based societies may be improved by incorporating trust models.

While the approaches above focus on trust between software agents, work in the area of social media aims to model trust between human users, see [16] or [17] for a survey investigating trust in social networks. Using algorithmic approaches or machine learning techniques, trust between users is derived from objective observations, such as behavior patterns in social networks. An example includes the work by Adali et al. [18] who assessed trust between two users based on the amount of conversation and the propagation of messages within the Twitter social network. Other approaches derive trust that is given to users from community-based reputation or social feedback, see, for example, the work by Ivanov et al. [19].

Unlike the above-mentioned approaches, our own research focuses on trust which users experience when interacting with a software system. Most work in this area aims to identify trust dimensions that influence the user's feeling of trust. Trust dimensions that have been researched in the context of internet applications and e-commerce include reliability, dependability, honesty, truthfulness, security, competence, and timeliness, see, for example, the work by Grandison and Sloman [20] or Kini and Choobineh [21]. Tschannen et al. [22], who are more interested in the sociological aspects of trust, introduce willing vulnerability, benevolence, reliability, competence, honesty, and openness as the constituting facets of trust. Researchers working on adaptive user interfaces consider transparency as a major component of trust, see, for example, the work by Glass et al. [7]. Trust dimensions have formed the basis of many conceptual models of trust. However, incorporating them into a computational model of trust is not a trivial task.

Indeed, computational models that assess trust felt by a user are rare. One of the few approaches in this area includes the work by Yan et al. [23]. Their computational model captures users' trust experience when interacting with mobile applications. In order to present users with appropriate recommendations that help increase the users' trust, they identified various user behaviors that can be monitored by a mobile device in addition to external factors, such as brand impact. The benefits of this approach have been shown by means of simulations. However, the approach has not been embedded in a pervasive environment to control the selection of system actions during an interaction. Since an offline evaluation may provide different results than a more challenging online evaluation with interacting users, the approach presented in this paper has been tested within live studies as well.

Trust management in ubiquitous display environments

Most work that investigates the phenomenon of trust in the context of ubiquitous display environments focuses on privacy issues, i.e. the distribution of private and public data over various displays. Often mobile phones are used as private devices that protect the personal component of interaction from public observation.

Röcker et al. [4] conducted a user study to identify privacy requirements of public display users. Based on the study, they developed a prototype system that automatically detects people entering the private space around a public display using infrared and RFID technology and adapts the information that is visible based on the privacy preferences of the users. An evaluation of the system revealed that privacy protection mechanisms may help increase user trust and thus improve the acceptance of public displays. While the system included mechanisms to enhance the user's privacy, it did not monitor the user's trust into the system during the interaction.

Based on the evaluation of two mobile guides, Graham and Cheverst [6] analyzed several types of mismatch between the users' physical environment and information given on the screen and their influence on the formation of user trust. Examples of mismatches included situations where the system was not able to correctly detect the user's current location or situations where the system conveyed a wrong impression about the accuracy of its descriptions. To help users form trust, Graham and Cheverst suggested to employ different kinds of guide, such as a chaperone, a buddy or a captain, depending on characteristics of the situations, such as accuracy and transparency. For example, the metaphor of a buddy was supposed to be more effective in unstable situations than the chaperone or the captain. However, their guides did not include any adaptation mechanism to maintain user trust in critical situations.

Cao et al. [24] proposed an approach that enabled users to access personalized information in public places through their mobile devices while ensuring their anonymity. The basic idea was to publicly present all information on a display, but to indicate to individual users only which part of the information is relevant to them by sending personal crossmodal cues (such as vibrations) to their mobile devices. In other words, the approach tried to enhance the users' privacy by obscuring the access to personal information to the public. Initial evaluations of the approach focused on usability issues, but not on the question of whether crossmodal cues appropriately address the users' privacy concerns.

All in all, there is a vivid research interest in the design of novel user interfaces for heterogeneous display environments. However, those few approaches that do address the user experience factor of trust in such environments do not attempt to explicitly model the user experience of trust as a prerequisite for a trust management system.

Research design and methodology
Modeling user trust through trust dimensions

Our trust management system is based on trust dimensions that allow us to derive user trust from relevant properties of a computer system. The trust dimensions are extracted from the literature (see Section 'Background and literature review') and our own user studies.

To identify a set of relevant trust dimensions, we conducted interviews with 20 students of computer science who were asked to indicate trust factors of user interfaces that they felt contributed to their assessment of trustworthiness. The choice of the study participants was motivated by the application domain, a university-wide ubiquitous display environment. The most frequent mentions fell into the following categories: comfort of use ("should be easy to handle"), transparency ("I need to understand what is going on"), controllability ("want to use a program without automated updates"), privacy ("should not ask for private information"), reliability ("should run in a stable manner"), security ("should safely transfer data"), credibility ("recommendation of friends") and seriousness ("professional appearance"). Less frequently mentioned trust factors included the visual appeal of a user interface and the brand of its developer.

The interviews gave a first impression on which factors influence the user's trust in a user interface. However, they did not provide any concrete information regarding their relative importance. To acquire more quantitative data, we designed a follow-up study which made use of a setting that was inspired by applications developed in the area of ubiquitous display environments. The setting consisted of a mobile phone and an interactive table. The table served as the central medium for showing and editing multimedia data whereas the mobile phone was used to send data to or receive data from the table. Thereby, the transmission and the point of time of the presentation of the data on the table were trust-critical moments for the user. In order to get a sufficient variety of user ratings, we built a number of prototypes where we manipulated the following variables: self-explainability, transparency, controllability and privacy.

We recruited 20 people of which the majority (16 people) had a background in computer science. Each participant had to perform various tasks for the single prototypes, such as transferring data between the table and the mobile phone. After completing all tasks for a single prototype, the participants had to rate the prototype according to the trust dimensions identified earlier (comfort of use, controllability, transparency, privacy, security, seriousness, credibility and trustworthiness) as well as their emotions (uneasiness, insecurity, irritation and surprise) on a five point Likert scale (from very low to very high).

The participants rated their general trust into software systems with a mean value of 3.10 (STD = 0.79) and their knowledge about secure data transmission with a mean value of 3.5 (STD = 1.05). To measure the degree of relationship between the ratings for trust and the ratings for the trust dimensions, we computed the Pearson product moment correlation coefficients. The test revealed a moderate to high positive correlation between the ratings for trust on the one hand and the ratings for seriousness ($r = 0.724$), controllability ($r = 0.70$), security ($r = 0.62$), privacy ($r = 0.61$), transparency ($r = 0.56$) and credibility ($r = 0.66$) on the other hand. For all items, the correlation was very significant ($p = 0.01$). The better the ratings for the trust dimensions, the better were also the ratings for trust.

In addition, we observed a moderate positive correlation ($r = 0.35$) between the users' ratings of their general trust into software and their reported trust into the presented system at the significance level of $p = 0.01$. We did not did not find any correlation between the user's self assessment of competence and their reported trust into the presented system. As a potential reason, we indicate that the majority of the users had a background in computer science. As a consequence, their self assessment of competence was rather high with a mean value of 4.03 (STD = 0.75).

Finally, our results revealed a moderate negative correlation between trust on the one hand and uneasiness ($r = -0.629$), insecurity ($r = -0.533$), irritation ($r = -0.484$) on the other hand. For all items the correlation was very significant ($p = 0.01$). We conclude that poor transparency, poor controllability, poor security, poor privacy and poor seriousness result into a loss of trust which in turn leads to a feeling of uneasiness.

Most of the results we obtained were in line with previous studies on the identification of trust factors even though we focused on a different application domain and target group. More information regarding the experiments described here can be found in [25] and [26].

Building the Bayesian network

As mentioned above, the identified trust dimensions form the basis of our computational trust model. Such a model should account for the following characteristics of trust:

Trust as a subjective concept: There is a consensus that trust is highly subjective. A person who is generally confiding is also more likely to trust a software program. Furthermore, users respond individually to one and the same event. While some users might find it critical if a software asks for personal information, others might not care. We aim at a computational model that is able to represent the subjective nature of trust.

Trust as a non-deterministic concept: The connection between events and trust is inherently non-deterministic. We cannot always be absolutely sure that the user notices a critical event or actually considers such an event as critical. As a consequence, it does not make sense to formulate rules that predict in a deterministic manner which level of trust a user has in a particular situation. A computational model of trust should be able to cope with trust as a non-deterministic concept.

Trust as a multifaceted concept: As shown above, trust is a multi-faceted concept. We therefore aim at a computational model that is able to explicitly represent the relative contribution of the trust dimensions to the assessment of trust. In particular, the model should help us predict the user's level of trust based on dimensions, such as the perceived transparency and controllability of a user interface. Furthermore, the model should allow us to easily add trust dimensions based on new experimental findings.

Trust as a dynamic concept: Trust depends on experience and is subject to change over time. Lumsden [27] distinguishes between immediate trust dimensions and interaction-based trust dimensions. Immediate trust dimensions, such as seriousness, come into effect as soon as a user gets in touch with a software system while interaction-based trust dimensions, such as transparency of system behavior, influence the users' experience of trust during an interaction. To model trust as a dynamic concept, we need to be able to represent how the user's level of trust depends on earlier levels of trust.

We have chosen to model the users' feelings of trust by means of Bayesian Networks. The structure of a Bayesian Network is a directed, acyclic graph in which the nodes represent random variables while the links or arrows connecting nodes describe the direct influence in terms of conditional probabilities (see [28]).

Bayesian Networks meet the requirements listed above very well: First of all, they allow us to cope with trust as a subjective concept. For example, we may represent the system's uncertain belief about the user's trust by a probability distribution over different levels of trust. Furthermore, the connection between critical events and trust is inherently non-deterministic. For example, we cannot always be absolutely sure that the user notices a critical event at all. It may also happen that a user considers a critical event as rather harmless. Bayesian Networks allow us to make predictions based on conditional probabilities that model how likely the value of the child variable is given the value of the parent variables. For example, we may model how likely it is that the user has a moderate level of trust if the system's behavior is moderately transparent. Furthermore, Bayesian Networks enable us to model the relationship between trust and its dimensions in a rather intuitive manner. For example, it is rather straightforward to model that reduced transparency leads to a decrease of user trust. The exact probabilities are usually difficult to determine. However, we derived the conditional probabilities from the user data we collected both in the study mentioned above, as well as the study described later in Section 'Gathering empirical data'.

In Figure 1, a Bayesian Network (BN) for modeling trust is shown. For each trust dimension, we introduced a specific node (second layer from the top, shown in blue). Following Lumsden [27], we distinguish between initial (immediate) and interaction-based trust dimensions. The left part of the network represents the factors influencing the establishment of *Initial Trust* that arises when a user gets a first impression of a system. Initial Trust consists of the trust dimensions *Security*, *Seriousness* and *Credibility*.

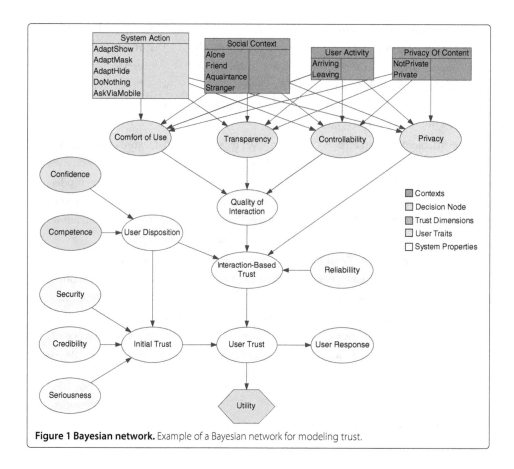

Figure 1 Bayesian network. Example of a Bayesian network for modeling trust.

Security, for example, could be conveyed by the use of certificates. A system's *Seriousness* is reflected, for example, by its look-and-feel. *Credibility* could be supported by additional information, such as a company profile. In this context, we would like to emphasize that trust dimensions may only affect the user's trust if the user is aware of them. For example, high security standards will only have an impact on user trust if the user knows that they exist. For the sake of simplicity, we assume that initial trust dimensions do not change over time. That is, we do not consider the fact that a user might notice references to security certificates only after working with a system over a longer period of time.

To describe the determinants of *Interaction-Based Trust*, we further distinguish between the *Quality of Interaction*, *Privacy* and *Reliability*. The *Quality of Interaction* is characterized by *Transparency*, *Controllability* and *Comfort of Use*. Both the establishment of *Immediate Trust* and *Interaction-Based Trust* depend on the users' *Trust Disposition* which is characterized by their *Competence* and general *Confidence* towards technical systems.

All of the single trust dimensions are treated as hidden variables that cannot be observed directly, but may be inferred from observable variables. Observable variables describe the current context: Examples include privacy level of data, presence of mobile devices, and social context. The latter reflects the social situation: whether the user is alone or not, how close the users are from the display, what the relationships between the present users are, which gender the users have, etc. Knowing the contextual situation, the BN can be used to estimate the impact that certain actions of the display will have on trust and trust dimensions. The trust dimension *Privacy*, for example, could be negatively affected by the display of private data in the presence of other people.

In order to use the BN for decision-making, we extended it to an influence diagram. We added the decision node *System Action*, representing all actions the display could choose to react on context changes and a *Utility* node that encodes the utilities of all these actions to maintain the user's trust. As an example, let us assume a user wishes to display data on a public display while other people are present. Such a situation could be described by the values of the BN's nodes *Social Context* and *Privacy of Content*. These have been determined by sensors or application data and are thus known by the system. The system may now consider three options to cope with the user's request: (1) transferring all data to the public display no matter whether they are private or not, (2) show only the information marked as non-private or (3) asking the user for a confirmation of one of these actions. Considering the example, option (1) may result in serious privacy concerns, option (2) may confuse the users if there is no plausible explanation for the adaptation, and option (3) could be less comfortable to use in a dynamic setting, such as the prototype settings described in this paper. Furthermore, if the system decides in favor of option (1) or (2), the users might perceive the system as less controllable. The arcs between the decision node and the nodes for the five dimensions of trust represent such influences. To choose the adaptation that is most useful for the system in a specific situation, the *Utility* node computes the utility of all possible actions and their consequences and returns the action with the highest utility. Since the goal of our work is to maintain and maximize user trust, the *Utility* node is attached to a node representing the *User Trust* and measures the utility of each single decision in terms of the resulting user trust - a combination of *Initial Trust* and *Interaction-Based Trust*.

Methods

Gathering empirical data

In order to be able to generate decisions, the BN needed to be initialized with empirical data. The data was collected through experiments conducted with potential users. The users were confronted with scenarios illustrating different contextual combinations (situations) and possible adaptive reactions of the displays in these situations that differed in the degree of transparency, user control, privacy and comfort of use. To discover which of the system reactions succeeded in maintaining users' trust and which did not, the users had to reflect on their perception of the display reactions in the specific situation and had to give insights into their feelings of trust and the related trust dimensions. The estimations served as a quantitative input for the initialization of the BN.

The collection of empirical data was arranged in two steps: First, an online survey targeting as many users as possible was conducted. This study presented a collection of applications demonstrating various content types typical of modern public displays: social networks, pictures and videos, maps and travel planning, and shopping items. These content types can be frequently found in real life projects [29,30] as well as in research works [31,32]. The applications showcased different trust critical situations in which an adaptation was necessary: space conflicts, privacy issues, and migration of data from public to mobile displays. The reason to involve several applications was based on our objective of verifying that the proposed approach works equally (or comparably) well for different kinds of content, different sources of social context, and different adaptation scenarios. If the approach indeed delivered robust results, we could generalize its applicability to a wide range of adaptive applications.

Since an online survey might not convey the experience of a real interaction and thus affect the ratings of the users, we also performed a live study. The experiments in this study involved two different applications that were also presented in the online survey. The live experiments were designed identically to the online surveys, but involved real user interactions.

All in all, the online survey was aimed to gather as much data as possible, involving online users. The live study was aimed to complement the online survey, supporting the results collected online by the evaluations of users during a real interaction. The studies were performed in compliance with the ethical guidelines set by Augsburg University. Below we describe both studies in detail and present the obtained results.

Prototypes employed for the studies

The first prototype, Friend Finder (FF), represents a public display supporting social networking [33]. Once a user comes closer, the large display shows the user's social network overlaid over a local map, depicting the status and locations of friends (see Figure 2 left). By selecting individual friends via their mobile phone users are able to display a route to the selected friend. The second prototype, Media Wall (MW), supports media exchange within a community [33]. It displays a gallery of private media items (pictures or videos) when a user approaches. Then the user, for example, can browse or rank the items via his mobile phone (see Figure 2 right). The third prototype, Travel Planner (TP), helps students arrange low-budget trips around Europe. By browsing the map on the large display map via their mobile phone, users can retrieve information on the cities and the estimated cost of a visit (see Figure 3 left). Apart from this neutral information, the application also is able to consider private budget-related data, if the user is logged in. In the budget-aware mode, the pop-up information is directly linked to the user's budget and shows whether the estimated costs are within budget. The fourth prototype, Shopping Mall display (SMD), aims at supporting customers of a shopping mall in finding products of their interests and the corresponding shops (see Figure 3 right) by displaying personalized information when a user approaches.

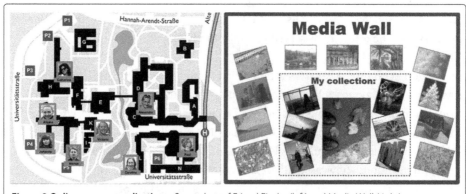

Figure 2 Online survey: applications. *Screenshots* of Friend Finder (left) and Media Wall (right).

Figure 3 Online survey: applications. *Screenshots* of Travel Planner (left) and Shopping Mall (right).

All four applications require mechanisms for deciding how to respond to trust-critical events, such as a passer-by approaching the display. Since all applications may disclose private information, such as a user's social network (FF) (see Figure 4 left), personal preferences (MW and SMD) or budget limitations (TP), they should be able to appropriately adapt to the surrounding social context in order to avoid potential privacy threats. Potential protection mechanisms include the migration of personal data from the public display to the user's mobile device, the hiding or masking of personal information (see Figure 4 middle) as well as offering these actions to the users via their mobile phones (see Figure 4 right). The corresponding scenarios in which users interact with a display while others pass or join will be in the following summarized under the common term "Spectator Scenario".

Besides people quickly passing the public display without taking notice of its content and people that may stop and watch, people may even engage in an interaction as well. In this case, the system does not only have to protect private information against unwanted disclosure, it should also account for strategies to accommodate the data and input originating from multiple users [2]. For example, several users may interact with the Shopping Mall display in parallel to exploring product information ("Space Scenario"). To accommodate the needs of multiple users, the size of the space allocated to particular users may be dynamically adapted. Alternatively, data may migrate to the user's mobile device. On the one hand, these strategies enable the simultaneous exploitation of a public display by

Figure 4 Possible display reactions (example). Examples of display reactions for Friend Finder (caused by privacy issues): Left: No reaction needed; Middle: Display Reaction: Mask private data on display and migrate data to the user's mobile phone; Right: Display Reaction: Present possible actions on the user's mobile phone.

multiple users. On the other hand, users might get irritated by the unsolicited customization. As a consequence, the system has to carefully balance the benefits and drawbacks of each action in order to come up with an optimized solution.

In addition, three of the applications (FF, MW and SMD) utilize additional sensors, such as cameras, to also offer proxemic interaction [2]. The corresponding scenarios for these applications will in the following be summarized under the term "Proximity Scenario". Whenever a user approaches the display, information relevant to him or her could be proactively presented on the screen. As soon as the user leaves the display, this information could be immediately removed again. On the one hand this feature offers great comfort. On the other hand, it limits the user's control over the system and might also be considered as opaque. Therefore, whenever a user approaches or leaves, the system could ask the user for confirmation via the user's mobile phone. Again this is a situation in which a system has to find a tradeoff between comfort of use, transparency and controllability to maximize the user's trust. The high dynamics in public places make this task even more difficult.

Online survey

The online survey was aimed at capturing the users' subjective assessment of display reactions in situations with changing social context. To this end, participants were shown videos clips of the four prototypes.

For each prototype, we recorded several short videos demonstrating scenarios in which a specific situation was given, the social context changed, and the display conducted a possible reaction. For example, the "Spectator Scenario" of the Friend Finder showed a single user interacting with the display in a public area (see Figure 5 left). The display recognized the arrival of an unknown person (change in social context) and masked the user's social network automatically (reaction) (see Figure 5 middle). Another video illustrated the same situation and context change, but a different display reaction: Instead of masking the data automatically, the data were blurred and the user was presented with various options on his mobile phone (see Figure 5 right).

Table 1 summarizes the recorded scenarios including possible situations which were represented by different settings of contextual variables, such as the social context and the privacy of the displayed content, and possible display reactions. Some scenarios were illustrated by different applications, in order to compare how people perceive the same

Figure 5 Online survey: screenshots of video (example). Screenshots of Video (Example) Screenshots of Video "Friend Finder - Approaching Stranger": Left: Single user interacting with private data on public display; Middle: Display Reaction: Mask private data; Right: Display Reaction: Blur private data and present possible actions on the user's mobile phone.

Table 1 Scenarios illustrated by videos: possible display reactions in different contextual combinations (situations)

Proximity scenario (privacy issues)			
User context	**Data context**	**Social context**	**Display reaction**
User approaching (FF, MW, SMD)	a) Private data b) Neutral data	a) User alone b) User not alone	a) Show user data automatically b) Ask via mobile device c) Do nothing
User leaving (FF, MW)	a) Private data b) Neutral data	a) User alone b) User not alone	a) Remove user data automatically b) Ask via mobile device c) Do nothing
Spectator scenario (privacy issues)			
User context	**Data context**	**Social context**	**Display reaction**
User interacts alone. (FF, MW)	a) Private data b) Neutral data	A person comes: a) Friend b) Acquaintance c) Stranger	a) Hide private data b) Mask private data c) Ask via mobile device d) Do nothing
User logged in (TP)	a) Private Data b) Neutral data	a) User alone b) User not alone	a) Show data on public display b) Show data on mobile device
Space scenario (space conflicts)			
User context	**Devices context**	**Social context**	**Display reaction**
User A interacts with the display. (SMD)	a) Mobile available b) not available	User B approaches the display: a) B is female b) B is male	a) Provide space for B, shrink data of A b) Provide space for B, move data of A to mobile c) Do nothing. B will wait

adaptations applied to different content. The applications illustrating the scenarios are indicated by the capital letters in the Scenario column.

All in all, four to six situations for each scenario (see Table 1 (Column 1–3)) and 22 situations in total were investigated. Considering two to four possible display reactions per situation (see Table 1 (Column 4)) this resulted in a total number of 68 recorded short videos. In order to reduce the time of the survey completion to about 10 minutes, we grouped the videos into six online surveys. Each survey contained about 8–12 videos. After an introductory page, the surveys provided a description of the used applications. Then, the user was confronted with the first scenario. The corresponding video illustrated the first situation and the first display reaction to the context change. After watching a video the user had to fill in a questionnaire. The questions aimed at capturing the participant's perception of the shown display reaction in terms of transparency, controllability, comfort of use, privacy, reliability, and trust. The questions represented statements which had to be ranked on a Likert scale from 1 ("absolutely disagree") to 5 ("absolutely agree"):

- Q1: I understood why the system was reacting in this way.
- Q2: I had control over the system.
- Q3: I found the system comfortable to use.
- Q4: The system protected my privacy in an appropriate way.
- Q5: I found the system reliable.
- Q6: I found the system trustworthy.

After presenting all possible display reactions for a particular situation, the users were asked to rank their preferences for it. The preferences also had to be estimated as statements of a 5-Likert scale. The statements emphasized the context of the given scenario, such as the presence of others or the privacy of data. For instance, a statement for the scenario of Friend Finder where the user was interacting with the display in a public area looked liked this:

"When I am watching my social network alone and a stranger approaches the display..."

- P1: I prefer to hide my data.
- P2: I prefer to mask my data.
- P3: I prefer no reaction from the display.
- P4: I prefer to be asked by my mobile phone.

Questions Q1-Q5 were aimed to collect empirical data to initialize the BN. Question Q6 was required to validate the network by checking whether the generated decisions matched the system action that created the highest user trust. Questions P1-P4 reflected subjective user preferences. In particular, we wanted to find out whether user preferences were in accord with the highest trust ratings and decisions generated by the BN. All in all, we collected evaluations of 85 online users and each video was seen by at least seven participants (Mean: 14). Supplying gender and age was not mandatory. The 73 users that provided demographic data included 24 women and 49 men. They were aged between 23 and 62 years, with an average age of 33.3 years.

Before using the data collected in these online studies for the initialization of the BN, we investigated whether the results of the online study were in line with the perception of users actually interacting with an adaptive system.

Live experiments

For the live experiments we picked two prototypes from the online studies that could be easily installed and tested in a university public area and that covered all scenarios related to privacy issues: Friend Finder and Travel Planner. The experiments were conducted individually in front of large displays that were installed in a university public area with a moderate circulation of researchers, students, and visitors. That is, the study participants were not just watching a video, but actively experiencing an application by interacting with it (see Figure 6). In each application, the users were confronted with a variety of trust-critical situations, such as the approach of another person, while they were viewing private information. As in the online survey, the users had to assess potential system reactions to these events. Hence, the procedure and the questions used in the live study reproduced the web-based study as closely as possible to control for any unintended side effects. Both prototypes were tested between groups: Every participant evaluated either Friend Finder or Travel Planner. Altogether, 36 people took part in the live experiments (FF: 16; TP: 20). Among them there were 16 female and 20 male persons, aged from 20 to 36 (mean 28.3).

The results of the live experiment generally matched the results obtained in the online study. Both experiments yielded similar distributions of user rankings of transparency, controllability, comfort of use, privacy and reliability. Moreover, we found similar distributions of trust and user preferences. Figure 7 shows the distributions of the user ratings for one particular situation in Friend Finder, namely the automated removal of data from a public display as soon as the user leaves. Most distributions are skewed to the right

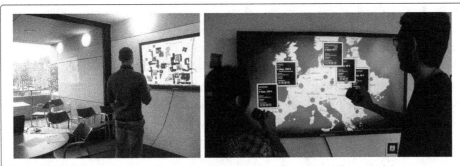

Figure 6 Life study: applications. Prototypes of Friend Finder (left) and Travel Planner (right).

reflecting positive user ratings both for the online and the live condition. Overall, the ratings in the online and in the live experiments show a similar trend. Similar observations could be made for the Travel Finder application.

Interestingly, the participants gave higher trust ratings in the live condition than in the online condition. For Friend Finder, a two-tailed t-test showed that the differences were significant with mean values of 3.66 (STD = 1.50) and 3.08 (STD = 1.27) in Friend Finder (t(238) = -2.46, $p < 0.02$) and mean values of 3.98 (STD = 0.84) and 3.14 (STD = 1.40) in Travel Planner (t(248) = 5.86, $p < 0.001$). Apparently, the fact that the participants had the chance to interact with the system had influenced their ratings positively.

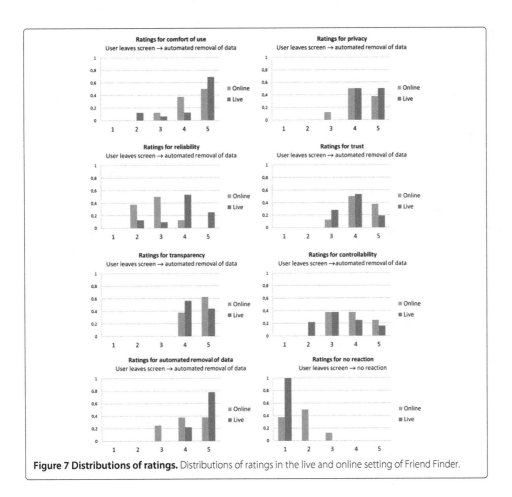

Figure 7 Distributions of ratings. Distributions of ratings in the live and online setting of Friend Finder.

However, the important result for us was to see that apart from a few exceptions the ranking of system reactions in the online experiments was in line with that obtained in the live experiments. Independently of whether users had to evaluate the online or the live setting, participants preferred the same system reaction. In the case of Travel Planner, this system reaction got significantly higher rankings than any other system reaction in all four situations for the live condition and in three out of four situations in the online condition. For example, people preferred private information to be displayed on a mobile phone in the presence of other people. Accordingly, performing a two-tailed paired t-test, we found that "Show on Mobile Device" got significantly higher ratings than "Show on Display" with mean values of 3.44 and 1.44 in the online scenario ($t(8) = -4.24, p < 0.01$) and mean values of 4.75 and 1.95 in the live scenario ($t(19) = -7.10, p < 0.001$). This system reaction also got the highest trust value in both conditions (albeit not significant). Similar observations could be made for Friend Finder even though less distinct. Again participants preferred the same system reaction in both conditions. Apart from two cases, the system reactions the users trusted most in the live setting matched the system reactions the users trusted most in the online setting. Overall, the results indicate that the online study provides realistic input for the initialization of the BN despite a few discrepancies.

Results and discussion

Initialization and validation of the Bayesian network

As the next step, the BN was populated with the empirically obtained data. For the creation of conditional probability tables, we employed the GeNIe (see http://genie.sis.pitt.edu) built-in algorithm for learning Bayesian Networks.

Overall, we constructed four different networks from the data received in the online studies, one for each row in Table 1, with the first two rows being combined into one network. While the basic structure was shared by all networks and was similar to the example network shown in Figure 1, each had different context nodes and possible adaptations, based on the respective scenario. For example, the first of the Spectator scenarios required one context node with two contexts and another one with three, as well as four different system reactions in the decision node. On the other hand, the second Spectator scenario required two context nodes with two contexts each and only two system reactions.

The quantitative data obtained in the evaluations enabled us to derive distributions for each trust dimension related to each contextual combination. For each trust dimension, we modeled the probability distribution for all combinations of context and display reaction in the BN after the data taken from both studies. The probability distributions for other node combinations were derived from the study described in Section 'Modeling user trust through trust dimensions'. In particular, dependency information from the earlier study was used to model (1) the relationship between the trust dimensions and user trust and (2) the relationship between the user's trust disposition and user trust.

Since knowledge about the user's trust disposition is hard to acquire in an ubiquitous display environment, it does not make sense to assume detailed knowledge about the trust disposition of a particular user. Rather, we created user trust profiles from empirical data acquired in the population that was of relevance to our application domain. That is the reasoning process of the BN did not start from "hard" evidence, but from distributions for user trust disposition. These distributions reflect the trust disposition of our users. However, data for other user groups can be easily integrated into the BN by replacing the corresponding distributions in the BN. An interesting resource to explore is the work by Westin who conducted a large number of studies to determine the percentage of people with certain levels of distrust or privacy concerns, see the paper by Kumaraguru and Cranor [34] for a survey of these studies.

Figure 8 shows an example of probability distributions for *Initial, Interaction-Based* and *User Trust* for a selected system reaction, assuming a very low *Trust Disposition* (blue) in one case and a very high one (red) in the other. As can be seen, we chose to model the distributions with a (skewed) bell curve, with a bias towards the lower end of trust scale. The utility function from *User Trust* to *Utility* maps "very low" to 1, "low" to 2 and so on, resulting into an overall trust value of 2.03 for the very low *Trust Disposition* and 3.34 for the very high one.

Although we also asked for the users' preferred display reaction for each context combination as well as their trust in the display reaction presented for each such combination, it should be noted that this information was not used to model the networks. As mentioned above, we only used the users' rankings of the different trust dimensions for each combination of context and display reaction. Instead, the data on user trust ratings and user preferences was used to validate the decisions generated by the BN. In this vein, we were able to check to what extent the relationship between trust and trust dimensions (see Section 'Modeling user trust through trust dimensions') was application-independent. For the validation of each created network, we generated decisions for all contextual combinations. These decisions were compared to the results from the user studies. In particular, we compared the decision obtained from the BN with the user's ratings of system actions and their own trust.

The contextual combinations were set by entering appropriate evidence into the matching context nodes. For example, for a specific situation in the Proximity scenario, the evidence would be set to "Privacy of Data → Private", "Movement → Arriving" and "Others Present → Yes". We only used "hard" evidence at this point, i.e. the corresponding values were set to 100%. For each of these combinations, the display reaction with the highest utility rating (which was directly based on the computed value of User Trust) was chosen as the system's decision.

First, we compared these generated reactions with those preferred by the participants in the studies. For each context combination, we selected the display reaction that received the highest average score in the surveys. When comparing the display reactions preferred by the users with those generated by the respective network, we found that they matched in 21 out of the 22 situations (95.45%). Second, we compared the generated

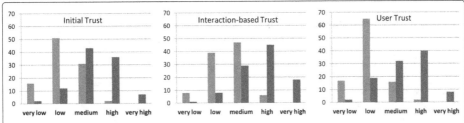

Figure 8 Impact of trust disposition on initial trust, interaction-based trust and overall user trust.
Probability distributions for very low (blue) and very high (red) Trust Disposition.

reactions with those that received the highest trust in the studies. They matched in all 22 situations.

These results show that the BN delivers good accuracy in the generated decisions. As an example from the results, let us take a look at the BN for the first Spectator scenario (the third row in Table 1) and its eight context combinations. Table 2 shows the different situations along with the respective display reactions which received the highest trust from the study participants. As mentioned above, these reactions matched those generated by the BN. For the preferred reactions, there was one mismatch. For the first situation (Data is private, Spectator is Friend), the study participants indicated a preference for "Hide private data" (even though they gave "Ask via mobile device" the highest trust value). Thus, the participants' trust ratings were in line with those determined by the BN while the favored reactions of the participants and the most appropriate reactions determined by the BN differed. It is worth mentioning that only two out of four possible system reactions for this scenario were among those favored (both preference- and trust-wise) by the study participants. As another, more diverse example, Table 3 shows the results for the Proximity scenario (the first two rows in Table 1).

However, this form of validation only validated our model within the same population and also the generated decisions were compared to average and not individual preferences. Thus we were also interested in how its generated decisions matched with the preferences of "new" and individual users. Therefore we also performed a leave-one-person-out cross-validation of our networks: For each network, we performed n validations, where n is the number of users that participated in the respective study for the scenario(s) in that network. In each of the n validations, the network was initialized with the data from (n - 1) users and then validated with the missing user. The final result for each network was the average of all n validations. The comparison of user preferences with the adaptations generated by the networks now resulted in 15.84 out of 22 matching situations (72.00%). The comparison with the highest-trust adaptations now matched in 17.26 out of 22 (78.45%). These results are in line with the percentages of study participants who individually preferred the system reaction which received the highest average score, 78.80% for preference and 82.58% for trust.

Finally, we were also interested in how the approach would perform in non-ideal situations, thus leveraging the BN's strength of decision-making under uncertainty. To test whether it still would be able to generate appropriate decisions in such situations, we simulated the following two problems (again using the leave-one-person-out cross-validation for all networks, as described above):

Table 2 Study results for display reactions in the first Spectator scenario

Context	Reaction with highest user ratings for trust
Data is private, Spectator is Friend	Ask via mobile device
Data is private, Spectator is Acquaintance	Hide private data
Data is private, Spectator is Stranger	Hide private data
Data is not private, Spectator is Friend	Ask via mobile device
Data is not private, Spectator is Acquaintance	Ask via mobile device
Data is not private, Spectator is Stranger	Ask via mobile device

Table 3 Study results for display reactions in the proximity scenarios

Context	Reaction with highest user ratings for trust
User is arriving, Data is private, User is alone	Ask via mobile device
User is arriving, Data is private, User is not alone	Ask via mobile device
User is arriving, Data is not private, User is alone	Do nothing
User is arriving, Data is not private, User is not alone	Do nothing
User is leaving, Data is private, User is alone	Remove user data automatically
User is leaving, Data is private, User is not alone	Remove user data automatically
User is leaving, Data is not private, User is alone	Remove user data automatically
User is leaving, Data is not private, User is not alone	Remove user data automatically

- No empirical data for certain context combinations: Especially for complex applications with many different contexts and system reactions, performing studies to obtain empirical data for each single situation might not be feasible. If a certain context combination (such as the transparency of a system action in a given situation) can not be initialized with empirical data, another solution, such as a uniform distribution, has to be chosen. Figure 9 shows the matching rates for trust and preference for an increasing number of uninitialized context combinations, using a uniform distribution when necessary.

- No context data for certain situations: If it is not possible to determine the context for a certain situation (e.g. the face-tracking sensor is not providing any data and thus the system cannot determine whether the user is alone or not) then only insufficient evidence can be entered into the network which will of course impact on the decision-making process. Figure 10 shows the matching rates for trust and preference for an increasing number of context nodes without evidence, using a uniform distribution instead of concrete evidence when necessary.

It is important to emphasize that a solution that results into the highest user trust is not necessarily the solution that the user actually prefers the most. The results of our online and live study support this fact: distributions of user preferences did not always reflect distributions of trust. From the comments of the live study participants, we found that the

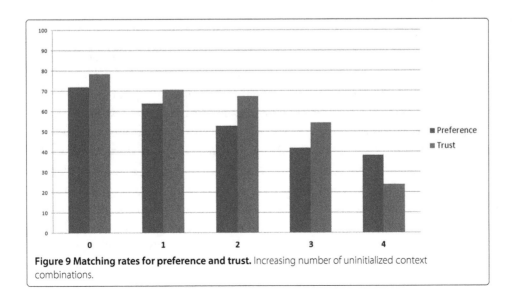

Figure 9 Matching rates for preference and trust. Increasing number of uninitialized context combinations.

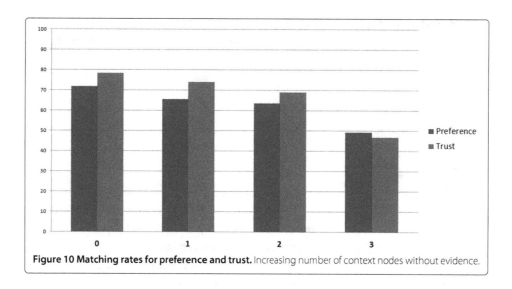

Figure 10 Matching rates for preference and trust. Increasing number of context nodes without evidence.

feeling of trust often depends on the person's ability to explain the system reaction and agree with it. For example, when a person comes closer to the display, it seems logical and expected that the display does not show any reaction. We learn this behavior from everyday life: Fixtures, even electronic ones, usually do not react. Apparently, the option "Do nothing" therefore received highest trust rankings. However, the most understandable reaction might not be the most preferred or the most convenient one. Here, the more creative (but less predictable) reactions were favored. For example, the users found it smart and convenient that the display noticed them and proposed via a mobile device to show their data on the large screen. Thus, the "Ask via mobile device" option was chosen as a preference.

Conclusion

The ability of ubiquitous display environments to dynamically adapt to changing social contexts comes with a lot of benefits. At the same time, it raises issues with user trust. In this paper we delineated a decision-theoretic mechanism to trust management based on Bayesian Networks that assesses user trust through trust dimensions, monitors it during the interaction and chooses appropriate measures to ensure user trust in critical situations. Using empirical data collected in online and live experiments, we demonstrated how the network was initialized and cross-validated. The evaluation revealed that the approach succeeded in determining system actions that obtained the highest value for trustworthiness from users. An interesting result obtained by the empirical validation of the Bayesian Network was the mismatch between the system reactions users *preferred* most and the system reactions resulting in the highest amount of user *trust*. A creative solution is more likely to impress users. At the same time, a surprising system response may have a negative impact on user trust. Future work should aim at gaining a deeper insight into this question, investigating which factor - trust or subjective preference - drives the user's ultimate choice of a system reaction. One limitation of our live studies is the homogeneity of the participants, since most of them were rather young students from the engineering sciences. Also, all interactive prototypes were deployed in a university setting. While we already reached a larger demographic variety with our online studies, future work should also extend the live studies in a similar fashion. So far, we do not exploit any knowledge about user-specific attitudes during the selection of system actions. Depending on their trust disposition, users might, however, favor different system responses. For example, users that tend to distrust technical systems might give more importance to a high level of control than to a high level of comfort. In our future work, we will investigate how to improve the accuracy of the user trust model by incorporating knowledge about user-specific attitudes. A promising approach might be to distinguish between different categories of users, such as privacy fundamentalists, pragmatics and unconcerned users, following Westin's privacy indices [34].

Unlike most earlier work, we focused on the challenge of modeling experience-based user trust. Since experience-based user trust refers to a psychological user state, it is hard to measure directly. The approach presented in the paper was based on the assumption that user trust may be assessed through trust dimensions that refer to trust-enhancing system properties. While the estimation based on trust dimensions gave promising results, more complex scenarios might require the consideration of additional trust indicators. For our future work, we plan two extensions. First of all, we aim to derive user trust not only from its causes, i.e. system properties, but also from its effects, i.e. observable user behaviors. In our earlier work [35], we investigated various physiological patterns as an indicator of trust felt by a user when viewing web pages. As a next step, we will concentrate on the identification of behavioral factors from which experience-based user trust might be derived in ubiquitous display environments, such as the time spent in front of a public display or the number of downloads. Secondly, we intend to extend the Bayesian Network to a Dynamic Bayesian Network in order to consider how user trust felt at a particular point in time depends on user trust experienced at an earlier point in time. While we presented the topology of such a network in [26], it has not yet been grounded and evaluated by user data.

Competing interests

The authors declare that they have no competing interests.

Authors' contributions

MW took over the lead of the design and the implementation of the trust management system based on Bayesian Networks. He also performed the statistical analysis for the online survey and the live studies. SH provided support in the implementation and the evaluation of the trust management approach. EK designed and implemented the scenarios which formed the basis of the evaluation. She was also involved in the conduction of the user studies. EA supervised the research. Also the concept of the decision-theoretic approach to trust management goes back to ideas from her. Finally, she acquired the funding from the German Science Foundation (DFG) for conducting the research. All authors collaborated in drafting and revising the manuscript and all authors read and approved the final manuscript.

Acknowledgments

This research is co-funded by OC-Trust (FOR 1085) of the German Research Foundation (DFG). The core of our implementation is based on the SMILE reasoning engine and the network shown in this paper was created using the GeNIe modeling environment. Both SMILE and GeNIe are developed and contributed to the community by the Decision Systems Laboratory, University of Pittsburgh and available at http://genie.sis.pitt.edu/.

References

1. Rothrock L, Koubek R, Fuchs F, Haas M, Salvendy G (2002) Review and reappraisal of adaptive interfaces: toward biologically inspired paradigms. Theor Issues Ergon Sci 3: 47–84
2. Greenberg S, Marquardt N, Ballendat T, Diaz-Marino R, Wang M (2011) Proxemic interactions: the new ubicomp? ACM Interact 18(1): 42–50
3. Müller J, Exeler J, Buzeck M, Krüger A (2009) ReflectiveSigns: digital signs that adapt to audience attention In: Proceedings of 7th International Conference on Pervasive Computing. Springer, Berlin, Heidelberg, pp 17–24

4. Röcker C, Hinske S, Magerkurth C (2007) Intelligent privacy support for large public displays In: Proceedings of Human-Computer Interaction International 2007 (HCII'07). Springer, Berlin, Heidelberg, Germany

5. Yan Z, Holtmanns S (2008) Trust modeling and management: from social trust to digital trust. IGI Global, Hershey

6. Graham C, Cheverst K (2004) Guides, locals, chaperones, buddies and captains: managing trust through interaction paradigms In: 3rd Workshop 'HCI on Mobile Guides' at the sixth international symposium on human computer interaction with mobile devices and services. ACM, New York, pp 227–236

7. Glass A, McGuinness DL, Wolverton M (2008) Toward establishing trust in adaptive agents In: Proceedings of the 13th international conference on Intelligent User Interfaces (IUI '08). ACM, New York, pp 227–236

8. Castelfranchi C, Falcone R (2010) Trust theory: a socio-cognitive and computational model. Wiley, Hoboken

9. Marsh S (1992) Trust in distributed artificial intelligence. In: Castelfranchi C, Werner E (eds) Artificial social systems, 4th European workshop on Modelling Autonomous Agents in a Multi-Agent World, MAAMAW '92, S. Martino al Cimino, Italy, July 29–31, 1992, selected papers. Lecture notes in computer science, vol. 830. Springer, Berlin, Heidelberg, pp 94–112

10. Wang Y, Vassileva J (2003) Bayesian network trust model in peer-to-peer networks. In: Moro G, Sartori C, Singh MP (eds) Agents and peer-to-peer computing, second international workshop, AP2PC 2003, Melbourne, Australia, July 14, 2003, Revised and invited papers. Lecture notes in computer science, vol. 2872. Springer, Berlin, Heidelberg, pp 23–34

11. Yu B, Singh MP (2002) An evidential model of distributed reputation management In: Proceedings of the first international joint conference on Autonomous Agents and Multiagent Systems: Part 1. AAMAS '02. ACM, New York, pp 294–301

12. Vogiatzis G, MacGillivray I, Chli M (2010) A probabilistic model for trust and reputation. In: van der Hoek W, Kaminka GA, Lespérance Y, Luck M, Sen S (eds) 9th international conference on Autonomous Agents and Multiagent Systems (AAMAS 2010), Toronto, Canada, May 10–14, 2010, Volume 1–3. IFAAMAS, Richland, pp 225–232

13. Jøsang A, Hayward R, Pope S (2006) Trust network analysis with subjective logic. In: Estivill-Castro V, Dobbie G (eds) Computer science 2006, Twenty-nineth Australasian Computer Science Conference (ACSC2006), Hobart, Tasmania, Australia, January 16–19 2006. CRPIT, vol. 48. Australian Computer Society, Darlinghurst, pp 85–94

14. Sankaranarayanan V, Chandrasekaran M, Upadhyaya SJ (2007) Towards modeling trust based decisions: a game theoretic approach. In: Biskup J, Lopez J (eds) Computer Security - ESORICS 2007, 12th European Symposium On Research In Computer Security, Dresden, Germany, September 24–26, 2007, Proceedings. Lecture Notes in Computer Science, vol. 4734. Springer, Berlin, Heidelberg, pp 485–500

15. Burnett C, Norman TJ, Sycara KP (2011) Trust decision-making in multi-agent systems. In: Walsh T (ed) IJCAI 2011, Proceedings of the 22nd International Joint Conference on Artificial Intelligence, Barcelona, Catalonia, Spain, July 16–22, 2011. IJCAI/AAAI, Palo Alto, California, USA, pp 115–120

16. Sherchan W, Nepal S, Paris C (2013) A survey of trust in social networks. ACM Comput Surv 45(4): 47:1-47:33

17. Bhuiyan T, Xu Y, Jøsang A (2010) A review of trust in online social networks to explore new research agenda. In: Arabnia HR, Clincy VA, Lu J, Marsh A, Solo AMG (eds) Proceedings of the 2010 International Conference on Internet Computing, ICOMP 2010, July 12–15, 2010, Las Vegas Nevada, USA. CSREA Press, Las Vegas, pp 123–128

18. Adali S, Escriva R, Goldberg MK, Hayvanovych M, Magdon-Ismail M, Szymanski BK, Wallace WA, Williams GT (2010) Measuring behavioral trust in social networks. In: Yang CC, Zeng D, Wang K, Sanfilippo A, Tsang HH, Day M-Y, Glässer U, Brantingham PL, Chen H (eds) IEEE international conference on Intelligence and Security Informatics, ISI 2010, Vancouver, BC, Canada, May 23–26, 2010, Proceedings. IEEE, s.l., Washington, DC, USA, pp 150–152

19. Ivanov I, Vajda P, Korshunov P, Ebrahimi T (2013) Comparative study of trust modeling for automatic landmark tagging. IEEE Trans Inf Forensics Secur 8(6): 911–923

20. Grandison T, Sloman M (2000) A survey of trust in internet applications. IEEE Commun Surv Tutorials 3(4): 2–16

21. Kini A, Choobineh J (1998) Trust in electronic commerce: definition and theoretical considerations In: Proc. of the Hawaii international conference on system sciences, vol. 31. IEEE Computer Society, Washington, DC, USA, pp 51–61

22. Tschannen-Moran M, Hoy WK (2000) A multidisciplinary analysis of the nature, meaning, and measurement of trust. Rev Educ Res 70(4): 547

23. Yan Z, Zhang P, Deng RH (2012) Truberepec: a trust-behavior-based reputation and recommender system for mobile applications. Pers Ubiquitous Comput 16(5): 485–506

24. Cao H, Olivier P, Jackson D (2008) Enhancing privacy in public spaces through crossmodal displays. Soc Sci Comput Rev 26(1): 87–102

25. Bee K, Hammer S, Pratsch C, Andre E (2012) The automatic trust management of self-adaptive multi-display environments In: Trustworthy ubiquitous computing. Atlantis ambient and pervasive intelligence, vol. 6. Atlantis Press, s.l., Paris, France, pp 3–20

26. Kurdyukova E, André E, Leichtenstern K (2012) Trust management of ubiquitous multi-display environments. In: Krueger A, Kuflik T (eds) Ubiquitous display environments. Cognitive technologies. Springer, Berlin, Heidelberg, pp 177–193

27. Lumsden J (2009) Triggering Trust: to what extent does the question influence the answer when evaluating the perceived importance of trust triggers? In: Proceedings of the 2009 British Computer Society Conference on Human-Computer Interaction (BCS HCI '09). British Computer Society, Swinton, pp 214–223

28. Russell SJ, Norvig P (2003) Artificial intelligence: a modern approach, 2nd international edn.. Prentice Hall, Upper Saddle River

29. Müller J, Krüger A, Kuflik T (2007) Maximizing the utility of situated public displays In: Proceedings of the 11th international conference on User Modeling (UM '07). Springer, Berlin, Heidelberg, pp 395–399

30. Peltonen P, Salovaara A, Jacucci G, Ilmonen T, Ardito C, Saarikko P, Batra V (2007) Extending large-scale event participation with user-created mobile media on a public display In: Proceedings of the 6th international conference on mobile and ubiquitous multimedia. ACM, New York, pp 131–138

31. Alt F, Balz M, Kristes S, Shirazi AS, Mennenöh J, Schmidt A, Schröder H, Goedicke M (2009) Adaptive user profiles in pervasive advertising environments In: Proceedings of the European conference on Ambient Intelligence (AmI '09). Springer, Berlin, Heidelberg, pp 276–286

32. Churchill EF, Nelson L, Denoue L, Girgensohn A (2003) The plasma poster network: posting multimedia content in public places In: In Proceedings of the IFIP International Conference on Human-Computer Interaction (INTERACT 2003). IOS Press, Amsterdam, The Netherlands, pp 599–606

33. Kurdyukova E, Bee K, André E (2011) Friend or foe? Relationship-based adaptation on public displays In: Proceedings of the second international conference on Ambient Intelligence (AmI'11). Springer, Berlin, Heidelberg, pp 228–237

34. Kumaraguru P, Cranor LF (2005) Privacy indexes: a survey of westin's studies. Technical Report CMU-ISRI-5-138, Technical Report, Institute for Software Research International (ISRI), Carnegie Mellon University

35. Leichtenstern K, Bee N, André E, Berkmüller U, Wagner J (2011) Physiological measurement of trust-related behavior in trust-neutral and trust-critical situations. In: Wakeman I, Gudes E, Jensen CD, Crampton J (eds) Trust Management V, 5th IFIP WG 11.11 international conference, IFIPTM 2011, Copenhagen, Denmark, June 29-July 1, 2011, proceedings. IFIP advances in information and communication technology, vol. 358. Springer, Berlin, Heidelberg, pp 165–172

4

Reusable components for online reputation systems

Johannes Sänger[*], Christian Richthammer and Günther Pernul

*Correspondence:
johannes.saenger@wiwi.
uni-regensburg.de
University of Regensburg,
Universitätsstraße 31, 93053
Regensburg, Germany

Abstract

Reputation systems have been extensively explored in various disciplines and application areas. A problem in this context is that the computation engines applied by most reputation systems available are designed from scratch and rarely consider well established concepts and achievements made by others. Thus, approved models and promising approaches may get lost in the shuffle. In this work, we aim to foster reuse in respect of trust and reputation systems by providing a hierarchical component taxonomy of computation engines which serves as a natural framework for the design of new reputation systems. In order to assist the design process we, furthermore, provide a component repository that contains design knowledge on both a conceptual and an implementation level. To evaluate our approach we conduct a descriptive scenario-based analysis which shows that it has an obvious utility from a practical point of view. Matching the identified components and the properties of trust introduced in literature, we finally show which properties of trust are widely covered by common models and which aspects have only rarely been considered so far.

Keywords: Trust; Reputation; Reusability; Trust pattern

Introduction

In the last decade, trust and reputation have been extensively explored in various disciplines and application areas. Thereby, a wide range of metrics and computation methods for reputation-based trust has been proposed. While most common systems have been introduced in e-commerce, such as eBay's reputation system [1] that allows to rate sellers and buyers, considerable research has also been done in the context of peer-to-peer networks, mobile ad hoc networks, social networks or ensuring data accuracy, relevance and quality in several environments [2]. Computation methods applied range from simple arithmetic over statistical approaches up to graph-based models involving multiple factors such as context information, propagation or personal preferences. A general problem is that most of the newly introduced trust and reputation models use computation methods that are designed from scratch and rely on one novel idea which could lead to better solutions [3]. Only a few authors build on proposals of others. Therefore, approved models and promising approaches may get lost in the shuffle.

In this work, we aim to encourage reuse in the development of reputation systems by providing a framework for creating reputation systems based on reusable components. Design approaches for reuse have been given much attention in the software engineering community. The research in trust and reputation systems could also profit from benefits like effective use of specialists, accelerated development and increased reliability. Toward this goal, we propose a *hierarchical taxonomy* for components of computation engines used in reputation systems. Thereto, we decompose the computation phase of common reputation models to derive single building blocks. The classification based on their functions serves as a natural framework for the design of new reputation systems. Moreover, we set up a *component repository* containing artifacts on both a conceptual and an implementation level to facilitate the reuse of the identified components. On the conceptual level, we describe each building block as a design pattern-like solution. On the implementation level, we provide already implemented components by means of web services.

The rest of this paper is based on the design science research paradigm involving the guidelines for conducting design science research by Hevner et al. [4] and organized as follows: Firstly, we give an overview of the general problem context as well as the relevance and motivation of our work. Thereby, we identify the research gap and define the objectives of our research. In the following section, we introduce our hierarchical component taxonomy of computation engines used in reputation systems. After that, we point out how our component repository is conceptually designed and implemented. Subsequently, we carry out a descriptive scenario-based analysis of our approach. At the same time, we match all components identified with the properties of trust introduced in literature. We show which properties of trust are widely covered by common models and which aspects have only rarely been considered so far. Finally, we summarize the contribution and name our plans for future work.

Problem context and motivation

With the success of the Internet and the increasing distribution and connectivity, trust and reputation systems have become important artifacts to support decision making in network environments. To impart a common understanding, we firstly provide a definition of the notion of trust. At the same time, we explain the properties of trust that are important with regard to this work. Then, we point out how trust can be established applying computational trust models. Focusing on reputation-based trust, we explain how and why the research in reputation models could profit from reuse. Thereby, we identify the research gap and define the objectives of this work.

The notion of trust and its properties

The notion of trust is a topic that has been discussed in research for decades. Although it has been intensively examined in various fields, it still lacks a uniform and generally accepted definition. Reasons for this circumstance are the multifaceted terms trust is associated with like credibility, reliability or confidence as well as the multidimensionality of trust as an abstract concept that has a cognitive, an emotional and a behavioral dimension. As pointed out by [5], trust has been described as being structural in nature by sociologists while psychologists viewed trust as an interpersonal phenomenon. Economists, however, interpreted trust as a rational choice mechanism. The definition often cited in literature regarding trust and reputation online that is referred to as *reliability trust* was proposed by Gambetta in 1988 [6]: *"Trust (or, symmetrically, distrust) is a particular level of the subjective probability with which an agent assesses that another agent or group of agents will perform a particular action, both before he can monitor such action (or independently of his capacity ever to be able to monitor it) and in a context in which it affects his own action."*

Multiple authors furthermore include security and risk which can lead to more complex definitions. Anyway, it is generally agreed that trust is multifaceted and dependent on a variety of factors. Moreover, there are several properties of trust described in literature (see Table 1). These properties are important with respect to this work because they form the basis for many applied computation techniques in trust and reputation systems described in Section 'Hierarchical component taxonomy'. Reusable components could extend current models by the ability to gradually include these properties.

Reputation-based trust

In recent years, several trust models have been developed to establish trust. Thereby, two common ways can be distinguished, namely policy-based and reputation-based trust

Table 1 Overview of properties of trust described in literature [14,41-46]

Dynamic	Trust can increase or decrease through gathering new experiences. Moreover, trust is said to decay with time (time-based aging [45]). Because of these characteristics, trust values strongly depend on the time they are determined. The greater importance of new experiences compared to old experiences has been widely studied and considered in many trust models such as [32,47] or [30].
Context-dependent	Trust is bound to a specific context. For example, Alice trusts Bob as her doctor. However, she might not trust him as a cook to prepare a delicious meal for her.
Multi-faceted	Even in the same context, a trust value may not reflect all aspects of this context [43]. For example, a customer may trust a particular restaurant for its quality of food but not for its quality of service. The overall trust on this restaurant depends on the combination of the amount of trust in the specific aspects.
Propagative	One property of trust made use of in several models is its propagativity. If Alice trusts Bob, who in turn trusts Claire, Alice can derive trust on Claire from the relationships between her and Bob as well as between Bob and Claire. Because of this propagative nature, it is possible to create trust chains passing trust from one agent to another agent. As clarified by Christianson and Harbison [48], trust is not automatically transitive although trust transitivity was assumed proven for a long time. If Alice trusts Bob, who in turn trusts Claire, it does not inherently mean that Alice trusts Claire. It follows from the foregoing that transitivity implies propagation. The reverse, though, is not the case.
Composable	When trust is propagated, a particular agent may be connected to multiple trust chains. To come up with a final decision whether to trust or distrust this agent, the trust information received from the different chains need to be composed in order to build one aggregated picture. In this context, trust statements propagated from nodes close to oneself should have greater influence on the aggregated value than the ones from distant nodes (distance-based aging [45]). Composition is potentially difficult if the trust statements are contradictory [14].
Subjective	The subjective nature of trust becomes clear if one thinks about a review on Amazon [26]. A book review that totally reflects Alice's opinion will probably resolve in a high level of trust against the reviewer Rachel. Bob, however, who disagrees with the review, will have a lower trust in Rachel although it bases on the same evidence.
Fine-grained	Although trust is sometimes modeled in a binary manner (i.e. either trust or distrust), it is possible that Alice trusts both Bob and Claire but that she trusts Bob more than Claire. Hence, there may be multiple discrete levels of trust such as high, medium and low [41]. Mapped to numbers, trust may also be a continuous variable taking values within a certain interval (e.g. between 0 and 1).
Event-sensitive	It can take a long time to build trust. One negative experience, though, can destroy it [23].
Reflexive	Trust in oneself is always at the maximum value.
Self-reinforcing	It is human nature to preferentially interact with other agents that are trusted. Analogously, agents will avoid interacting with untrustworthy agents. Thus, the trustworthiness of other agents is inherently taken into consideration.

establishment [7]. Policy-based trust is often referred to as a *hard security mechanism* due to the exchange of hard evidence (e.g. credentials). Reputation-based trust, in contrast, is derived from the history of interactions. Hence, it can be seen as an estimation of trustworthiness (*soft security*). In this work, we focus on reputation-based trust. Reputation is defined as follows: *"Reputation is what is generally said or believed about a person's or thing's character or standing."* [8].

It is based on referrals, ratings or reviews from members of a community. Therefore, it can be considered as a collective measure of trustworthiness [8]. Trustworthiness as a global value is objective. However, the trust an agent puts in someone or something as a combination of personal experience and referrals is subjective.

Research gap: design of reputation systems with reuse

It has been argued (e.g. by [3]) that most reputation-based trust models proposed in the academic community are built from scratch and do not rely on existing approaches. Only a few authors continue their research on the ideas of others. Thus, many approved models and promising thoughts go unregarded. The benefits of reuse, though, have been recognized in software engineering for years. However, there are only very few works that proposed single components to enhance existing approaches. Rehak et al. [9], for instance, introduced a generic mechanism that can be combined with existing trust models to extend their capabilities by efficiently modeling context. The benefits of such a component that can easily be combined with existing systems are obvious. Nonetheless, research in trust and reputation still lacks in sound and accepted principles to foster reuse.

To gradually close this gap, we aim to provide a framework for the design of new reputation systems with reuse. As described above, we thereto propose a hierarchical component taxonomy of computation engines used in reputation systems. Based on this taxonomy, we set up a repository containing design knowledge on both a conceptual and an implementation level. On the one hand, the uniform and well-structured artifacts collected in this repository can be used by developers to select, understand and apply existing concepts. On the other hand, they may encourage researchers to provide novel components on a conceptual and an implementation level. In this way, the reuse of ideas, concepts and implemented components as well as the communication of reuse knowledge should be achieved. Furthermore, we argue that the reusable components we identify in this work could extend current reputation models by the ability to gradually include the properties of trust described above. To evaluate whether our taxonomy/framework can cover all aspects of trust, we finally provide a table matching our component classes with trust properties.

A hierarchical component taxonomy for computation methods in reputation systems

To derive a taxonomy from existing models, our research includes two steps: (1) the analysis of the generic process of reputation systems and (2) the identification of logical components of the computation methods used in common trust and reputation models. A critical question is how to determine and classify single components. Thereto, we follow an approach to function-based component classification, which means that the taxonomy is derived from the functions the identified components fulfill.

The generic process of reputation systems

The generic process of reputation systems, as depicted in Figure 1, can be divided into three steps: (1) *collection & preparation*, (2) *computation* and (3) *storage & communication*. These steps are adapted from the three fundamental phases of reputation systems identified by [10] and [11]: feedback generation/collection, feedback aggregation and feedback distribution. Feedback aggregation as the central part of every trust and reputation system is furthermore divided into the three process steps *filtering*, *weighting* and *aggregation* taken together as computation. The context setting consists of a trustor who wants to build a trust relation toward a trustee by providing context and personalization parameters and receiving a trustee's reputation value.

Collection and preparation

In the collection and preparation phase, the reputation system gleans information about the past behavior of a trustee and prepares it for subsequent computing. Although personal experience is the most reliable, it is often not sufficiently available or nonexistent. Therefore, data from other sources needs to be collected. These can be various, ranging from public or personal collections of data centrally stored to data requested from different peers in a distributed network. After all available data is gathered, it is prepared for further use. Preparation techniques include normalization, for instance, which brings the input data from different sources into a uniform format. Once the preparation is completed, the reputation data serves as input for the computation phase.

Computation

The computation phase is the central part of every reputation system and takes the reputation information collected as input and generates a trust/reputation value as output. This phase can be divided into the three generic process steps *filtering*, *weighting* and *aggregation*. Depending on the computation engine, not all steps have to be implemented. The first two steps (filtering and weighting) preprocess the data for the subsequent aggregation. The need for these steps is obvious: The first question to be answered is *which* information is useful for further processing (filtering). The second process step concerns the question of *how relevant* the information is for the specific situation (weighting). In line with this, Zhang et al. [12] pointed out that current trust models can be classified into the two broad categories *filtering-based* and *discounting-based*. The difference between filtering and weighting is that the filtering process reduces the information amount while

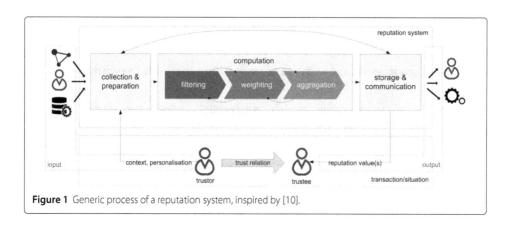

Figure 1 Generic process of a reputation system, inspired by [10].

it is enriched by weight factors in the second case. Therefore, filtering can be seen as *hard selection* while weighting is more like a *soft selection*. Finally, the reputation values are aggregated to calculate one or several reputation scores. Depending on the algorithm, the whole computation process or single process steps can be run through for multiple times.

Storage and communication

After reputation scores are calculated, they are either stored locally, in a public storage or both depending on the structure (centralized/decentralized/hybrid) of the reputation system. Common reputation systems not only provide the reputation scores but also offer extra information to help the end-users understand the meaning of a score. They should furthermore reveal the computation process to accomplish transparency.

In this work, we focus on the computation phase, since the first phase (collection & preparation) and the last phase (storage & communication) strongly depend on the structure of the reputation system (centralized or decentralized). The computation phase, however, is independent of the structure and can look alike for systems implemented in both centralized and decentralized environments. Therefore, it works well for design with reuse.

Hierarchical component taxonomy

In this section, the computation process is examined in detail. We introduce a novel hierarchical component taxonomy that is based on the functional blocks of common reputation systems identified in this work. Thereto, we clarify the objectives of the identified classes (functions) and name common examples. Our analysis and selection of reputation systems is based on different surveys [2,3,8,13,14]. Figure 2 gives an overview of the primary and secondary classes identified.

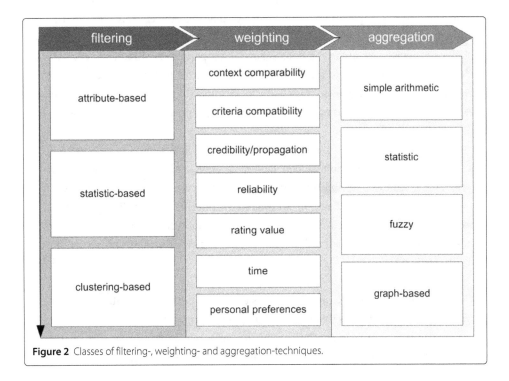

Figure 2 Classes of filtering-, weighting- and aggregation-techniques.

Beginning with the filtering phase, the three broad classes *attribute-based, statistic-based* and *clustering-based* filtering can be identified:

1. **Attribute-based filtering**: In several trust models, input data is filtered based on a constraint-factor defined for the value of single attributes. Attribute-based filters mostly implement a very simple logic, in which an attribute is usually compared to a reference value. Due to their lightweight, they are proper for reducing huge amounts of input data to the part necessary for the reputation calculation. Besides the initial filtering of input data, it is often applied after the weighting phase in order to filter referrals that have been strongly discounted. Time is an example of an attribute that is often constrained because it is desirable to disregard very old ratings. eBay's reputation system, for instance, only considers transactions having occurred in the last 12 months for their overview of positive, neutral and negative ratings. Other models such as Sporas [15] ignore every referral but the latest, if one party rated another party more than once. In this way, simple ballot stuffing attacks can be prevented. In ballot stuffing attacks, parties improve their reputation by means of positive ratings after fake transactions.

2. **Statistic-based filtering**: Further techniques that are used to enhance the robustness of trust models against the spread of false rumors apply statistical patterns. Whitby et al. [16], for example, proposed a statistical filter technique to filter out unfair ratings in Bayesian reputation systems applying the majority rule. The majority rule considers feedback that is far away from the majority's referrals as dishonest. In this way, dishonest or false feedback can easily be detected and filtered.

3. **Clustering-based filtering**: Clustering-based filter use cluster analysis approaches to identify unfair ratings. These approaches are comparatively expensive and therefore rarely used as filtering techniques. An exemplary procedure is to analyze an advisor's history. Since a rater never lies to himself, an obvious way to detect false ratings is to compare own experience with the advisor's referrals. Thus, both fair and unfair ratings can be identified. iCLUB [17], for example, calculates clusters of advisors whose evaluations against other parties are alike. Then, the cluster being most similar to the own opinion is chosen as fair ratings. If there is no common experience (e.g. bootstrapping), the majority rule will be applied. Another example for an approach using cluster filtering was proposed by Dellarocas [18].

Once all available information is reduced to those suitable for measuring trust and reputation in the current situation, it becomes clear that various data differ in their characteristics (e.g. context, reliability). Hence, the referrals are weighted in the second process step based on different factors. In contrast to the filtering step, applied techniques differ strongly. For that reason, our classification of weighting techniques is based on the properties of referrals that are analyzed for the discounting. We distinguish between the following classes:

1. **Context comparability**: Reputation data is always bound to the specific context in which it is created. Ratings that are generated in one application area might not be automatically applicable in another application area. In e-commerce, for instance, transactions are accomplished involving different prices, product types, payment

methods, quality or time. The non-consideration of this context leads to the value imbalance problem where a malicious seller can build a high reputation by selling cheap products while cheating on expensive ones. To increase comparability and avoid such situations, context has become a crucial attribute for many current approaches like [19] or [9].

2. **Criteria comparability**: Besides the context in which feedback is created, the criteria that underlie the evaluation are important. Particularly, if referrals from different application areas or communities are integrated, criteria comparability can be crucial. In file-sharing networks, for instance, a positive rating is often granted with a successful transaction independent of the quality of service. On e-commerce platforms, in contrast, quality may be a critical factor for customer satisfaction. Other distinctions could be the costs of reviews, the level of anonymity or the number of peers in different communities or application areas. Weighting based on criteria comparability can compensate these differences.

3. **Credibility/propagation**: In network structures such as in the web-of-trust, trust can be established along a recommendation or trust chain. Obviously, referrals that have first-hand information about the trustworthiness of an agent are more credible than referrals received at second-hand (with propagation degree of two) or higher. Therefore, several models apply a propagation (transitivity) rate to discount referrals based on their distance. The biometric identity trust model [20], for instance, derives the reputation-factor from the distance of nodes in a web-of-trust.

4. **Reliability**: Reliability or honesty of referrals can strongly affect the weight of reviews. The concept of feedback reputation that measures the agents' reliability in terms of providing honest feedback is often applied. As a consequence, referrals created by agents having a low feedback reputation have a low impact on the aggregated reputation. The bases for this calculation can be various. Google's PageRank [21], for instance, involves the position of every website connected to the trustee in the web graph in their recursive algorithm. Epinions [22], on the other hand, allows users to directly rate reviews and reviewers. In this way, the effects of unfair ratings are diminished.

5. **Rating value**: Trust is event sensitive. For stronger punishment of bad behavior, the weight of positive ratings compared to negative ratings can be calculated asymmetrically. An example for a model using an "adaptive forgetting scheme" was proposed by Sun et al. [23], in which good reputation can be built slowly through good behavior but easily be ruined through bad behavior.

6. **Time**: Due to the dynamic nature of trust, it has been widely recognized that time is one important factor for the weighting of referrals. Old feedback might not be as relevant for reputation scoring as new referrals. An example measure for time-based weighting is the "forgetting factor" proposed by Jøsang [24].

7. **Personal preferences**: Reputation systems are used by various end-users (e.g. human decision makers, services). Therefore, a reputation system must allow the adaptation of its techniques to subjective personal preferences. Different actors might have different perceptions regarding the importance of direct experience and referrals, the significance of distinct information sources or the rating of newcomers.

The tuple of reputation data and weight-factor(s) serve as input for the third step of the computation process - the aggregation. In this phase, one or several trust/reputation values are calculated by composing the available information. In some cases, the weighting and the aggregation process are run through repetitively in an iterative manner. However, the single steps can still be logically separated. The list of proposed algorithms to aggregate trust and reputation values has become very long during the last decade. Here, we summarize the most common aggregation techniques and classify them into the four blocks *simple arithmetic*, *statistic*, *fuzzy* and *graph-based models*:

1. **Simple arithmetic**: The first class includes simple aggregation techniques like ranking, summation or average. Ranking is a very basic way to measure trustworthiness. In ranking algorithms, ratings are counted and organized in a descending order based on that value. This measure has no exact reputation score. Instead, it is frequently used as a proxy for the relative importance/trustworthiness. Examples for systems using ranking algorithms are message boards like Slashdot [25] or citation counts used to calculate the impact factor in academic literature. Other aggregation techniques that are well known due to the implementation on eBay or Amazon [26] are the summation (adding up positive and negative ratings) or the average of ratings. Summation, though, can easily be misleading, since a value of 90 does not reveal the composition of positive and negative ratings (e.g. +100,-10 or +90,0). The average, on the other hand, is a very intuitive and easily understandable algorithm.

2. **Statistic**: Many of the prominent trust models proposed in the last years use a statistical approach to provide a solid mathematical basis for trust management. Applied techniques range from *Bayesian probability* over *belief models* to *Hidden Markov Models*. All models based on the beta probability density function (beta PDF) are examples for models simply using Bayesian probability. The beta PDF represents the probability distributions of binary events. The *a priori* reputation score is thereby gradually updated by new ratings. The result is a reputation score that is described in a beta PDF function parameter tuple (α, β), whereby α represents positive and β represents negative ratings. A well known model using the beta PDF is the Beta Reputation system [24]. A weakness of Bayesian probabilistic models, however, is that they cannot handle uncertainty. Therefore, belief models extend the probabilistic approach by Dempster-Shafer theory (DST) or subjective logic to include the notion of uncertainty. Trust and reputation models involving a belief model were proposed by Jøsang [27] or Yu and Singh [28]. More complex solutions that are based on machine learning, use the Hidden Markov Model, a generalization of the beta model, to better cope with the dynamic behavior. An example was introduced by Malik et al. [29].

3. **Fuzzy**: Aggregation techniques classified as fuzzy models use fuzzy logic to calculate a reputation value. In contrast to classical logic, fuzzy logic allows to model truth or falsity within an interval of [0,1]. Thus, it can describe the degree to which an agent/resource is trustworthy or not trustworthy. Fuzzy logic has been proven to deal well with uncertainty and mimic the human decision making process [30]. Thereby, a linguistic approach is often applied. REGRET [31] is one prominent example of a trust model making use of fuzzy logic.

4. **Graph-based**: A variety of trust models employ a graph-based approach. They rely on different measures describing the position of nodes in a network involving the flow of transitive trust along trust chains in network structures. As online social networks have become popular as a medium for disseminating information and connecting people, many models regarding trust in social networks have lately been proposed. Graph-based approaches use measures from the field of graph theory such as centrality (e.g. Eigenvector, betweenness), distance or node-degree. Reputation values, for instance, grow with the number of incoming edges (in-degree) and increase or decrease with the number of outgoing edges (out-degree). The impact of one edge on the overall reputation can depend on several factors like the reputation of the node an edge comes from or the distance of two nodes. Popular algorithms using graph-based flow model are Google's PageRank [21] as well as the Eigentrust Algorithm [32]. Other examples are the web-of-trust or trust models particularly designed for social networks as described in [14]. As mentioned above, the weighting and aggregation phases are incrementally run through for several times due to the incremental nature of these algorithms.

The classification of the computation engine's components used in different trust models in this taxonomy is not limited to one component of each primary class. Depending on the computation process, several filtering, weighting and aggregation techniques can be combined and run through more than once. Malik et al. [29], for instance, introduced a hybrid model combining heuristic and statistical approaches. However, our taxonomy can reveal the single logical components a computation engine is built on. Moreover, it serves as an overview of existing approaches. Since every currently known reputation system can find its position, to the best of our knowledge, this taxonomy can be seen as complete. Though, an extension by new classes driven by novel models and ideas is possible. Our hierarchical component taxonomy currently contains 3 primary component classes, 14 secondary component classes, 23 component terms and 29 subsets. Table 2 shows an excerpt of the hierarchical component taxonomy with building blocks of the primary class "weighting". The full taxonomy is provided in Additional file 1: Table S1.

The component taxonomy as a framework for design with reuse

The hierarchical component taxonomy introduced in the former section serves as a natural framework for the design of reputation systems with reuse. To support this process, we set up a component repository combining a knowledge and a service repository. Thus, it does not only contain information about software components on implementation level but also provides extensive descriptions of the ideas applied on a conceptual level. This comprehensive set of fundamental component concepts and ideas combined with the related implementation allows the reuse of both ideas and already implemented components.

In this section, we firstly describe the conceptual design of our component repository in detail. Then, we elaborate on the implementation of a web application employing our thorough repository to provide design knowledge for reuse on a conceptual and an implementation level.

Table 2 Excerpt of the hierarchical component taxonomy with descriptions

Primary component class	Secondary component class	Component term	Subset	Description
weighting	credibility/ propagation	propagation discount		Discount referrals along trust chains
	reliability	subjective reliability	property similarity	Discount based on similarity of personal properties
			rating similarity	Discount referrals based on similarity of ratings toward other agents
		objective reliability	Explicit	Discount based on explicit reputation information like referrals or certificates
			Implicit	Discount based on implicit reputation information like profile age, number of referrals or position
	rating value	asymmetric rating		Strongly discount positive ratings compared to negative ratings (event sensitive)
…	…	…	…	…

Conceptual design of the component repository

Reuse-based software engineering can be implemented on different levels of abstraction, ranging from the reuse of ideas to the reuse of already implemented software components for a very specific application area. In this work, we want to apply our taxonomy for reuse on two levels – a conceptual level and an implementation level. Therefore, the developed repository provides design knowledge for reuse on two logical layers (see Figure 3).

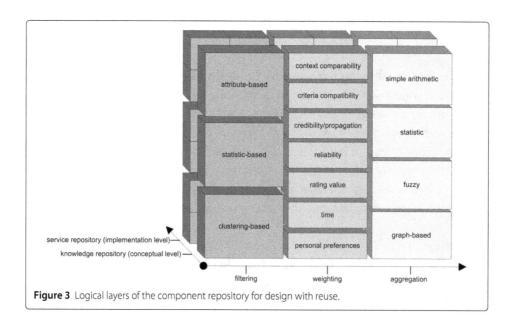

Figure 3 Logical layers of the component repository for design with reuse.

Reuse on conceptual level

When reusing an implemented component, one is unavoidably constrained by design decisions that have been made by the developer. A way to prevent this is to conceive more abstract designs that do not specify the implementation. Thus, we provide an abstract solution to a problem by means of design pattern-like concepts. Design patterns are descriptions of commonly occurring problems and a generic solution to the problems that can be used in different settings [33]. Our design pattern-like concepts consist of essential elements that are exemplary depicted in Table 3.

Reuse on implementation level

On implementation level, we provide fully implemented reusable components by means of web services in a service-orientated architecture. These services encapsulate the concepts' logic and functionality in independent and interchangeable modules to achieve the separation of concerns. The web services are incorporated via well-defined interfaces. All services provided are registered as artifacts in the service repository. An artifact contains essential information about one live reachable service such as ID, type (REST or ws), URL, description, parameters, example calls, example output, the design pattern that is implemented by the service, and tags describing the functionality. Table 4 shows an example artifact for the design pattern described above.

Table 3 Design pattern on the conceptual level (example)

Component term	Context similarity
Subset	**Absolute congruence**
Description	This component uses an absolute congruence metric as similarity measure to identify context similarity.
Problem description	Reputation data is always bound to the specific context in which it was created. Ratings that were generated in one application area might not be automatically applicable in another application area which can result in the value imbalance problem.
Solution description	Apply similarity measurement between context c_i (reference context) and context c_j of referrals in the referral set to deliver a weight-factor for each item of the referral set using the following formula: $$w(c_1, c_2) := \frac{k(c_i) \cap k(c_j)}{k(c_i) \cup k(c_j)}$$ $k(c_i)$ denotes the total number of keywords describing context c_i.
Applicability	Set of nominal context attributes.
Code example (php)	```php function calculate_values($reference, $context_sets) { $reference_context = $reference['context_attributes']; $return_values = array(); while(!empty($context_sets)) { ...shortened... } return $return_values; } ```
Implementation	Context similarity-based weighting service (absolute congruence)
Literature	• Mohammad Gias Uddin, Mohammad Zulkernine, and Sheikh Iqbal Ahamed. 2008. CAT: a context-aware trust model for open and dynamic systems. In Proceedings of the 2008 ACM symposium on Applied computing (SAC '08). ACM, New York, NY, USA, 2024–2029.
Tags	weighting, context, similarity, congruence

Table 4 Web service description on implementation level (example)

Component term	Context similarity
Subset	Absolute congruence
Type	REST
Demo	http://trust.bayforsec.de/ngot/webservice/Client/?=Weighting-congruence-absolute-call.php
Description	This service provides an absolute similarity measurement between a reference context and a context-set of referrals. Example: The sets 'registered','charged', 'verified' and 'registered', 'costless', 'unverified' have a similarity of 1/3.
Parameters	

```
// define words that describe the quality of a referall
$reference_context : array("words" => array (TEXT));

$referral_sets = array( $context_set );

$referral_set = array( "id" => NUMBER, "words" => array (TEXT));
```

Example call

```
require_once('WebserviceCallHelper.php');

$arguments = array("words" => array ("registered","charged","verified"));
$referral_set = array();
$referral_set[0] = array( "id" => "10000", "words" =>
    array ("registered","costless", "unverified"));
$referral_set[1] = array( "id" => "10001", "words" =>
    array ("registered","charged", "verified"));
$referral_set[2] = array( "id" => "10002", "words" =>
    array ("registered","costless", "verified"));

$webservice_call = new WebserviceCallHelper(array(
    'base_url' => WEBSERVICE_URL,
    'format' => "html",
    'component' => "Weighting\CongruenceAbsolute"
));
$webservice_call->get_result($arguments, $referral_set);
```

Example output

```
Array
(
    [status] => 200
    [data] => Array
        (
            [0] => Array
                (
                    [0] => 10000
                    [1] => 0.2
                )
            [1] => Array
                (
                    [0] => 10001
                    [1] => 1
                )
            [2] => Array
                (
                    [0] => 10002
                    [1] => 0.5
                )
        )
)
```

Pattern Implemented	Context similarity (Absolute congruence)
Tags	weighting, context, similarity, congruence

Implementation of the repository

To demonstrate the feasibility of our approach, we have prototypically implemented the repository as a web-based application in a three-tier client-server-architecture [34]. To give an overview of the chosen architecture, we distinguish between server-side and client-side implementation.

Server-side

On server-side, the logic is implemented in PHP on an Apache server (logic layer) connecting to a MySQL database (persistent layer). The MySQL database contains all data regarding the design patterns as described in Table 2. Each of these design patterns is also implemented in a web service. To enable a standardized realization of new web services and a flawless call via standardized interfaces, we employ an abstract class *Component*. All components (implemented as web services) must inherit from this class, which particularly requires overwriting the function *calculate_values*. To make the generic component independent of the input data, developers are advised to make use of the PHP function *func_get_args()*. In this way, distinct components can receive a variety of arguments. To consistently handle client calls, our architecture is extended by a *WebserviceCallHandler*. Figure 4 depicts the schematic layout.

All web services implementing the trust pattern currently described in our knowledge repository have been created and registered as artifacts in our service repository [34]. Furthermore, these artifacts are described in detail including a definition of input, output and example calls as defined in Table 4.

Client-side

On client-side (presentation layer), we employ the current web standards HTML5, JavaScript and CSS (Bootstrap). The front end is divided into three main pages – "overview", "knowledge repository" and "service repository" – which provide information on the general concept, the trust patterns and the web services. To enable a standardized call of a web service from client-side, a *WebserviceCallHelper* allows a simple call of each component by configuration and provides all functions necessary to establish a connection to the repository. The configuration details are passed to the constructor, which requires a *base_url*, an output *format* (HTML, XML or JSON) and a unique *component* name as illustrated below.

Example call of a filtering component via the WebserviceCallHelper

```
$webservice_call = new WebserviceCallHelper(array(
        'base_url' => "http://trust.bayforsec.de/ngot/webservice/",
        'format' => "html",
        'component' => "Filtering\AgeBasedAbsolute"
    ));
$webservice_call->get_result($arguments, $referral_set);
```

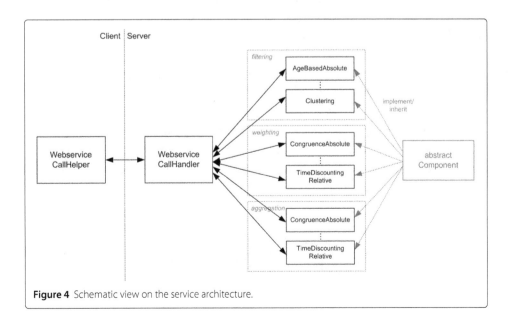

Figure 4 Schematic view on the service architecture.

Evaluation

To rigorously demonstrate the proper functioning and quality of our approach, we carry out a two-part evaluation of our artifact in this section. As there is currently no comparable framework, we firstly perform a descriptive scenario-based evaluation. According to Hevner et al. [4], this is a standard approach for innovative artifacts like ours. To demonstrate the completeness of our taxonomy, we secondly conduct a static analysis [4], in which we match all components to the trust properties described in Section 'The notion of trust and its properties'.

Scenario analysis: Reputation system development

The fictitious web developer John Gray runs an electronic marketplace platform for philatelists and numismatics. The platform has been launched with his friends as the first users but has been growing fast. Meanwhile, most users do not know each other in person anymore. As a result, many of the initial users have stopped interacting with the newcomers as they do not trust them. After realizing this problem, John decides to introduce an online reputation system in order to establish trust among the strangers. In the following, we describe how our knowledge and service repository can help him to build a reputation system that perfectly meets his requirements.

Having read the basics on our component model, John concludes that he wants to build a computation engine that makes use of components of all three phases – filtering, weighting and aggregation. Thinking about the experiences made with sellers on the platform, he recognizes that most of them do not deliver the same quality all the time. Thus, an *age-based filter* should be employed to make old referrals less important than new ones. Furthermore, there are sellers that usually deliver high quality stamps while offering poor quality coins. Therefore, a weighting component based on *context similarity (absolute congruence)* should be selected. Regarding the aggregation alternatives, John decides to make use of the *average* component as the simple average is probably the most intuitive and most transparent aggregation technique for the users. Finally, the single components are combined in sequence to a fully functional computation engine as depicted in Figure 5.

The code listed below shows an example for the implementation of John's computation engine. Here, the WebserviceCallHelpers for each of the selected components have to be instantiated first as described in Section 'Client-side'. Secondly, the referral set needs to be loaded and prepared according to input parameter descriptions provided for each web service in the component repository. In its current form, the framework does not provide any classes to automatically plug single components together (glue class). Thus, the developer has to ensure that the output of one component is correctly provided as an input for the following component. This lose coupling, however, allows for more flexibility. All details on the input and output format can be found in the artifact description of each component. While the input data varies from component to component, the output is alike for components of each primary class.

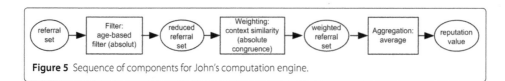

Figure 5 Sequence of components for John's computation engine.

Example code for the computation engine described above

```
//create helper for filtering component
$webservice_filter = new WebserviceCallHelper(array(
          'base_url' => WEBSERVICE_URL,
          'format' => "html",
          'component' => "Filtering\AgeBasedAbsolute"
      ));
//create helper for weighting component
$webservice_weight = ...as above...

//create helper for aggregation component
$webservice_aggregate = ...as above...

//define referral_set
$referral_set = array("id" => NUMBER, "time" => DATE, "context" => array (TEXT), "
    rating" => NUMBER);

//call computation
$reputation_value = $webservice_aggregate(
              $glue->prepare_for_aggregation($webservice_weight(
                  $glue->prepare_for_weighting($webservice_filter->get_result(
                      $referral_set))
                      ))
              );
```

This scenario elucidates that our knowledge and service repository has an obvious utility from a practical point of view since developers can easily access it and gain knowledge about online reputation systems. Thereby, we may help to better spread innovative ideas and allow developers to experiment with different computation techniques. However, our approach requires specific knowledge on the structure of the repository, the functioning of each component and details on how to plug components together. Developers need to manually combine components and take care, whether they use valid input data and a feasible combination of reputation system components. In its current form, our framework is not very "developer friendly". Therefore, further research will be necessary in order to improve the practical usability of our component repository. In Section 'Contribution and future work', we discuss open issues in more detail.

Static analysis: Matching components and trust properties

To guarantee the proper generation of computational trust, trust-enforcing mechanisms such as reputation systems should be able to consider and address all properties of trust. As our component taxonomy serves as a framework for the design of new reputation systems with reuse, it should enable developers to extend current reputation models by the ability to gradually include the various properties of trust. Therefore, a way to evaluate the completeness of our solution is to review whether a trust system that is built according to our framework could meet this standard. In Table 5, we match the computation components identified above to the properties of trust introduced in Section 'The notion of trust and its properties'. Since our taxonomy is based on reputation systems analyzed in various surveys, this approach also enables us to identify aspects of trust that have only rarely been considered in research so far.

Examining Table 5, we find that all trust properties listed are widely covered. There is at least one component addressing each single characteristic. Going into more detail, we find that there are many proposals that have developed components to personalize reputation systems, thus covering the subjective property of trust. This reflects a general trend to an enhanced personalization of reputation systems. Furthermore, it becomes clear that all of our weighting and aggregation components follow the fine-grained property of trust, i.e. that trust can be modeled as a continuous variable. For the filtering components, the fine-grained property is not entirely applicable in the same meaning as filtering has no direct influence on the trust value of referrals. Since the effect of filtering is that a referral

Table 5 Matching reputation system components and trust properties

Primary component class	Secondary component class	Trust properties									
		Dynamic	Context-dependent	Multi-faceted	Propagative	Composable	Subjective	Fine-grained	Event-sensitive	Reflexive	Self-reinforcing
Filtering	attribute-based	●	○	○	○	◐	●	○	○	○	○
	statistic-based	●	○	○	○	○	●	○	○	○	◐
	clustering	○	○	○	○	○	●	○	○	●	◐
	context comparability	◐	●	◐	○	○	○	●	○	○	◐
	criteria comparability	○	◐	●	○	○	●	●	○	◐	○
Weighting	credibility	○	○	○	●	●	●	●	○	○	○
	reliability	○	○	○	◐	◐	●	●	○	◐	●
	rating value	○	○	○	○	○	○	●	●	○	◐
Computation components	time	●	○	○	○	○	○	●	○	○	○
	personal preferences	○	○	○	○	○	●	●	○	○	○
Aggregation	simple arithmetic	○	○	○	○	●	○	●	○	○	◐
	statistic	○	○	○	○	●	○	●	○	○	◐
	fuzzy	○	○	○	○	●	○	●	○	○	◐
	graph-based	○	○	○	○	●	◐	●	○	○	◐

○ not addressed.
◐ partly addressed.
● completely addressed.

either is further considered or not, it shows a binary character rather than being fine-grained. In contrast to the subjective and fine-grained properties of trust, other properties such as context-dependent, multi-faceted and event-sensitive are particularly addressed by only one or two components. Note that this does not automatically mean that there is an increased necessity for future research concerning these properties. It may also be possible that one component is enough to cover one trust property. More detailed studies on this could be part of future work.

Overall, we can say that computational trust can be represented quite accurately when using our taxonomy and the provided components as a basis for the development of new reputation systems or the extension of existing models. Note, however, that this is only one view on our taxonomy. Conducting a comparable analysis from the viewpoint of attacks and defense mechanisms, for instance, the outcomes may vary greatly.

Contribution and future work

Many surveys of trust and reputation systems give an overview of existing trust and reputation systems by means of a classification of existing models and approaches. In contrast to this, we provide a collection of ideas and concepts classified by their functions. Furthermore, these ideas are not only named but also clearly described in well-structured design pattern-like artifacts which can easily be adapted to a specific situation. Therewith, we reorganized the design knowledge for computation techniques in reputation systems and translated the most common ideas into a uniform format. To directly make use of novel components, the web services created on implementation level can instantly be reused and integrated in existing reputation systems to extend their capabilities. This approach (i.e. publicly providing implemented computation components as web services) may help to better spread innovative ideas in trust and reputation systems and give system builders a better choice allowing to experiment with different computation techniques. Moreover, we encourage researchers to focus on the design of single components by providing a platform on which concepts and their prototypical implementation can be made publicly available.

Nonetheless, there are still some unexplored areas regarding the design with reuse in trust and reputation systems. Firstly, reusability could play a role in process steps other than the computation phase. To clarify the opportunities, further research is necessary in this area. Secondly, our hierarchical taxonomy is currently limited to a functional view on the identified components but developers may also benefit from additional views. Because of the importance of the robustness of trust and reputation systems [35], we are particularly interested in an attack view. In [36], we present first ideas on this issue. We propose a taxonomy of attacks on reputation systems and then refer to the single components of our repository as solutions to the specific attack classes. In this way, we not only support reputation system designers in the development of more reliable and more robust reputation systems with already existing components but also help to identify weaknesses that have not been addressed so far. Thirdly, the selection and interpretation of adequate components for new reputation systems in a particular application area requires time, effort and – to some extent – knowledge of this research area. To increase usability, a software application is needed to support a user in this development process. Ultimately, the application may even be able to automatically find the most qualified composition for specific requirements and input data. This, in turn, demands for generic testbeds that enable objective evaluations of reputation systems because so far, researchers have mainly been developing their own testing scenarios favoring their own work [37]. The most well-known proposals regarding independent testbeds are ART [38] and TREET [37]. Recently, Irissappane and Zhang [39,40] made another important step forward by introducing a publicly available testbed that is able to reflect real environmental settings. We plan to use their tool in future studies. Finally, we need to observe the usage of our repository in practice to learn from how users deal with it. This can either be done through conducting experimental user studies or by interviewing developers who use our repository in a real environment. In this way, we can run through a continuous improvement process.

Conclusion

The research in trust and reputation systems is still growing. In this paper, we presented concepts to foster reuse of existing approaches. We provided a hierarchical taxonomy of computation components from a functional view and described the implementation of a component repository that serves as both a knowledge base and a service repository. In this way, we communicate design knowledge for reuse, support the development of new reputation systems and encourage researchers to focus on the development of single components that can be integrated in various reputation systems to easily extend their capabilities by new features. Matching the identified components and the properties of trust, we found that integrating existing ideas and concepts can lead to a reputation system that widely reflects computational trust by addressing all properties of trust described in literature.

Additional file

Additional file 1: Table S1.

Competing interests
The authors declare that they have no competing interests.

Authors' contributions
JS proposed the initial idea of this paper. He developed the hierarchical component taxonomy and implemented the component repository. CR and JS conducted the evaluation of the proposed ideas. CR and JS furthermore revised this paper according to reviewers' comments. GP supervised the research, contributed to the paper writing and made suggestions. All authors read and approved the final manuscript.

Acknowledgment
The research leading to these results was supported by the Bavarian State Ministry of Education, Science and the Arts" as part of the FORSEC research association.

References
1. Electronics, Cars, Fashion, Collectibles, Coupons and More | eBay. http://www.ebay.com
2. Yao Y, Ruohomaa S, Xu F (2012) Addressing common vulnerabilities of reputation systems for electronic commerce. J Theor Appl Electron Commerce Res 7(1):1–20
3. Tavakolifard M, Almeroth KC (2012) A taxonomy to express open challenges in trust and reputation systems. J Commun 7(7):538–551
4. Hevner AR, March ST, Park J, Ram S (2004) Design science in information systems research. MIS Quarterly 28(1):75–105
5. McKnight DH, Chervany NL (1996) The Meanings of Trust. Technical report. University of Minnesota, Management Information Systems Research Center
6. Gambetta D (1988) Can we trust trust? In: Gambetta D (ed). Trust: making and breaking cooperative relations. Basil Blackwell, Oxford. pp 213–237
7. Artz D, Gil Y (2007) A survey of trust in computer science and the semantic web. Web Semantics 5(2):58–71
8. Jøsang A, Ismail R, Boyd C (2007) A survey of trust and reputation systems for online service provision. Decis Support Syst 43(2):618–644

9.   Rehak M, Gregor M, Pechoucek M, Bradshaw J (2006) Representing context for multiagent trust modeling. In: Skowron A, Barthès JP, Jain LC, Sun R, Morizet-Mahoudeaux P, Liu J, Zhong N (eds). Proceedings of the 2006 IEEE/WIC/ACM International Conference on Intelligent Agent Technology, Hong Kong, China. IEEE Computer Society, Washington, DC. pp 737–746

10.   Swamynathan G, Almeroth KC, Zhao BY (2010) The design of a reliable reputation system. Electron Commerce Res 10(3–4):239–270

11.   Resnick P, Kuwabara K, Zeckhauser R, Friedman E (2000) Reputation systems. Commun ACM 43(12):45–48

12.   Zhang L, Jiang S, Zhang J, Ng WK (2012) Robustness of trust models and combinations for handling unfair ratings. In: Dimitrakos T, Moona R, Patel D, McKnight DH (eds). Trust Management VI: Proceedings of the 6th IFIP WG 11.11 international conference (IFIPTM). Springer, Berlin, Heidelberg, Surat, India. pp 36–51

13.   Noorian Z, Ulieru M (2010) The state of the art in trust and reputation systems: a framework for comparison. J Theor Appl Electron Commerce Res 5(2):97–117

14.   Sherchan W, Nepal S, Paris C (2013) A survey of trust in social networks. ACM Comput Surv 45(4):1–33

15.   Zacharia G, Moukas A, Maes P (2000) Collaborative reputation mechanisms for electronic marketplaces. Decis Support Syst 29(4):371–388

16.   Whitby A, Jøsang A, Indulska J (2004) Filtering out unfair ratings in Bayesian reputation systems. In: Falcone R, Barber S, Sabater J, Singh M (eds). Proceedings of the third international joint conference on autonomous agents and multi agent systems, New, York, USA. IEEE Computer Society, Washington, DC. pp 106–117

17.   Liu S, Zhang J, Miao C, Theng Y-L, Kot AC (2011) iCLUB: an integrated clustering-based approach to improve the robustness of reputation systems. In: Sonenberg L, Stone P, Tumer K, Yolum P (eds). Proceedings of the 10th international conference on Autonomous Agents and Multiagent Systems (AAMAS), Taipei, Taiwan. IFAAMAS, Richland, SC. pp 1151–1152

18.   Dellarocas C (2000) Immunizing online reputation reporting systems against unfair ratings and discriminatory behavior. In: Jhingran A, MacKie J, Tygar D (eds). Proceedings of the 2nd ACM conference on electronic commerce, Minneapolis, MN. ACM, New York. pp 150–157

19.   Zhang H, Wang Y, Zhang X (2012) A trust vector approach to transaction context-aware trust evaluation in e-commerce and e-service environments. In: Shih C, Son S, Kuo T, Huemer C (eds). Proceedings of the 5th IEEE international conference on Service-Oriented Computing and Applications (SOCA). IEEE Computer Society Washington, DC, Taipei, Taiwan. pp 1–8

20.   Obergrusberger F, Baloglu B, Sänger J, Senk C (2013) Biometric identity trust: toward secure biometric enrollment in web environments. In: Yousif M, Schubert L (eds). Proceedings of the 3rd international conference on Cloud Computing (CloudComp), Vienna, Austria. Springer, Berlin, Heidelberg. pp 124–133

21.   Brin S, Page L (1998) The anatomy of a large-scale hypertextual web search engine. Comput Networks 30(1-7):107–177

22.   Epinions.com: Read expert reviews on Electronics, Cars, Books, Movies, Music and More. http://www.epinions.com/

23.   Sun Y, Han Z, Yu W, Ray Liu K (2006) Attacks on trust evaluation in distributed networks. In: Proceedings of Th 40th annual Conference on Information Sciences and Systems (CISS), Princeton, NJ, USA, IEEE Computer Society Washington, DC. pp 1461–1466

24.   Jøsang A, Ismail R (2002) The beta reputation system. In: Proceedings of the 15th bled conference on electronic commerce, Bled, Slovenia. pp 41–55

25.   Slashdot: News for nerds, stuff that matters. http://www.slashdot.org/

26.   Amazon.com: Online Shopping for Electronics, Apparel, Computers, Books, DVDs & more. http://www.amazon.com

27.   Jøsang A (2001) A logic for uncertain probabilities. Int J Uncertainty Fuzziness Knowledge-Based Syst 9(3):279–311

28.   Yu B, Singh MP (2002) An evidential model of distributed reputation management. In: Proceedings of the first International Joint Conference on Autonomous Agents and Multiagent Systems (AAMAS), Bologna, Italy. ACM, New York, NY. pp 294–301

29.   Malik Z, Akbar I, Bouguettaya A (2009) Web services reputation assessment using a Hidden Markov Model. In: Baresi L, Chi CH, Suzuki J (eds). Service-oriented computing: Proceedings of the 7th International Joint Conference on Service-Oriented Computing (ICSOC-ServiceWave), Stockholm, Sweden. Springer Berlin, Heidelberg. pp 576–591

30.   Song S, Hwang K, Zhou R, Yu-Kwong K (2005) Trusted P2P transactions with fuzzy reputation aggregation, Vol. 9

31.   Sabater J, Sierra C (2002) Reputation and social network analysis in multi-agent systems. In: Proceedings of the first International joint conference on Autonomous Agents and Multiagent Systems (AAMAS), Bologna, Italy. ACM, New York, NY. pp 475–482

32.   Kamvar SD, Schlosser MT, Garcia-Molina H (2003) The Eigentrust algorithm for reputation management in P2P networks. In: Hencsey G, White B, Chen YF, Kovács L, Lawrence S (eds). Proceedings of the 12th International Conference on World Wide Web (WWW), Budapest, Hungary. ACM, New York, NY. pp 640–651

33.   Gamma E (1995) Design patterns: elements of reusable object-oriented software. Addison-Wesley, Reading

34.   Next Generation Online Trust. http://trust.bayforsec.de

35.   Jøsang A (2012) Robustness of trust and reputation systems: does it matter? In: Dimitrakos T, Moona R, Patel D, McKnight DH (eds). Trust management VI: Proceedings of the 6th IFIP WG 11.11 International Conference (IFIPTM), Surat, India. Springer, Berlin, Heidelberg. pp 253–262

36.   Sänger J, Pernul G (2015) Reusable defense components for online reputation systems. In: Marsh S, Jensen CD, Murayma Y, Dimitrakos T (eds). Trust management IX: Proceedings of the 9th IFIP WG 11.11 International Conference (IFIPTM), Hamburg, Germany. Springer, Berlin, Heidelberg

37.   Kerr R, Cohen R (2010) TREET: The Trust and Reputation Experimentation and Evaluation Testbed. Electron Commerce Res 10(3–4):271–290

38.   Fullam KK, Voss M, Klos TB, Muller G, Sabater J, Schlosser A, Topol Z, Barber KS, Rosenschein JS, Vercouter L (2005) A specification of the Agent Reputation and Trust (ART) Testbed. In: Dignum F, Dignum V, Koenig S, Kraus S, Singh MP, Wooldridge M (eds). Proceedings of the 4th international joint conference on Autonomous Agents and Multiagent Systems (AAMAS), Utrecht, Netherlands. ACM, New York, NY, USA. pp 512–518

39. Irissappane AA, Jiang S, Zhang J (2012) Towards a comprehensive Testbed to evaluate the robustness of reputation systems against unfair rating attacks. In: Herder E, Yacef K, Chen L, Weibelzahl S (eds). Workshop and Poster Proceedings of the 20th conference on User Modeling, Adaptation, and Personalization (UMAP), Montreal, Canada. Springer Berlin, Heidelberg

40. Irissappane AA, Zhang J (2014) A Testbed to evaluate the robustness of reputation systems in e-Marketplaces. In: Bazzan A, Huhns MN, Lomuscio A, Scerri P (eds). Proceedings of the 13th international conference on Autonomous Agents and Multiagent Systems (AAMAS), Paris, France. ACM, New York, NY, USA. pp 1629–1630

41. Grandison T, Sloman M (2000) A survey of trust in internet applications. IEEE Commun Surv Tutorials 3(4):2–16

42. Yu B, Singh MP (2000) A social mechanism of reputation management in electronic communities. In: Goos G, Hartmanis J, van Leeuwen J (eds). Proceedings of the 4th international workshop on cooperative information agents IV - The future of information agents in cyberspace (CIA), Boston, USA, Springer, London, UK. pp 154–165

43. Wang Y, Vassileva J (2003) Trust and reputation model in peer-to-peer networks. In: Shahmehri N, Graham RL, Caronni G (eds). Proceedings of the 3rd international conference on Peer-to-Peer Computing (P2P), Linköping, Sweden. IEEE Computer Society Washington, DC. pp 150–157

44. Golbeck JA (2005) Computing and applying trust in web-based social networks. PhD thesis, University of Maryland, College Park, MD, USA

45. Haque MM, Ahamed SI (2007) An omnipresent Formal Trust Model (FTM) for pervasive computing environment. In: Proceedings of the 31st annual international Computer Software and Applications Conference (COMPSAC), Bejing, China. IEEE Computer Society Washington, DC. pp 49–56

46. Uddin MG, Zulkernine M, Ahamed SI (2008) CAT: a context-aware trust model for open and dynamic systems. In: Wainwright RL, Haddad H (eds). Proceedings of the 2008 ACM Symposium on Applied Computing (SAC), Fortaleza, Brazil. ACM, New York, NY. pp 2024–2029

47. Wishart R, Robinson R, Indulska J, Jøsang A (2005) Superstringrep: reputation-enhanced service discovery. In: Estivill-Castro V (ed). Proceedings of the 28th Australasian conference on computer science, Newcastle, NSW, Australia. Australian Computer Society, Inc, Darlinghurst, Australia. pp 49–57

48. Christianson B, Harbison WS (1997) Why Isn't trust transitive? In: Christianson B, Crispo B, Lomas T, Roe M (eds). Proceedings of the 2nd international workshop on security protocols, Paris, France. Springer, London, UK. pp 171–176

5

Two sides of the coin: measuring and communicating the trustworthiness of online information

Jason RC Nurse[1*], Ioannis Agrafiotis[1], Michael Goldsmith[1], Sadie Creese[1] and Koen Lamberts[2]

* Correspondence:
jason.nurse@cs.ox.ac.uk
[1]Cyber Security Centre, Department of Computer Science, University of Oxford, Oxford, UK
Full list of author information is available at the end of the article

Abstract

Information is the currency of the digital age – it is constantly communicated, exchanged and bartered, most commonly to support human understanding and decision-making. While the Internet and Web 2.0 have been pivotal in streamlining many of the information creation and dissemination processes, they have significantly complicated matters for users as well. Most notably, the substantial increase in the amount of content available online has introduced an information overload problem, while also exposing content with largely unknown levels of quality, leaving many users with the difficult question of, what information to trust? In this article we approach this problem from two perspectives, both aimed at supporting human decision-making using online information. First, we focus on the task of measuring the extent to which individuals should trust a piece of openly-sourced information (e.g., from Twitter, Facebook or a blog); this considers a range of factors and metrics in information provenance, quality and infrastructure integrity, and the person's own preferences and opinion. Having calculated a measure of trustworthiness for an information item, we then consider how this rating and the related content could be communicated to users in a cognitively-enhanced manner, so as to build confidence in the information only where and when appropriate. This work concentrates on a range of potential visualisation techniques for trust, with special focus on radar graphs, and draws inspiration from the fields of Human-Computer Interaction (HCI), System Usability and Risk Communication. The novelty of our contribution stems from the comprehensive approach taken to address this very topical problem, ensuring that the trustworthiness of openly-sourced information is adequately measured and effectively communicated to users, thus enabling them to make informed decisions.

Keywords: Information trustworthiness; Information quality; Trust metrics; Trust visuals; Decision-making; Social-media content; Risk communication

Introduction

We live in a world where the ability to access and publish information is practically considered a human right. The adoption of the Internet into our daily lives has facilitated this capability, leading to the creation of a global information marketplace that has become central to decision-making online and offline. There remain, however, significant concerns regarding the quality of online information, and thus its trustworthiness, that cannot be overlooked. Numerous real-life cases have highlighted this misinformation problem within social-media sites, and more recently we have even witnessed the severe impact which inaccurate information can have; that is, in the Boston bombings case, where an individual, after being wrongly identified as a suspect by a popular social site, was found dead [1]. Here, poor quality information resulted not only in an ill-judged decision, but a tragic loss of an innocent life.

To address the issues surrounding the quality and trustworthiness of online content, there have been a number of proposals focusing on various aspects of the problem. Agichtein et al. [2] for instance, propose a system that can automatically identify high-quality content items in question-and-answer networks using several contextual and intrinsic features. This drive towards automated assessment of social content can also be seen in Castillo et al. [3] as applied to analysing the credibility of Twitter data, and in Suzuki and Yoshikawa [4], who focus on evaluating editor and text features to determine the quality of Wikipedia articles. These proposals all draw on well-defined sets of sub-factors – e.g., provenance, reputation, competence, corroboration and recency – which tend to be indicative of quality and trust [5], and from these deduce useful metrics and approaches to arrive at a trustworthiness score that may be associated with the online content.

One aspect not covered by these and similar works, however, is the fact that trust, credibility and quality (and the sub-factors of which they are comprised) are intrinsically subjective, i.e., they can be perceived and interpreted in different ways, and arguably may have varying levels of importance depending on the user of the information or the context. One user may rely heavily on the reputation of its source in determining how much to trust content, while another user may be more concerned with how up-to-date it is. With this in mind, we believe that there is substantial value in allowing users of information-trustworthiness measures to influence the scores which they will receive from automated tools, so as better to represent their individual preferences and situation. User influence could be realised at several levels – as simplistic as disregarding some trustworthiness/quality sub-factors completely, or as complicated as defining ranges of weights (i.e., importance) for trust sub-factors depending on scenario and decision context.

Measuring information trustworthiness is only one half of the problem. Once trustworthiness scores have been calculated, it is crucial that they are appropriately communicated to users in such a way as to enable them to make well-informed decisions. Although not extensive, there has been some work on this task. In Idris et al. [6], for example, authors present a simple traffic-light system (with red, amber and green, thus drawing on the real-world metaphor) to convey quality. Adler et al. [7] take a finer-grained approach to presenting trust as they colour the text background of Wikipedia content – from white (high trustworthiness) to dark orange (low trustworthiness) dependent on how trustworthy their system deems that segment of the information to be. Although useful approaches, these proposals at times lack the strong foundation in Cognitive Science and HCI that is imperative to designing interfaces and visuals that will ultimately be effective in communicating trust. This risks the possibility of confusing users even more, thus resulting in bad decisions and ill-informed actions.

The aim of this paper is therefore to present our comprehensive, interdisciplinary approach to address the shortcomings highlighted above, and to support decision-making that takes advantage of online content. This article brings together and consolidates a number of our previous contributions, while also reflecting on their utility with the overall problem in mind. We begin in Section 2 by briefly recapping our policy-based approach to measuring the degree to which users should trust openly-sourced information (e.g., tweets, Facebook updates, and blog posts) – this takes into account information provenance, quality and infrastructure-integrity factors and metrics, along with the individual's preferences and situation. Section 3 then considers visual approaches for communicating trustworthiness, i.e., those that predate ours and our previous work on this topic, and subsequent evaluations and reflections. In Section 4, we enter the core of the paper, which focuses on radar graphs and their use as a visual mechanism for communicating detailed trustworthiness information effectively. The discussion here highlights their advantages and shortcomings, but also covers general points applicable to any technique to communicate trust via visuals. Finally, Section 5 concludes the article and presents directions for extending this work.

An approach to calculate information's trustworthiness

Assessing the quality and trustworthiness of information is not a new problem. Early articles such as Wang and Strong [8] (on data quality) and Chopra and Wallace [9] (on trust) have researched this at length and identified several sub-factors that could be used to assess and measure these aspects. Examples of sub-factors within these areas include the level of competence of a source, their reputation and authority, the recency of information, how well corroborated the information is, and even how information is presented. In more recent articles, these and other sub-factors have been applied to automatically analyse and rate the trustworthiness of content, with commendable degrees of accuracy; cf. Castillo *et al.* [3]. The shortcoming with these specific automated types of proposals, however, is the lack of explicit appreciation of the subjective nature of trust (and related concepts) thereby overlooking the importance of allowing a user to influence the final information-trustworthiness score that is presented to them.

To address this problem, we have devised a policy-based approach and framework through which the trustworthiness of information can be measured [10,11]. As it is a framework, we allow for the 'plug-in' of any of the variety of techniques currently used to measure sub-factors of trust, such as those by Agichtein *et al.* [2] and Castillo *et al.* [3]. Most importantly, this approach allows users to specify their preferences via policies, and then have these applied to trustworthiness calculations to guide the calculation of a final content trustworthiness score. This may mean attenuation or accentuation of the scores given to specific sub-factors (e.g., weighting the information's calculated recency score higher than its corroboration score), or indeed, changing the way that they are combined to arrive at the single trust score. This is somewhat similar to the idea of personalisation systems for news and other such information (e.g., [36]).

Broadly, we assess information trustworthiness in three domains: the provenance of information, its quality, and the integrity of the information infrastructure used to communicate the content from author to final consumer (hereafter, referred to as III). While there are several publications focused on the first two of these domains, the third has thus far largely been neglected. As such, we have outlined a preliminary technique for accounting for attacks detected against the information infrastructure (e.g., information poisoning) – practically limited to local technology deployed within the user's network – which takes into account known and unknown threats, vulnerabilities in local infrastructure, and probabilities of attacks [11]. This will allow users to attain a better understanding of the environment they are operating in as well as assisting them to decide whether or not to believe associated provenance or quality scores. At this point, our research in this area is still on-going as we aim to better comprehend infrastructure scopes, and automated linkage to vulnerability and attack databases (e.g., CVE [12], NVD [13] and CAPEC [14]), en route to proposing a viable III metric.

As we envisage our general approach and any developed tools to be used within organisations as well (e.g., an Emergency Operations Centre (EOC) trying to understand an on-going crisis situation using live Twitter and Facebook data), we also allow organisations to define policies that reflect their beliefs. For instance, an EOC may always want tweets from the BBC to be rated as highly competent or, equally, may prefer that its employees never listen to some blacklisted information sources. Of course, the danger with allowing this personalisation of trust scores – by user or organisation – is that calculated information trustworthiness values are highly biased and ultimately unreliable. It remains our opinion however, that users of this system will be more focused on the ground truth, i.e., what is actually happening regarding a topic, situation or scene, and therefore doctoring content's trust scores will only put them at a disadvantage; the adage, 'garbage in garbage out' applies here.

Figure 1 presents the approach, with a simple example.

As illustrated in Figure 1, the approach starts with openly-sourced information being fed into the system. This could be from any source, including content on Twitter,

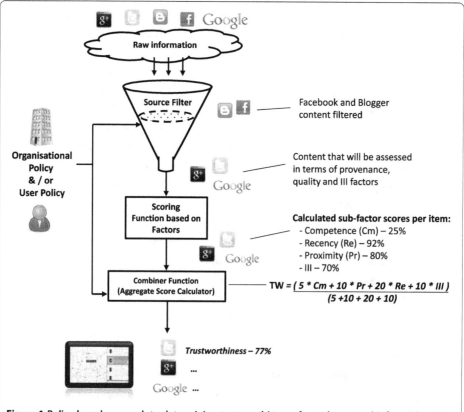

Figure 1 Policy-based approach to determining trustworthiness of openly-sourced information. This approach utilises an information filter, scoring function and combiner function, while also considering the organisational and user policies of its users.

Facebook and Google+, and could either be directly entered or gathered by a Web crawler or from an RSS feed. Information is then filtered according to the specific source, e.g., the tweeter on Twitter, or by source type, so as to remove content from unwanted sources. In the figure, the organisation, an EOC, has set a company-wide policy to block content from Facebook and Blogger, but allow content from Twitter, Google Plus and Google. Next, the filtered information (and any associated metadata) is assessed using several trust metrics to gain sub-factor ratings for each piece of information. These metrics can be drawn from existing work (e.g., [2,3,7]), or contributions by the efforts of our research consortium [11]. In the figure, we see examples of scores that can result for each information item: 25% for the Competence of a source (i.e., they have been found not to be very competent), 92% for information Recency (meaning the information is quite up to date), 80% for Proximity (i.e., the source is physically fairly close to the event of interest), and III of 70% (therefore although generally good, there may be some concerns about the integrity of the information infrastructure).

The approach then combines the sub-factor scores into a single trustworthiness score. Crucially, this combination can be influenced by the organisation's policy and any specific user policies that have been set beforehand [15]. We allow two types of configuration input at this stage. The first enables organisations and users to assign importance levels to the different sub-factors, to define their weight and ultimate impact on the final trustworthiness score. In the example in Figure 1, the user has assigned Competence to have a weight of 5; Proximity, 10; Recency, 20; and III, 10. Other research that we have been involved in [16] actually looks in detail at this notion of importance of factors and understanding people's perceptions; we expect that this could be used in the future to help specify importance policies. The second configuration available is the ability to select different types of combiner functions. In the illustration above we use the weighted arithmetic mean, however, there are numerous others including geometric mean, harmonic mean, and variations on root-mean-square (quadratic mean) that may be of use [17]. The advantage in having this range of functions available is that they all offer nuances that may be preferred by different users and contexts. In the case of crisis response, one could imagine an EOC preferring that trustworthiness scores associated with information items are slightly underestimated rather than overestimated, given that human lives are at stake. As a result, the harmonic mean would be a better choice than the quadratic mean because of its tendency to consistently underrate combined values [17].

After the policies have been applied and the combiner function executed, the output is a trustworthiness score for each piece of information. This score would have made use of the range of novel techniques to automatically measure quality and trust, but also would accommodate organisational and user preferences and context. In Section 3, we take the trustworthiness score, as it is here – a percentage – and consider whether and how visuals may be applied to allow for effective communication of the associated information risk.

Visuals for communicating trustworthiness

Over the last few years, there have been an increasing number of articles using visuals to communicate the quality and trustworthiness of information. In our review in

Section 1, we highlighted the work of Idris *et al.* [6] and the use of traffic-lights, and that of Adler *et al.* [7] that advocates changing the background colour of related text to indicate trust. Another notable approach is that of Chevalier *et al.* [18]. In their article, they concentrate heavily on visuals, particularly charts and graphs, as a support tool to assist information users to assess the quality of openly-sourced content. While these articles are indeed valuable, assumptions are often made regarding users and their cognitive abilities and preferences for interfaces, inclusive of visuals for trust. Unfortunately, ill-conceived assumptions may introduce other problems for users, such as information overload and confusion, which can negatively affect decision-making.

As a result of this, we have pursued a research agenda focused specifically on understanding ways in which information could be effectively communicated to users, in light of their cognitive abilities, perceptions and biases. Two well-established fields were central to this work: (1) Risk Communication, given that our aim of presenting users with trustworthiness data is in effect, to mitigate the risk of believing and acting on that information; (2) HCI and System Usability, for general guidance and principles of interface design. Having critically reflected on these and related domains, we engaged in several exercises to evaluate existing and new visual techniques for conveying information trustworthiness. Broadly, our investigative approach involved gathering a large number of visualisation techniques (e.g., iconography, glyphs, charts, and imagery), assessing them in terms of accepted Risk Communication and Usability guidelines and in the context of trust, and lastly, conducting user experiments to test a subset of the more useful visual approaches.

In detail, our user experiments tested four techniques for visualising the trustworthiness of information. These were: traffic lights (with red, amber and green indicating low, medium and high trustworthiness respectively), transparency (where highly trustworthy information would be shown normally, medium trustworthy content would be made 30% transparent, and low trustworthy content 70% transparent), stars (using size of star to indicate trustworthiness, the bigger, the better), and test-tubes (filled to portray trustworthiness – the fuller it was the higher the trust). As indicated, these all operated on three levels of trustworthiness, namely, high, medium and low; the assumption being that the percentage score calculated would have to be mapped to these levels. Figure 2 displays the visuals in the context of the experiment which was conducted on a tablet PC device; full details are available in [20].

From our analysis of the experimental results, traffic lights were found to be the most preferred technique for presenting trustworthiness, while transparency was the least preferred. Participants' choice of traffic lights was reportedly linked to modern man's instilled behaviour towards them and the colours they presented; in society today, a red traffic light is the universal sign to stop. The use of real-world metaphors is heavily advocated in Usability and Risk Communication principles but it was good to actually verify these recommendations. The poor performance by the transparency method was surprising, given analogous approaches have been used before [21] with some success. Feedback from individuals pointed to the difficulty in perceiving and understanding the degree of trustworthiness actually being conveyed, i.e., perceiving the difference between being 30% or 70% transparent. Moreover, if we were to allow five levels of trust as opposed to three – the positive there being further granularity to trust scores – it would be even more challenging for individuals to perceive. Of course, there would also be a challenge with regards to using traffic lights.

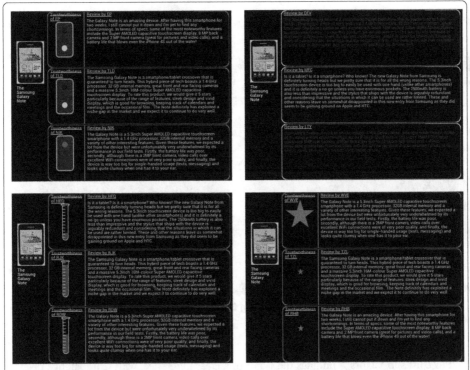

Figure 2 Screenshots of the tool's prototype interface for visually communicating information trustworthiness using traffic lights, transparency, test-tubes and stars.

Other general points worth noting include the fact that transparency appears to subconsciously direct participants away from low trustworthy content (a potentially good feature depending on where the tool is deployed and the level of subconscious persuasion desired); different visuals may elicit varying interpretations from users (i.e., even though participants were told beforehand about the three levels of trust, some perceived a low test-tube as worse than a red traffic light); and often, individuals desire more information on trustworthiness scores (i.e. how it was determined, what factors led to it). It is the last of these points that has given rise to the work presented in the next section.

Communicating trustworthiness with radar graphs

As mentioned above, a key finding in our experiments was that users would like more information about how the trustworthiness score was calculated by the system, to help them determine how confident they could be in the trust score presented. From a human trust perspective, this is perfectly reasonable, as understanding is a common antecedent to trust [5]. To assist users with building confidence in trust scores, we engaged in two experiments. The first experiment explored people's perception of a set of trust factors using radar graphs as visuals. Figure 3 shows the interface that was presented to study participants. This allowed us to assess: (i) whether individuals could understand the detailed factors that they were requesting – we found that they could; (ii) their ability to perceive and comprehend radar graphs to deduce trust – generally, also positive conclusions were drawn; and (iii) the existence of variations in the levels of importance

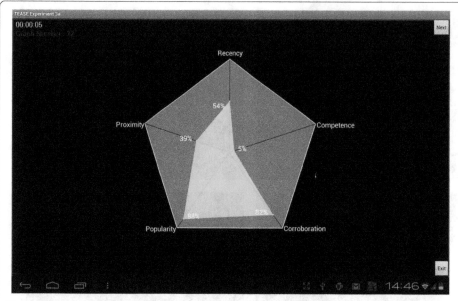

Figure 3 Radar graphs application interface displaying five detailed information-trustworthiness sub-factors: Recency, Proximity, Popularity, Corroboration and Competence.

attached to trust sub-factors – findings did point to a clear difference, with Competence being the most important of the five and Popularity being the least important [22].

The second experiment, which built on the first, sought to use radar-graph visuals to allow users to 'drill-down' into trustworthiness scores shown initially as traffic lights. The context of the experiment was crisis-response and users had the task of making decisions on the level of risk in a scenario containing openly-sourced information with associated trust scores; a screenshot of the interface used is shown in Figure 4. Trustworthiness was visualised at three levels: at the highest level, there was a traffic light symbol; the second level showed radar graphs with associated measures for provenance, quality and III (users could tap the traffic light to drill down to this level of detail); and the third level displayed a radar graph with the actual factors used to calculate each of these measures. The purpose of allowing drill-down to radar graphs was to build confidence in the higher-level trust scores, where and when necessary; a goal that was achieved according to the results from the study [16].

One crucial finding from these experiments, especially the first, was that people's perceptions of particular graph schemas could actually be quite varied and also subject to visual biases. To understand why this was the case and when it was likely to occur, we focused on these graphs and explored the nuances in schemas that might have led to these differences in perceptions. Below, we describe that work in detail and reflect on key findings that will be useful for any future work on visualisations for trustworthiness.

Experiment background and context

The aim of our radar graphs experiment was to explore people's perception of five trust factors, which our previous findings suggest are key to trust online [5,22], and also to assess their importance to individuals in so far as they pertain to judgements on trustworthiness. The factors were: Competence (*Cm*), the level of knowledge of a person or

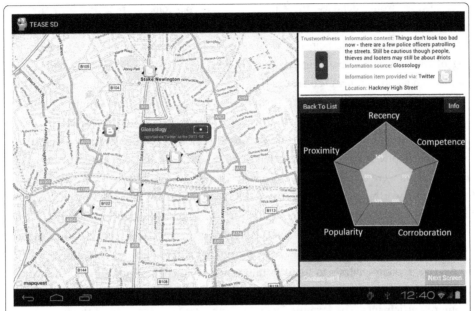

Figure 4 Crisis management application interface that allows the tool's users to drill-down into trustworthiness scores (initially represented by traffic lights) to get more detail on how scores were conceived. This detail is presented in the context of the trustworthiness sub-factors of Recency, Proximity, Popularity, Corroboration and Competence.

information source; Proximity (Pr), the geographical closeness of a source to an event of interest; Popularity (Po), how well-known is a source; Recency (Re), how recent or up-to-date is information to the event of interest; and Corroboration (Cr), how well supported the information is by a variety of different sources. The experiment design consisted of 200 radar graphs, each presenting ranges of values between 0-100% for the five factors; Excel's $RAND()$ function was used to produce a set of 200 random values which was then implemented in our application for experimentation. In Figure 3, we show an example visual, which displays Graph #22; with Recency at 54%, Competence at 5%, Corroboration at 82%, Popularity at 88%, and Proximity at 39%. Further below we present graphs exactly as they were presented to study participants, to give readers the best insight into the conditions and tasks of the experiment.

A total of 40 individuals (29 females, 11 males, mean age of 23.7, age range: 18–58 years) participated in the study. Recruitment was conducted through the use of flyers posted within the University of Warwick and the University of Oxford. Participants were from a variety of disciplines (sciences, humanities, and social sciences) and there was also a diversity of levels, i.e., students were both postgraduates and undergraduates, and working professionals spanned from hospitality clerks to personal assistants, researchers and administrators. Participants were compensated for assisting with the experiment.

The experiment consisted of participants being presented with each of the 200 graphs and then given a maximum of 10 seconds before they were asked to give a rating of 0–100 (100 being the maximum trustworthiness) to represent the level of trustworthiness the graph conveyed to them. A timer was displayed on screen and therefore participants were always aware of the time remaining. The restricted time allowed served two purposes. Firstly, we were aiming to get participants' first and instinctive impression, and secondly, we would decrease the chances of study participants recalling how they assessed similarly shaped graphs, thereby avoiding them simply using their memory.

To present the graphs to participants, we used a Motorola Xoom tablet PC. At the beginning of the experiment, participants were briefed on the goals of the study and requested to sign a consent form. To ensure that they had a clear understanding of the five trust factors, they were also shown short definitions and examples of how the terms could be used. As there were a large number of graphs, participants were advised that in case of discomfort (e.g., tired eyes), they were free to take a break at any time. Regarding the responses to the graphs, it was emphasised that there were no correct or incorrect answers. Once participants were comfortable, the experiment commenced, and they were asked to evaluate the trustworthiness degree represented by each of the 200 radar graphs by assessing measures of the five factors included and any personal preferences they held.

The findings from the analysis, as reported initially in [16], were very encouraging and highlighted distinct significance levels of factors across participants. Specifically, we used linear regression analysis to identify importance (via coefficients) for each factor per participant, and then averaged across the sample to define a regression formula for the group of participants. The formula for trustworthiness (as a function of the five factors) that resulted is shown below:

Equation (1) presented in [16]:

$$Trustworthiness = -5.425 + 0.176\,Re + 0.405\,Cm + 0.235\,Cr + 0.127\,Po + 0.141\,Pr$$

Coefficients preceding each factor were taken to define factor importance. Thus, Competence was the most influential factor, followed by Corroboration, Recency, Proximity and Popularity. Finally, it is worth mentioning that participants did not report any significant difficulties in understanding the factors (or their relation to trustworthiness), graphs or combining them to deduce an overall trust score. This built our confidence in the findings above.

Detailed radar graph analysis

In addition to the more general evaluation in [16], we have subsequently engaged in several smaller and more focused statistical analyses pertaining to graphs and respective participants' scores. In the first investigation, we conducted a basic relationship analysis to verify that values produced by the formula derived from the sample above (hereafter, 'expected values') correlated with participants' trustworthiness scores for each of the 200 graphs. This was to establish some link between expected values and participants' actual scores rather than an influence or causal association; although both types of values would have the underlying trust-factor scores as a basis. Another key benefit was also the potential to identify any outlying participants (i.e., those with different opinions than the general populous) that might have been marginalised after averaging across coefficients to define the trustworthiness formula for the sample.

The analysis consisted of first computing expected values (using the formula in (1) and respective factor scores) for all of the graphs, and running a Pearson product–moment correlation [23] to determine the relationship between these values and each of the 40 participants' graph scores. As an example, in Table 1 we present the details of

Table 1 Data table which shows the graph data (i.e., scores for Recency, Competence, Corroboration, Popularity, and Proximity), expected trustworthiness values (based on the trustworthiness formulae proposed in equation (1)) and actual trustworthiness scores provided by two participants in the study

Graph #	Re	Cm	Cr	Po	Pr	Expected	P1	P2
22	54	5	82	88	39	42	40	40
33	1	14	12	30	9	8	9	5

two graphs, their respective trust-factor scores, the expected value for the graphs and the actual scores given by Participants #1 (P1) and #2 (P2).

From the analysis conducted, we found a positive correlation between the expected and actual scores, with all Pearson correlation coefficients statistically significant at p < 0.001. This confirmed a link between these two values and suggested that there were no extreme outliers (i.e., participants with very contrary opinions and perceptions of factor importance). To reinforce our findings and focus more on an evaluation of the similarity of expected and given scores, we also calculated the *deviation* from the expected value for every graph, per participant. The equation we used is presented below, where *n* is the number of the graphs, *x* is the score that the participant gave to the graph and *E* is the expected value for the specific graph. The findings from this calculation did highlight some deviation across participants; however, the results were supportive of the similarity of values in general.

Equation (2):

$$\sqrt{\frac{1}{n}\sum_{i=1}^{n}(x_i - E_i)^2}$$

From the correlation analysis, we did identify a participant with a Pearson coefficient of *0.353*, which was much smaller than the average across the sample of *0.745*. Not surprisingly, the same participant had the highest *deviation* value, a score of *24.49*, as compared to the sample average of *15.93*. Upon further investigation, we found that this participant viewed the importance of trust factors very differently, with Recency being most important (*0.385*), followed by Proximity (*0.184*), Corroboration (*0.162*), Competence (*0.135*) and then Popularity (*0.081*). This variation could therefore explain the lowest Pearson coefficient and the highest deviation value. Generally however, the strong correlation in other scores did emphasise the utility of the main formula presented in (1).

From our in-depth analysis of graphs and scores assigned to them (in addition to deviation analyses mentioned above), we were able to identify a set of graphs that were persistent outliers where some participants allocated much higher or lower scores than expected. Our further assessment therefore focused on understanding the cause of these outliers (i.e. graphs where the expected and actual score differ more than 50%) in an attempt to comprehend their nature and, if possible, mitigate their future effects.

Elaborating on the outliers, we noted that in 4 graphs, at least 40% of participants agreed in their reporting of scores greater than 50% different to expectations. Specifically: for Graph #3, 53% of participants provided scores 50% or more greater than the expected value; for Graph #45, 45% of individuals gave scores of at least 50% smaller; for Graph #52, 40% of study participants supplied scores of at least 50% greater than expected; and for Graph #66, 45% of participants reported scores of 50% or more smaller than the expected values. We noted two potential reasons for these significant variations. Either, there was a marked deviation in factors' importance (i.e., coefficients) for those groups of participants, or possibly the overall size or area of the radar graph (i.e., the filled part of the pentagon) or indeed, its schema, influenced individuals. An example of the latter case is that smaller-sized graphs, independent of specific factor importance levels, subconsciously swayed participants to give lower scores than normal for the sample.

To ascertain which of these (if any) may have been true, we first calculated the average coefficient value for each trust factor, for the four groups of participants that gave the differing scores to the graphs. One should recall that coefficients resulted from linear regression analysis on each participant's 200 graph scores. Next, we compared these coefficients (i.e., levels of importance) to those of the main sample. This assessment highlighted several variations in factors' importance, to the extent that it could have been the reason for differing final graph scores.

In Graph #66 (in Figure 5) for instance, where 45% of participants gave scores 50% or more lower than expected, we found that these participants felt that Recency and Popularity were respectively 11% and 17% less important than in the overall sample formula and Corroboration was 9% more important. Reflecting on the graph itself, one can begin to understand why a lower score from those participants might therefore have resulted. That is, the factors with higher graph values were less important and those with lower values (here, Corroboration only) were more important. Similar observations were apparent with the other three graphs. This was a notable finding that pointed to deviation in factors' importance as the actual reason for different (or outlier) scores, and potentially not subconscious influences of graph size. A possible solution to mitigate the effect of this specific outlier could be to allow users to customise the importance of the five factors according to their trust perceptions.

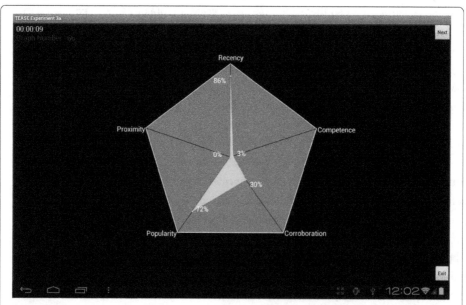

Figure 5 Screenshot of Graph #66, where the high percentage of Recency among extremely low percentages of Competence and Proximity results in a very small volume.

Apart from comparing participants' scores to the expected values for the sample, another more focused approach to determine whether size of graphs subconsciously influenced participants was to compare their individual scores to their expected values (i.e., values calculated based on their own trustworthiness formulae). This was therefore moving away from assessing outliers as it pertains to the expected score across the sample, to identifying and evaluating outliers relating to the respective participant's expected graph score. For this investigation, therefore, we used the formula generated for each participant based on the linear regression analysis, and compared the new expected values to the actual scores that were given to the respective graphs. To gather an idea of whether graph size or area might have influenced participants, we checked for cases where actual scores were 50% or more different to the expected scores, *and* size of the graph (or more accurately, the calculated area of the filled graph) was at least 25% different to the expected value. To calculate the filled area, we used the equation presented below in (3). This splits the pentagon into five triangles, calculates the blue-shaded area in each, sums these, then divides by the total pentagon area to determine the size percentage filled.

Equation (3):

$$\frac{{}^1\!/_2 \times \sin 72 \times (Re \times Cm + Cm \times Cr + Cr \times Po + Po \times Pr + Pr \times Re)}{{}^5\!/_2 \times 100 \times 100 \times \sin 72}$$

Therefore, if a participant gave an actual graph score 65% greater than their expected value for that graph, and the graph size was 40% bigger than that expected score, we hypothesised this to mean that size may have had some impact on their decision to award that higher graph score.

The results from this analysis indicated that there were a significant number of cases – i.e., 49% of the cases where there was larger than a 50% difference – where this situation occurred, which led us to believe that graph size may have had some noteworthy impact on participants' scores. Considering the situations where this transpired, we became interested in the respective graphs and whether a particular type of schema (i.e., graph arrangement) or area may have resulted in under or overestimations in scores. This could give us valuable further insight into how graphs were perceived by participants in addition to allowing us to look in more detail at the outliers present.

In testing for this, we found that for a number of the cases particularly small sizes did feature. The graphs most underestimated by participants, and therefore those where size may have had a real influence, were Graph #45 shown in Figure 6 and Graph #66 previously presented in Figure 5; 17 participants underestimated these graphs. Assessing Graph #45's schema, the very low values for Recency, Popularity and Competence led to a particularly small graph size with considerably thin filled areas for even the higher rated factors of Proximity and Corroboration. Graph #66 exhibited a similar size phenomenon just with different trust factors. The other graphs which may have been particularly influenced by graph area are documented in Table 2; incidentally, all of these graphs result in underestimations of trustworthiness scores. Readers can easily recreate the graphs to view their schemas as necessary.

Further to the test above, we also considered the possibility that extremely low levels of Competence (generally the most important factor) may have been the cause of low

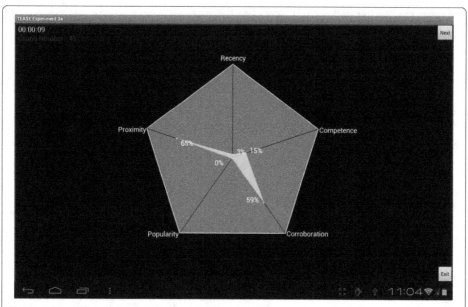

Figure 6 Screenshot of Graph #45, where factors with high percentages are adjacent to factors with low percentages, resulting in a very low volume.

scores across the participants. This would be easily conceivable, as a low score in the most important factor may have led to individuals completely discounting the graph. As can be seen in Graph #2 in Table 2 and Figure 7 however, even in cases where Competence was extremely high, there was some level of understatement in participants' scores. The outliers identified in this case will require further research to fully characterise and mitigate their effects.

The final cause that we considered as a potential source of outliers was the time constraint of 10 seconds within which participants had to provide their answers for each graph. We observed, however, that all the participants would respond within the first five to seven seconds, thus rendering the effect of time probably insignificant.

Next steps in using radar graphs and other visuals for trust

There are several avenues for further research which we intend to pursue, in order to follow up on the analyses and exploratory findings in terms of communicating

Table 2 Graphs (and their associated values for Recency, Competence, Corroboration, Popularity, and Proximity) where there is a possibility that graph size may have impacted trustworthiness scores given by study participants

Graph #	Re	Cm	Cr	Po	Pr	Number affected by size	Expected value	Average deviation of scores from the expected value
2	13	94	20	33	46	9	51	21
15	21	0	31	70	15	9	17	16
33	1	14	12	30	9	11	8	5
106	19	14	30	0	32	10	15	8
143	63	0	2	57	37	10	19	18
148	63	2	25	25	1	11	16	16
150	35	1	73	35	7	9	24	20

We also show the expected trustworthiness value and the average deviation of scores given by participants to that value.

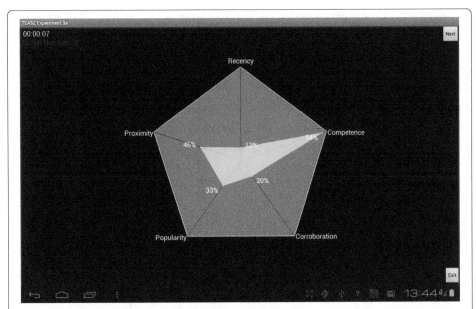

Figure 7 Screenshot of Graph #2, where an extremely high value on Competence is among very low values of the adjacent factors Recency and Corroboration, resulting in underestimations due to low volume of the graph.

trustworthiness especially using radar graphs. The first pertains to the layout of the graph itself – i.e., the position and ordering of each trust factor and its axis – and what happens when the positioning or ordering is changed. To take Graph #66 as an example, if Recency (86%), Popularity (72%) and Corroboration (30%) were next to each other, the graph's schema would be noticeably different and the area would jump from 5% to 17%. Figure 8 shows a mocked-up example of this altered format.

The research question therefore remains, might these variations in ordering have an impact on participants' perceptions and the scores that they award? Or, do people see

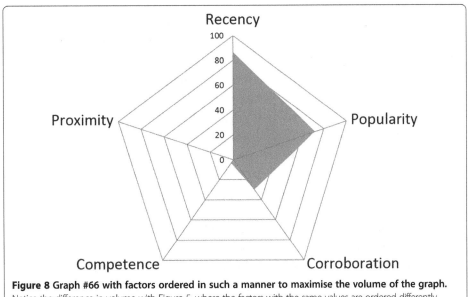

Figure 8 Graph #66 with factors ordered in such a manner to maximise the volume of the graph.
Notice the difference in volume with Figure 5, where the factors with the same values are ordered differently.

past the area and schema differences and award similar scores regardless of ordering? If ordering does have an impact then we would need to consider whether there are any 'better' orderings or indeed, whether the choice of ordering should be left to system users to decide. Finding the optimal ordering solution may mitigate the outlier effect caused by the graph size as well, thereby potentially rendering future attempts to communicate trustworthiness as effective instead of problematic, as they seem to be now.

We have already started to consider orderings that would maximise graph size, where the graph might be unduly underestimated by some individuals because of its schema. Graph factors ordered in the following way may result in a consistently maximised graph area: largest factor, second largest factor, fourth largest factor, fifth largest factor and then third largest factor (i.e., 1-2-4-5-3). We need to be careful however, because this approach could lead to consistent overestimations in the trustworthiness of graphs and related information, since the participants will always view a maximum area for the graph. Moreover, users might become confused with the constant change of the position of the trustworthiness factors in the edges of the pentagon; usability will also therefore be an issue.

One possibility is to assess whether placing the trust factors with the same ordering in the radar graph (i.e., 1-2-4-5-3) but focusing on the importance of the trustworthiness factors to the participants. This approach could allow the system to provide higher volume in graphs that should be trusted and lower volumes in graphs that should not be trusted. Unfortunately, a side effect of this is that it leads to system biases, not to mention the initial task of ascertaining how important individual factors are to users (although, this could arguably be expressed by them at system setup). Nonetheless, as mentioned above, continued work on this and other approaches will be necessary.

Another avenue for follow-up research picks up on a feedback point from interviews with participants who have undertaken the graphs experiment. There were suggestions that we should investigate the potential of additional axes in radar graphs to represent more factors. Our current emphasis on 5 factors was based on simplicity and reducing cognitive effort required by system users (a guideline from the Risk Communication and Usability fields), but as several research articles have suggested (e.g., Miller [24] and Saaty and Ozdemir [25]), the human brain may be capable of coping with possibly 7 or 9 items. Future experiments might therefore seek to evaluate people's ability and desire to assess additional trust factors – of which there are many [5] – and assess whether there is as preferred number of factors that should be displayed. This could also allow us to further validate our existing work and investigate the importance of other factors as it pertains to trustworthiness. Dependent on the research available, we may need to conduct a broader study on the importance of factors outside of graphs and then use a subset (e.g., the most important) for display within graphs during decision-making. In terms of graphs, the field of Risk Communication (especially seminal research work such as Lipkus and Hollands [19]) will undoubtedly continue to be a key area of reference during our study design and subsequent user experimentation.

An area where we may also conduct further research is to consider the impact of *context* on individuals, and assess the influence it has on people's perception of trust factors and their importance both within and outside of visuals and graphs. For the previous experiments, we specifically avoided context as a variable because we were more focused on how people perceived the importance of those factors generally. In the real-world however, as has been highlighted in existing research [26,27], context is crucial and is likely to have a notable influence on the importance of factors and perceived trust. This was also hinted at in interviews with participants as some said that they may have allocated different scores to the same graphs if they were presented with different scenarios. It will also be intriguing to investigate whether individuals' perceptions concur regarding factors' importance levels within specific contexts.

Finally, in terms of radar graphs, we aim to assess the impact that cognitive biases may have on the perception of graphs within our experiments. Cognitive biases refer to systematic weaknesses in human's cognitive processing and have been discussed at length in several articles [28-30]. The bias of most immediate interest is the *anchoring effect*, which defines the tendency of decision-makers to systematically base judgements on initial (and potentially even irrelevant) information [30]; future decisions are 'anchored' or biased to that starting information. We would therefore be specifically investigating (using quantitative – i.e., scores – and interview-based approaches) whether such an effect is prevalent when individuals score graphs, and if it is, to what extent. Key questions include, assessing whether we could find clear links between this and incorrect perception of certain graphs. A good reference point for this information is Furnham and Boo [31] and their recent, comprehensive review on the anchoring effect, its causes and attempts to tackle it in the past.

Conclusions and future work

The proliferation of information in online environments has rendered the designing of tools able to support decision-making using this information more crucial than ever. Towards this end, exploring the notion of trustworthiness of information is a vital step. Many researchers investigating this multidimensional concept have thus far focused either on proposing novel information-trustworthiness metrics, or on visuals through which quality and trustworthiness scores can be presented to users.

In this article, we have taken a lateral approach, synthesising a number of our previous contributions and presenting our comprehensive approach to measuring *and* visualising trust, in an attempt to address 'both sides of the coin'. We first recapped our policy-based approach which evaluates the degree of trustworthiness which users should place in online information. This is comprised of a number of quality and trust factors and respective metrics, and of the preferences of decision-makers, i.e., the users of the system. In addition to the application of policies, our approach also benefits from allowing any metric to be plugged into our framework to measure quality and trust. As these techniques mature, therefore, our approach will become more efficient and accurate. This will result in better support for system users when drawing on online information to assist decision-making online and offline.

Presenting a method to calculate trustworthiness addresses only one dimension of the problem at hand. To address the other main issue, i.e., effective communication of information-trustworthiness scores, we have taken steps towards understanding how best to communicate trustworthiness to individuals, by exploring and experimenting with various visualisation techniques including traffic lights, transparency, stars, and more recently, radar graphs. Apart from presenting and discussing our general two-pronged approach to the problem, this paper focused in detail on these radar graphs and evaluated their use as techniques for effectively and efficiently communicating trustworthiness information. We were also able to use graphs to assess the importance of trust factors to ranges of test participants, while also identifying challenges to communication realised via inconsistencies in human perceptions (in schemas, etc.). Most importantly, these irregularities could also apply to other visual techniques, and so wider research should note and consider these issues. Section 4.3 outlined several steps that we intend to take to further these discussions and address how misperceptions could be handled across ranges of similar visualisation approaches.

Briefly commenting on the use cases for our system, we believe that there are several of interest. The most compelling one, however, is that of crisis management and response, as alluded to in the various experiments conducted. Here, responders would be able to use a tool implemented on a tablet device, for instance, en route to or at a crisis scene. This could inform them of related content, who is posting content in or about the area, and how trustworthy that content is (likely strongly influenced by an Emergency Operations Centre's overarching organisational policy). Other cases include supporting decision-making when doing online research for the purchase of a new device or searching for quality information about an emerging topic.

Reflecting on our work in general, there are underlying issues which raise further challenges to be addressed, some practical and others requiring further novel research. One practical challenge is that we assume that the information upon which our approaches are applied is readily consumable. While this may be the case in some situations, there may be practical difficulties in gathering, parsing and reading information in an automated fashion, e.g.: How are topics searched? Is the system real-time? Is information persisted? Typically, we envisage that our system assessing trustworthiness will reside in the user domain and therefore, initial queries could dictate what information to gather and when to access it. There are solutions suggested that constantly scan sources (mainly focusing on social media) that are of specific interest [32,33], searching for information containing particular words. These will be considered in future work, as well as the notions of real-time monitoring, parsing and rating of information. There is also the possibility of drawing on advances in Natural Language Processing (NLP) and Semantic analysis to give further insight into information content, what is being said, and what exactly is meant.

Regarding the processing of the information and acquiring the necessary data to determine the score for the trust and quality factors, proposed methods for measurement rely heavily on the metadata (e.g. timestamps to determine information's recency, or geo-tags to determine the proximity of a source to a reported event). There can be cases, however, where such metadata is absent (the dearth of geo-tagged tweets is a good example) or has been maliciously tampered with, in the case of direct attacks on our system, for instance. For malicious tampering, we hope that the III score assigned to information will be able to reflect this, but where metadata is completely absent, this will be more difficult to handle. There are some approaches we have been considering to address this gap, such as that proposed by Sultanik and Fink [34], and this and other techniques are directly within the scope of future work.

Catering for users' needs when faced with information of unknown quality, albeit of crucial importance, is not the only research area where our approaches could be applied. We envisage adapting the knowledge from our research in understanding and visually communicating trust and quality to explore whether it could be beneficial to other disciplines, such as Cybersecurity; an initial exploration into that problem is presented in [35]. Opportunities have arisen in that field in particular because of the increase in attacks which target human weaknesses, both perceptual and cognitive. If systems and interfaces could be designed that better take these weaknesses into account and also understand what makes users trust or ignore security warnings and messages, this should lead to better security decisions and behaviour.

Competing interests
The authors declare that they have no competing interests.

Authors' contributions
All authors listed contributed significantly in the research and experimentation leading to this article, and the preparation of the manuscript itself. All authors read and approved the final manuscript.

Acknowledgements
This work was conducted as a part of the TEASE project, a collaboration between the University of Oxford, University of Warwick, HW Communications Ltd and Thales UK Research and Technology. The project was supported by the UK Technology Strategy Board's Trusted Services Competition (www.innovateuk.org) and the Research Councils UK Digital Economy Programme (www.rcuk.ac.uk/digitaleconomy).

Author details
[1]Cyber Security Centre, Department of Computer Science, University of Oxford, Oxford, UK. [2]Department of Psychology, University of York, York, UK.

References
1. BBC (2013) Falsely accused student of Boston attacks confirmed dead. In: Falsely accused student of Boston attacks confirmed dead. http://www.bbc.co.uk/news/world-us-canada-22297568. Accessed 30 Sept 2013
2. Agichtein E, Castillo C, Donato D, Gionis A, Mishne G (2008) Finding high-quality content in social media. In: Proceedings of the International conference on Web search and web data mining. pp 183–194, ACM
3. Castillo C, Mendoza M, Poblete B (2011) Information credibility on twitter. In: Proceedings of the 20th international conference on World Wide Web. pp 675–684, ACM
4. Suzuki Y, Yoshikawa M (2012) Mutual evaluation of editors and texts for assessing quality of Wikipedia articles. In: Proceedings of the 8th Annual International Symposium on Wikis and Open Collaboration. ACM
5. Nurse JRC, Rahman SS, Creese S, Goldsmith M, Lamberts K (2011) Information Quality and Trustworthiness: A Topical State-of-the-Art Review. In: Proceedings of the International Conference on Computer Applications and Network Security (ICCANS). IEEE
6. Idris NH, Jackson MJ, Abrahart RJ (2011) Colour coded traffic light labeling: A visual quality indicator to communicate credibility in map mash-up applications. In: Proceedings of International Conference on Humanities Social Sciences, Science & Technology
7. Adler BT, Chatterjee K, De Alfaro L, Faella M, Pye I, Raman V (2008) Assigning trust to Wikipedia content. In: Proceedings of the 4th International Symposium on Wikis. ACM
8. Wang RY, Strong DM (1996) Beyond accuracy: What data quality means to data consumers. J Manag Inform Syst 12(4):5–33
9. Chopra K, Wallace WA (2003) Trust in electronic environments. In: Proceedings of the 36th Annual Hawaii International Conference on System Sciences. p 10–19, IEEE
10. Rahman SS, Creese S, Goldsmith M (2012) Accepting information with a pinch of salt: handling untrusted information sources. In: Security and Trust Management (pp. 223–238). Springer, Berlin Heidelberg
11. Nurse JRC, Creese S, Goldsmith M, Rahman SS (2013) Supporting Human Decision-Making Online Using Information-Trustworthiness Metrics. In: Human Aspects of Information Security, Privacy, and Trust (pp. 316–325). Springer, Berlin Heidelberg
12. MITRE (n.d.) Common Vulnerabilities and Exposures (CVE). http://cve.mitre.org/. Accessed 30 Sept 2013
13. NIST (n.d.) National Vulnerability Database (NVD). http://nvd.nist.gov/. Accessed 30 Sept 2013
14. MITRE Common Attack Pattern Enumeration and Classification. http://capec.mitre.org/. Accessed 4 Sept 2013
15. Helfert M, Foley O, Ge M, Cappiello C (2009) Limitations of weighted sum measures for information quality. In: Proceedings of the 15th Americas Conference on Information Systems
16. Nurse JRC, Agrafiotis I, Creese S, Goldsmith M, Lamberts K (2013) Building Confidence in Information - Trustworthiness Metrics for Decision Support. In: Proceedings of 12th IEEE International Conference on Trust, Security and Privacy in Computing and Communications (IEEE TrustCom-13). IEEE
17. Agarwal B (2007) Programmed Statistics. New Age International Ltd, New Delhi.
18. Chevalier F, Huot S, Fekete JD (2010) Wikipediaviz: Conveying article quality for casual Wikipedia readers. In: IEEE Pacific Visualization Symposium (PacificVis). pp 49–56, IEEE
19. Lipkus IM, Hollands JG (1999) The visual communication of risk. JNCI Monographs 1999(25):149–163

20. Nurse JRC, Creese S, Goldsmith M, Lamberts K (2012) Using Information Trustworthiness Advice in Decision-Making. In: Proceedings of the International Workshop on Socio-Technical Aspects in Security and Trust (STAST) at the 25th IEEE Computer Security Foundations Symposium (CSF-2012), (pp. 35–42). IEEE

21. Bisantz AM, Stone RT, Pfautz J, Fouse A, Farry M, Roth E, Nagy AL, Thomas G (2009) Visual representations of meta-information. J Cognit Eng Decis Making 3(1):67–91

22. Nurse JRC, Agrafiotis I, Creese S, Goldsmith M, Lamberts K (2013) Communicating Trustworthiness using Radar Graphs: A Detailed Look. In: Proceedings of 11th International Conference on Privacy, Security and Trust (PST-2013), (pp. 333–339). IEEE

23. Howell DC (2011) Fundamental statistics for the behavioral sciences, 7th edn. Wadsworth Publishing Company, Belmont, CA.

24. Miller GA (1956) The magical number seven, plus or minus two: some limits on our capacity for processing information. Psychol Rev 63(2):81

25. Saaty TL, Ozdemir MS (2003) Why the magic number seven plus or minus two. Math Comput Model 38(3):233–244

26. Kelton K, Fleischmann KR, Wallace WA (2008) Trust in digital information. J Am Soc Inf Sci Technol 59(3):363–374

27. Marsh S, Basu A, Dwyer N (2012) Rendering unto Caesar the Things That Are Caesar's: Complex Trust Models and Human Understanding. In: Proceedings of 6th IFIP International Conference on Trust management (IFIPTM 2012). Springer, Berlin

28. Tversky A, Kahneman D (1974) Judgment under uncertainty: Heuristics and biases. Science 185(4157):1124–1131

29. Croskerry P (2002) Achieving quality in clinical decision making: cognitive strategies and detection of bias. Acad Emerg Med 9(11):1184–1204

30. Peters E, McCaul KD, Stefanek M, Nelson W (2006) A heuristics approach to understanding cancer risk perception: contributions from judgment and decision-making research. Ann Behav Med 31(1):45–52

31. Furnham A, Boo HC (2011) A literature review of the anchoring effect. J Socio Econ 40(1):35–42

32. Indiana University Bloomington (2012) Truthy - Information diffusion research, http://truthy.indiana.edu. Accessed 30 Sept 2013

33. Streams K (2012) LazyTruth Chrome Extension Fact Checks Chain Emails. http://www.theverge.com/2012/11/14/3646294/lazytruth-fact-check-chain-email. Accessed 30 Sept 2013

34. Sultanik EA, Fink C (2012) Rapid Geotagging and Disambiguation of Social Media Text via an Indexed Gazetteer. In: Rothkrantz L, Ristvej J, Franco Z (eds) Proceedings of the 9th International Conference on Information Systems for Crisis Response and Management ISCRAM-2012, vol 190. pp 1–10

35. Nurse JRC, Creese S, Goldsmith M, Lamberts K (2011) Trustworthy and Effective Communication of Cybersecurity Risks: A Review. In: Proceedings of the International Workshop on Socio-Technical Aspects in Security and Trust (STAST) at the 5th International Conference on Network and System Security (NSS-2011), (pp. 60–68). IEEE

36. Streibel O, Alnemr R (2011) Trend-based and reputation-versed personalized news network. In: Proceedings of the 3rd International Workshop on Search and Mining User-generated contents at the 20th ACM Conference on Information and Knowledge Management. pp 3–10, ACM

6

A decentralized trustworthiness estimation model for open, multiagent systems (DTMAS)

Abdullah M Aref[*] and Thomas T Tran

*Correspondence:
a.m.aref@ieee.org
School of Electrical Engineering and
Computer Science (EECS), University
of Ottawa, 800 King Edward Ave.
Ottawa, Ontario, K1N 6N5, Canada

Abstract

Often in open multiagent systems, agents interact with other agents to meet their own goals. Trust is, therefore, considered essential to make such interactions effective. However, trust is a complex, multifaceted concept and includes more than just evaluating others' honesty. Many trust evaluation models have been proposed and implemented in different areas; most of them focused on algorithms for trusters to model the trustworthiness of trustees in order to make effective decisions about which trustees to select. For this purpose, many trust evaluation models use third party information sources such as witnesses, but slight consideration is paid for locating such third party information sources. Unlike most trust models, the proposed model defines a scalable way to locate a set of witnesses, and combines a suspension technique with reinforcement learning to improve the model responses to dynamic changes in the system. Simulation results indicate that the proposed model benefits trusters while demanding less message overhead.

Keywords: Trust evaluation; Multiagent systems; Locating witnesses

Introduction

In many systems that are common in virtual contexts, such as peer-to-peer systems, e-commerce, and the grid, elements act in an autonomous and flexible way in order to meet their goals. Such systems can be molded as open, dynamic multi-agent systems (MASs) [1]. In open, dynamic MASs, agents can represent software entities or human beings. Agents can come from any setting with heterogeneous abilities, organizational relationships, and credentials. Furthermore, the decision-making processes of individual agents are independent of each other and agents can join or leave the system. As each agent has only bounded abilities, it may need to rely on the services or resources of other agents in order to meet its objects [2]. Agents cannot take for granted that other agents share the same core beliefs about the system or that other agents make accurate statements regarding their competencies and abilities. In addition, agents must accept the possibility that others may intentionally spread false information, or otherwise behaving in a harmful way, to meet their own aims [3]. Therefore, trust evaluating agents, also referred to as trusters (TRs), should use a trust estimation model that allows them to recognize reliable partners in their systems. The estimated assessment should be sufficiently accurate to allow TRs, to distinguish honest trustees (TEs) in the system. In open MAS, the trust evaluation model should not rely on centralized entities but should dynamically update the agents' knowledge sets to take into account new characteristics of the environment. The failure or takeover of any agent must not lead to the failure of the whole system.

TRs use trustworthiness estimation to resolve some of the uncertainty in their interactions and form expectations about the behaviors of others [3]. Trust has been defined in many ways in different domains [1]. For this work the definition used in [4] for trust in MASs, will be adapted. A TE's trustworthiness is considered as a measurement of the TE's possibility to do what it is supposed to do.

Unlike most trust models, DTMAS defines a scalable way to locate a set of witnesses, where there exist a network structure, to consult for indirect trust information. The model uses of a semi-hierarchical structure for MASs, coupled with the notion of the small world networks [5] and the concept of contacts [6]. Furthermore, a suspension technique is used and combined with reinforcement learning (RL) to improve the model responses to dynamic changes in the system. This parameter is used to address the short-term relationship between a TR and the TE under consideration. It helps the TR to address a recently malfunctioning TE that used to be honest for a relatively large number of transactions. The idea is that a TR will stop interacting with a misbehaving trustee immediately, and wait utile it is clear whether this misbehavior is accidental or it is a behavioral change. Because the suspension is temporary, and because TR uses information from witnesses, the effect of accidental misbehavior will phase out, but the effect of a behaviour change will be magnified.

Background and related work

Reinforcement learning (RL)

The reinforcement learning attempts to solve the problem of learning from interaction to achieve an object. An agent starts by observing the currents state s of the environment, then performs an action on the environment, and later on receives a feedback r from the environment. The received feedback is also called a reinforcement or reward. Agents aim to maximize their cumulative reward they receive in the end [7].

There are three well-known, fundamental classes of algorithms for solving the reinforcement learning problem, namely dynamic programming, Monte Carlo, and temporal-difference (TD) learning methods [7]. Unlike other approaches, TD learning algorithms can learn directly from experience without a model of the environment. TD algorithms do not require an accurate model of the environment (contrary to Dynamic Programming) and are incremental in a systematic sense (contrary to Monte Carlo methods). However, unlike Monte Carlo algorithms, which must wait until the end of an episode to update the value function (only then is the return r known), TD algorithms only need to wait until the next time step. TD algorithms are thus incremental in a systematic sense [7].

One of the most widely used TD algorithms is known as the Q-learning algorithm. Q-learning works by learning an action-value function based on the interactions of an agent with the environment and the instantaneous reward it receives. For a state s, the Q-learning algorithm chooses an action a to perform such that the state-action value $Q(s, a)$ is maximized. If performing action a in state s produces a reward r and a transition to state s', then the corresponding state-action value Q (s, a) is updated accordingly. State s is now replaced by s' and the process is repeated until reaching the terminal state [7]. The detailed mathematical foundation and formulation, as well as the core algorithm of Q-learning, can be found in [8] therefore it is not repeated here.

Q-learning is an attractive method of learning because of the simplicity of the computational demands per step and also because of proof of convergence to a global optimum, avoiding all local optima, as long as the Markov Decision Process (MDP) requirement is met; that is the next state depends only on the current state and the taken action (it is worth noting that the MDP requirement applies to all RL methods) [9].

Clearly, a MAS can be an uncertain environment, and the environment may change any time. Reinforcement learning explicitly considers the problem of an agent that learns from interaction with an uncertain environment in order to achieve a goal. The learning agent must discover which actions yield the most reward via a trial-and-error search rather than being told which actions to take as in most forms of machine learning. It is this special characteristic of reinforcement learning that makes it a naturally suitable learning method for trust evaluating agents in MASs. Furthermore, the suitability of RL can also be seen if we note that a TR observes the TEs, selects a TE, and receives the service from that TE. In other words, these agents get some input, take an action, and receive some reward. Indeed, this framework is the same framework used in reinforcement learning, which is why we chose reinforcement learning as a learning method for our proposed agents model [10].

Related work

A wide variety of trust and reputation models have been developed in the literature. Different dimensions to classify and characterize computational trust and reputation models were presented in different surveys [11]. One of the most cited and used general purpose surveys is the one developed by Sabater and Sierra [12]. Their dimensions of analysis were prepared to enhance the properties of the Regret model [13] and show basic characteristics of trust models [11]. The dimensions proposed in [12] are:

- Paradigm type, where models are classified as cognitive and numerical. The numerical paradigm includes models that do not have any explicit representation of cognitive attitudes to describe trust. On the other hand, cognitive paradigm includes models in which the notion of trust or reputation is built on beliefs and their degrees [11].
- Information sources where a set of models use direct experiences while other models use third-party testimonials from other agents in the same environment, refered to as witness. Yet, others depend on the analysis of social relations among the agents [11].
- Visibility, where the trust information of an agent is be considered a private property that each agent build or a global property that all other agents can observe.
- Granularity, which refers to the context-dependence of trust and reputation models.
- Cheating behavior, which refers to the models' assumptions regarding information from witnesses. According to [12] a model may assume that witnesses are honest, or that witnesses may hide information but never lies or, alternatively, that witnesses can be cheaters.
- Type of exchanged information, where information assumed to be either boolean, or continuous estimations.

In addition to the those dimintions, [11] added the procedural dimension to reflect weather or not a bootstrap mechanizime is embeded within the model. Furthermore, they introduced generality dimension to classify models that are general purpose versus the ones that focus on very particular scenarios.

Form architectural point of view, [11,14-16], among others, differentiated between centralized and distributed models. Typically, a central entity manage the reputation of all agents in the first approach, but each agent performs its trust estimations without a central entity in the second approach [16]. Decentralized systems may use flat or hierarchical architectures. Generally speaking, decentralized models are more complex than centralized models. But Single point of failure and performance bottleneck are major concerns for centralized models [17]. centralized models are subject to single point of failure and need powerful and reliable central entities and communication bandwidth [16].

Witnesses locating dimension was described in [14] to reflect weather or not a mechanism is embedded within the model for locating third party information sources. Few general purpose trust, such as FIRE [15] use a distributed approach for this purpose.

This section reviews a selection of decentralized models, and not meant to provide a comprehensive survey of trust modeling literature in MASs. Recent surveys such as [2,11,14] provide further detailed overview of the literature.

A decentralized, subjective, RL based trustworthiness estimation model for buying and selling agents in an open, dynamic, uncertain and untrusted e-marketplace is described in [18] and further elaborated in [7]. This model is based on information collected from past direct experiences where buyers model the trustworthiness of the sellers as trustworthy, untrustworthy and neutral sellers. A buying agent chooses to purchase from a trustworthy seller. If no trustworthy seller is available, then a seller from the list of non-untrustworthy sellers is chosen. The seller's trustworthiness estimation is updated based on whether the seller meets the expected value for the demanded product with proper quality. The update process is maintained after comparing the obtained information about the reliability of a seller against the obtained product quality from the same seller. The model described in [7,18], uses some certain thresholds set to categorize TEs to trustworthy and untrustworthy agents. TRs do not interact with the untrustworthy TEs and among the trustworthy ones, TEs with the highest values are selected as interaction partners. The information is based on TR's personal interaction experience, so the new entry TR has lack of knowledge about different TEs. This model has limited applicability, if repeated transactions between traders are rare [19].

A decentralized, subjective, extension to the model used in [18] is describe in [20,21], to enable indirect trustworthiness based on third party witnesses in e-marketplace. In this model, witnesses are partitioned into trustworthy, untrustworthy and neutral sets to address buyers' subjectivity in opinions. However, the authors did not present any experimental results to justify their theoretical approach [22].

A combined model based on direct and indirect trustworthiness estimation is described in [23] as an extension to [20,21] where advising agents are partitioned into trustworthy, untrustworthy and neutral sets. To address the subjectivity of witnesses, the mean of the differences between the witness's trustworthiness estimation and the buyer's trustworthiness estimation of a seller is used to adjust the advisory's trustworthiness estimation for that seller. Nevertheless, how witnesses are located was not specified.

All those RL based modes [18,21] and [22] classify TEs into three non overlapping sets namely trusted, distrusted, and neutral, also referred to as neither trusted nor untrusted [18]. Similarly, the computational model of [24], classifying TEs as trusted, distrusted or untrusted, where the last one means neither trusted nor distrusted. The authors extend the model of [25] and enriched their model with the use of regret and forgiveness to aid TRs classifying TEs. Their trust estimation at time instance $t + 1$ depends of the current estimation (at time t) and a forgiveness function. The forgiveness function, in turn, depends on both the regret the TR has because it trusted a TE that does not fulfill its needs, and the regret that the corresponding TE express, if any, for not satisfying the demand of the TR. However, this later factor, the regret of the TE, can be misleading if the TE communicate false regret value. The model does not use third party witnesses.

TRAVOS [26] is a well-known decentralized, general purpose trustworthiness estimation model for MASs. The model depends on beta distributions to predict the likelihood of honesty of a TE [19]. If the TR's confidence in its evaluation is below a predefined threshold, the TR seeks advices from witnesses. In TRAVOS, trust is a private and subjective property that each TR builds. The model computes the reliability of witnesses via the direct experience of interaction between the TR and witnesses, and discards inaccurate advices [4]. Unfortunately, it takes certain time for the TR to recognize the inaccuracy of the provided reports from the previously trusted witness agents [4]. The model does not describe how witnesses are located.

Regret [13] is a decentralized, general purpose trustworthiness estimation model for open MASs that takes into account direct experiences, witness information and social structures to calculate trust, reputation and levels of credibility [11]. The model assumes that witnesses are willing to cooperate, and depends on social networks among agents to find witnesses, then uses a set of fuzzy rules to estimate the credibility of witness and therefore there testimonies [2]. Even though the model heavily depends on agents' social networks, it does not show how TRs may build them [15].

Yu and Singh [27], presented a decentralized, subjective trustworthiness estimation model where a TR estimates the trustworthiness of a TE using both its own experience, and advices from witnesses. The model use social network concepts in MASs, where it incorporates for each agent a TrustNet structure. Each agent in the system maintains a set of acquaintances and their expertise. The set of neighbors is a subset of the acquaintances set. The model locate witnesses based on individual agents' knowledge and help through each agent's neighbors without relying on a centralised service [15]. Thus, when looking for a certain piece of information, an agent can send the query to a number of its neighbors who will try to answer the query if possible or, they will refer the requester to a subset of its neighbors [15]. The requester considers the information only if the referred witnesses are whiten a limit in the social tree [11]. To address the subjectivity of witnesses, agents model acquaintances expertise [27]. An agent's expertise is then used to determine how likely it is to have interaction with or to know witnesses of the target agent [15]. The model uses Dempster Shafer evidence theory to aggregate the information from different witnesses.

FIRE [15] is a well-known, general purpose, decentralized, trustworthiness estimation model for open MASs. The model takes into account multiple sources of information. FIRE categorizes trust components into four categories; direct experience called Interaction Trust, Witness Reputation, Role-based Trust and Certified Reputation. The model assumes that witnesses are honest and willing to cooperate and use weighted summation to aggregate trust components [15]. In FIRE, trust is a private and subjective property that each TR builds [11] .

To locate witnesses, FIRE uses a variant of the referral system used by [27], but does not model witnesses experties the same way as in [27]. Instead, FIRE assumes that addressing subjectivity of witnesses is application dependent. To address resources limitations; the branching factor and the referral length threshold parameters were used. The first used to limit the breadth of search and the second is used to limit the depth of search [15]. An important aspect of FIRE is that a TR does not it does not create a trust graph, as in [27], and therefore may quickly evaluates the TE's trust value using a relatively small number of transactions [4]. Unfortunately, if a TE proposes some colluding referee for certified reputation, this source of information and be misleading to the TR [4].

To address the subjectivity of witnesses, most models allows a TR to evaluate the subjectivity of witnesses simply based on their deviations from its own opinions [28]. Most models of trustworthiness estimation allow the communication of trustworthiness information regardless of their contexts, even though trustworthiness estimations are context-dependent [28]. A functional ontology of context for evaluating trust (FOCET), a context-aware trustworthiness estimation model for multi-agent systems, is described in [28] to address the case where a TE may offer different kinds of services in different contexts. These contexts might be totally different or have some features in common.

To measure the effect of a particular context, two individual metrics were defined: 1) a weight matrix (WM) that includes the importance level of each feature of context; and 2) a relevancy matrix (RM) that indicates the degree of similarity of each feature in the first context with the corresponding one in the second context. The WM is a 1∗n matrix, where n is the number of FOCET context features and matrix entry w_i is in [0, 1]. The RM is an n∗1 matrix where matrix entry v_i is in [0, 1] and refers to the degree of importance of the corresponding feature. For example, an agent, called B1, may consider the "fast-enough" delivery of a specific transaction very important and uses 0.9 as the corresponding value in its WM. Similarly, another agent, called B2, may also consider the "fast-enough" delivery of another transaction very important and uses 0.9 as the corresponding value in its WM. However, for B1, "fast enough" means: within one week. On the other hand, for B2, "fast enough" means: within one day. Therefore, B1 will use a lower value for "delivery time" feature in its RM (e.g. 0.2) whereas, B2 will use a higher value for "delivery time" feature in its RM (e.g. 0.7).

Given the WM and RM matrixes, the influence of the context of the direct interaction between the witness agent and the TE in which the trustworthiness of the TE is estimated, known as the context effect factor (CEF), is computed in [28] by

$$CEF = \frac{\sum_{i=1}^{n}(1 - w_i) + w_i * v_i}{n} \qquad (1)$$

TRs subjectively specify a degree of decay p ($0 \leq p \leq 1$) that is based on their policies in order to reduce the influence of the old trustworthiness estimation information adaptively. Time decaying is used to emphasize that utility gain (UG) from recent transaction weigh more compared to UG from old transactions if they have the same absolute value [28].

$$CEF' = e^{(-p\Delta t)} CEF \qquad (2)$$

where Δt indicates the time elapsed since previous interactions took place and can be determined according to the temporal factor concept in FOCET.

A common issue with RL based trust models that TRs do not quickly recognize the environment changes and adapt with new settings. To address this shortcoming, DTMAS uses a technique similar to regret described in [24] in order to improve the model responses to dynamic changes in the system. We propose suspending the use of a TE as a response to unsatisfactory transaction with the TE. The suspension is temporary, and its period increases as the transaction importance increases. Similar to regret [24], it represent an immediate reaction of a TR when it is not satisfied with an interaction with a TE. However, unlike the use of regret in [24], TRs do not depend of any expressed feel of sorry from TEs. Furthermore, suspension is more aggressive. No interactions with suspended TEs as long as it is suspended. On the other hand, while forgiveness is used to reduce the effect of regret in [24], our suspension decays with time only. This is to avoid being mislead by false feel of sorry expressed by the TE, and to allow the effect of accidental misbehavior to phase out, and to magnify the effect of a behavior change as testimonies form witnesses are aggregated. Furthermore, DTMAS integrates context-dependency of third party testimonies [28] together with reinforcement learning for MASs. Similar to [13,15,27] DTMAS defines a way to locate a set of witnesses to consult for indirect trust information. Like [15], using DTMAS a TR does not create a trust graph, as in [27], and therefore may quickly evaluates the TE's trust value using a relatively small number of transactions. Unlike existing trust models, DTMAS uses of a semi-hierarchical structure for MASs, coupled with the notion of the "small world" [5] to help reducing the communication overhead associate locating witnesses.

Framework

In this section, we will outline some general notation, and outline the necessary components and assumptions we make about the underlying trust estimation model, which we will use in the remainder of this work. For the complete list of abbreviation terms used in this study, please see Table 1.

Agent architecture

Based on the agent's architecture described in [29], we assume that each agent has an embedded trust management module. This module stores models of other agents and interfaces both with the communication module and the decision selection mechanism. The subcomponents of the trust management module, in compliance with [29], are listed in the following:

- Evaluate: This component is responsible for evaluating the trustworthiness of other agents using different information sources such as direct experience and witness testimonies. Trust models described in [13,15,18,26,27] are well-known models that belongs mainly to the evaluation component. The proposed DTMAS belong is a trust evaluation model.
- Establish: This component is responsible for determining the proper actions to establish the agent to be trustworthy to others. The work of Tran, et al. [30] is an example of a model designed mainly to address this component.
- Engage: This component is responsible for allowing rational agents to decide to interact and engage others with the aim of estimating their trustworthiness. In the literature, this component is usually referred to as trust bootstrapping and cold start problem. Bootstrapping Trust Evaluations Through Stereotypes [31] is an example model that belongs mainly to this component.

Table 1 Abbreviations

Abbreviation	Description
A	Society of Agents
AD	Honest witness
BSI	Basic Suspension Interval
D	Depth
DT	The direct trust estimation
DTMAS	Decentralized Trustworthiness Estimation Model for Open, Multi-agent Systems
FOCET	Functional Ontology of Context for Evaluating Trust
FT	Fraudulent Threshold
HT	Honesty Threshold
IT	The Indirect Trust estimation
IV	Transaction Importance
MANET	Mobile Ad-hoc NETwork
MAS	Multi-agent System
MC	Monte Carlo
MDP	Markov Decision Process
PNT	The reduction fraction of the reported trust
r	rating
RF	Referee
RL	Reinforcement Learning
RM	Relevancy Matrix
RT	Reported Trust
ST	Satisfactory Threshold
SUS	Suspension penalty
T	Set of possible tasks
TD	Temporal-difference
TE	Trustee
TR	Truster
TRAVOS	Trust and Reputation in the Context of Inaccurate Information Sources
IT	Integrated Trustworthiness Estimation
UG	Utility Gain
TD	Temporal-difference
WDT	Witnesses Differences Threshold
WFT	Witnesses Fraudulence Threshold
WHT	Witnesses Honesty Threshold
WM	Weight Matrix
ZRP	Zone Routing Protocol

- Use: This component is responsible for determining how to select prospective sequences of actions meant on the trust models of other agents that have been learned. The model described in [32] is an example model that belongs mainly to this component.

Agents and tasks

We assume a society of agents, $A = \{a_1, a_2, ...\}$ which is referred to as the global society. We assume a set of possible tasks $T = \{s_1, ..., s_n\}$. The nature of tasks in T are application dependent. A TR that desires to see some task accomplished, considers depending on a trustee to perform the task on its behalf [32].

Agents can communicate with each other in a distributed manner. No central entity exists to facilitate trust-related communications. No service level agreement or contract exists between TRs and TEs. We assume that witnesses are willing to cooperate.

DTMAS
Architectural overview of DTMAS

Finding the set of witnesses that previously interacted with a specific TE, in a pre-request before a TR can use indirect estimation for the trustworthiness of the TE. While many decentralized trust models offer a variety of approaches for trustworthiness estimation, few of them define how to locate the set of witnesses to contact for indirect trust information, and simply assume the availability of this set. Even though a simple broadcast may be used for this purpose, the overhead associated with that may limit the scalability of the model.

We propose the use of a semi-hierarchical model for MASs influenced by Zone Routing Protocol (ZRP)[33], coupled with the notion of the small world networks [5] and the concept of contact [6]. In the context of Mobile Ad-hoc NETworks (MANETs), the ZRP defines a zone for each node as the number of nodes reachable within a radius of R edges (links or hops in MANETs' terminology). Nodes obtain routes to all nodes within their zone in a proactive approach. A reactive routing approach is employed to discover routes to nodes outside a zone [33]. It was suggested in [5] that introducing a small amount of long-range edges is enough to make the world "small", while having short paths between each pair of nodes. In the context of MANETs, [6] suggested the use of a few nodes away from the querying node, which act as shortcuts to convert a MANET into a 'small world'. He referred to those nodes as contacts of the querier.

In the architecture of DTMAS, a zone is defined for each TR as the number of neighboring agents within a radius of R edges. Each TR broadcasts to its neighbors within its zone that it has interacted with a TE whenever such interaction takes place for the first time. This information can be refreshed periodically, or when a change takes place; e.g., when the agent moves into a different neighborhood. Therefore, each TR knows which of its neighboring agents interacted with a particular TE(s). If a TR did not find proper information locally, the TR starts searching outside its zone through its contacts. For DTMAS, contacts are a few agents away from the querying agents, which act as shortcuts to convert a MAS into a small world in order to help the querying agents in locating witnesses, if any. This is useful for highly dynamic systems where agents may change their locations frequently and/or agents frequently enter and leave the system. To alleviate potential overhead and enhance the scalability of the model, a TR can use a number of "contacts", typically far away from itself, to inquire instead of inquiring every node in its neighborhood and the query may be forwarded up to a maximum number of agents called search depth. This has a similar effect to the use of branching factor in Yu and Sing model [27] and in FIRE model [15]. After the presentation of the trustworthiness estimation in subsection "Trustworthiness estimation", the algorithm for locating witnesses is presented in subsection "Locating witnesses" followed by the algorithm for selecting contacts in subsection "Selecting contacts". Both the number of contacts and the search depth, explained in subsection "Locating witnesses", can be used to control overhead, in the MAS.

Trustworthiness estimation

Q-learning based trustworthiness estimation is deemed suitable for uncertain environments in an electronic marketplace where agents discover which actions yield the most satisfying results via a trial-and-error search [34]; therefore, we make use of Q-learning for trustworthiness estimation in DTMAS, for simplicity, we will use RL to refer to Q-learning in this work.

In addition to the use of RL for trustworthiness estimation and the integration of direct and indirect trust estimation without assuming the honesty of witnesses, we propose the integration of a suspension technique to enhance the model responses to dynamic changes in the system.

Employing DTMAS, a TR implement immediate, temporary suspension of the use of a TE if a transaction results in an unsatisfactory result for the TR. The suspension period increases as the transaction importance of the unsatisfactory transaction increases. The objective is to reduce the side effects associated with a TE that built a good reputation, and then, for some reason, began to misbehave. However, suspension should be temporary to avoid excluding a good TE that accidently misbehaved.

If an honest witness a_1 considers a TE as suspended, according to direct transaction between a_1 and TE, then, whenever a TR consults a_1 about TE during the suspension period, $a1$ will report the trustworthiness estimation of TE as -1 (the lowest limit of possible credibility). Furthermore, an honest witness A will reduce the reported trustworthiness estimation of a TE after the end of the suspension period. This reduction is inversely proportional to the time elapsed since the end of suspension. In other words, the reported trustworthiness estimation of a TE will equal the calculated trustworthiness estimation of the TE, based on the history of interaction between a_1 and TE, minus a penalty (i.e. punishment) amount related to time elapsed since the end of suspension period.

When considering the credibility of witnesses, a suspension policy similar to the one implemented in the direct trust component of the model is used. That is, a TR will suspend the use of any witness whose advice is the opposite of the actual result of interaction with the TE. The suspension period increases as the transaction importance increases. Initially all witnesses are considered neutral. In case no witness found the TR depends on the direct experience component alone. The default value of the direct trust value of a TE is the neutral value. Zero is used as the neutral value in DTMAS.

When a TR wants to interact with a TE at time t, the TR avoids any TE that is untrustworthy or suspended and estimates the trustworthiness of TEs using integrated direct and indirect trust components, but avoids the advice of all untrustworthy or suspended witnesses. Then, the TR selects the TE that maximizes its UG of the interaction subject to the constraint that the integrated trustworthiness estimation of the TE is not less than a satisfactory threshold (ST).

Integrated trustworthiness estimation TT(TR,TE)

The trust equation we are interested in should take into consideration TRs' direct trust of TE(s), testimonies from witnesses, subjectivity in witnesses' opinions and credibility of witnesses. Therefore, the total trust estimate can be calculated using Eq (3).

$$TT(TR, TE) = x * DT(TR, TE) + (1 - x) * IT(TR, TE) \qquad (3)$$

- DT(TR,TE) is the direct trust estimation component of the TR for the TE.
- IT(TR,TE) is the indirect trust estimation component of the TR for the TE.
- x is a positive factor, chosen by the TR, which determines the weight of each component in the model.

Direct trustworthiness estimation DT(TR, TE)

TRs use RL to estimate the direct trust of TEs in a way similar to the process in [7]. If the TR is satisfied by the interaction with the TE, Eq. (4) is used to update the credibility of the TE as viewed by the TR.

$$DT_t(TR, TE) = DT_{t-1}(TR, TE) + \alpha\,(1 - |DT_{t-1}(TR, TE)|) \qquad (4)$$

- $DT_t(TR, TE)$ is the direct trust estimation of the TE by the TR at instant $Time_t$.
- The cooperation factor α is positive ($1 > \alpha > 0$) and the initial value of the direct trustworthy estimation is set to zero.

The value of DT(TR, TE) varies from -1 to 1. A TE is considered trustworthy if the trustworthiness estimation is above an honesty threshold (HT), which is similar to the cooperation threshold in [24]. The TE is considered untrustworthy if the trustworthiness estimation value falls below a fraudulent threshold (FT), which is similar to the forgiveness limit in [24]. TEs with trustworthiness estimation values between the two thresholds are considered neutral.

If the TR is not satisfied by the interaction with the TE, Eq. (5) is used to update the credibility of the TE as viewed by TR.

$$DT_t(TR, TE) = DT_{t-1}(TR, TE) + \beta\,(1 - |DT_{t-1}(TR, TE)|) \qquad (5)$$

- β is a negative factor called the non-cooperation factor ($0 > \beta > -1$).

Furthermore, the TR suspends the use of the TE for a period of time determined by equation (6).

$$SUS_t(TE) = SUS_{t-1}(TE) + BSI * IV \qquad (6)$$

- $SUS_t(TE)$ is the suspension penalty associated with the TE at instant $Time_t$.
- The basic suspension interval (BSI) is application dependent, and could be days in an e-marketplace or seconds in a robotics system that has a short life time.
- The transaction importance (IV) is how much the TR values the transaction, not the actual utility gain of the interaction.

We believe that the cooperation and non-cooperation factors are application dependent and should be set by each agent independently. In general, we agree with [7] that the factors should be related to the value gain of the transaction.

When a TR wants to interact with a TE at instant $Time_t$, the TR avoids any TE that is untrustworthy (i.e., $DT_t(TR, TE) < FT$) or suspended (i.e., $SUS_t(TE) > Time_t$).

Indirect trustworthiness estimation

To estimate indirect trust, a TR consults other witnesses who interacted previously with the TE. To adopt different context elements with different importance levels relating to their subjective requirements and environmental conditions, FOCET [28] will be used. An overview of FOCET is presented in subsection Related work.

To reduce the effect of fraudulent and outlying witnesses, a TR excludes reports from any witness where the mean of the differences between the witness's trustworthiness estimation and the TR's trustworthiness estimation of TEs other than the one under consideration is above the witnesses differences threshold (WDT).

To protect the model from attacks in which a TE would obtain some positive ratings and participates in a bad interaction that actually causes large damage, the importance of transactions is considered when estimating the trust. An honest witness AD reports its testimony (RT) about a TE as

$$RT(AD, TE) = \frac{\sum_{tr=1}^{NI} \left(CEF'_{tr} * IV_{tr} * UG_{tr}\right)}{MaxUG * \sum_{tr=1}^{NI} \left(CEF'_{tr} * IV_{tr}\right)} * PNT \tag{7}$$

- PNT=(1-DD(AD,TE)).
- DD (AD, TE) is the reduction fraction of the reported trust of TE because of previous suspension(s).
- DD= 0 if TE has never been suspended previously; otherwise $DD = SUS(TE)/Age(AD)$.
- NI is the number of transactions between the AD and the TE,
- CEF' is the decay factor applied to the CEF. as calculated by equation 2.
- UG_{tr} is the utility gain of the transaction tr with the TE
- and MaxUG is the maximum possible UG of a transaction. Obviously, MaxUG is application dependent.

A TR will calculate the indirect trust (IT) component as

$$IT(TR, TE) = \frac{\sum_{i=1}^{N} RT(AD_i, TE)}{N} \tag{8}$$

- N is the number of trustworthy witnesses.
- RT (AD_i, TE) is the testimony of witness i about TE

Each TR updates its rating for the witnesses after each interaction as follows:

- If the transaction was satisfactory for the TR and the witness AD had recommended TE or If the transaction was NOT satisfactory and AD's opinion was "not recommend", then the trustworthiness estimation of witness AD is incremented by

$$DT(TR, AD) = DT(TR, AD) + \gamma \left(1 - |DT(TR, AD)|\right) \tag{9}$$

- Otherwise, the trustworthiness estimation of AD is decremented by

$$DT(TR, AD) = DT(TR, AD) + \zeta \left(1 - |DT(TR, AD)|\right) \tag{10}$$

Furthermore, the TR suspends the use of the witness for a period of time determined by

$$SUS_t(AD) = SUS_{t-1}(AD) + WBSI * IV \tag{11}$$

- γ and ζ are positive and negative factors respectively and chosen by the TR as cooperation and noncooperation factors.
- SUS_t(AD) is the suspension penalty associated with AD at time instant t
- As with the BSI, the Witnesses Basic Suspension Interval (WBSI) is application dependent.

- Transaction importance (IV) is the how much the TR values the transaction, not the actual UG of the interaction.
- $SUS_t(AD)$ is decremented by one each time step. However, it can not be less than zero.

The value of DT (TR, AD) varies from -1 to 1. A witness is considered trustworthy if the trustworthiness estimation is above the witnesses honesty threshold (WHT). A witness is considered untrustworthy if the trustworthiness estimation falls below the witnesses fraudulence threshold (WFT). Witnesses with trustworthiness estimation values in between the two thresholds are considered neutral.

When a TR wants to interact with a TE at instant $Time_i$, the TR avoids any AD that is untrustworthy or suspended.

Locating witnesses

Algorithm 1 Witnesses Locating Algorithm

---

1. The TR (A) sends a witnesses-locating request to its contact agents
2. The request contains the depth of search (D).
3. Upon receiving the request, each contact (Ci) checks the value of D.

    (a)   If D > 1, the contact agent decrements D by 1 and forwards the request to all its contacts.

    (b)   If D is equal to 1, Ci sends to A the set of witnesses in its zone (if they exist).

4. The reply takes the reverse path of the request.
5. As the reply travels back to A, each intermediate contact agent on the way to A appends the list of witnesses in its zone that match the request.

A TR can use Algorithm 1, to find witnesses who interacted previously with a TE. The algorithm is inspired by the routing protocol for MANETs in [35]. The TR a first initiates the witnesses locating request with search depth D_1 = initial_value to its contacts, if it does not receive satisfying feedback within a specified time, it creates a new request with $D_i = 2*D_i-1$ and sends it again to its contacts. Each contact observes that $D_i \neq 1$, reduces the value of D_i in the request by 1 and forwards it to its contacts that serve as second-level contacts for a. In this way the request travels through multiple levels of contacts until D reduces to 1. Depending on the quality of the provided information (if any), a may choose to continue searching for other alternatives probably with larger D up to a predefined upper level for D. In this way the value of D is used to query multiple levels of contacts in a manner similar to that of the expanding ring search. However, this would be more efficient than a system-wide broadcast search as the request is directed to individual agents (the contacts).

In addition to the described mechanism for locating witnesses, a TR can request the TE to provide a list of referee agents where a referee RF of a TE; is a TR that previously interacted with TE, and willing to share its experience with other TRs.

Selecting contacts

Each TR can decide on the number of contacts K to use depending on how cautious the agent is, how important the interaction is, and how much resources the agent has. To reduce the maintenance overhead, contacts can be selected dynamically, when a TR requests an advice on a TE using the Contacts Selection Algorithm (Algorithm 2).

Algorithm 2 Contacts Selection Algorithm

---

1. If positional information is available for agents: The TR (A) views the area around itself as a set of sectors each with angle equal $2\pi/K$

    (a) A border agent B_i is a TR that is R hops from A. Agent A determines the sector in which B_i is located as the sector of the angle $\tan^{-1}(\triangle Y/\triangle X)$ where $\triangle Y$ is the vertical difference between B_i and A, and $\triangle X$ is the horizontal difference between B_i and A.

    (b) Then, for each sector, agent A selects a "non-untrustworthy" and "non-suspended" border agent B_i in the sector that maximize the distance $B_i\text{-A} = \sqrt{(Y_{B_i} - Y_A)^2 + (X_{B_i} - X_A)^2}$

    (c) Each B_i will select a "non-untrustworthy" and "non-suspended" border agent C_j such that C_j is located in the same sector as B_i from the point of view of A, and C_j maximize the distance $C_j\text{-A} = \sqrt{(Y_{c_i} - Y_A)^2 + (X_{C_i} - X_A)^2}$

2. If positional information is not available for agents: We use an algorithm adapted from [35].

    (a) The querying agent (A) select a number of "non-untrustworthy" and "non-suspended" border nodes equal to the number of contacts (K), such that the querying agent (A) has disjoint paths to border agents.

    (b) Each selected border agent B_i then selects "non-untrustworthy" and "non-suspended" border agent C_j such that C_j has the maximum number of hops to A and B_i has disjoint paths to both C_j and A with the hope to reducing the overlap between areas covered by different contacts

3. If the querying agent (A) cannnot select the required number of contacts by either alternative 1 or alternative 2

    (a) Requesting agent (A) randomly select a number of "non-untrustworthy" and "non-suspended" agents from its zone to satisfy the number of contacts K.

    (b) Each randomly selected agent B_i randomly selects a "non-untrustworthy" and "non-suspended" agent C_j from its zone as the contact for A.

Performance analysis

It is often difficult to find suitable real world data set for comprehensive evaluation of trust models, since the effectiveness of various trust models needs to be assessed under different environmental conditions and misbehaviors [2]. Therefore, in trust modeling for MASs research field, most of the existing trust models are assessed using simulation or synthetic data [2]. One of the most popular simulation test-beds for trust models is the agent reputation and trust (ART) test-bed proposed in [36]. However, even this test-bed does not claim to be able to simulate all experimental conditions of interest [2].

Simulation environment

We use simulation to evaluate the performance of the proposed model for distributed, multi-agent environment using the discrete-event multi-agent simulation toolkit MASON [37] with TEs, as agents that provide services, and TRs, as agents that consume services. As with [15], we assume that the performance of a TE in a particular service is independent from that in another service. Therefore, without loss of generality, and in order to reduce the complexity of the simulation environment, it is assumed that there is only one type of service in the system simulated and all trustees offer the same service with, possibly, different performance. In order to study the performance of the proposed trust model for TE selection, we compare the proposed model with the well known FIRE trust model [15], one of the well-known trust models for MASs and among the few models that define a mechanism to locate witnesses.

All agents are placed randomly in a rectangular working area. Each TR has a radius of direct communication to simulate the agent's capability in interacting with others and all other agents in that range are direct neighbors of the TR. The simulation step is used as the time value for transactions. Interactions that take place in the same simulation step are considered simultaneous. TRs evaluate the trustworthiness of the TE(s), and then select the one that promise the maximum transaction importance. Locating TEs is not part of the trust model; therefore TRs locate TE(s) through the system. Table 2 gives the number of agents, the dimensions of the working area and other parameters used for DTMAS and those used for the environment. FIRE-specific parameters are similer to those used in [15].

Having selected a provider, the TR then uses the service and gains some benefits from the interaction. This benefit is referred to as UG. A TE can serve many users in a single step, and all TRs attempt to use the service in every step. For DTMAS, after each interaction, the TR updates the credibility of the provider and the credibility of witnesses. We did not consider the case where a TE can record all or part of the history of interactions to be able to provide referee lists to other TRs upon request.

We consider a mixture of well behaving and poorly behaving TEs in addition to those who alter their behavior randomly. Witnesses are categorized as agents who are honest, agents who strictly report negative feedback, agents who strictly report positive feedback, agents who report honestly with probability 0.5, or agents who strictly lie in that they always report the opposite of their beliefs. TRs are associated with nine different context categories randomly.

Since agents can freely join and leave, and they may be moving, the agent population can be very dynamic and agents can break old relationships and make new ones during their lifetimes. To address this, in our simulation, agents change their locations in the working area. When a TR changes its location, it will have a new set of neighbors. Therefore, changing an agent's location changes its relationships with others, as well as its individual situation.

In each step, TRs are assumed to move random distances between 0 and MaxMove in a random direction between 0 and 2π. When they reach an edge of the working area, they simply enter the working area from the opposite edge.

When bidding, an honest TE bids its UG category. This value is considered the transaction importance, whereas the UG of the interaction for the TR is the transaction importance divided by the context category of the TR to address its subjectivity.

Table 2 Values of used parameters

Parameter	Value
Working area diminutions	1000 X 1000
Total number of TE	12
Total number of TR	81
Zone radius	3
Number of contacts	5
direct communication radius	100
MaxMove	707.1
Depth of contacts' level	2
Number of TE changing behavior	7
Number of context categories	10
Basic suspension interval	10
Number of utility gain categories	9
Witnesses changing behavior	10
Witnesses always report negative	7
Witnesses always report positive	7
Witnesses report neutral 50%	7
Witnesses always lie	7
Maximum utility gain	10
Inerval of TE changing behavior	10
TE cooperation factor	0.01
TR non-cooperation factor	-0.03
Witnesses cooperation factor	0.01
Witnesses non-cooperation factor	-0.03
Direct trust fraction	0.5
Degree of decay	0.01
HT	0.5
FT	-0.5
WHT	0.5
WFT	-0.5
ST	0
WDT	0.5
FIRE -Specific Parameters	
Local rating history size	10
DT recency scaling factor	$-(5/\ln(0.5))$
Branching factor	2
Referral length threshold	5
Interaction trust coefficient	2
Role-base trust coefficient	2
Witness reputation coefficient	1
Certified reputation coefficient	0.5
Reliability function parameter: Interaction trust	$-\ln(0.5)$
Reliability function parameter: Role-base trust	$-\ln(0.5)$
Reliability function parameter: Witness reputation	$-\ln(0.5)$
Reliability function parameter: Certified reputation	$-\ln(0.5)$

Experimental results

We analyze the performance of DTMAS in terms of UG, and the overhead of locating witnesses, and we compare the performance of DTMAS with that of FIRE. However, because FIRE assumes that witnesses are honest, we present the performance comparison of DTMAS with the use of honest witness as well as with the use of witnesses who are not necessarily honest. We refer those two variates as "DTMAS - 2" and "DTMAS - 1" respectively.

Figure 1 shows that selecting TEs using DTMAS performs consistently better than FIRE in terms of UG per agent, which indicates that DTMAS helps TRs select honest TEs from the population and gain better utility than that gained using the FIRE model. This is because DTMAS prefers TEs who have not been suspended for a longer time over those who promise higher benefits but have been suspended within a shorter period, in order to reduce the effect of a TE whose performance starts to reduce. DTMAS integrates FOCET [28] to adopt different context elements with different importance levels relating to their subjective requirements and environmental conditions. Additionally, using DTMAS, a TR excludes reports from any witness where the mean of the differences between the witness's trustworthiness estimation and the TR's trustworthiness estimation of TEs other than the one under consideration is above the witnesses differences threshold (WDT).

Figure 2 shows the average communication overhead per transaction per agent, calculated as the total number of messages passing over all edges divided by multiplication of the number of transactions by the number of TRs, when employing the witnesses locating strategy. The figure shows that DTMAS with contact-based architecture has lower overhead than FIRE for locating witnesses. This is due to the contact selection strategy, which attempts to reduce the overlapping of contacts' zones. Suspending the use of unreliable witnesses reduces the overhead associated with consulting a larger number of witnesses, slightly as shown in the figure. It worth noting that the two variants of DTMAS used in this study, the one with honest witnesses and the one with witnesses who are not necessarily honest, achieve a comparable results in terms of average UG and communication overhead. This indicates the ability of DTMAS to reduce the effect dishonest witnesses, and work in an environment where a subset of witnesses may provide misleading information.

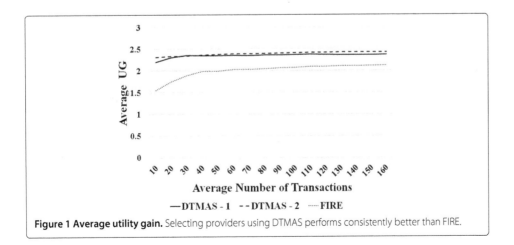

Figure 1 Average utility gain. Selecting providers using DTMAS performs consistently better than FIRE.

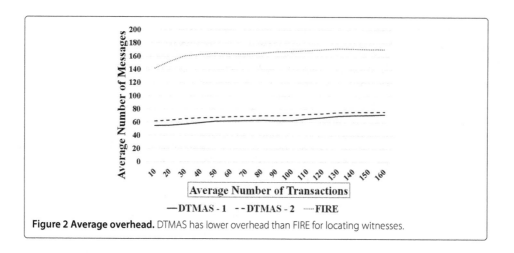

Figure 2 Average overhead. DTMAS has lower overhead than FIRE for locating witnesses.

Conclusions and future work

This paper presented DTMAS; a scalable, decentralized model for trust evaluation. We presented a generic architecture that reduces the overhead of locating witnesses, which enhances the scalability of the architecture of the model. DTMAS allows direct and indirect sources of trust information to be integrated, thus providing a collective trust estimation. Additionally, we introduced a temporary suspension mechanism to reduce the harm of misbehaving TEs and misbehaving witnesses. In short, we believe DTMAS can provide a trust measure that is sufficiently useful to be used in an open and dynamic MAS.

Dynamically determining parameter values such as the weight of each component in the model (x), HT, FT, etc., enabling TEs to actively promote their honesty to allow new and honest TEs to enter the system, and enhancing the scalability of the proposed architecture are considered as future work.

Competing interests
The authors declare that they have no competing interests.

Authors' contributions
AA participated in the creation of the model, carried out the simulation studies, and drafted the script. TT participated in the creation of the model and supervised the research. All authors read and approved the final manuscript.

References
1. Ramchurn SD, Huynh TD, Jennings NR (2004) Trust in multi-agent systems. Knowledge Eng Rev 19(1):1–25
2. Yu H, Shen Z, Leung C, Miao C, Lesser VR (2013) A survey of multi-agent trust management systems. Access, IEEE 1:35–50
3. Burnett C (2011) Trust assessment and decision-making in dynamic multi-agent systems. PhD thesis, Department of Computing Science, University of Aberdeen
4. Khosravifar B, Bentahar J, Gomrokchi M, Alam R (2012) Crm: An efficient trust and reputation model for agent computing. Knowl-Based Syst 30:1–16
5. Watts DJ, Strogatz SH (1998) Collective dynamics of 'small-world' networks. Nature 393(6684):409–10
6. Helmy A (2002) Architectural framework for large-scale multicast in mobile ad hoc networks. In: IEEE International Conference on Communications, ICC 2002, April 28 - May 2, 2002, New York City, NY, USA Vol. 4. pp 2036–2042. doi:10.1109/ICC.2002.997206
7. Tran TT (2010) Protecting buying agents in e-marketplaces by direct experience trust modelling. Knowl Inf Syst 22(1):65–100
8. Sutton RS, Barto AG (1998) Introduction to Reinforcement Learning. ISBN0262193981, 1st edition. MIT Press, Cambridge, MA, USA

9. Georgoulas S, Moessner K, Mansour A, Pissarides M, Spapis P (2012) A fuzzy reinforcement learning approach for pre-congestion notification based admission control. In: Proceedings of the 6th IFIP WG 6.6 International Autonomous Infrastructure, Management, and Security Conference on Dependable Networks and Services, AIMS'12. Springer, Berlin, Heidelberg. pp 26–37

10. Tran TT (2004) Reputation-oriented reinforcement learning strategies for economically-motivated agents in electronic market environments. PhD thesis, David R. Cheriton School of Computer Science, University of Waterloo

11. Pinyol I, Sabater-Mir J (2013) Computational trust and reputation models for open multi-agent systems: a review. Artif Intelligence Rev 40(1):1–25. doi:10.1007/s10462-011-9277-z

12. Sabater J, Sierra C (2005) Review on computational trust and reputation models. Artif Intell Rev 24(1):33–60

13. Sabater J, Sierra C (2001) Regret: A reputation model for gregarious societies. In: Fourth Workshop on Deception Fraud and Trust in Agent Societies Vol. 70

14. Noorian Z, Ulieru M (2010) The state of the art in trust and reputation systems: A framework for comparison. J Theor Appl Electron Commer Res 5(2):97–117

15. Huynh TD, Jennings NR, Shadbolt NR (2006) An integrated trust and reputation model for open multi-agent systems. Autonomous Agents Multi-Agent Syst 13(2):119–154

16. Wang Y, Vassileva J (2007) Toward Trust and Reputation Based Web Service Selection: A Survey. Int Trans Syst Sci Appl 3(2):118–132

17. Wang Y, Zhang J, Vassileva J (2014) A super-agent-based framework for reputation management and community formation in decentralized systems. Comput Intell 30(4):722–751

18. Tran T, Cohen R (2004) Improving user satisfaction in agent-based electronic marketplaces by reputation modelling and adjustable product quality. In: 3rd International Joint Conference on Autonomous Agents and Multiagent Systems (AAMAS 2004), 19-23 August 2004, New York, NY, USA. IEEE Computer Society, Los Alamitos, CA, USA. pp 828–835. ISBN0-7695-2092-8

19. Kerr RC (2007) Toward secure trust and reputation systems for electronic marketplaces. Master's thesis, Computer Science, University of Waterloo

20. Regan K, Cohen R, Tran T (2005) Sharing models of sellers amongst buying agents in electronic marketplaces. In: Proceedings of Decentralized, Agent Based, and Social Approaches to User Modelling Workshop, Edinburgh, UK Vol. 1. pp 75-79

21. Regan K, Cohen R (2005) Indirect reputation assessment for adaptive buying agents in electronic markets. In: Proceedings of business agents and the semantic web workshop (BASeWEB 05) Decentralized Agent Based Social Approaches User Modell Workshop, Victoria, British Columbia, Canada Vol. 1. pp 121–130

22. Beldona S (2008) Reputation based buyer strategies for seller selection in electronic markets. PhD thesis, Electrical Engineering & Computer Science, University of Kansas

23. Beldona S, Tsatsoulis C (2007) Reputation based buyer strategy for seller selection for both frequent and infrequent purchases. In: ICINCO 2007, Proceedings of the Fourth International Conference on Informatics in Control, Automation and Robotics, Robotics and Automation 2, Angers, France, May 9-12, 2007. INSTICC Press, Portuga. pp 84–91. ISBN978-972-8865-83-2

24. Marsh S, Briggs P (2009) Examining trust, forgiveness and regret as computational concepts. In: Golbeck J (ed). Computing with Social Trust. Human Computer Interaction Series. Springer. pp 9–43

25. Marsh SP (1994) Formalising trust as a computational concept PhD thesis Department of Mathematics and Computer Science, University of Stirling, Scotland , UK

26. Teacy WL, Patel J, Jennings NR, Luck M (2006) Travos: Trust and reputation in the context of inaccurate information sources. Autonomous Agents Multi-Agent Syst 12(2):183–198

27. Yu B, Singh MP (2002) An evidential model of distributed reputation management. In: Proceedings of the First International Joint Conference on Autonomous Agents and Multiagent Systems: Part 1, AAMAS '02. ACM, New York, NY, USA. pp 294–301. doi:10.1145/544741.544809. http://doi.acm.org/10.1145/544741.544809

28. Mokhtari E, Noorian Z, Ladani BT, Nematbakhsh MA (2011) A context-aware reputation-based model of trust for open multi-agent environments. In: Cory B, Pawan L (eds). Advances in Artificial Intelligence - 24th Canadian Conference on Artificial Intelligence, Canadian AI 2011, St. John's, Canada, May 25-27, 2011. Proceedings. Springer, Heidelberg, Berlin Vol. 6657. pp 301–312. ISBN:978-3-642-21042-6

29. Sen S (2013) A Comprehensive Approach to Trust Management. In: International conference on Autonomous Agents and Multi-Agent Systems, AAMAS 13, Saint Paul, MN, USA, May 6-10. International Foundation for Autonomous Agents and Multiagent Systems, St. Paul, MN, USA. pp 797–800. ISBN:978-1-4503-1993-5

30. Tran T, Cohen R, Langlois E (2014) Establishing trust in multiagent environments: realizing the comprehensive trust management dream. In: Paper presented at the 17th International Workshop on Trust in Agent Societies, Paris, France, on the 6th May 2014

31. Burnett C, Norman TJ, Sycara K (2010) Bootstrapping Trust Evaluations Through Stereotypes. In: Proceedings of the 9th International Conference on Autonomous Agents and Multiagent Systems: Volume 1 - Volume 1. International Foundation for Autonomous Agents and Multiagent Systems, Series AAMAS '10, Richland, SC. p 8. ISBN:978-0-9826571-1-9

32. Burnett C, Norman TJ, Sycara KP (2011) Trust decision-making in multi-agent systems. In: Walsh T (ed). IJCAI 2011, Proceedings of the 22nd International Joint Conference on Artificial Intelligence, Barcelona, Catalonia, Spain, July 16-22, 2011. AAAI Press/International Joint Conferences on Artificial Intelligence, Menlo Park, California. pp 115–120

33. Haas ZJ (1997) A new routing protocol for the reconfigurable wireless networks. In: Proceedings of IEEE 6th International Conference on Universal Personal Communications, 12-16 October San Diego, CA, USA Vol. 2. pp 562–566. doi:10.1109/ICUPC.1997.627227, ISSN:1091-8442

34. Tran TT, Cohen R (2002) A reputation-oriented reinforcement learning strategy for agents in electronic marketplaces. Comput Intelligence 18(4):550–565

35. Helmy A (2005) Contact-extended zone-based transactions routing for energy-constrained wireless ad hoc networks. Vehicular Technol, IEEE Trans 54:307–319

36. Fullam KK, Klos TB, Muller G, Sabater J, Schlosser A, Topol Z, Barber KS, Rosenschein JS, Vercouter L, Voss M (2005) A specification of the agent reputation and trust (art) testbed: Experimentation and competition for trust in agent societies. In: Proceedings of the Fourth International Joint Conference on Autonomous Agents and Multiagent Systems, AAMAS '05. ACM, New York, NY, USA. pp 512–518. doi:10.1145/1082473.1082551

37. Luke S, Cioffi-Revilla C, Panait L, Sullivan K, Balan G (2005) Mason: A multiagent simulation environment. Simulation 81(7):517-527

7

Understanding user perceptions of transparent authentication on a mobile device

Heather Crawford[1]* and Karen Renaud[2]

*Correspondence:
hcrawford@fit.edu
[1] Department of Computer Sciences
and Cybersecurity, Florida Institute
of Technology, 150 W. University
Blvd., Melbourne, FL 32901, USA
Full list of author information is
available at the end of the article

Abstract

Due to the frequency with which smartphone owners use their devices, effortful authentication methods such as passwords and PINs are not an effective choice for smartphone authentication. Past research has offered solutions such as graphical passwords, biometrics and password hardening techniques. However, these solutions still require the user to authenticate frequently, which may become increasingly frustrating over time. Transparent authentication has been suggested as an alternative to such effortful solutions. It utilizes readily available behavioral biometrics to provide a method that runs in the background without requiring explicit user interaction. In this manner, transparent authentication delivers a less effortful solution with which the owner does not need to engage as frequently. We expand the current research into transparent authentication by surveying the user, an important stakeholder, regarding their opinions towards transparent authentication on a smartphone. We asked 30 participants to complete a series of tasks on a smartphone that was ostensibly protected with varying degrees of transparent authentication. We then surveyed participants regarding their opinions of transparent authentication, their opinions of the sensitivity of tasks and data on smartphones, and their perception of the level of protection provided to the data and apps on the device. We found that 90% of those surveyed would consider using transparent authentication on their mobile device should it become available. Furthermore, participants had widely varying opinions of the sensitivity of the experiment's tasks, showing that a more granular method of smartphone security is justified. Interestingly, we found that the complete removal of security barriers, which is commonly cited as a goal in authentication research, does not align with the opinions of our participants. Instead, we found that having a few barriers to device and data access aided the user in building a mental model of the on-device security provided by transparent authentication. These results provide a valuable understanding to inform development of transparent authentication on smartphones since they provide a glimpse into the needs and wants of the end user.

Keywords: Usability; Usable security; Authentication; Transparent; Mobile

Introduction

The popularity of mobile devices is undeniable. According to the International Data Corporation (IDC), more smartphones were sold in 2012 than desktop and laptop computers combined [1]. Their popularity may be attributed in part to their increasing functionality – technological advances in computing have allowed smartphones to become increasingly powerful, which in turn supports greater functionality. Smartphones offer a wide range of capabilities, such as email account access, news updates, access to the Internet and device location via GPS. As a result of their increased (and increasing) functionality, smartphones are able to access and store personally identifying information. Potentially private data such as medical details, sensitive business information, personal pictures and voicemails have been recovered from mobile devices, despite being deleted [2]. This confirms that users do indeed store these kinds of data on their devices.

The sensitivity and amount of information stored on smartphones underscores the need for an effective, flexible method of managing device access. Historically, passwords (including sketched varieties) and PINs have been used to protect smartphones from unauthorized access, but they are easily cracked or weakened through sharing, reuse or using weak secrets [3,4]. The cumbersome nature and unpopularity of repeatedly typing a password on a mobile device has led users to avoid accessing business data on their mobile devices [5]. Furthermore, such secret knowledge techniques provide *point-of-entry* security: once the secret has been entered, the user has access to all on-device services and data.

A better method for providing mobile device security would be to use the data-rich interactions a user has with their device to create a pattern which acts as a baseline to support comparison with users in order to verify that the current user is the owner. Such authentication, which may be based on behavioral biometrics such as keystroke dynamics and speaker verification, allow for *transparent, continuous authentication* that runs in the background as the user goes about using their device as usual. With transparent authentication, the user is no longer required to explicitly authenticate because the uniqueness in their device interactions provides the basis for authentication decisions. The biometric information may be gathered via the rich set of input sensors that characterize modern mobile devices, such as microphones, keyboards, screen-based touch input and gyroscopes. These multimedia-based sensors have the benefit of familiarity to the user since they are already used for a variety of on-device functions. The rich and potentially seamless nature of sensor-based biometric data provides transparent authentication with the possibility of providing a more granular approach to application and data access by thresholding tasks. This scheme implies that the device maintains an ongoing level of confidence that the current user is also its owner, referred to as *device confidence*. It is continuously updated based on biometric matches and non-matches. If device confidence is above a defined certainty level, called *task confidence*, then the task (or data access) is allowed; otherwise it is denied.

Transparent authentication has the following benefits over traditional methods:

Effortless: Since the behavioral biometrics are gathered in the background during regular device use, the user does not need to interrupt their tasks to authenticate.

Fine-grained access control: Traditional authentication mechanisms allows for point-of-entry authentication; once the user has provided the correct shared secret, all data and functionality on the device is accessible. Transparent authentication has the capability of providing access control on a per-task or per-data basis.

Continuous: The utilized behavioral biometrics may be selected to take advantage of the most frequently performed tasks such as typing or speaking. In this way, there is a rich source of information used to authenticate, which supports a continuous authentication model. More information about transparent authentication on mobile devices can be gained from these publications [6,7].

Transparent authentication may elicit concerns regarding privacy, among others, that could lead users to reject it due to its utilization of behavioral biometrics [8]. In order for transparent authentication to gain support, users will have to accept it and consent to have the mechanism installed on their device, potentially barring their legitimate access to their own applications and services. The user is an important stakeholder in the implementation of transparent authentication; thus, their opinions and needs must be considered early in the design process to encourage acceptance. In this paper, we present the findings of a study carried out to determine whether transparent, continuous authentication is likely to be accepted by users. Finally, we elicit initial impressions regarding the use of transparent authentication on a mobile device as an alternative to traditional access control.

Study goals

Alternative authentication methods have been widely researched over the last decade [9-12], but rarely deployed outside a lab setting. In general, researchers might not fully understand how or if users will use, bypass or accept new security mechanisms. Feasibility studies demonstrate that behavioral biometrics show potential as the basis for the decision–making in a transparent authentication system [13,14]. The outstanding question is whether mobile device users would choose to use such a method to protect their devices and data.

Our study has two purposes: (1) to determine whether the participants feel a transparent authentication method on a mobile device provides adequate security, and, if so, whether they would consider using it on their own mobile devices; (2) to elicit user opinions and suggestions to inform the design of a mobile device transparent authentication mechanism. Our study was designed to answer the following related research questions:

- What are the participant's opinions of, and reactions to, using a transparent authentication method on a mobile device?
- What is the participant's perceived level of security while using a mobile device that employs transparent authentication?
- How do participants react to barriers blocking them from completing their intended tasks?

These questions are intended to examine *user opinions* of a possible transparent authentication mechanism, and not the security provision of such a mechanism. The security provision can be carried out once a prototype system has been made available.

Background and literature review
Smartphone authentication
Mobile devices are rapidly changing the landscape for interactive computing. The technology provided by Google Android, Apple iOS, Blackberry, and Microsoft Windows Phone has enabled smartphones and tablets to become the computing device of choice for mobile workers. The success of these devices, and the applications that run on them, is largely due to the multitude of sensors embedded in them. These sensors, such as

the microphone, camera, gyroscope and accelerometer, not only provide information to applications but the sensed information can also be leveraged to facilitate continuous authentication by taking advantage of the unique patterns that exist in the user's interaction with the device.

Despite the range of interactions available due to mobile device sensors, passwords and PINs remain commonplace authentication methods due to their familiarity, ease of use and the existence of code libraries, widgets and development toolkits that support them as authenticators. The availability of development tools that support password use is bolstered by corporate policies that mandate password use on mobile devices that store or access corporate information, despite studies that have shown that these policies can produce passwords that are less secure than expected [15]. Such policies often dictate the length and required characters in a password, but do not allow for alternative authentication methods. Interestingly, corporate password policies have been shown to negatively impact employee productivity due to their strict, inflexible nature [16]. Identifying the issues and limitations of passwords with respect to mobile devices may provide information for corporations, enabling updates to their corporate policies to include authentication alternatives.

While passwords and PINs may be a commonly used means of authentication on mobile devices due to their simplicity and familiarity, studies have shown that they are often slow and cumbersome to type on a soft keyboard [17,18]. Add to this the commonality of mistakes when typing on a mobile device keyboard [19,20] and it becomes clear that passwords and PINs are not the most effective means of authentication for mobile devices. Bao *et al.* performed a user study into the use of passwords as an authenticator on mobile devices, and found that users find passwords on mobiles so cumbersome and slow that they avoided accessing data on their devices unless necessary [5].

Passwords and PINs have the benefit of being familiar to users, as well as being easy to use and implement, even in legacy systems. In order to retain these benefits, research has been performed to attempt to strengthen passwords and PINs rather than replacing them. Vibrapass uses haptic interaction with a separate mobile device to improve the secrecy of entering a password or PIN into an easily observed public terminal, such as an ATM [21]. The mobile device, which is linked to the terminal during the interaction, vibrates to indicate that the user should enter an incorrect secret (i.e., an incorrect character in a password or PIN), while lack of vibration indicates that a correct entry is expected. Their study showed that the system was acceptable to users with about half the characters as incorrect secrets, while providing a higher security level. Such a system could easily be used for password and PIN entry on a mobile device, as was studied by Bianchi *et al.* in creating the Phone Lock method [22]. Phone Lock takes advantage of smartphone sensors to add non-visual audio and haptic cues, such as spoken numbers audible via earphones and vibrations linked to numbers, to PINs of various lengths. Their goal is to provide a PIN entry mechanism that is resistant to shoulder-surfing attacks, but retains the familiarity and ease-of-use attributed to PINs. Their results showed that the users were significantly faster entering the PIN via audio rather than vibration cues, and that the error rate remained insignificantly different between the two modalities [22]. These methods provide valuable insight into how passwords and PINs may be strengthened by using sensor information, but are not necessarily useful for transparent authentication. It may be argued that these methods are *more* invasive than simple passwords or

PINs because they require additional knowledge or interaction as the price for increased security.

Alternatives to passwords and PINS

Graphical passwords [9,23], gestures and screen interaction [24-27] and biometric authentication [28,29], among others, are emerging as viable alternatives to passwords and PINs as smartphone authenticators. Biometrics, in particular, have seen much research interest in terms of authentication, likely due to the range of sensors available on modern mobile devices. Since more than one sensor is usually available, research has focused on using the fusion of multiple biometrics to downplay any limitations that a single biometric may have. For instance, Hazen *et al.* have studied a method that fuses facial and speech recognition [30]; their results show that error rates can be reduced by up to 90% when compared to the error rates for each individual biometric. Trewin *et al.* compared three biometric modalities (face, voice and gestures) to the use of passwords as authenticators on mobile devices in terms of the effects of each on the time, effort, number of errors and task disruption [29]. Their study showed that the biometric modalities facilitated speedier authentication as compared to password entry. Their results enforce the idea that user frustration with password and PIN-based authentication on smartphones provides a possibility for a change in authentication modality, but that a high level of usability must be achieved and maintained to encourage user acceptance of the new method.

Transparent authentication

Both secret knowledge-based methods and the methods suggested to strengthen them require the user to explicitly authenticate prior to using their device. This effortful authentication is unsuited to the mobile device environment, which is characterized by a bursty use pattern – the smartphone is used very frequently but for short periods of time [31,32]. Generally, with each new interaction the user must re-authenticate, which may become frustrating or annoying to the device owner. The purpose of transparent authentication is to remove the barriers often caused by security tasks – a user rarely picks up a device with the intention of performing security measures. Instead, the user has some other task to accomplish, and authentication is a barrier that must be overcome in order to achieve their intended task.

Research into the area of transparent authentication has begun to gain attention as mobile devices become increasingly ubiquitous, store increasingly private information, and as the shortcomings of passwords and PINs on these devices becomes abundantly clear. Hocking *et al.* have introduced a transparent authentication method called Authentication Aura, in which the user is authenticated by polling the area around the device to determine whether known devices associated with the owner are in close proximity [33]. Their results show that such initial polling can reduce the number of explicit authentication requests by up to 74%, which significantly reduced user frustration with authentication. Similarly, De Luca *et al.* have studied a transparent authentication method that is based on patterns in how the user interacts with the touch screen on a mobile device [25]. Their study found that adding such a behavioral biometric to password use increased security and made the device more resistant to attacks. Clarke *et al.* have performed significant research into transparent authentication, both in terms of assessing frameworks and prototypes [34] and possible biometrics for use in transparent authentication, such as facial recognition [35] and keystroke dynamics [36]. Karatzouni *et al.* have expanded upon the work of Clarke *et al.* to assess user opinions of both current authentication methods and transparent methods [37]. They found that users envisage a need for increased security on mobile devices due to the nature of the data kept on them, and that biometrics and transparent authentication were feasible replacements for traditional authentication methods. These results show that user privacy, and how they perceive the risks to their personal information, is an important consideration in deploying a transparent authentication method.

User privacy on smartphones

Frequent pop-ups and warnings desensitize the user to the risks they are accepting, particularly if no immediate negative consequences are seen as a result [38]. Therefore, a warning system that uses fewer warnings may help increase security on smartphones. Furthermore, users are confused by permission warning systems such as those used by Android [39,40], in which the user is notified about the particular services an app wishes to access for each app installed. Apps that provide fine-grained privacy control have been examined and found useful in managing app permissions [41], but allowing the user to remove Android permissions statically has been found to cause instability in app functionality [42]. Centralized permission systems, such as those used by the Apple App Store in which the app and its use are governed by a centralized body, remove the burden of judging an app's need for access to potentially private or sensitive information. While this seems to be a positive benefit, it may be the case that the body making the ultimate decision has different sensitivities regarding what is private, offensive or potentially risky. Research has been performed to examine this gap between the user and the decision-making body's concerns regarding smartphone privacy and security, as summarized in the following sections.

Smartphone user privacy concerns

Building upon research that shows privacy and security are concerns to mobile device owners, recent work has identified some of the specific threats that concern users. Chin *et al.* found that users are more concerned about privacy on their smartphones compared to their laptops [43]. They report that users are significantly less willing to perform tasks such as making purchases and accessing their bank accounts or medical records on their mobile devices. They found no significant difference, however, when the users were asked about sharing photos and viewing work-related email on their smartphones versus laptops [43].

Similarly, Felt *et al.* surveyed 3115 smartphone users about 99 selected risks associated with their smartphone and ranked them according to the number of users who would be "very upset" if the risk occurred [44]. They found that the warnings presented to users upon installing an app in both Android and iOS do not correspond to user concerns regarding privacy and security on mobile devices.

Mobile devices, when compared to desktop and laptop computers, have been shown to have different needs in terms of privacy and security [45]. Many smartphones have two types of mobile device PINs [46,47]; the handset PIN, which protects the handset itself and the data stored in its memory from unauthorized use, and the SIM PIN, which protects the use of, and data stored on, the SIM. Kowalski and Goldstein found that most users did not understand the difference between (and the existence of) the SIM and handset PINs [48]. They further found that only 32% of users in their study were aware of the SIM PIN, and none of them chose to use it. Similarly, Botha *et al.* distinguish between SIM and handset PINs and recognize that these are simply point-of-entry security mechanisms that have limited ability to provide content security [49]. They also found that PIN entry on mobile platforms may be tedious and annoying to the owner because "mobile users may simply wish to take the device out of their pocket to check a schedule entry and could therefore find that entering the password takes longer than the task itself". ([49], p.3). These findings suggest the need for a more nuanced and effortless mechanism for mobile devices.

User opinions of transparent authentication

Biometrics are one way of providing transparent authentication. Jones *et al.* performed a survey of respondents to determine what, if any, technologies were familiar and acceptable to respondents as a potential authenticator [50]. They found that biometrics such as fingerprints were nearly as acceptable to users as passwords (67% for fingerprints compared to 70% for passwords), but that smart cards, other tokens and biometrics such as iris and retina scans were far less acceptable (32%, 27% and 44%, respectively).

In order to determine the current (at the time) use of authentication on mobile devices, Clarke and Furnell conducted a survey of 297 mobile device owners to determine mobile device use frequency, the type of authentication they used, and their attitudes toward future authentication options [46]. They found that 83% of respondents favored the use of biometrics-based authentication. They further found that approximately 33% of respondents did not use a password or PIN at all.

As a follow-up study, Clarke *et al.* performed an evaluation of a behavioral biometrics-based transparent authentication framework called Non-Intrusive and Continuous Authentication (NICA) [6]. Their evaluation found that 92% of the 27 participants reported that the NICA prototype provided a more secure environment when compared to other forms of authentication such as passwords and PINs.

Our study builds upon research in mobile authentication, behavioral biometrics and transparent authentication by determining whether users might accept transparent authentication on smartphones, what their attitudes are towards the use of behavioral biometrics to authenticate themselves on a smartphone, and what their opinions are towards having a more granular (rather than binary) approach to smartphone authentication and security.

Research design and methodology

We performed a lab-based, between-groups study ([51], p. 74) in which 30 participants were asked to complete seven tasks using an Apple iPhone provided by the experimenter. The seven tasks were divided into three security levels (Low, Medium, and High) that represented the level of device confidence the device must have before the task is allowed. *Device confidence* is a term that defines the certainty the device has that its current user is also the device owner. Each participant was randomly assigned to one of three groups that determined the level of transparent authentication they experienced. After the participant completed the tasks, we asked them a series of questions in a semi-structured interview about their experiences with the transparent authentication mechanism, their general impressions of, and perceived needs for, smartphone security. Figure 1 depicts the interplay between the different aspects of the experimental setup.

Our study was designed with three main constraints in mind. First, we intended to elicit information about the users' opinions of the *privacy and security* provided by the mobile device, rather than their opinions of the functionality of or applications on the device. Second, because the users were given an iPhone, we made it clear that the device itself was unimportant to their opinions and that a similar security method may be available for Android or Blackberry devices. Finally, since our study did not make use of a real transparent authentication method on the provided device, we had to be very careful to maintain the impression that one was there, even in the face of questions from participants.

We obtained IRB permission to perform the study prior to its start. All personally identifying information was coded to protect the identity of the participant, and all interviews, which were recorded with the participant's permission, were deleted after transcription.

Participants

The 30 participants ranged in age from 20 to 58 years (median = 26.5, mean = 29.4). 60% of the respondents were Android users with various handset models, 13% were iPhone users, 10% used a Blackberry and the remaining 17% used a feature phone (e.g., non-smart phone). 17% of the participants were female and 83% were male. Participants were recruited in August and September 2012 using convenience sampling methods, through a combination of email invitations and requests for participation to university classes. Participants were not required to own or use a smartphone, and were paid an honorarium for their time.

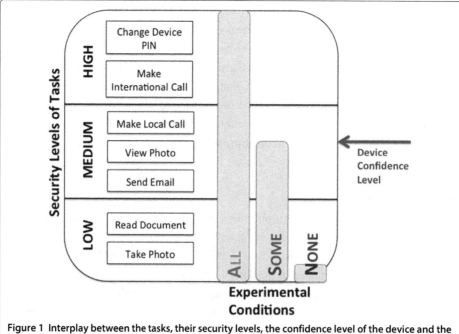

Figure 1 Interplay between the tasks, their security levels, the confidence level of the device and the confidence level of the authentication mechanism.

On their own devices, 27% of participants used a 4-digit PIN, with the same percentage using a sketched password. 30% used no security method, and the remaining 16% used another method, such as encryption and passwords.

Apparatus and materials

Participants used an Apple iPhone 4 with iOS version 5.1.1 during the experiment. It was pre-loaded with the study application and preset with the participant's randomly assigned category and a starting device confidence of "Low". This made it possible to remove potential confounding effects of different operating system versions, and the presence of current applications and stored data on the device. It also limited potential interference from other applications on the participant's own device. The experimenter recorded the interviews using the Voice Memo application on another iPhone. Afterwards, participants were asked a series of questions in a semi-structured interview. The study was conducted in an on-campus meeting room, with one participant and one experimenter per interview; each session lasted 60 to 90 minutes.

Methods

The study began with a short demographic-style questionnaire. The participant was then given an introduction to transparent authentication, introduced to the Apple iPhone and told that a transparent authentication method was running on the device. Transparent authentication was described to the participant as a method that works in the background and allows or disallows access to apps and services such as WiFi or 3G by using the way the device is used to determine if the current user is the legitimate device owner. They were told that the biometrics used were how you speak (voice) and how you type (keystroke dynamics), and that as more and more of these were gathered, the device would become increasingly certain as to who was using the device. Participants were also told that, due to study constraints, no biometrics had been pre-gathered about them so the study would start with a device confidence of Low. Finally, they were told to use a challenge question to explicitly authenticate where they felt it was needed (i.e., if they thought it might help them complete a task).

The participant was told how to turn off or override the transparent authentication mechanism should they wish to at any point during the experiment. This was implemented via a Settings button that popped up a view that asked the participant to confirm that they wanted to turn off security. The transparent authentication could be turned on via the same set of steps. The ability to turn off transparent authentication was provided to build a mental model of the intended transparent authentication method, although the actual working of the application depended on the category to which the participant had been assigned. Each participant began the study with a combination of a "Low" security level and whichever category they had been randomly allocated to.

Upon launching the study application, the participant was prompted via an alert box to set the answer to their challenge question, as a backup to the transparent authentication method. If a task was not allowed because device confidence was lower than the required task confidence, the participant was notified via an alert that stated the required task confidence and the current device confidence, and asked if the participant wanted to answer their challenge question. If the participant said yes (and answered it correctly), the device confidence was increased by one level (i.e., from Low to Medium or Medium to High).

After providing a baseline answer to the challenge question, the participant saw the main "Tasks" screen. All participants completed the tasks in the same order. The order of the tasks were from low to high security, and dictated whether or not explicit authentication was required.

Tasks

Participants completed seven tasks that were classified into one of three security levels: Low, Medium and High based on the general level of privacy or sensitivity a particular task warranted. The task security required a matching device confidence level for the participant to be able to carry them out. The transparent authentication mechanism needs to have that level of confidence that the participant is indeed the authorized device owner. Since the experiment does not last long enough for the participant to build up a device confidence of sufficient level, the device confidence was initially set to "Low" and the participant was instructed to assume that it was based on previous interaction with the device.

The tasks were chosen to represent commonly-used mobile device functionality, as well as for their familiarity to participants. Since one of the study goals was to determine how easy or difficult each task was for the participants, by selecting familiar tasks we hoped that an observed increase in task difficulty could be attributed to additional steps required by the underlying security provision. Participants were reminded that the purpose of the study was to assess their impressions of the security features of the transparent authentication method as described to them, and not their ability to achieve the tasks, nor the user interface of the application itself.

The tasks given to each participant are detailed below.

Low security tasks

Read Document: The participant was asked to open and read the contents of an ostensibly private document from a list. The document titles, such as "PasswordList", "PrivateThoughts" and "BankStatement", were chosen to create a sense of privacy; while the documents did not actually belong to the participant, they were asked to assume that they did. This task was intended to determine whether assigning security levels by *task* was a realistic way of mapping device confidence to device functionality, since we expected that different participants would prefer to have the ability to place documents at different security levels.

Take Photo: The participant was asked to use the mobile device to take a photo of a diagram on a whiteboard in the study locale. Taking a photo on a device may not be a high-security task since it is unlikely to cause the device owner undue concern since the photos can simply be deleted. Exceptions exist, especially in cases of applications where a photo can be immediately uploaded to social networking sites, for example. However, it is envisaged that the ability to view photos rather than take them would fall under a higher security level; this task was included to test this assumption.

Medium security tasks

Send Email: The participant was asked to send an email to a particular email address, with text provided by the experimenter. The text was intended to be somewhat private to give the participant a feeling that they would want to prevent others from seeing it. This task was used to provide a way for the user to type during the study in order to provide a biometric match or non-match based on their typing pattern. No biometric classification was actually performed; either match or non-match was randomly selected after typing. After the task was completed, the participant was told whether their keystroke dynamics biometric was a match or non-match and the device confidence level was adjusted up or down accordingly.

View Photo: The participant was asked to view a photo, generally the one of the diagram that had been taken in the "Take Photo" task. This task was intended to get the participant thinking about viewing photos versus taking photos and the security ramifications of others viewing their (potentially private) photos.

Make Local Call: The participant was asked to dial a local phone number provided by the experimenter and leave a message of a private nature. The financial aspect of making a call was of interest in this task; the assumption was that a local call would have a lower fee associated with it compared to a long distance call. This task also allowed the participant to speak and thus (theoretically) provide a biometric sample. The participant was informed whether their speaker verification biometric was a match or a non-match, with the accompanying adjustment of the device confidence level.

High security tasks

Make International Call: The participant was asked to dial a long-distance telephone number and leave a message provided by the experimenter. Dialing a long-distance call may have a high cost associated with it compared to making a local call, which allowed us to explore participant opinions on financial risks. This task also allowed another speaker verification match or non-match, much like as described for the Make Local Call task.

Change Device PIN: The participant was asked to change the device PIN. This task was included to assess how participants perceive the value of the PIN mechanism and the security it provides.

Each participant was allocated randomly to one of three categories, which affected their ability to complete the tasks. The participant was able to perform the tasks firstly based on the current device confidence and secondly on their pre-set category, as described below:

None: Participants were unable to complete any task, regardless of their current device confidence. This category is intended to assess the level of frustration seen in a seemingly broken authentication method – one that prevents task completion. This category tested whether the participant would choose to turn off or override the mechanism in frustration. This level of authentication mimics the first stages of using a transparent method, when the device owner has not yet provided sufficient biometric samples to create a baseline for future comparison.

All: Participants were able to complete *all* on-device tasks regardless of device confidence. This category tested whether the participant becomes distrustful of the security provided, since they are neither challenged nor denied access to data or device functionality. This level is meant to mimic the situation in which the mobile device user suspects the security method is malfunctioning and allowing full access to all users.

Some: Participants were able to complete the tasks that were at their current or lower device confidence only. As such, the application compared the current device confidence to that of their current task, and allowed access if the task level was lower than or equal to the current device confidence. The participant could raise the device confidence by answering their challenge question or by having a matching keystroke or speaker biometric result. This category mimics the real design and use of a transparent authentication method, where the current device confidence is matched to a pre-chosen task authentication level.

The participants were asked to attempt all tasks on the device via the custom designed application and in the same order. Observations were recorded throughout. In particular, the number of times the challenge question was used per task was recorded, as was the number of times the transparent authentication method was deactivated. These values were expected to vary depending on category. Those in the "All" category, for instance, should not have needed to turn off security or answer the challenge question. The participants in the "None" category, however, may have overridden the mechanism by using the challenge question several times before turning off the mechanism altogether. Once the participants had completed all tasks, they were asked a series of questions about their experience in a semi-structured interview (see Appendix A for interview questions). Interview questions explored candidate attitudes towards mobile phone security in general and attempted to gauge initial impressions about the acceptability of a transparent authentication mechanism controlling access on a mobile device.

The participants were debriefed after the interview: they were told that no transparent authentication mechanism had actually been running on the device and that none of their details had actually been collected. They were informed of the three participant categories, and to which category they had been allocated.

Analysis

The independent variable for this study is the level of transparent authentication the user sees: a high level (the "None" category), a moderate level (the "Some" category) or a low level (the "All" category). The dependent variables were their subjective perceptions of transparent authentication and their subjective beliefs about the security level provided by a transparent authentication method. These were measured using ordinal-answer questions (i.e., Likert scale questions) as well as a semi-structured interview. The recordings were transcribed for analysis purposes. We thus had three kinds of data to inform our analysis:

1. Transcribed interviews;
2. Data recorded by the application about what the participants actually did; and
3. Demographic data from the applicants.

We analyzed the data quantitatively and qualitatively. The demographic and descriptive data was charted and analyzed in order to ensure that we understood what the participants did during the experiment. The interview transcripts were analysed using the Grounded Theory approach ([52], p. 101) to elicit themes in the answers. We worked first through the transcripts of the interviews line by line, coding the data. This process was repeated to ensure that all codes had been identified. The codes were then grouped into themes.

Statistical significance of the ordinal data was determined initially using the Kruskal-Wallis test. This test was chosen for its applicability to non-parametric data with three or more independent participant categories. In cases where the Kruskal-Wallis test indicated statistical significance, the inter-category significance was tested in a pairwise manner using the Mann-Whitney test, which is suitable for use on non-parametric data where there are two independent groups.

Results

No participants withdrew, and each participant was paid £6 for their time. The final themes that emerged from the qualitative analysis are discussed below.

The first theme, *basis for security level choice*, provides an insight into user perceptions when choosing security levels. The second theme, *security as a barrier*, answers the questions about the helpful nature of removing security barriers, and whether they use or override transparent authentication and why. Questions regarding perceived security are answered by the final theme, *user perceptions of authentication*.

Theme 1: basis for security level choice

Participants expressed concerns regarding data and functionality on current mobile devices, and expressed the desire to protect them. One reason given for not using an access control mechanism on their own devices was the inconvenience of having repeatedly to enter a password or PIN. This confirms the arguments of [31,32] about the impact of the bursty usage pattern on the inconvenience imposed by current access control mechanisms that require authentication at each use.

Figure 2 depicts the participant responses for the required security confidence level for each experimental task, grouped into *High, Medium* and *Low* as an aggregate of the three participant categories.

All participants, regardless of category, considered "Change Device PIN" a high security task. This result indicates that changing PINs was considered a "meta-security" task, in that use of a PIN controls access to device data, functionality and settings as well as providing point-of-entry access control. Some participants noted that control over the device and its functionality belongs to the person who knows the PIN. One participant referred to a PIN-locked device as a "brick": essentially useless.

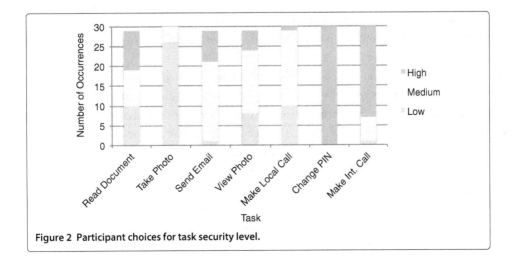

Figure 2 **Participant choices for task security level.**

Participants did not consider the "Take a Photo" task to be high security. Taking a photo adds data to the device rather than editing or exposing existing data, and is easily deleted by the device owner. Therefore, this task is not a source of data leakage or privacy concerns to the participants in our study.

The "Read Document" task had a relatively even split between high, medium, and low security. This shows the link between the *contents* or *subject* of the document and the preferred level of security. Participants preferred to have the ability to assign a more fine-grained security level based on the sensitivity of each document's contents, rather than based on the meta-task. When they were required to choose an overall level, many participants chose the higher security level with the intention of better protecting any private or sensitive information that might reside in one of the documents. A clear distinction was made between personal and business-related documents: the former were referred to using the terms "personal" or "private", which denote a sense of ownership. Work-related documents, on the other hand, were referred to as "sensitive" and "dangerous", which imply that the participant understood that there was some risk associated with their being exposed, but this does not suggest a sense of ownership.

The differences between the preferred security levels per task reveal a number of considerations that participants implicitly took into account to determine the sensitivity of a given task. Some major themes emerged during the analysis of the responses. When participants were asked why they chose a particular security level for the task in question, responses fell into one of the following categories.

Perceived risks

The study participants cited the following risks that affected the levels to which they allocated the tasks:

Data Loss or Exposure: This risk is strongly linked to data ownership. For example, participants drew a clear distinction between loss of personal data as opposed to work–related data. Loss of personal data, they considered, implied loss of reputation or "face" that could be difficult to overcome in the device owner's social circles. Loss of business data, on the other hand, could result in loss of a job and professional reputation.

Impersonation: The risk of impersonation was a strong theme, particularly with respect to sending email. The anticipated severity ranged from pranks by friends who may send a false email to a mutual friend, to more serious examples that included sending negative or derogatory email to the owner's boss, or using the owner's email as a way of "doing evil things" or committing fraud.

Financial Loss: This risk was prevalent when discussing making telephone calls, both international and local. The perceived risk of financial loss was directly proportional to the chosen security level. For instance, international calls were considered more expensive than local calls, and thus were assigned a higher security level. Thus, associating financial loss with a particular task makes it more likely that device owners would be prepared to perform specific actions in order to protect the data or to authorise the task.

Embarrassment (Misinterpretation of Actions): Strongly related to impersonation and loss of reputation, embarrassment was a risk factor that was associated with many of the tasks. Participants were particularly concerned with embarrassing or compromising photos and other images, as opposed to emails, text messages, or documents. The embarrassment risk was not in the subject of the photo itself, but with the risk that others may see it, or perhaps pass it onto mutual friends via email or MMS.

Identity Theft and Fraud: Identity theft differs from impersonation in that the latter is single instance and ID theft encompasses multiple instances and has much more serious consequences due to the importance of identity in transactions such as banking.

Damage control after data compromise: Once a person's identity is stolen, it can take a significant amount of time to reclaim the identity and to rebuild reputation and credibility including aspects such as credit ratings and credit card ownership. In less far-reaching situations, there is an aspect of damage control linked to the embarrassment and reputation risks, since time and effort must go into rebuilding status in both social and professional spheres.

Access to some data or tasks may imply access to others: Coupling of tasks and data access is common on mobile devices. For instance, access to email probably permits access to the device owner's address book. It was unclear to many study participants whether protecting one task implied protection of all associated tasks or data, so they tended to assign a higher required security level in these cases.

Data/task sensitivity

If a task or data were considered sensitive, personal or private, the participants in all three categories felt that the device confidence level required to access the task or data should be higher than that of a non-sensitive task or data. This expressed desire to protect themselves is understandable, yet we found that many of the participants did not consider their own on-device data either important or sensitive. Many expressed the belief that there was little data of value on their device. They were also generally uninformed about how much data their own device actually held at the time of the experiment.

Control over device & data

Device owners expressed a strong need to control physical access to their own device and the data it contained. Some participants achieved this simply by keeping the device on their person all the time.

"...it never really leaves my pocket..."

Techniques such as supervision and physical possession of the device were used to ease security concerns. Device sharing was cited as a motivation for assigning security levels according to perceived data sensitivity. Participants stated that implementing public and private folders or memory locations would allow them to share their device without risking sensitive data exposure. Such sharing was done in a very controlled fashion: participants supervised device use and considered this non-negotiable.

The sense of control over the device and data extended to the choice of security mechanism. When asked whether they would consider using a transparent authentication method on their own mobile device, 90% of the participants answered in the affirmative, at least on a trial basis. The participants stated that they would "play around with" the method to "see how it worked". Such a statement shows the owner's desire to know how the security provisions work, and this applies equally to a transparent method. They clearly wanted to have control over its operation and access to data. Furthermore, our interpretation suggested that they might well also want to understand how intrusive the security provision will be before committing to its use. Reasons advanced for why they would subsequently remove such a transparent authentication mechanism included annoyance, too-frequent explicit authentication requests, or if they believed the method was not restricting access with sufficiently rigour: "allowed anybody to access my stuff". Interestingly, many participants stated that their feeling of device and data security was enhanced by barriers existing to control data access, even though some considered such barriers annoying and frustrating.

One participant suggested that since biometric usage data was already on the device, it would be a positive benefit to the device owner to have this data used to enhance security provision:

> "In the past people might have raised concerns about storing that kind of information [keystrokes and voice] on a mobile device, but ...if it's already on there, why not use it to provide additional security? It's practically already recording your voice, and it's already recording what you're typing and things like that, so, I'm not sure the objection of storing that information on a mobile device is valid."

Theme 2: security as a barrier

There was a clear theme of security being a barrier, or hurdle, that emerged from the analysis. Participants seemed somewhat conflicted about this. On the one hand the perceived access control delivered by said barrier gave them a sense of security. On the other hand, these barriers sometimes prevented them from accessing their own data and device functionality. Many stated that they would remove access control software if it got "too annoying", or required them to explicitly authenticate too often, something that they considered would be "frustrating".

The "Some" category had a large number of explicit authentication requests, as shown in Figure 3. This stands to reason since this category had the least access to tasks out of all categories when transparent authentication was enabled. The "None" category also had a large number of explicit authentication uses because they too saw its use as a means of accomplishing their task. It was expected that they would quickly learn that using explicit authentication did not allow them to complete the tasks. This assumption held for all but one participant, who felt that repeatedly entering the challenge question was providing the mechanism with keystroke biometric information. The differences between

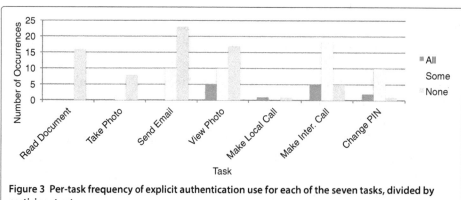

Figure 3 Per-task frequency of explicit authentication use for each of the seven tasks, divided by participant category.

the "Some" and "None" groups and supporting comments show that the device owner's threshold for interruption is relatively low. They also reinforce the "security as a barrier" mental model, and confirm that their usual tasks are the main goal when using a mobile device.

To determine the effect of barriers on security provision, the participants in all categories were able to disable transparent authentication. Figure 4 shows the frequency with which participants disabled transparent authentication on a per-task basis. The "Some" category participants did not disable transparent authentication at all. Their mental model matched the actual operation of transparent authentication; therefore they were able to complete all tasks using explicit authentication and biometric matches only. The "All" category members chose to disable transparent authentication before the tasks that required higher device confidence. The "None" category disabled transparent authentication frequently for the first task, and increasingly less with subsequent tasks. Participants in the "None" group chose to disable transparent authentication permanently early in the experiment, which suggests that task completion might well trump precaution, especially when security becomes intrusive and overly arduous.

The theme of security as a barrier is strongly supported by the behavioral recording data. Explicit authentication requests force the user to stop the task they intend to complete and resume it once authentication is complete. The perceived level of frustration with such interruptions was cited as a major reason that participants in this study would consider disabling a transparent authentication method on their device.

One of the main reasons for the amount of frustration felt when security provision was seen as a barrier was lack of access to the data on the device. Figure 5 shows the participants' perceived levels of data protection provided by transparent authentication, per category. Participants in the "All" category thought the data was poorly protected since they indicated an answer higher than neutral in only two cases. This category had the fewest security barriers with which to contend. Conversely, many of the "None" category members, who had the most security barriers, considered the data very or somewhat well protected. The "Some" category members ranged somewhere between the "All" and "None" extremes. They had a moderate number of security barriers, and largely considered the data either somewhat protected or not protected, but never very well protected.

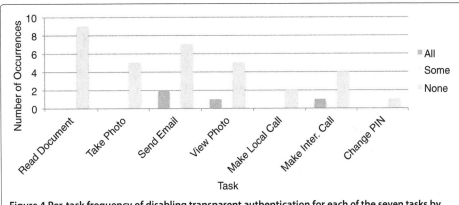

Figure 4 Per-task frequency of disabling transparent authentication for each of the seven tasks by participant category.

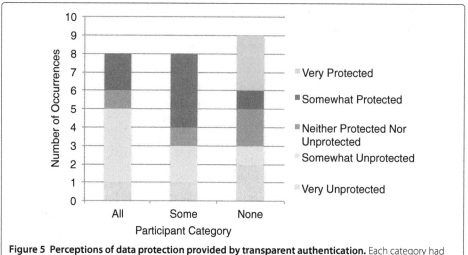

Figure 5 Perceptions of data protection provided by transparent authentication. Each category had 10 participants; some declined to provide a specific value, as shown by the shorter bars.

Theme 3: perceptions of authentication

The participants seemed to believe that "something is better than nothing" in terms of security provision. This, however, does not explain the actions of those participants who chose to use no security at all on their own device. Other things, perhaps the barriers provided by explicit authentication methods, discourage them from using security on their devices even though they seem to believe that it is useful. This theme can also be seen in the previously stated opinions on PIN use. Participants saw the PIN as a powerful overarching security method for protecting the functionality and data on their own device. It seemed, however, that the other side of the coin, not being able to access their own data, outweighed the need for this barrier being put in the way of potential thieves. The barrier was too uni-dimensional: it offered the same obstacle to intruder and legitimate user.

When they had expressed their opinion of their own device's access control offerings, including whether they used it or not, we asked them directly about whether they thought transparent authentication would be an attractive alternative. Figures 6 and 7 show participant opinions on transparent authentication provision compared to either their current mobile device security method (Figure 6) or to no security at all (Figure 7). These figures show that the majority of participants felt that the security provided by transparent authentication was at least as good as what they currently use on their own device, and much better than no security at all. This feeling of a secure environment may encourage users to adopt transparent authentication as an alternative to traditional passwords and PINs.

The overwhelming majority of the participants would consider using a transparent authentication method. However, the participants offered several areas of improvement for transparent authentication, as follows:

1. Assign required device confidence on a per-task or per-folder basis, in addition to by task or application. Have pre-set values that can be changed by owner to reduce initial setup effort.

2. Minimize the number of explicit authentication interruptions as much as possible as these are considered frustrating and intrusive.

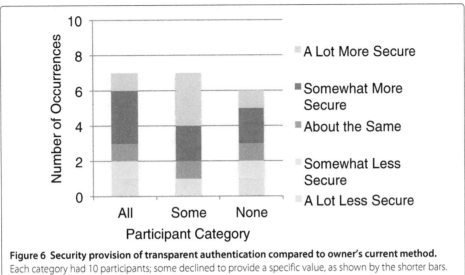

Figure 6 Security provision of transparent authentication compared to owner's current method. Each category had 10 participants; some declined to provide a specific value, as shown by the shorter bars.

3. Keep the owner's data on the owner's device. Do not share it with others, or remove it from the device in order to implement a security mechanism.
4. Minimize effort for frequent tasks. This can be managed by allowing the device owner to select a lower device confidence for tasks that are accessed frequently.

Quantitative analysis

We analysed the information gathered by the application itself while the participants used it, in order to determine whether there were differences between the different experimental groups. Table 1 shows the frequency of explicit authentication use per task; the majority of explicit authentication use occurred from participants in the "Some" and "None" groups. This is an expected result since they were the groups that experienced the most barriers when attempting to complete tasks. It can be argued that the "Some" group should see the most explicit authentication use because its use actually helped the

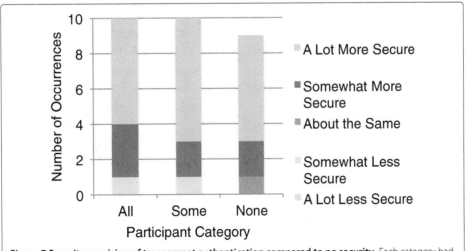

Figure 7 Security provision of transparent authentication compared to no security. Each category had 10 participants; some declined to provide a specific value, as shown by the shorter bars.

Table 1 Total number of explicit authentication attempts per experimental group (All, Some and None) for each task

Task	Group			ρ Value
	All	Some	None	
Read document	0	0	16	**< 0.0001**
Take photo	0	1	8	**0.0436**
Send email	0	10	23	**0.0008**
View photo	5	10	17	0.1290
Make local call	1	0	1	0.5958
Change device PIN	2	10	1	**0.0009**
Make international call	5	19	5	**< 0.0001**
Totals	13	50	71	
Median	1	10	8	
Mode	0	10	1	
Std. Dev.	2.27	7.13	8.61	

The last column shows statistical significance calculated using the Kruskal-Wallis test. ρ < 0.05 are significant (bolded values).

participants to complete their tasks, where the use in the "None" group was not reinforced by being able to then complete the task. Table 1 shows that the "None" group (71 instances, median = 8, mode = 1, SD = 8.61) actually had more instances of explicit authentication use than the "Some" group (50 instances, median = 10, mode = 10, SD = 7.13). However, this result is affected by the contribution of one study participant who misunderstood the function of the challenge question. During the semi-structured interview, the participant stated that they chose to enter their answer repeatedly because they thought that their typing biometrics were being sampled and that task access would be granted when the mechanism had "enough" biometric information. This had the result of artificially increasing the total number of explicit authentication requests seen for the "None" group. This participant's data is included in this analysis rather than being removed as an outlier because the data the participant contributed in other parts of the study (frequency of turning off transparent authentication, qualitative answers to semi-structured interview questions) showed no such bias, and were valuable in assessing other aspects of the hypotheses that drove this work.

There were significant differences in the frequency of explicit authentication use in all tasks except *View Photo* and *Make Local Call* (see Table 1). The order of the tasks had an effect on these values, since all participants began the study at a Low device confidence, and thus had access to at least the first two tasks as they were Low security. The exception is the "None" category, since they were unable to complete any tasks while the transparent authentication was in operation. The significance in explicit authentication frequency per task can be interpreted as the number of barriers presented to participants in various categories; the "All" category had no barriers at all, the "Some" category had a moderate number, and the "None" category had a large number. It is interesting to note that some participants in the "All" category decided to use the explicit authentication despite having task access without it. This shows that they had a strong mental model of the transparent authentication mechanism, and attempted to work within it.

To determine which categories contained the significant results for frequency of using explicit authentication, pairwise comparisons between the frequency data for the "All",

"Some", and "None" categories were performed using the Mann-Whitney test, as shown in Table 2. The View Photo and Make Local Call tasks have been excluded from Table 2 because there was no indication of statistical significance revealed by the Kruskal-Wallis tests.

Per Table 2, most of the categories were significantly different from each of the other categories in terms of the number of times explicit authentication was used per task (see Table 1 for the per-task frequencies). The exceptions are when comparing "All" and "None" for the *Change PIN* and *Make International Call* tasks, and "All" and "Some" and "Some" and "None" for the *Take Photo* task. These differences show that barriers presented before allowing tasks were significantly more frequent for "Some" and "All". This represents a potentially annoying amount of intrusion into the participants' attempts to complete the assigned tasks, a notion that was supported in the participants' comments.

The total number of times a participant chose to turn off transparent authentication is depicted in Table 3. As is expected, due to the barriers put in place for the "None" group, they had the highest instance of disabling transparent authentication. Thus, task completion was considered more important, at least in the experimental setting, than the security of the device and its data.

Perceiving tasks as the main goal is supported by the significant differences between the "None" and "All" and "None" and "Some" categories for the tasks in Table 4. In both cases, many participants in the "All" category did not feel the need to disable transparent authentication since all tasks were accessible with it enabled. In the "None" category, the only way to complete the tasks was to disable transparent authentication, so the difference between these occurrences is understood. Similarly, there would also be many instances in the "Some" category where disabling transparent authentication aided the participant in completing tasks, therefore explaining the statistically significant differences between

Table 2 Pairwise ρ values calculated using the Mann-Whitney test for number of times explicit authentication was used for the tasks that were significantly different

Task	Group	Participant category		
		All	Some	None
Read document	All	–	NaN	**< 0.0008**
	Some	–	–	**< 0.0008**
	None	–	–	–
Take photo	All	–	0.3681	**0.0347**
	Some	–	–	0.1224
	None	–	–	–
Send email	All	–	**< 0.00002**	**0.0147**
	Some	–	–	0.7066
	None	–	–	–
Change PIN	All	–	**< 0.0005**	0.5828
	Some	–	–	**< 0.00008**
	None	–	–	–
Make international call	All	–	**0.0012**	1.000
	Some	–	–	**0.0012**
	None	–	–	–

$\rho < 0.05$ are significant (bolded values). The comparison between the "All" and "Some" categories for the *Read Document* task is NaN because there were no occurrences of explicit authentication for either category.

Table 3 Total number of times transparent authentication was turned off per group for each task

Task	Group			ρ Value
	All	Some	None	
Read document	0	0	9	**< 0.0001**
Take photo	0	0	5	**0.0030**
Send email	2	0	7	**0.0025**
View photo	1	0	5	**0.0146**
Make local call	0	0	2	0.1260
Change device PIN	0	0	1	0.3679
Make international call	1	0	4	**0.0490**
Totals	4	0	33	
Median	0	0	5	
Mode	0	0	5	
Std. Dev.	0.79	0	2.75	

The last column shows statistical significance calculated using the Kruskal-Wallis test. $\rho < 0.05$ are significant (bolded values).

these occurrences and the "None" category. These results reinforced the finding that disabling transparent authentication, and leaving it off for subsequent tasks, was considered the correct course of action, and that completing the tasks was more important than protecting the information and accessibility of tasks on the device.

Study limitations

The convenience sampling methods used represent a potential source of study bias since the participants were skewed towards technically-minded males that were younger than an unbiased distribution. However, the age of the participants is in-line with the average

Table 4 Pairwise ρ values calculated using the Mann-Whitney test for frequency that transparent authentication was turned off for the tasks that were significantly different

Task	Group	Participant category		
		All	Some	None
Read document	All	–	NaN	**< 0.0001**
	Some	–	–	**< 0.0001**
	None	–	–	–
Take photo	All	–	NaN	**0.0137**
	Some	–	–	**0.0137**
	None	–	–	–
Send email	All	–	0.1675	**0.0318**
	Some	–	–	**0.0016**
	None	–	–	–
View photo	All	–	0.3681	0.0636
	Some	–	–	**0.0137**
	None	–	–	–
Make international call	All	–	0.3681	0.1444
	Some	–	–	**0.0336**
	None	–	–	–

$\rho < 0.05$ are significant. The two NaN values mark cases where both categories had no instances of turning off security.

age of UK mobile device owners [53]. Since this study is introductory in nature, this source of bias can be considered acceptable.

The majority of the data gathered in this study is of a subjective nature; it is the participants' opinions and perceptions and is thus subject to their own beliefs and knowledge. The same study conducted on a larger or differently populated group (as the group sampled here was UK-centric) could well result in a different range of opinions. Asking participants to express opinions is a widely-used mechanism for gauging mental models of particular concepts and, as such, was warranted here. The UK-centric nature of the participants clearly signals the need for a wider ranging study but does not detract from the value of the insights we gained from this study.

Discussion

It is curious that participants, in general, did not feel their data was valuable, were not entirely sure how much data they held, yet were concerned about other people accessing this data. Their expressed preference might be a manifestation of their fear of the unknown [54], a vague sense of being at risk and needing to take action to prevent harm. Perhaps their behavior is rooted in loss aversion, and is not really linked to the actual value of their data. On the other hand, it might be that participants were giving the answers that they think the experimenter might want to hear by claiming that security barriers are desirable, since they were aware of her research speciality.

As imperfect as our findings may be, they do, nevertheless, deliver valuable insights into participants' thought processes. Device owners clearly have a sense of identity associated with their mobile devices, as demonstrated by their unwillingness to allow others to use their devices. That they are frustrated with frequent authentication attempts is also clear. Even if they were demonstrating a social desirability response by claiming a need for authentication their own annoyance with it came across very clearly. Rather than merely being lazy, it became clear that users had very good reasons for their so-called "insecure" behaviors. Security researchers need to consider such rationales when designing security mechanisms, or these will be subverted or discarded if they become too arduous to use.

The participants in this study were open to the idea of an alternative mechanism, especially if such a mechanism intruded as little as possible, yet at the same time did provide a measure of protection. However, the sense of identity they associate with their devices means that an transparent mechanism is going to have to treat the behavioral biometric data with respect, and not remove it from the device.

Our main findings are as follows:

Security Barriers Need to be Visible: While removing security barriers such as effortful authentication and warning messages may simplify security provision while limiting user frustration with barrier frequency, this study has shown that removing *all* barriers is probably unwise. Participants indicated that having a few barriers was desirable to show that the security mechanism is working as intended. Barriers also help users build a mental model of the security provided, and may help build user trust that their data and device are adequately protected. To our knowledge, this result is novel.

Secret Knowledge is Problematic: We found that users were fearful of forgetting secret knowledge such as PINs and passwords because they linked that knowledge to the ability to use their device at will. Removing the dependence on remembering a secret, while still adequately protecting the device functionality and data, may help relieve the user of this fear. This result goes beyond other research that states that users *do* forget passwords and PINs [55] to state that users are *fearful* of forgetting, and thus allow this fear to inform their security provision on their mobile device. We also believe this result is in line with other studies that state the user does not wish to act in an insecure manner, but perhaps chooses to do so to make up for failings in the security provisions afforded them [3].

Biometrics are Acceptable: We found that users were willing to try transparent methods based on biometrics, although they wished to have a period of evaluation before making a final decision. This result is similar to those found by Clarke *et al.* [46], and show that a plausible authentication solution that uses biometrics and is also acceptable to users has not yet been discovered. Furthermore, we found that users are willing to consider trying transparent authentication, as they see a need for alternatives to passwords and PINs. This finding supports similar results reported by Clarke *et al.* in their evaluation of the NICA method [6].

Recommendations

Based on these findings, we recommend the following considerations for those providing an alternative mobile device authentication mechanism:

Use what we have: Mobile devices gather a significant amount of potentially private information about the user and their preferences, such as typing patterns, speech, accelerometer and gyroscope data and to whom and when they call or text. Future authentication methods can use this information as a way of determining who is using the device at a given time via behavioral biometrics such as keystroke dynamics, speaker verification and device use patterns. Since this information is already gathered, users tend to support its use as a potential authenticator.

Respect the mobile device environment: Since mobile devices are characterized by a bursty use pattern in which users access them frequently for short periods of time [31,32] authentication methods should not represent a barrier with each use or it may encourage users to not use security provisions. Mobile devices also have limitations in processor speed and memory, which is one reason for use of easy authentication methods. Alternatives to these easy methods should work in the background, but not overtax processors and memory.

Keep data on-device: Participants reported that they were uncomfortable with personally-identifying information leaving their device. Since this data is already gathered, future authentication methods that use it should process it on the device itself. This has far-reaching privacy implications since the data remains under its owner's control at all times.

Remove *most* barriers, but not *all*: Our study has shown that participants choose not to use provided security methods on their mobile device because they quickly become frustrated with entering authentication details repeatedly. Such barriers to task completion are common in security. Since the mobile device environment is characterized by frequent use, owners are asked to authenticate frequently. Removing some of these barriers may help reduce user frustration with authentication, but removing all barriers may have the effect of changing the user's mental model of the security provided. Participants opined that they would like to test, or experiment with, any new method before adopting it; this supports the creation of a mental model of security. Therefore, we should give clear signals as to the current state of security on the device, and give feedback in a non-intrusive manner as to the success or failure of authentication methods.

Conclusions and future work

Mobile devices represent a unique environment that is not well-suited to repeated entry of secret knowledge-based authentication methods. Consequently, we require alternative authentication methods that respect both the bursty nature of this environment, as well as the device owner's need for a reliable, non-intrusive authentication method. Respecting both the needs of the user and the limitations of the mobile device environment may lead to methods that are both more usable and more acceptable to device owners.

As a first step towards realizing transparent authentication on mobile devices, we conducted a user study with 30 participants to understand their opinions of transparent mobile device authentication that is based on behavioral biometrics. Our results show that 30% of participants used no security method on their mobile device, despite the opinion that their device stored sensitive information that should be protected. Overall, 73% of study participants felt transparent authentication was more secure than traditional methods such as secret knowledge techniques, although many of them wished to test the new system first before making a final decision on its security provision. Finally, 90% of participants stated that they would consider using a transparent authentication method on their own mobile device, should one be made available to them.

Through our qualitative analysis of interview questions, we found that participants are fearful and distrustful of PINs and other secret knowledge methods, that they often depend on physical proximity to the device to limit unauthorized access, and that having a few barriers helps them feel that the mechanism is working as designed. We recommend that future work in creating alternative authentication methods for mobile devices respect the limitations of the mobile device environment while limiting the effort that a user must make in order to protect their device. Furthermore, we recommend that any method be completely transparent to the user in its workings while providing a clear indication of the current security state of their device at any given time. Finally, we recommend that new authentication methods keep the user's personally identifying information on the device; this respects the owner's privacy and ensures that the authentication mechanism does not empower identity thieves.

Future work

The study reported here has several interesting avenues for future work, as follows:

- Perform a related study on tablets to see whether users express the same concerns on more powerful and functional (but still portable) devices;
- Examine whether putting apps into particular user-chosen security levels reduces the amount of access an application has to potentially private data/functionality. This study examined the feelings of users to other *people* having access to functionality on their device. The difference is that *apps* may also have that functionality and data access. Can we also protect the user from automated data access, access to device functionality that they have accepted due to blanket acceptance of warning messages?

Appendix A: interview questions

- Were you able to complete all the tasks given to you? Why or why not?
- Did you turn off the transparent authentication system? Why or why not?
- Did you use the challenge question feature? Why or why not?
- Assume for a moment that you were placing each task from the study into a security level that you think is most appropriate given how you use your mobile device and how sensitive you think each task is. Use the 3-point Likert scale to assign each task from the study into what level you think it should be in.
- How many security level choices would you like to have? Is Low/Med/High accurate enough, or should there be more choices?
- What did you like about using the transparent authentication system?
- What did you dislike about using the transparent authentication system?
- Would you use a transparent authentication method on your own mobile device? Why or why not?
- Using the 5-point Likert scale, indicate how well protected you thought the data on the device was. 1 is very unprotected, 2 is somewhat unprotected, 3 is neither protected nor unprotected, 4 is somewhat protected and 5 is very protected. Why did you select this level?
- What security mechanism do you currently use on your mobile device?
- When compared to using your usual security mechanism as the sole security method on a mobile device, did you feel that using a transparent authentication method was more secure, less secure, or about the same? Use the Likert scale for this 1 is a lot less secure, 2 is somewhat less secure, 3 is about the same, 4 is somewhat more secure, and 5 is a lot more secure. Why?
- When compared to using no security method at all on a mobile device, did you feel that using a transparent authentication method was more secure, less secure, or about the same? Use the Likert scale for this 1 is a lot less secure, 2 is somewhat less secure, 3 is about the same, 4 is somewhat more secure, and 5 is a lot more secure. Why?

Competing interests
The authors declare that they have no competing interests.

Authors' contributions
The majority of the work was done by the first author (HC), as is expected given that the work presented in this manuscript is a part of the first author's Ph.D. dissertation. HC conceived the study, designed the interview questions, designed and wrote the required mobile device application, undertook all participant meetings and interviews and compiled the first pass of qualitative data analysis. HC also performed all quantitative statistical analysis, including the first draft of the results. KR made suggestions that improved the clarity and neutrality of the interview questions, performed the second pass of qualitative data analysis, and refined the results that are based on both qualitative and quantitative analysis. Both authors wrote parts of, edited and approved the final manuscript.

Author details
[1] Department of Computer Sciences and Cybersecurity, Florida Institute of Technology, 150 W. University Blvd., Melbourne, FL 32901, USA. [2] School of Computing Science, University of Glasgow, Sir Alwyn Williams Building, Lilybank Gardens, Glasgow G12 8QQ, UK.

References
1. IDC (2013) Mobility reigns as the smart connected device market rises. Online: http://www.idc.com/getdoc.jsp?containerId=prUS23958513#.UTCkuDd4DlZ. Last checked: August 21, 2013
2. Glisson WB, Storer T, Mayall G, Moug I, Grispos G (2011) Electronic retention: what does your mobile phone reveal about you? Int J Inform Secur 10(6): 337–349
3. Adams A, Sasse MA (1999) Users are not the enemy. Comm ACM 42(12): 40–46

4. Gaw S, Felten EW (2006) Password management strategies for online accounts In: Proceedings of 2nd symposium on usable privacy and security, pp 44–55

5. Bao P, Pierce J, Whittaker S, Zhai S (2011) Smartphone use by non-mobile business users In: Proceedings of the 13th international conference on human computer interaction with mobile devices and services, pp 445–454

6. Clarke N, Karatzouni S, Furnell S (2009) Emerging challenges for security, privacy and trust, Volume 297/2009 of IFIP advances in information and communication technology. chap. Flexible and Transparent User Authentication for Mobile Devices. Springer Boston, pp. 1–12

7. Crawford H, Renaud K, Storer T (2013) A framework for continuous, transparent mobile device authentication. Comput Secur 39, Part B: 127–136

8. Prabhakar S, Pankanti S, Jain AK (2003) Biometric recognition: security and privacy concerns. IEEE Secur Privacy 1(2): 33–42

9. Chiasson S, van Oorschot PC, Biddle R (2007) Graphical password authentication using cued click points. In: Proceedings of the 2007 European symposium on research in computer security, volume 4734/2007 of Lecture Notes in Computer Science. Springer Berlin / Heidelberg, pp 359–374

10. O'Gorman L (2003) Comparing passwords, tokens, and biometrics for user authentication. Proc IEEE 91(12): 2019–2040

11. Patel SN, Pierce JS, Abowd GD (2004) A gesture-based authentication scheme for untrusted public terminals In: Proceedings of the 17th annual ACM symposium on user interface software and technology, pp 157–160

12. Shi E, Niu Y, Jakobsson M, Chow R (2011) Implicit authentication through learning user behavior. In: Burmester M, Tsudik G, Magliveras S (eds) Information security, Volume 6531 of Lecture Notes in Computer Science. Springer Berlin / Heidelberg, pp 99–113

13. Rokita J, Krzyzak A, Suen C (2008) Image analysis and recognition volume 5112 of Lecture Notes in Computer Science. chap. Cell Phones Personal Authentication Systems Using Multimodal Biometrics. Springer Berlin / Heidelberg, pp 1013–1022

14. Snelick R, Indovina M, Yen J, Mink A (2003) Multimodal biometrics: issues in design and testing In: Proceedings of the 5th international conference on multimodal interfaces, pp 68–72

15. Komanduri S, Shay R, Kelley PG, Mazurek ML, Bauer L, Christin N, Cranor LF, Egelman S (2011) Of passwords and people: measuring the effect of password-composition policies In: Proceedings for the SIGCHI conference on human factors in computing systems, pp 2595–2604

16. Inglesant PG, Sasse MA (2010) The true cost of unusable password policies: password use in the wild In: Proceedings of SIGCHI conference on human factors in computing systems, pp 383–392

17. Azenkot S, Zhai S (2012) Touch behavior with different postures on soft smartphone keyboards In: Proceedings of 14th international conference on human computer interaction with mobile devices and services, pp 251–260

18. Hoggan E, Brewster SA, Johnston J (2008) Investigating the effectiveness of tactile feedback for mobile touchscreens In: Proceedings of the SIGCHI conference on human factors in computing systems, pp 1573–1582

19. Allen JM, McFarlin LA, Green T (2008) An in-depth look into the text entry user experience on the iPhone In: Proceedings of the human factors and ergonomics society annual meeting, Volume 52(5): 508–512. SAGE Publications

20. Chen T, Yesilada Y, Harper S (2010) What input errors do you experience? Typing and pointing errors of mobile web users. Int J Hum Comput Stud 68(3): 121–182

21. Luca AD, von Zezschwitz E, Hussmann H (2009) Vibrapass: secure authentication based on shared lies In: Proceedings of the SIGCHI conference on human factors in computing systems, pp 913–916

22. Bianchi A, Oakley I, Kostakos V, Kwon DS (2011) The phone lock: audio and haptic shoulder-surfing resistant pin entry methods for mobile devices In: Proceedings of the 5th international conference on tangible, embedded and embodied interaction, pp 197–200

23. Dunphy P, Heiner AP, Asokan N (2010) A closer look at recognition-based graphical passwords on mobile devices In: Proceedings of the 6th symposium on usable privacy and security, pp 26–38

24. Cai L, Chen H (2011) Touchlogger: inferring keystrokes on touch screen from smartphone motion In: Proceedings of 6th USENIX workshop on Hot Topics in Security (HotSec'11), pp 9–9

25. Luca AD, Hang A, Brudy F Lindner C, Hussmann H (2012) Touch me once and I know it's you!: implicit authentication based on touch screen patterns In: Proceedings for the SIGCHI conference on human factors in computing systems, pp 987–996

26. Frank M, Biedert R, Ma E, Martinovic I, Song D (2012) Touchalytics: on the applicability of touchscreen input as behavioral biometric for continuous authentication In: IEEE transactions on information forensics and security, Volume 8, pp 136–148

27. Uellenbeck S, Dürmuth M, Wolf C, Holz T, Görtz H (2013) Quantifying the security of graphical passwords: the case of android unlock patterns In: Proceedings of the 20th ACM conference on computer and communications security, pp 161–172

28. Allano L, Morris AC, Sellahewa H, Garcia-Salicetti S, Koreman J, Jassim S, Ly-Van B, Wu D, Dorizzi B (2006) Non-intrusive multi-biometrics on a mobile device: a comparison of fusion techniques In: Proceedings of the SPIE conference on biometric technology for human identification III

29. Trewin S, Swart C, Koved L, Martino J, Singh K, Ben-David S (2012) Biometric authentication on a mobile device: a study of user effort, error and task disruption In: Proceedings of the annual computer security applications conference, pp 159–168

30. Hazen T, Weinstein E, Heisele B, Park A, Ming J (2007) Face biometrics for personal identification: multi-sensory multi-modal systems. chap. Multimodal face and speaker identification for mobile devices. Springer

31. Falaki H, Mahajan R, Kandula S, Lymberopoulous D, Govindan R, Estrin D (2010) Diversity in smartphone usage In: Proceedings of the 8th international conference on mobile systems, applications and services, pp 179–194

32. Jo HH, Karsai M, Kertèsz J, Kaski K (2012) Circadian patterns and burstiness in mobile phone communication. New J Phys 14(1): 013055

33. Hocking C, Furnell S, Clarke N, Reynolds P (2013) Cooperative user identity verification using an authentication aura. Comput Secur in press
34. Clarke N, Furnell S (2007) Advanced user authentication for mobil devices. Comput Secur 26(2): 109–119
35. Clarke N, Karatzouni S, Furnell S (2008) Transparent facial recognition for mobile devices In: Proceedings of the 7th international information security conference
36. Clarke N, Furnell S, Lines B, Reynolds P (2003) Keystroke dynamics on a mobile handset: a feasibility study. Inform Manag Comput Secur 11(4): 161–166
37. Karatzouni S, Furnell S, Clarke N, Botha RA (2007) Perceptions of user authentication on mobile devices In: Proceedings of the 2007 ISOneWorld conference. CD Proceedings
38. Stewart DW, Martin IM (1994) Intended and unintended consequences of warning messages: a review and synthesis of empirical research. J Publ Pol Market 13(1): 1–19
39. Felt AP, Ha E, Egelman S, Haney A, Chin E (2012) Android permissions: user attention, comprehension and behavior In: Proceedings of the eighth symposium on usable privacy and security, pp 1–3:14
40. Kelley PG, Consolvo S, Cranor LF, Jung J, Sadeh N, Wetherall D (2012) A conundrum of permissions: installing applications on an android smartphone In: Proceedings of 16th international conference on financial cryptography and data security, pp 68–79
41. Zhou Y, Jiang X, Freeh VW, Zhang X (2011) Taming information-stealing smartphone applications (on android) In: Proceedings of the 4th international conference on trust and trustworthy computing, pp 93–107
42. Kennedy K, Gustafson E, Chen H (2013) Quantifying the effects of removing permissions from android applications In: Proceedings of Mobile Security Technologies (MOST)
43. Chin E, Felt AP, Sekar V, Wagner D (2012) Measuring user confidence in smartphone security and privacy In: Proceedings of the eighth symposium on usable privacy and security, pp 1–1:16
44. Felt AP, Egelman S, Wagner D (2012) I've got 99 problems, but vibration ain't one: a survey of smartphone users' concerns In: Proceedings of 2nd ACM workshop on security and privacy in smartphones and mobile devices, pp 33–44
45. Ben-Asher N, Kirschnick N, Sieger H, Meyer J, Ben-Oved A, Möller S (2011) On the need for different security methods on mobile phones In: Proceedings of 13th international conference on human computer interaction with mobile devices and services, pp 465–473
46. Clarke N, Furnell S (2005) Authentication of users on mobile telephones - a survey of attitudes and practices. Comput Secur 24(7): 519–527
47. Herley C, van Oorschot PC, Patrick AS (2009) Passwords: if we're so smart, why are we still using them? In: Proceedings of the 13th international conference on financial cryptography and data security Volume 5628/2009 of Lecture Notes in Computer Science, pp 230–237
48. Kowalski S, Goldstein M (2006) Consumers' awareness of, attitudes towards, and adoption of mobile phone security In: Proceedings of the 20th international symposium on human factors in telecommunication
49. Botha RA, Furnell S, Clarke N (2009) From desktop to mobile: examining the security experience. Comput Secur 28(3–4): 130–137
50. Jones LA, Antòn AI, Earp JB (2007) Towards understanding user perceptions of authentication technologies In: Proceedings of the 2007 ACM workshop on privacy in electronic society, pp 91–98
51. Field A, Hole G (2008) How to design and report experiments. SAGE Publications
52. Strauss A, Corbin JM (1998) Basics of qualitative research: techniques and procedures for developing grounded theory 2nd edition. SAGE Publications
53. The Deloitte Consumer Review (2013) Beyond the Hype: The True Potential of Mobile. Online: Last checked: June 25, 2014 http://www.deloitte.com/assets/Dcom-UnitedKingdom/Local%20Assets/Documents/Industries/Consumer%20Business/uk-cb-consumer-review-edition-5.pdf
54. Cao HH, Han B, Hirshleifer D, Zhang HH (2011) Fear of the unknown familiarity and economic decisions. Rev Finance 15: 173–206
55. Florêncio D, Herley C (2007) A large-scale study of web password habits In: Proceedings of the 16th international conference on World Wide Web (WWW '07), pp 657–666

8

How buyers perceive the credibility of advisors in online marketplace: review balance, review count and misattribution

Kewen Wu[*], Zeinab Noorian, Julita Vassileva and Ifeoma Adaji

* Correspondence:
kew259@mail.usask.ca
Department of Computer Science,
University of Saskatchewan,
Saskatoon, Canada

Abstract

In an online marketplace, buyers rely heavily on reviews posted by previous buyers (referred to as advisors). The advisor's credibility determines the persuasiveness of reviews. Much work has addressed the evaluation of advisors' credibility based on their static profile information, but little attention has been paid to the effect of the information about the history of advisors' reviews. We conducted three sub-studies to evaluate how the advisors' review balance (proportion of positive reviews) affects the buyer's judgement of advisor's credibility (e.g., trustworthiness, expertise). The result of study 1 shows that advisors with mixed positive and negative reviews are perceived to be more trustworthy, and those with extremely positive or negative review balance are perceived to be less trustworthy. Moreover, the perceived expertise of the advisor increases as the review balance turns from positive to negative; yet buyers perceive advisors with extremely negative review balance as low in expertise. Study 2 finds that buyers might be more inclined to misattribute low trustworthiness to low expertise when they are processing high number of reviews. Finally, study 3 explains the misattribution phenomenon and suggests that perceived expertise has close relationship with affective trust. Both theoretical and practical implications are discussed.

Keywords: Source credibility; Misattribution; Online marketplace; Review balance

Introduction

In an online marketplace, buyers rely heavily on reviews posted by advisors. A recent business survey reported that 92% of online consumers read advisors' reviews before they make purchase decisions [1]. Literature also suggests that advisors' reviews significantly influence consumers' attitudes towards the products or sellers, which ultimately influence sales [2,3].

The extent to which a buyer accepts or follows an opinion presented in a review is a matter of persuasiveness. The persuasiveness of an online review is determined by the credibility of its source (the advisor), because online reviews are written by advisors with varied backgrounds and motivations [4]. Advisors can write reviews no matter if they are capable of assessing a product critically or not (e.g., layperson versus expert). Moreover, many intentional and unintentional factors can influence the writing of a review [5-7]. For instance, an advisor's account may be controlled by a seller to write positive reviews and promote himself (known as ballot stuffing); and it may also be controlled to write negative reviews to attack competitors (known as bad-mouthing). These reputation manipulation activities have been identified as a pervasive phenomenon in online marketplaces [5,8]. Even if an advisor is a real buyer, he may still be influenced by others and write reviews that do not represent his actual experience (e.g., herd effect).

Given the uncertainty regarding the source of online reviews, buyers are motivated to assess the credibility of advisors based on accessible pieces of information [9]. Many online marketplaces (e.g., Amazon, Taobao) allow buyers to visit advisors' profile page. To evaluate an advisor's credibility, buyers are inclined to seek and use profile information as cues, other than the review itself. A number of studies have been conducted to evaluate how advisors' profile influences buyers' perception of credibility [10,11]. Advisors' static profile information, such as real name, location, nickname and hobbies, have been found to be helpful in supporting consumers' judgment [11,12]. However, current studies on advisors' review history mainly come from computer science field, and little is known about the impact of advisors' review history on buyers' perception of advisors' credibility. Analyzing an advisor's review history could provide useful information (e.g., purchase frequency, areas of interests or even background) about the advisor, which can be helpful for buyers to make judgement on advisors' credibility.

In this paper, we segment advisors into five types based on the ratio of positive to negative reviews (referred to as review balance). If the proportion of positive (negative) reviews is extremely higher than, substantially higher than, or almost equal to the proportion of negative (positive) reviews, the review balance is respectively defined as extreme positive (negative), positive (negative), or neutral. We choose review balance as representative of review history because it can be easily noticed by buyers through direct scanning of an advisor's review history list or a summary table provided by the platform. Prior studies indicate that buyers usually do not scrutinize reviews [13,14]; they form attitude only based on the information they gain easily. Intuition also suggests that it is unrealistic for a buyer to conduct a comprehensive evaluation of review history for each advisor in the product page.

We conducted three sub-studies to explore how different review balances signal different meanings to buyers regarding the advisors' trustworthiness and expertise (two dimensions of credibility). Study 1 aims to gain a preliminary knowledge about buyers' perception of advisor's trustworthiness and expertise. Study 2 extends study 1 by using larger sample size and considering more variables. Finally, study 3 is conducted to further explain the results of previous two sub-studies.

Research background
Source credibility: trustworthiness and expertise
The concept of source credibility has received much attention from various fields related to communication, such as politics, human-computer interaction, marketing and information system. It is a multifaceted term suggesting that the positive characteristics of a message source can enhance the perceived value of message information, and thus increase the persuasiveness of the message [15,16]. Expertise, trustworthiness and attractiveness are commonly reported as three dimensions of source credibility [17]. In this study, we considered source credibility as a two-dimensional construct, since expertise and trustworthiness

are more relevant to online review context [18]. Trustworthiness describes the receiver's confidence in a source's objectivity and honesty in providing information [15]. There is a wide consensus on the positive relationship between trustworthiness and source credibility [19].

Expertise refers to a source's capability of providing correct and valid information [15]. Such capability can be technical-oriented or practical-oriented [20]. Technical expertise reflects the skillfulness of processing special knowledge required by writing comments towards a given product (e.g., an advisor who majors in acoustics writes a review about a headphone). Practical expertise is the skills that are gained from direct participation in related activities (e.g., an advisor who has tried many headphones writes a review about one headphone). The characteristics of online communication (e. g., limited availability of personal information) make it difficult to identify whether an advisor is an expert or not. As a result, in online context, different results have been found regarding the relationship between expertise and source credibility. For example, some studies found that expert endorsers can lead to higher source credibility than laypersons; others found that layperson can induce higher credibility than experts; yet others found that the levels of expertise make no difference in determining the perceived source credibility [19,21].

The complex findings on expertise imply that other dimensions of source credibility might disturb the effects of expertise. As mentioned earlier, attractiveness is not relevant to online review context. Here we only take trustworthiness as an example. On one hand, high expertise can lead to increased trust because assessments of expertise and trust both employ an attribute evaluation of trustee's identifiable actions [22]. For example, a seller's expertise reflects a buyer's identification of competencies associated with the transaction. On the other hand, as suggested by the attribution theory [23], people attribute a review to both stimulus and non-stimulus causes. When the consumer suspects that the review is not drawn based on product performance (stimulus) but on the advisors' unknown intentions (non-stimulus), they will discredit the review message. In some cases, a source may be perceived to be high in expertise but low in trustworthiness [24]. For example, people trust an expert because they think expert statements are true; however, if this expert's motivation to share is reasonably suspected, people's perception of this expert's trustworthiness will decrease. The contradictory effects (e.g., high on expertise but low on trustworthiness) may cancel each other out [25].

The above mentioned two circumstances only address the impacts of expertise on trustworthiness, that high expertise can lead to both high trust (because of belief in competency) and low trust (because of suspicious motivation). However, little is known about how trustworthiness affects expertise.

Advisors profile and credibility

Previous work on credibility of online reviews can be divided into two streams. The first stream of work focuses on review itself; studies have addressed many factors such as sequence of reviews [26,27], valence [26], volume [28], information depth [29], attribution (e.g., experience issue or product issue) [26,27]. However, these studies generally assume reviews come from credible sources.

The second stream of work deals with the credibility of advisors. Much work has been done on evaluating the effects of advisors' profile. In real online review systems, a profile usually includes an advisor's identity-related information and review history. Advisors' identity-related information, such as real name, gender, location, nickname, hobbies and reputation (e.g., special badges such as top 50 reviewers), has been proven to be helpful for buyers' judgment [11,12,10]. However, limited attention has been paid on the effects of review history.

The social exchange theory suggests that people develop trust based on behavioral characteristics observed from direct experiences with the trustee [30]. The history of experience facilitates the accumulation of knowledge and thus increases the validity of knowledge-based attribution [31]. Compared to static characteristics (e.g., gender, location), buyers are able to make rational credibility judgment as they obtain greater knowledge from the review history.

Positive or negative reviews could signal different meanings to buyers, for instance, a reviewer who gives negative feedback might be perceived to be high in expertise [32]. However, few studies have considered how buyers perceive expertise from advisor's review history (e.g., review balance). Moreover, current studies on the perception of trustworthiness from advisors' review history mainly come from computer science area. The basic assumptions regarding trustworthiness and advisors' review behavior are based on three points: (1) Similarity. According to social identity theory [33], a buyer may categorize an advisor who has similar purchase history and review opinions into the same social group, resulting in increased trust towards this advisor [34,35]. (2) Social consensus, that if an advisor holds the same opinions with the majority of advisors, his/her review is perceived as correct and would be accepted [36]. (3) Social network, that dishonest advisors (e.g., fake buyers' accounts), may share the same review behavioral pattern [37]. Given the fact that related human studies are scarce, this paper evaluates buyers' perception of advisors' credibility based on review history.

Data source

The review dataset used in this paper is built upon Taobao review data. We selected Taobao as our target online marketplace based on two reasons. First, Chinese online marketplaces have been growing rapidly in recent years. Taobao is the leading platform with about 90% market share. Its transaction volume is estimated to have more sales than Amazon and eBay combined in 2013 [38]. Taobao is well known among Chinese communities (half a billion registered users) and it is usually considered as a typical e-commerce sample in previous studies [39]. Second, despite the huge number of transactions, Chinese online marketplaces face serious reputation manipulation problem [5]. For example, some critics estimate that about 80% of *Taobao* sellers have committed reputation manipulation activities during their businesses [40]. And it has been reported that over 1000 active trust fraud companies provide services to help sellers increase reputation and whitewash negative feedback [5]. But a recent official report shows that more than 70% online buyers choose Taobao as their primary choice [41]. Therefore, the high transaction volume, serious trust issue and being buyers' primary choice jointly make Taobao a valuable target to investigate.

We use a self-developed crawler to download real review data from Taobao during 2014-04-01 and 2014-4-20. This dataset includes the latest 180-day detailed review information about 24,287 sellers and 1,686,870 advisors who are willing to show their profile. The average number of reviews per advisor in our dataset is 116.

To prepare the dataset for our experiment, we invited four master's students to select 200 positive and 200 negative reviews from our Taobao review database. The selection of reviews was based on two criteria: (1) previous studies have shown that the different review targets (product and service) have different impacts on consumer's decision-making process [26]. Therefore, we decided to only consider product attribute-based reviews to serve as data source in our experiment. Service-based reviews were excluded because service quality is usually unstable across different buyers (e.g., delivery service might be excellent in some areas but much worse in other areas) and buyers' perception of service quality contains many subjective factors. (2) We set the length of each review to be around 30 Chinese characters (about 60 English characters), and the reasons described in each review should be clear. We built advisors' profiles based on five types of review balances (See Table 1). In the following experiment, we did not set the ratio between number of positive ratings (R) and number of negative ratings (S) close to threshold values (e.g., 0.2 for Type I), because we wanted to make different types of review balance distinguishable. For example, we set the ratio of a Type I advisor's R/S to 0.05, rather than 0.19.

Study 1

Study 1 was designed to gain a preliminary knowledge about buyers' perception of advisor's source credibility regarding different review balances.

Hypotheses

Previous studies suggest that the proportion of positive reviews is much higher than negative reviews in online review systems [42,43]. People are reluctant to give negative feedback unless they encounter terrible experience [44]. A content analysis of eBay comments shows that 72.5% of negative reviews were related to unsatisfactory product and service, while the other 27.5% were related to sellers' attempts to exploit buyers [43]. This result suggests that terrible experience (negative feedback) usually happens due to the poor product or service quality that cannot meet buyer's expectation.

Table 1 Five types of advisors based on different review balance

Type	Description
I. Extremely negative Balanced	$R < < S^a$: number of positive ratings are significantly lower than number of negative ratings ($R/S < 0.2^b$)
II. Negative balanced	$R < S$: number of positive ratings are lower than number of negative ratings ($0.2 \leq R/S < 0.7$)
III. Neutral balanced	$R \approx S$: number of positive ratings are approximately the same as number of negative ratings ($0.7 \leq (R/S \text{ or } S/R) \leq 1$)
IV. Positive balanced	$R > S$: number of positive ratings are larger than number of negative ratings ($0.2 \leq S/R < 0.7$)
V. Extremely positive Balanced	$R > > S$: number of positive ratings are significantly larger than number of negative ratings ($S/R < 0.2$)

Note: [a]: R refers to number of positive ratings/reviews; S refers to number of negative ratings/reviews; [b]: this ratio is only used to describe a phenomenon (e.g., R < <S) and used to manipulate of advisors' profiles. It is not a strict classification of advisors.

The reviewers who give negative feedback are perceived as brighter and more intelligent than those who give positive feedback [32]. They give negative reviews because they have enough knowledge to identify product issues. For instance, as a domain expert, an acoustics enthusiast gives negative feedback to a headphone due to its poor performance, while non-experts could not notice the pros and cons of this headphone. In this view, an advisor with a negative review balance might be perceived as a strict expert who is hard to be satisfied. Therefore, we hypothesize that:

H1: The level of perceived expertise of an advisor increases as the review balance changes from extremely positive to extremely negative.

Negative feedback usually contains distinctive information than positive ones, therefore, it is perceived to be more accurate, trustworthy and helpful for buyers to make decisions [42]. Absence of negative feedback may have nothing to do with the judgment of review authenticity [19]. An advisor who has almost all positive feedback (review balance: extreme positive) may be considered as a malicious account controlled by a dishonest seller to do self-promotion, or as a "Mr. Goody-goody" who always gives positive feedback regardless of his actual experience. Similarly, an advisor who gives all negative feedback (review balance: extreme negative) may be judged to be a malicious account used to attack competitors, since the case that a buyer always experiences unsatisfactory transactions is unrealistic. Previous studies have found that buyers are more likely to form positive attitudes (e.g., trust, purchase intention) towards a product which receives a mix of positive and negative reviews [45,46,19]. Therefore, it is reasonable to assume that an advisor who posts both positive reviews and negative reviews would be perceived as trustworthy. We hypothesize that:

H2: The level of perceived trustworthiness is high when an advisor's review balance is neutral, and the level of perceived trustworthiness is low when an advisor's review balance is either extremely positive or extremely negative. Especially, an advisor with extreme negative review balance is perceived to be most untrustworthy.

Experiment and result

In order to reduce cognitive load, we only considered ratings in this sub-study. We created two sets of advisors' profiles based on our review dataset. Advisors in each set have entirely different review balances (see Table 2). Although these advisors' profiles cannot present the characteristics of the whole dataset, using a small amount of typical experiment material is acceptable in many studies [9,47].

Twenty experienced online buyers were invited to evaluate the impacts of review balance on perceived trustworthiness and expertise. These participants were all aware of

Table 2 Advisors' profile used in study 1

Type	Description	Set 1 (R,S)	Set 2 (R,S)
I	R < <S[a]	(5, 86), (0, 103)	(2, 42) ,(0, 63)
II	R < S	(31, 57), (38, 64)	(13, 30)
III	R ≈ S	(51, 43), (58, 42)	(29, 24), (43, 32)
IV	R > S	(68, 31), (72, 23)	(37, 13), (64, 14), (56, 16)
V	R > > S	(104, 0), (115, 1)	(49, 1), (43, 1)

Note[a]: R refers to number of positive ratings/reviews; S refers to number of negative ratings/reviews.

unfair rating/review phenomenon in online marketplaces, they were told that the rating history of each advisor in this survey was based on real data gained from Taobao. The interface of the experiment system is shown in Figure 1.

For the judgement of perceived trustworthiness, we randomly assigned 10 participants to check the rating history of advisors in Set 1 and asked them to rank advisors based on their perceived trustworthiness from the lowest (1) to the highest (10) on a ten-point scale (we used a computer program to ensure that each ranking position has only one advisor). Then we assigned the remaining 10 participants to rate advisors in Set 2 and rank advisors in the same way.

For the judgement of perceived expertise, we used the same advisors' profiles and the same subjects (however, two of them quitted). We randomly assigned 9 participants to check advisors in Set 1 and asked them to rank advisors based on perceived expertise from the highest to the lowest on the ten-point scale (1 shows the least expertise and 10 shows the highest expertise). Then we assigned the remaining 9 participants to check Set 2 and rank advisors, respectively.

We used Kendall's coefficient of concordance (W) to measure the degree of agreement among participants with the rankings of advisors. The capability of W in performing multiple judgments (more than two) makes it the most suitable tools to test inter-judge reliability [48]. Past studies suggest that the value of $W > 0.7$ shows strong consensus; $W = 0.5$ shows moderate consensus; and $W < 0.3$ shows weak consensus amongst different users on their ranked data [48].

In the test regarding perceived trustworthiness, for Set 1 we achieved $W = 0.7578$ ($p < 0.0001$), and for Set 2 we achieve $W = 0.7345$ ($p < 0.0001$). Therefore, there is a strong consensus between participants in terms of ranking different groups of advisors. The average ranking result shown in Figure 2 suggests that the relationship between review balances (from extremely negative to extremely positive) and perceived trustworthiness follows an inverted-U shape, and an extremely negative balanced review history is perceived as the most untrustworthy profile by buyers (2 versus 3.4 and 2.3 versus 2.95).

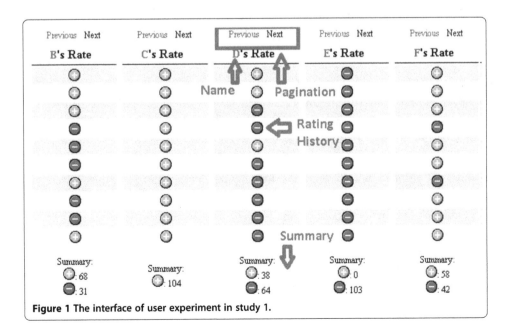

Figure 1 The interface of user experiment in study 1.

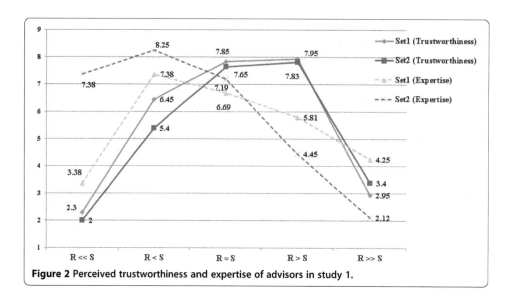

Figure 2 Perceived trustworthiness and expertise of advisors in study 1.

In the test regarding perceived expertise, for Set 1 we achieved $W = 0.2867$ ($p < 0.05$), and for Set 2 we achieve $W = 0.6451$ ($p < 0.0001$). This result indicates that the levels of consensus in Set 1 and Set 2 are weak and moderate, respectively. The averaged ranking result is shown in Figure 2, which suggests that perceived expertise does not increase linearly when review balance ranged from extremely positive to extremely negative. Meanwhile, participants' rankings about advisors with almost all negative reviews (Type I) are different (7.38 versus 3.38) across two sets.

In summary, the results from study 1 reject H1 because advisors with extremely negative review balance (Type I) were perceived to be low in expertise. H2 is supported, suggesting that advisors who always give the same ratings (either negative or positive) are not trustworthy to buyers.

Considering that the participants did not gain high consensus regarding the expertise of the advisors, it is interesting to further explore the influences of review balances on perceived credibility (especially expertise) of advisors.

Study 2

There are at least four issues in study 1, which limit the explanation power of the result. First, the sample is relatively small (20 participants). Second, the list of reviews only contains ratings, and it is not clear what the results would be when both ratings and comments are displayed (a real online review system usually displays both ratings and comments). Third, the measurements of trustworthiness and expertise are based on ranking, not on pre-validated questions. Ranking has its limitations, for example, it uses a one-to-one matching method between an advisor and a position and therefore, it might be difficult for participants to choose between two or more advisors when their trustworthiness/expertise perceived to be similar. Moreover, rankings only provide sequential data within a set but little is known about the differences across two sets. And fourth, the total number of reviews is not controlled.

The aim of study 2 is to further verify the results of study 1 by considering the limitations of study 1. First, a large sample was organized, including 200 participants; second, both ratings and review comments were displayed to participants; third, pre-validated questions and Likert scale were used to measure participants' opinions. And fourth, perceived trustworthiness and expertise were evaluated in both high and low review count conditions.

Experiment preparation

To determine appropriate number of reviews in two conditions (high and low number of reviews), we manipulated five lists of advisors' review history, which contained 10, 40, 80, 120 and 200 reviews. We provided these review history lists to three Ph.D. students who were experienced online buyers. Their feedback suggested that 10 and 40 reviews could be treated as low number of reviews, but a list with only 10 reviews was usually not enough to form an attitude towards an advisor. Therefore, we set the value of low review number to 40. The feedback also suggested that a list with 200 reviews was beyond normal processing capacity, so we set the value of high review number to 200.

We built 10 advisors' review history lists based on selected 400 reviews. The details are shown in Table 3. We edited some of the reviews to make sure that these reviews did not conflict with each other. For example, one review may indicate that an advisor is a mother, but another review may indicate that the advisor is a father.

Details of experiment

We designed an online survey system which consisted of two parts: an advisor's review history and questions regarding trustworthiness and expertise. In the review history page, participants were told to imagine that they were shopping in Taobao as usual, and need to evaluate the credibility of an advisor. They should use the same amount of time to judge the advisor in our survey as in their regular purchase, and they could go to the questionnaire page as soon as they felt they have finished their judgment.

All questions in the survey were measured with 7-point Likert scale. Trustworthiness was measured by five items (dependable, honest, reliable, sincere and trustworthy); expertise was also measured by five items (expert, experienced, knowledgeable, qualified, skilled). These items were originally developed by Ohanian [25], and they have been adopted by many studies [49]. In order to do manipulation check, we used a question to ask participants to select one of the five conditions ($R < < S$; $R < S$; $R \approx S$; $R > S$; $R > > S$) which best fits what they see.

We invited 200 participants into our experiment. They were undergraduate students and they all had purchase experience in Taobao. Each participant was randomly

Table 3 Advisors' profile used in study 2

Type	Low review count (R,S)	High review count (R,S)
$R < < S$ [a]	(1, 39)	(4, 196)
$R < S$	(12, 28)	(59, 141)
$R \approx S$	(19, 21)	(98, 102)
$R > S$	(29, 11)	(136, 64)
$R > > S$	(40, 0)	(198 , 2)

Note[a]: R refers to number of positive ratings/reviews; S refers to number of negative ratings/reviews.

assigned into one of the ten conditions (5 types of review balance × 2 types of review count). Therefore, each condition had 20 participants. This sample size provided an acceptable level of statistical power with an effective size of 0.50 at a two-tailed 5% significance level [50]. We selected undergraduate students as research subjects based on following two reasons: first, students provided an accessible sample when an experiment requires a large sample size [51]; second, young adults and university students are a typical group of online buyers, and similar sampling approach has also been employed in previous studies [52,51,17]. Moreover, a recent official survey shows that 56.4% of Chinese buyers in online marketplaces are aged between 20 and 29, 35.9% of consumers have (or are pursuing) bachelor degrees [41].

Analysis and result

All participants could correctly select the condition they were assigned to, indicating that our manipulations were successful. Table 4 shows the results of factor analysis (CFA) for both high and low review count conditions. All factor loadings were significant ($p < 0.01$), and ranged from 0.73 to 0.93. The composite reliability and Cronbach's alpha of each factor ranged from 0.86 to 0.94, demonstrating acceptable levels for internal reliability (the recommended threshold for these two indices is 0.7). All values of AVE shown in Table 4 are greater than the recommended value (0.5), suggesting that the latent constructs account for the majority of the variance in their indicators on average [53]. As a common rule, the presence of multi-collinearity issue is confirmed if Variance Inflation Factor (VIF) is higher than 10 [54]. More strictly, the VIF threshold of 3.3 has been recommended by Cenfetelli & Bassellier [55]. Table 4 shows that only two items (EXP2 and EXP3) from the high number reviews group are larger than 3.3 (but smaller than 10), indicating that multi-collinearity is not a serious issue.

We conducted two 5 × 2 ANOVA analyses on trustworthiness and expertise respectively. For trustworthiness, both review count ($F_{(1,190)} = 4.045$, $p < 0.05$) and review balance conditions ($F_{(4,190)} = 109.159$, $p < 0.001$) have significant main effects, but no significant interaction effect ($F_{(4,190)} = 1.231$, $p > 0.05$). This result suggests that in general the participants perceived higher trustworthiness under the high review count

Table 4 Results from confirmation factor analysis in study 2

Constructs		Loading	C.R.	C.A.	AVE	VIF
Trustworthiness	TRU1	0.83/ 0.87[a]	0.91/0.93	0.87/0.91	0.66/0.74	2.19/2.65
	TRU2	0.77/0.83				1.80/2.10
	TRU3	0.75/0.89				1.74/2.99
	TRU4	0.83/0.87				2.13/3.09
	TRU5	0.87/0.85				2.41/2.59
Expertise	EXP1	0.77/0.79	0.90/0.94	0.86/0.92	0.65/0.76	1.79/2.53
	EXP2	0.87/0.93				2.56/4.42
	EXP3	0.86/0.92				2.57/3.83
	EXP4	0.73/0.91				1.80/2.47
	EXP5	0.78/0.78				1.94/2.15

Note[a]: the value on the left side of "/" is from the low number of reviews condition; the value on the right side of "/" is from the high number of reviews condition.

conditions than under low review count conditions (mean differences = 0.178, p < 0.05). And in both low and high review count conditions, the values of perceived trustworthiness are distributed in an inverted-U curve (see the repeated contrast of means shown in Table 5).

For expertise, both the review count (F(1,190) = 5.656,p < 0.05) and review balance conditions (F(4, 190) = 35.906, p < 0.001) have significant main effects. Moreover, a significant interaction effect is observed (F(4, 190) = 13.05, p < 0.001). This result suggests that the advisor's expertise is perceived to be higher under low number of reviews condition than under high number of reviews condition (mean differences = 0.288, p < 0.05). And the values of perceived expertise are distributed differently across high and low number of reviews conditions. In low number of reviews condition, only the difference between means in conditions "R < <S" and "R < S" is negative (–0.36, but insignificant), suggesting that the perceived expertise linearly increases when review balance ranges from extremely positive to extremely negative. However, in the high number of reviews condition, the values of perceived expertise are distributed differently (an inverted-U shape). Especially when advisors have almost all negative reviews, they are perceived to be very low in expertise (see Table 5, repeated contrast of means between conditions "R < <S" and "R < S": –2.64, p < 0.001).

In line with study 1, study 2 supports H2 but rejects H1. The results from both study 1 and study 2 show that buyers might misattribute low trustworthiness to low expertise, and this case might happen when buyers check an advisor who has a high number of reviews.

Study 3

The misattribution phenomenon found in study 1 and study 2 suggests that it is necessary to further explore the interplay between sub-dimensions of trust and expertise. Previous studies indicate that misattribution is usually a kind of affective response to a stimulus [56]. Similar to source credibility, trust is also a multifaceted variable, including both cognitive dimension and affective dimensions [22].

Cognitive trust is a kind of prediction based on people's accumulated knowledge gained through observation of trustee's behavior [22]. Affective trust is generated based on the positive emotions in the judgement process. Previous studies assume a positive impact of cognitive trust on affective trust because cognitive trust is a prerequisite for

Table 5 Means and repeated contrast results in study 2

Review balance	Perceived trustworthiness				Perceived expertise			
Condition	Low count[a]	Repeated contrast[b]	High count	Repeated contrast	Low count	Repeated contrast	High count	Repeated contrast
R < <S	3.49 (0.72)	_	3.42 (1.06)	_	5.07 (0.56)	_	3.04 (0.73)	_
R < S	4.82 (0.66)	–1.33***	5.10 (0.54)	–1.68***	5.43 (0.57)	–0.36[N.S.]	5.68 (0.73)	–2.64***
R ≈ S	5.37 (0.54)	–0.55*	5.79 (0.50)	–0.69*	4.58 (1.05)	0.85*	4.70 (1.07)	0.98**
R > S	6.09 (0.39)	–0.72**	6.39 (0.39)	–0.60*	4.40 (0.92)	0.18[N.S.]	4.61 (1.01)	0.09[N.S.]
R> >S	4.90 (0.57)	1.19***	4.86 (0.60)	1.53***	3.34 (0.81)	1.06**	3.35 (0.89)	1.26***

Note: ***:p < 0.001;**:p < 0.01;*:p < 0.05; [N.S.]: p > 0.05; [a.] the values with parenthesis are standard deviations.
[b]:The mean value in latter condition minus the mean value in former condition.

affective trust [57,22]. Cognitive trust has clear distinctions with expertise [7]. However, affective trust may have close relationship with expertise because of buyer's misattribution. Therefore, we conducted study 3 to explore the relationships among affective trust, cognitive trust and expertise in high number of reviews condition.

Details of experiment

A survey-based experiment was conducted. Detailed content of measurable items are shown in Table 6. Three measureable items (AFF3, AFF4, AFF5) for trust are extracted from previous study [57], while others are self-developed. Self-developed measures were used because no relevant items can be found in previous studies, and these items were developed to fit our research context well. Items used to measure expertise are extracted from Ohanian [25].

The experiment procedure is similar to the procedure in study 2. We invited 100 undergraduate students with Taobao purchase experience to take part in our experiment. The demographic information of participants is shown in Table 7. The number of participants meets the requirement of Partial Least Squares (PLS) analysis. Each participant was randomly assigned into one of the five review balance conditions with an advisors' review history containing 200 reviews. Participants were told to imagine that they were shopping in Taobao and need to judge the credibility of the advisor. Survey was provided as soon as the participants finished their judgement.

Table 6 Results of measurement model in study 3

Construct	Items	Content	C.R	C.A.	AVE	Loading	VIF
Cognitive trust	COG1	I see no reason to doubt his motivation to write reviews	0.94	0.91	0.75	0.77	2.26
	COG2	I think taking his review into consideration is a good decision				0.95	2.53
	COG3	I think I can rely on his reviews				0.77	2.79
	COG4	I think what he write in the reviews (pros and cons) is reasonable				0.92	2.79
	COG5	I think the review content and review activities make him a trustworthy advisor.				0.88	3.09
Affective trust	AFF1	I can feel his sincerity in writing reviews.	0.93	0.92	0.76	0.84	2.77
	AFF2	I am confident that he writes reviews based on his real experience.				0.95	3.51
	AFF3	I feel comfortable about relying on him for my purchase decision.				0.87	1.79
	AFF4	I feel secure about relying on him for my purchase decision				0.83	3.38
	AFF5	I feel content about relying on him for my purchase decision				0.85	3.64
Perceived expertise	EXP1	Expert-not an expert	0.93	0.91	0.74	0.88	2.94
	EXP2	Experienced-inexperienced				0.89	2.39
	EXP3	Knowledgeable-unknowledgeable				0.86	2.83
	EXP4	Qualified-unqualified				0.83	2.58
	EXP5	Skilled-unskilled				0.83	2.79

Note: S.D.: standard deviation. C.R.: Composite reliability. C.A.: Cronbach's alpha.

Table 7 Demographic information of participants

Items	Mean	S.D.	Min	Max	Comment
1. Age	22.24	1.11	19	25	
2. Gender	0.49	0.50	0 (female)	1 (male)	Male:49; Female:51
3. How much Taobao purchase experience do you have?	4.95	0.76	4	6	7 point scale (rarely–very frequently)

Structural equation modeling (SEM)-based PLS analysis was chosen to process survey data. This method was chosen in this study because it is suitable for exploratory study, and it requires neither large sample size nor multivariate normality of distribution [44]. We used WarpPLS 4.0 with bootstrapping to conduct PLS analysis. In line with other PLS softwares, the classic PLS algorithm was adopted.

Analysis and result

The analysis procedure is divided into two steps: test for measurement model and structural model. Table 6 shows the results of measurement model. All factor loadings were significant ($p < 0.001$), and ranged from 0.77 to 0.95. The composite reliability and Cronbach's alpha of each factor ranged from 0.91 to 0.94. All values of AVE are greater than 0.5. Finally, multi-collinearity is not a serious issue because the highest value of VIFs is only 3.64. These results indicate that our self-developed questions have good reliability and our survey data are suitable for further analysis.

In the test of structural model, first, age, gender and purchase experience are included as control variables. Results show that p values for these three variables are 0.06, 0.35 and 0.19. Therefore, no significant effects ($p > 0.05$) of control variables are found. As it is shown in Figure 3, the impact of cognitive trust on expertise is not significant (Beta = 0.05, $p > 0.05$). Cognitive trust has positive impact on affective trust (Beta = 0.76, $p < 0.001$), and affective trust positively influences expertise (Beta = 0.45, $p < 0.001$). The percentage of the variance explained (R^2) of affective trust and perceived expertise are 57% and 29%, indicating good explanation power.

The results of study 3 confirm the assumption of misattribution from trustworthiness to expertise, and further suggest that affective trust plays a significant role in determining expertise.

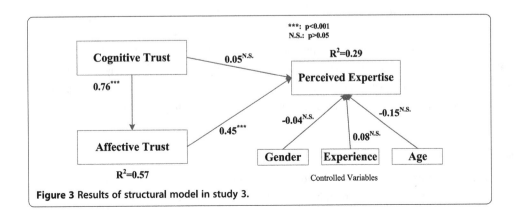

Figure 3 Results of structural model in study 3.

Summary and discussions

In online marketplaces, an advisor's credibility is important because buyers rely on advisor's reviews to make purchase decision. An advisor's profile is a major way for buyers to assess advisor's credibility. A profile usually includes identity-related information and review history. Disclosure of identity-related information has been found to be helpful in supporting buyers' judgment, however, the impacts of the review history remains unclear. In this research, we investigated the effects of review balance, an important aspect of review history. Study 1 investigated how buyers perceive advisors' trustworthiness and expertise based on different review balances. The results support H2 and show that perceived trustworthiness distributes in an inverted U-shaped curve when review balance ranges from extremely negative to extremely positive. Advisors with almost all positive or negative reviews are perceived to be not trustworthy, while advisors who write mixed reviews are perceived to be trustworthy. This result is in line with psychological studies [45], suggesting that mixed positive and negative reviews could enhance buyers favorable judgement towards a target (a seller, a product or an advisor). The finding is also supported by data mining studies, which treat advisors with all negative reviews as unusual cases with low trustworthiness [30,31,34,58,59]. An unexpected result in study 1 is that perceived expertise does not decrease linearly when review balance ranges from extremely negative to extremely positive. Therefore H1 is rejected.

An advisor with almost all positive reviews might be seen as an easy-to-satisfy buyer. As the proportion of negative reviews increases, advisor's perceived strictness on evaluating product increases. However, an advisor with extremely high proportion of negative reviews is perceived to be low in expertise. This result implies that buyers might misattribute low trustworthiness to low expertise. Many trust-related misattributions have been mentioned in previous studies. For example, alcoholism, drug abuse, and mental illness among managers can harm employee's trust towards the organization [60]; people with positive emotions (e.g., happiness and gratitude) are more inclined to trust than people with negative emotions (e.g., anger, sadness) [20]. This phenomenon occurs because affective states, even if they are caused by unrelated events, usually serve as an information aid in people's judgement.

Study 2 addresses some limitations of study 1 by incorporating larger sample size and more variables. The results of study 2 are consistent with those found in study 1, and again reject H1 but support H2. Study 2 further suggests that buyer's misattribution behavior is more likely to happen under high processing effort condition (advisor with high number of reviews). Currently there is little evidence to support the direct relationship between stress and misattribution. However, processing a high number of reviews can cause low processing fluency, which then leads to negative affective states [61].

The result of study 3 shows that expertise is positively related to affective trust, while not significantly related to cognitive trust. It provides evidence to explain why low trustworthiness leads to low expertise. Previous studies, however, neglect the affective aspect of trust and argue that trustworthiness and expertise are clearly distinguishable [7].

Implications

The results of this study yielded a couple of theoretical implications. First, previous studies on online marketplace mainly focus on the importance of advisors' review for potential buyers in evaluating the trustworthiness of sellers. They advocate that the existence of inconsistent reviews, rather than majority positive or majority negative reviews, better reflects the seller's credibility. However, they did not consider different credibility of advisors. This study explores how the advisor's profile signals credibility meaning to buyers. Second, a large amount of work on advisors' credibility focuses on static personal information (e.g., gender, hobbies). This study moves a step further to evaluate the impact of review balance shown in review history. It is worthwhile to explore review history since it can provide valuable information to judge advisors' credibility. Third, this study enriches extant knowledge about the relationship between trustworthiness and expertise. Previous studies mention that people can easily distinguish between trustworthiness and expertise [7], and in some experiment, manipulations of trustworthiness and expertise were not found to influence each other [62]. However, in this study, low expertise is found to easily be misattributed from low trustworthiness, especially when buyers face advisors with a high number of reviews.

This study also generates practical implications for the design of mechanisms to support credibility judgement. First, there are many ways to assigning trust value when buyers and sellers are strangers, including initializing trust values based on beta distribution, and incorporating social network attributions. We argue that assigning trust values should take subjective perception into consideration. The results of this study could serve as a reference for assigning credibility values of advisors. Second, some trust models compute advisors' trustworthiness based on the degree of consensus among advisors [36]. Such method might not be suitable in a marketplace with a high proportion of fake positive reviews, because these models assume other advisors are credible. The results of this study could be helpful to refine existing trust models by reducing the importance of consensus in considering trustworthiness. For example, a malicious advisor with all positive reviews might be judged in existing models as highly trustworthy because his reviews are in agreement with others, however, he will be considered to be less trustworthy in revised trust model.

Limitations and future work

This study has five limitations, which affect the generalizability of our findings. First, although our research participants (mostly undergraduates) reflect a typical group of buyers in online marketplace, they cannot be representative of the whole consumer community. Moreover, our participants were required to have purchase experience and they were aware of unfair/review issues in online marketplace, therefore our findings cannot fully explain how new buyers perceive credibility of advisors with different review histories. We will extend our work by inviting participants with various backgrounds in future work. Second, in our experiment, an advisor's reviews for all sellers were listed together, but the differences (e.g., reputation) among different sellers were not considered. We argue that discarding sellers' difference does not significantly affect our result because it is unlikely for a buyer to further judge characteristics of sellers who are listed in an advisor's profile page. This issue will be considered in future work as a pretest before formal experiment. Third, our results cannot explain how buyers perceive an advisor who only has a few reviews. Buyers usually cannot make judgement based on a short review history list (e.g., only one or two reviews). Fourth, different online marketplaces have different characteristics. Our target platform (Taobao) has serious unfair rating/review problem, while this issue might not be a problem in other platforms. Therefore, buyers in Taobao are assumed to have more knowledge about identifying advisors with low credibility. Fifth, in real purchase, buyers usually have to judge a list of advisors, while our experiments (study 2 and 3) only required participants to judge one advisor. The judgement of a list of advisor might be affected by the sequence of the list (primacy effect: buyers can only remember the credibility of the first advisor) and the information overload (e.g., buyers only judge a few advisors in the list). In future study, we will aim at measuring trust attitude towards a seller by providing buyers with a list of advisors.

Competing interests
The authors declare that they have no competing interests.

Authors' contributions
KW and ZN proposed initial idea of this paper. JV provided comments and helped KW and ZN with the formulation of research framework. KW and ZN conducted study 1 and KW conducted study 2 and 3. KW and ZN drafted the paper. IA proofread the draft and provided comments and suggestions. KW revised this paper according to reviewers' comments. JV supervised the revising process, proofread revised paper and confirmed responses to review comments. KW was in charge of submitting the paper and corresponding with the editors of the journal and Springer Open Production Team. All authors read and approved the final manuscript.

Acknowledgement
This work has been supported by NSERC through a Discovery Grant and a Discovery Accelerator Supplement Grant.

References
1. Li M, Huang L, Tan C-H, Wei K-K (2013) Helpfulness of online product reviews as seen by consumers: Source and content features. Int J Electron Commer 17(4):101–136
2. Lee J, Park D-H, Han I (2008) The effect of negative online consumer reviews on product attitude: An information processing view. Electron Commer Res Appl 7(3):341–352
3. Park D-H, Lee J, Han I (2007) The effect of on-line consumer reviews on consumer purchasing intention: The moderating role of involvement. Int J Electron Commer 11(4):125–148
4. Chua AYK, Banerjee S (2014) Understanding review helpfulness as a function of reviewer reputation, review rating, and review depth. Journal of the Association for Information Science and Technology
5. Zhang Y, Bian J, Zhu W (2012) Trust fraud: A crucial challenge for china's e-commerce market. Electron Commer Res Appl 12(5):299–308
6. Dellarocas C (2000) Immunizing online reputation reporting systems against unfair ratings and discriminatory behavior. In: Proceedings of the 2nd ACM conference on Electronic commerce. ACM, New York, pp 150–157
7. Sprecker K (2002) How involvement, citation style, and funding source affect the credibility of university scientists. Sci Commun 24(1):72–97
8. Chen Z, Yang J (2009) Credit fraud control and credit system optimization on c2c marketplaces. In: Proceedings of the 42nd Hawaii International Conference on System Sciences. Hawaii, HI, IEEE Computer Society Press, Washington
9. Lim Y-S, Van Der Heide B (2014) Evaluating the wisdom of strangers: The perceived credibility of online consumer reviews on yelp. Journal of Computer-Mediated Communication
10. Park H, Xiang Z, Josiam B, Kim H (2013) Personal profile information as cues of credibility in online travel reviews. Anatolia 25(1):13–23
11. Forman C, Ghose A, Wiesenfeld B (2008) Examining the relationship between reviews and sales: The role of reviewer identity disclosure in electronic markets. Inf Syst Res 19(3):291–313
12. Ghose A, Ipeirotis PG (2011) Estimating the helpfulness and economic impact of product reviews: Mining text and reviewer characteristics. IEEE Trans Knowl Data Eng 23(10):1498–1512
13. Heesacker M, Petty RE, Cacioppo JT (1983) Field dependence and attitude change: Source credibility can alter persuasion by affecting message-relevant thinking. J Pers 51(4):653–666
14. Tintarev N, Masthoff J (2007) A survey of explanations in recommender systems. In: IEEE 23rd International Conference on Data Engineering Workshop. IEEE Computer Society Press, Washington, pp 801–810
15. Rezaei S (2015) Segmenting consumer decision-making styles (cdms) toward marketing practice: A partial least squares (pls) path modeling approach. J Retail Consum Serv 22:1–15
16. Mcallister DJ (1997) The second face of trust:Reflections on the dark side of interpersonal trust in organizations. Res Negotiation Organ 6:87–111
17. Tarnanidis T, Owusu-Frimpong N, Nwankwo S, Omar M (2015) Why we buy? Modeling consumer selection of referents. J Retail Consum Serv 22:24–36
18. Park J, Gunn F, Han S-L (2012) Multidimensional trust building in e-retailing: Cross-cultural differences in trust formation and implications for perceived risk. J Retail Consum Serv 19(3):304–312

19. Willemsen LM, Neijens PC, Bronner F (2012) The ironic effect of source identification on the perceived credibility of online product reviewers. J Comput-Mediat Commun 18(1):16–31

20. Dunn JR, Schweitzer ME (2005) Feeling and believing: the influence of emotion on trust. J Pers Soc Psychol 88(5):736

21. Willemsen LM, Neijens PC, Bronner F, De Ridder JA (2011) "Highly recommended!" the content characteristics and perceived usefulness of online consumer reviews. J Comput-Mediat Commun 17(1):19–38

22. Johnson D, Grayson K (2005) Cognitive and affective trust in service relationships. J Bus Res 58(4):500–507

23. Heider F (2013) The psychology of interpersonal relations. Psychology Press, New Jersey

24. Pornpitakpan C (2004) The persuasiveness of source credibility: a critical review of five decades' evidence. J Appl Soc Psychol 34(2):243–281

25. Ohanian R (1990) Construction and validation of a scale to measure celebrity endorsers' perceived expertise, trustworthiness, and attractiveness. J Advert 19(3):39–52

26. Sparks BA, Browning V (2011) The impact of online reviews on hotel booking intentions and perception of trust. Tour Manag 32(6):1310–1323

27. Huang L, Tan C-H, Ke W, Wei K-K (2014) Do we order product review information display? How? Information & Management

28. Khare A, Labrecque LI, Asare AK (2011) The assimilative and contrastive effects of word-of-mouth volume: An experimental examination of online consumer ratings. J Retail 87(1):111–126

29. Mudambi SM, Schuff D (2010) What makes a helpful online review? A study of customer reviews on amazon.com. Manag Inf Syst Q 34(1):185–200

30. Metzger MJ, Flanagin AJ, Medders RB (2010) Social and heuristic approaches to credibility evaluation online. J Commun 60(3):413–439

31. Chou SY, Picazo-Vela S, Pearson JM (2013) The effect of online review configurations, prices, and personality on online purchase decisions: a study of online review profiles on ebay. J Internet Commer 12(2):131–153

32. Amabile TM (1983) Brilliant but cruel: perceptions of negative evaluators. J Exp Soc Psychol 19(2):146–156

33. Ashforth BE, Mael F (1989) Social identity theory and the organization. Acad Manag Rev 14(1):20–39

34. Jindal N, Liu B, Lim E-P (2010) Finding unusual review patterns using unexpected rules. In: Proceedings of the 19th ACM international conference on Information and knowledge management. ACM, New York, pp 1549–1552

35. Ziegler C-N, Golbeck J (2007) Investigating interactions of trust and interest similarity. Decis Support Syst 43 (2):460–475

36. Zhang J, Cohen R (2008) Evaluating the trustworthiness of advice about seller agents in e-marketplaces: a personalized approach. Electron Commer Res Appl 7(3):330–340

37. Zhu Y, Zhang W, Yu C (2011) Detection of feedback reputation fraud in taobao using social network theory. In: 2011 International Joint Conference on Service Sciences (IJCSS). IEEE Computer Society Press, Washington, pp 188–192

38. Popper B (2014) Alibaba has more sales than amazon and ebay combined, but will americans trust it? http://www. theverge.com/2014/5/7/5690596/meet-alibaba-the-ecommerce-giant-with-more-sales-than-amazon-and-ebay.

39. Clemes MD, Gan C, Zhang J (2014) An empirical analysis of online shopping adoption in beijing, china. J Retail Consum Serv 21(3):364–375

40. Moneyweek (2011) Gray industry cluster parasitism: Four complicated interest chains on taobao. http://finance. stockstar.com/MS2011050300000899.shtml.

41. Cnnic (2014) 2013 statistical report on chinese internet shopping https://www.cnnic.net.cn/hlwfzyj/hlwxzbg/ dzswbg/201404/t20140421_46598.htm.

42. Sen S, Lerman D (2007) Why are you telling me this? An examination into negative consumer reviews on the web. J Interact Mark 21(4):76–94

43. Pavlou PA, Dimoka A (2006) The nature and role of feedback text comments in online marketplaces: Implications for trust building, price premiums, and seller differentiation. Inf Syst Res 17(4):392–414

44. Kallweit K, Spreer P, Toporowski W (2014) Why do customers use self-service information technologies in retail? The mediating effect of perceived service quality. J Retail Consum Serv 21(3):268–276

45. Ein-Gar D, Shiv B, Tormala ZL (2012) When blemishing leads to blossoming: the positive effect of negative information. J Consum Res 38(5):846–859

46. Berger J, Sorensen AT, Rasmussen SJ (2010) Positive effects of negative publicity: when negative reviews increase sales. Mark Sci 29(5):815–827

47. Xie H, Miao L, Kuo P-J, Lee B-Y (2011) Consumers' responses to ambivalent online hotel reviews: the role of perceived source credibility and pre-decisional disposition. Int J Hosp Manag 30(1):178–183

48. Nevo D, Chan YE (2007) A delphi study of knowledge management systems: scope and requirements. Inform Manag 44(6):583–597

49. Senecal S, Nantel J (2004) The influence of online product recommendations on consumers' online choices. J Retail 80(2):159–169

50. Cohen J (2013) Statistical power analysis for the behavioral sciences. Academic, Routledge

51. Liqiong D, Poole MS (2010) Affect in web interfaces: a study of the impacts of web page visual complexity and order. MIS Q 34(4):711–A710

52. Kim DJ, Ferrin DL, Rao HR (2008) A trust-based consumer decision-making model in electronic commerce: The role of trust, perceived risk, and their antecedents. Decis Support Syst 44(2):544–564

53. Mackenzie SB, Podsakoff PM, Podsakoff NP (2011) Construct measurement and validation procedures in mis and behavioral research: Integrating new and existing techniques. MIS Q 35(2):293–A295

54. Mason CH, Perreault WD Jr (1991) Collinearity, power, and interpretation of multiple regression analysis. J Mark Res 28(3):268–280

55. Cenfetelli RT, Bassellier G (2009) Interpretation of formative measurement in information systems research. MIS Q 33(4):7

56. Payne BK, Hall DL, Cameron CD, Bishara AJ (2010) A process model of affect misattribution. Bulletin, Personality and Social Psychology

57. Sun H (2010) Sellers' trust and continued use of online marketplaces. J Assoc Inf Syst 11(4):2

58. Mukherjee A, Liu B, Wang J, Glance N, Jindal N (2011) Detecting group review spam. In: Proceedings of the 20th international conference companion on World Wide Web. ACM, New York, pp 93–94

59. Lim E-P, Nguyen V-A, Jindal N, Liu B, Lauw HW (2010) Detecting product review spammers using rating behaviors. In: Proceedings of the 19th ACM international conference on Information and knowledge management. ACM, New York, pp 939–948

60. Speller JL (1989) Executives in crisis: Recognizing and managing the alcoholic, drug-addicted, or mentally ill executive. Jossey-Bass, San Francisco

61. Mosteller J, Donthu N, Eroglu S (2014) The fluent online shopping experience. J Bus Res 67(11):2486–2493

62. Wiener JL, Mowen JC (1986) Source credibility: on the independent effects of trust and expertise. Adv Consum Res 13(1):306–310

Local user-centric identity management

Audun Jøsang[1]*, Christophe Rosenberger[2], Laurent Miralabé[3], Henning Klevjer[4], Kent A Varmedal[5], Jérôme Daveau[6], Knut Eilif Husa[7] and Petter Taugbøl[8]

*Correspondence: josang@ifi.uio.no
[1] University of Oslo, Oslo, Norway
Full list of author information is available at the end of the article

Abstract

Identity management is a rather general concept that covers technologies, policies and procedures for recognising and authenticating entities in ICT environments. Current identity management solutions often have inadequate usability and scalability, or they provide inadequate authentication assurance. This article describes local user-centric identity management as an approach to providing scalable, secure and user friendly identity management. This approach is based on placing technology for identity management on the user side, instead of on the server side or in the cloud. This approach strengthens authentication assurance, improves usability, minimizes trust requirements, and has the advantage that trusted online interaction can be upheld even in the presence of malware infection in client platforms. More specifically, our approach is based on using an OffPAD (Offline Personal Authentication Device) as a trusted device to support the different forms of authentication that are necessary for trusted interactions. A prototype OffPAD has been implemented and tested in user experiments.

Keywords: Authentication; Trust; OffPAD

Introduction and background

Trusted interaction between users and service providers in online environments depends on robust mutual authentication. Given the exponential growth in the number of interconnected online entities, where each entity often gets multiple and changeable identities, the challenge of ensuring robust authentication between all these identities is daunting. Because authentication involves two parties - the relying verifier as well as the authenticated target - identity management requires process components at each location at least, and possibly at third-party locations as well. All parties that engage in online activities have identities that need to be managed. In the traditional client-service architecture, the identities of both the client and server must be considered. In addition, it must also be taken into consideration that there are people, organisations and systems with identities that need to be managed, both on the client and server sides. Finally, it is necessary to consider data authentication as a separate security service in the context of identity management. This is because the origin of data can not be derived from entity authentication alone. A realistic threat is for example that malware on a client platform could modify data provided by a user even if the user has been correctly authenticated. From these simple observations we quickly realise that the general identity management problem is quite complex.

Identity management can be defined as the set of technologies, processes, policies and standards that enables identification and authentication of entities as digital identities. Entities are typically persons or computer systems, where either can be active on the client side or on the server side. An identity is a set of attributes that characterise the entity, where one of the attributes typically is a name that serves as an identifier for the entity within a domain. Figure 1 below illustrates how the concepts of entity, identity, and attributes are related.

A digital entity is a set of digitally expressed attributes of an entity, where one of the attributes typically is a name or identifier for uniquely selecting the entity within a name-space domain. Identity attributes can be self-assigned such as usernames on social website, assigned by an authority such as social security numbers, dictated by circumstances such as a home address, or be intrinsically linked to the entity such as biometric characteristics. Identities can be transient (shorter period than the entity's lifetime), permanent (as long as the entity exists) or persistent (remains even after the entity no longer exists). Each entity can have multiple identities simultaneously or at different points in time. For example, a person's professional and private identities are typically partially overlapping (i.e. with some common attributes), and a person's various digital online identities can be partially overlapping or even totally separate without any common attributes.

Identity management for online services has traditionally focused on managing user identities through processes located on the server side, where solutions are optimized for simple management from the service providers' point of view. The *silo model* is the traditional identity management model used in this approach where each service provider (hereafter abbreviated as SP) governs a separate 'silo domain' with its own name space of user identities. A specific user normally has separate identities and names in different silo domains, and in addition must use a different authentication credential for each identity. The silo domain model results in severe usability problems due to the identity overload that it generates, i.e. that users accumulate a high number of identities.

Online activity typically leads to the accumulation of so many digital identities and passwords that it becomes a real challenge to manage them in an efficient and secure way. In recent years, security architects have therefore focused on new solutions that can improve the user experience, often dubbing such solutions as *'user centric'*. One of the main approaches to user-centric identity management is identity federation where the basic

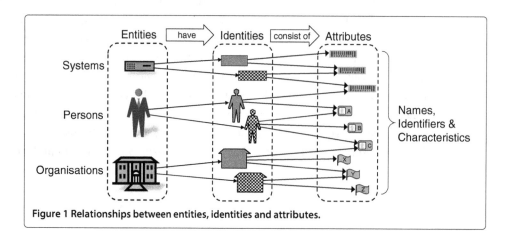

Figure 1 Relationships between entities, identities and attributes.

idea is to let users access multiple separate service domains with the same identity and credential. This is made possible by interconnecting the federated service domains with a common security protocol and by agreeing on a common security policy whereby user authentication by one identity provider is accepted by all other SPs (service providers) in the federation domain. Identity federation comes in many variations but is typically based on the SAML[a] standard which is implemented in applications such as Shibboleth, OpenId, YouProve, as well as FacebookConnect.

Identity federation can certainly simplify the user experience in many situations, but it does not fundamentally solve the problem of identity overload. There will always be different federation domains, because not all SPs will merge their respective user identity domains into a single federated domain. In addition, a side-effect of identity federation is that it requires additional trust in specific third parties, and can give monopolistic business power to specific parties in the federation. The identity provider in a federation is for example able to collect information about user activity. Selling this information for profit or using it for targeted advertisement constitutes a privacy breach in many jurisdictions. It is commonly assumed that users would abandon identity providers that fail to protect user privacy. Paradoxically, federated identity providers seem to be only minimally affected by trust erosion caused by such privacy breaches, which is a serious trust management problem. Finally, identity federation processes are mostly located on the server side or at some other location in the Internet cloud, which means that identity federation which is typically dubbed as user-centric in reality is network-centric.

We argue that there is a need for identity management solutions that can really solve the identity overload problem, that have simple trust requirements, that lead to balanced business power between SPs, and that are user-centric from both a practical and technical point of view. We use the term *local user-centric identity management* (abbreviated Lucidman) in order to distinguish between this identity management model and other models that are often called user-centric in the literature. More specifically, Lucidman not only provides robust security and adequate security usability, it is also based on placing technology and computing processes for identity management locally on the user side in the client-server architecture. An essential element of the user-side technology is the OffPAD (Offline Personal Authentication Device) which acts as a trusted device that can support strong multilateral authentication even in situations of compromised client platforms. This article describes Lucidman as a principle for identity management based on the OffPAD to support secure and user friendly mutual entity authentication as well as data authentication.

Our proposed solution is based on an external trusted device called an OffPAD (Offline Personal Authentication Device) as shown in Figure 2. The OffPAD enables different authentication classes described in more detail below.

A paradox in today's Internet computing environment is that we continue to build vulnerable client platforms while still expecting them to support trusted online interactions. According to PandaLabs' estimates, approximately one third (31.63%) of the world's PCs are infected with some sort of malware (Q2 2012) of which most (78.92%) are Trojans [1]. It must therefore be assumed that sooner or later a client platform will be infected by malware, which means that it can never be trusted. In order to ensure resilience in such adverse situations Lucidman also ensures trusted interactions even when it is assumed that client platforms are infected by malware.

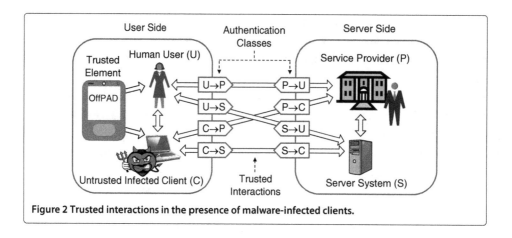

Figure 2 Trusted interactions in the presence of malware-infected clients.

The OffPAD is not connected to the Internet nor to other public communication networks, but it can communicate with the human user and with local client platforms in a controlled way. The network architecture in Figure 2 consists of two entities (client and user) on the client side, and of two entities (server system and SP organisation) on the server side, which thereby extends the traditional client-server architecture that only has one entity on each side. The term *ceremony* [2] is typically used to denote network protocols that involve entities and interactions external to the traditional system entities, i.e. where nothing is out-of-band. The solutions described in this article consists of ceremonies that are described on a relatively high level of abstraction.

Below is first described related work. Subsequently are described the different authentication classes and authentication modalities, the OffPAD device itsefl, the ceremonies for local user-centric identity management, a security analysis of the OffPAD, the user experiment with the prototype OffPAD, and finally the discussion and conclusion.

The principles and technologies for local user-centric identity management and trusted interaction based on the OffPAD have been developed within the Lucidman project (Eureka project number 7161) which is a collaborative research project supported by the Franco-Norwegian Foundation in the period 2011-2013. Partners in the project have been the University of Oslo, Tellu and Vallvi in Norway, and ENSICAEN, TazTag and CEV in France.

Related work

Several authentication solutions (particularly unimplemented designs and recommendation) relying on an external device are present in the literature. Examples include the Pico by Stajano [3], MP-Auth by Mannan and van Oorschot [4] and Nebuchadnezzar by Singer and Laurie [5]. However, these devices only support authentication of client-side entities to server-side parties, i.e. typically user authentication, in contrast to the OffPAD which also supports the authentication of server-side entities to client-side parties, as well as data authentication. Below we briefly summarise related work on external authentication devices.

Pico

The Pico [3] is a device that authenticates a user through a challenge-response protocol. It stores private keys for communication with every application it supports authenticating to, in its on-board encrypted memory. Each supported application has one asymmetric key pair to communicate with Picos.

Challenges are presented as 2D visual codes (e.g. QR codes) to the Pico, and collected by the device's embedded camera. Transmission of the response is done over Bluetooth. The Pico solution requires changes to both the client and the server side. Most SPs are probably reluctant to consider changing their visual appearance to support another authentication scheme. Where the Pico is restricted to its own authentication scheme, the OffPAD authentication is done building on a pre-existing technology. Also, the Pico only supports user authentication, whereas the OffPAD supports multilateral authentication.

MP-Auth

The MP-Auth (Mobile Password Authentication) protocol was proposed as a means for moving password authentication (not the passwords themselves) to a personal device, protecting them against being collected by malware. In this protocol, an SSL tunnel is established between the user's mobile phone and the server to which he wants to authenticate. The user's password or credential is then entered on the phone and transmitted, protected by the SSL tunnel, to the server, authenticating the user [4].

MP-Auth's solution relays the communication and entering of a password to a mobile phone, but does not provide the benefit of identity management. This solution only supports user authentication.

Nebuchadnezzar

The authors of Nebuchadnezzar assume that trying to establish a trusted path of communication between a general purpose operating system and a server is a bad idea. They also assume that the other extreme: trying to run every application on a minimal, secured, locked down operating system, is also a bad idea. They therefore propose that the only sensible solution is a combination of the two. The position paper [5] describes the principles of the Nebuchadnezzar, which much like the OffPAD is an external device, and which is minimized with regard to features. The Nebuchadnezzar may be seen as a the OffPAD part that supports user authentication. However, our OffPAD concept also supports additional types of authentication, not just user authentication.

Trusted platform module

The TPM is mentioned here because it represent a security module integrated on computing platforms and that is resistant to malware attacks. The TPM also provides a method for cryptographic authentication of client platforms. The term 'TPM' is at the same time the name of a set of specifications [6] issued by the Trusted Computing Group, as well as the name of the hardware chip that implements these specifications. TPM chips are commonly installed in computer systems shipped since 2006, with the purpose of providing a robust hardware based mechanism for obtaining security assurance about various integrity aspects of systems. The TPM chip can e.g. be used to verify that the OS loader has not been modified by malware, and can also be used to authenticate (client) systems to external parties, which corresponds to client authentication (class $[C \rightarrow S]$) in Figure 2. TPM based system authentication relies on the EK (Endorsement Key) pair which is a public/private key pair that is unique for each TPM, generated and installed by the manufacturer or the vendor of the TPM. However, the TPM can not support user authentication as $[U \rightarrow S]$, server authentication as $[S \rightarrow U]$, nor cognitive data authentication.

Authentication classes and modalities

This section explains the concepts of entity and data authentication, and introduces three distinct modalities of authentication called syntactic, semantic, and cognitive authentication.

Entity authentication

The distinction between a system entity (client or server) and a legal/cognitive entity (person or organisation) brings into play multiple entities on each side in the client-server model, as illustrated in Figure 2. A requirement for trusted interaction in this scenario is to have mutual authentication between pairs of interacting entities whenever relevant, leading to 4 possible types of mutual entity authentication as shown in Figure 2 and described in Tables 1 and 2.

Some of the entity authentication classes in Tables 1 and 2 are relatively impractical, such as [C → P] and [P → C], but they illustrate the generality of entity authentication with non-atomic user and server sides. The authentication class [U → P] is e.g. practiced when authenticating customers over the phone by asking about customer number, date of birth, etc. The X.800 standard focuses on entity authentication classes [C → S] and [S → C] which take place at the network protocol layers and are typically transparent to the human user.

For online service access the entity authentication classes [U → S] (user authentication) and [S → U] (cognitive server authentication, defined below) are the most relevant. The importance of these authentication classes emerges from the need for end-to-end security. End-to-end communication between the human user (U) and the server system (S) takes place during online service access. It is therefore pragmatic to require mutual authentication between those two entities. Traditional user authentication can provide [U → S] authentication. It is often incorrectly assumed that traditional server authentication with Browser PKIX[b] server certificates and TLS[c] provides [S → U] authentication, however in reality it does not. This might seem surprising but is in fact easy to understand [7].

For example, phishing attacks normally start with spam email messages that invite people to access a fake web site masquerading as a genuine web site that e.g. tricks the user into providing user Id and password. In a syntactic sense the fake phishing website can be correctly authenticated through TLS because the server certificate is validated by the browser. However, from a cognitive point of view this is not authentication because the website's identity is different from that intended by the user. The problem is due to the poor usability offered by current implementations of TLS [8,9] which does not facilitate cognition of identities nor any understanding of what they represent.

Table 1 Authentication classes for user-side entities as illustrated in Figure 2

Class	Authentication of user-side entities
[U → P]	User (U) authentication by the service provider (P)
[U → S]	User (U) authentication by the server system (S) (commonly called *user authentication*)
[C → P]	Client (C) authentication by the service provider (P)
[C → S]	Client (C) authentication by the server system (S)

Table 2 Authentication classes for SP-side entities as illustrated in Figure 2

Class	Authentication of SP-side entities
[P → U]	Service provider (P) authentication by the human user (U)
[P → C]	Service provider (P) authentication by the user client (C)
[S → U]	Server (S) authentication by the human user (U)
	(here called *cognitive server authentication*)
[S → C]	Server (S) authentication by the user client (C)

According to the X.800 standard, entity authentication is *"the corroboration that a peer entity in an association is the one claimed"* [10]. Here, 'association' means a connection, a session or a single instance of communication. We use the term 'interaction' as a general term for the same thing. So in case a victim user intends to connect to `https:\\www.paypal.com`, but is tricked into connecting to a phishing website called `https:\\www.peypal.com`, then the server certificate claims that the server identity is `www.peypal.com` which then is correctly authenticated according to X.800. However, something is clearly wrong here, and the failure to capture this obvious security breach indicates that the above definition of entity authentication is inadequate. What is needed is a richer modality of authentication. We define three authentication modalities where *syntactic authentication* is the poorest, where *semantic authentication* is intermediately rich, and where *cognitive authentication* is the richest modality, as described next.

Authentication modalities:

- **Syntactic entity authentication:** *The verification by the relying entity that the unique name of the remote entity in an interaction is as claimed.*
  This basic form of entity authentication is equivalent to peer-entity authentication as in X.800. Syntactic authentication alone does not provide any meaningful security and can e.g. not prevent phishing attacks since the relying party is indifferent to the identity of the authenticated entity.

- **Semantic entity authentication:** *The verification by the relying entity that the unique name of the remote entity in an interaction is as claimed, and in addition the verification by the relying entity that semantic characteristics of the remote entity are compliant with a specific security policy.*
  Semantic entity authentication can be enforced by an automated system e.g. with a white list of identities that have been authorized for interaction.

- **Cognitive entity authentication:** *The verification by the cognitive relying party that the unique name of the remote entity in an interaction is as claimed, and in addition the verification by the relying party that semantic characteristics of the remote entity are compliant with a specific security policy, where the latter is supported by presenting in a user-friendly way identity attributes that enable the cognitive relying party to recognise relevant aspects of the remote entity and to judge policy compliance.*
  Cognitive entity authentication requires the relying party to have cognitive reasoning power, such as in humans, animals or advanced AI systems. This authentication modality effectively prevents phishing attacks because users recognise the identity of a server and decide whether it is the intended one.

Technologies for SP authentication are very different from those of user authentication, because user authentication (class [U → S]) typically takes place on the application layer e.g. with passwords, whereas SP authentication – interpreted as server system authentication (class [S → C]) – typically takes place on the transport layer e.g. with TLS.

User identity management is frequently discussed in the identity management literature, whereas SP identity management is mostly discussed in the network security literature. Lucidman applies to both types because users must manage their own identities as well as those of SPs, in order to be authenticated by server systems on a semantic level, and to authenticate the server systems on a cognitive level. Lucidman is aimed at providing adequate security assurance and usability for the management of both user identities and server identities, with the goal of enabling trusted interaction between online entities.

Data authentication

According to the X.800 standard data origin authentication is *"the corroboration that the source of data received is as claimed"* [10]. This is different from entity authentication because knowing the identity of a remote entity in a session is different from knowing whether the data received through a session with a specific remote entity genuinely originates from that entity. This difference might seem subtle at first glance but it is in fact fundamental for security, as explained below.

Malware infection on client platforms opens up for attacks against data authentication that entity authentication can not prevent. More specifically, entity authentication is insufficient for ensuring trusted interaction in case the client platform is compromised. A typical example is the situation of online banking transactions with mutual entity authentication. Even with strong 2-factor user authentication, and users' correct interpretation of server certificates, there is the possibility that malware on the client platform can modify data communicated between client and server platforms, and thereby compromise transactions. Current attacks against online banking are typically mounted in this way. Such attacks lead to breach of data integrity, but not a breach of entity authentication.

The preparation for this type of attacks typically includes tricking the user into installing a Trojan, i.e. a program that really or seemingly does something useful, but that in addition contains hidden malicious functionality that allows the attacker to take control of the client platform. During an online banking transaction the attacker uses the Trojan program to change transaction details without the user's knowledge. SpyEye, Zeus, IceIX, TDL, Hiloti, Carberp, and many others [11,12] are concrete examples of malware that enable such attacks.

The separation between the human/legal entity and the system entity on each side of a client-server session – as illustrated by Figure 2 – makes it necessary to specify which entity in particular is the assumed origin of data. In case e.g. the human user is assumed to be the origin, and the client system modifies data input by the user before it is sent to the server system, then this would be a breach of data origin authentication. However, in case the client system is assumed to be the origin, the same scenario would not be a breach of data authentication. The general rule is that the object of entity authentication must also be the origin of data authentication. For typical online transactions where the human user is directly involved and authenticated, the user must also be seen as the origin of data for data authentication purposes. Unfortunately current solutions for user data origin authentication are either non-existent or inadequate because they assume the client system to be the origin of data [13].

Users rely on visual cues to know whether a browser session is secured with TLS. After verifying that TLS is enabled, averagely security aware users will comfortably input their banking account and transaction details into the browser window. However, many users ignore that malware like those mentioned above has functionality commonly known as a 'web inject' that can change the behaviour of the browser and modify input and output data arbitrarily.

The fact that entity authentication and data authentication are two separate security functions implies that it is necessary to have specific security mechanisms to ensure data integrity in online transactions. The OffPAD enables data origin authentication with high assurance and usability, as explained below.

Data origin authentication can also be implemented with different modalities, similarly to entity authentication. It is thus meaningful to speak about syntactic, semantic or cognitive data authentication.

OffPAD – the Offline Personal Authentication Device

The PAD (Personal Authentication Device) is described by Jøsang and Pope [14] as a secure device external to the client computer platform. It functions as a user-friendly personal identity manager for automated user authentication to any online service. The PAD is the conceptual predecessor to the OffPAD.

The OffPAD (Offline Personal Authentication Device) described by Klevjer *et al.* [15] and Varmedal *et al.* [16] is an enhanced version of the PAD, where an essential characteristic is to be offline, i.e. not connected to the Internet. Keeping the OffPAD offline strengthens its security by eliminating exposure to Internet threats. The requirement of being offline means that the OffPAD should not have Wi-Fi or wireless broadband capabilities, but can e.g. support limited use of NFC in short periods. The OffPAD represents local user-centric identity management because it enables secure and user friendly management of digital identities and credentials locally on the user side. The OffPAD supports authentication of both user and SP identities (i.e. mutual authentication) and can in addition support data authentication. For access to the OffPAD, the user must unlock the device by using e.g. a PIN, pass phrase, biometrics or other adequate authentication credentials. A possible OffPAD design is illustrated in Figure 3.

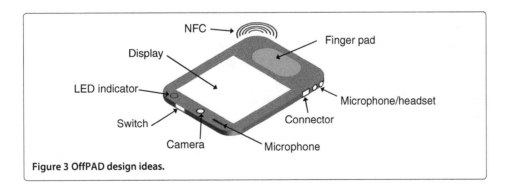

Figure 3 OffPAD design ideas.

The OffPAD is a trusted device, meaning that it is assumed to function as intended and to be adequately protected against relevant attacks. Attacks originating from the Internet are effectively eliminated by keeping the OffPAD offline. The OffPAD has limited connectivity to client platforms e.g. through wireless NFC or through USB cable which theoretically represents an attack channel. These communication channels must therefore be carefully controlled, e.g. by sanitizing the received data. Protection against attacks resulting from physical theft is to have traditional access control based on PIN and biometrics [17,18], combined with some level of physical tamper resistance.

It is not required that the OffPAD operating system and applications are free from vulnerabilities, because it is assumed that attackers are unable to exploit such vulnerabilities since the OffPAD is offline. In that sense, a specific software bug which would have been a vulnerability in an online system is strictly speaking not a vulnerability in the OffPAD because it can not be exploited. In other words, security vulnerabilities are eliminated simply by keeping the OffPAD offline.

The OffPAD may have several interfaces for communication. Microphone, touch screen and camera may be used for voice and face recognition, and a fingerprint reader may be used for both authenticating to the device and elsewhere.

The requirement of being offline does not totally exclude electronic communication with the OffPAD, but means that the communication follows controlled formats and takes place in short, restricted time periods. This decoupling from networks strengthens security as it removes threats from outside attacks.

Although electronic communication channels is normally be disconnected, limited communication is possible. NFC (Near Field Communication) as well as a backup USB connection are seen as the most suitable communication technologies for the OffPAD. Both technologies are fast, USB guarantees (physically) that the correct device is connected, and NFC gives high visual assurance that the correct device is connected. This limits the threat of a man-in-the-middle attack when connecting an OffPAD to a computer.

The first connection to the OffPAD requires Trust-On-First-Use (TOFU), also known as leap-of-faith [19]. On first use, there is no cryptographic way to verify the connection between the device and the client platform, the trust must simply be based on the physically observed set-up. On the first connection, pairing between the device and computer occurs, so that the subsequent connections can be verified to be between the same device and computer.

For our prototype implementations the TazCard device produced by TazTag[d] was used as a prototype OffPAD. The TazCard does not have all the functions described above which must be understood as an ideal OffPAD that currently does not exist. The TazCard is an android device with a touch screen that communicates via NFC and USB, which means that it has the basic characteristics of an OffPAD.

Local user-centric identity management

The OffPAD represents technology for improving the user experience and for strengthening security, which already makes it user centric. Since the OffPAD in addition is located on the user side, it is physically local to the user, and thereby represents technology for local user-centric identity management. The OffPAD can be used for a number of different security services [16], but this article only focuses on how it enables trusted interaction through mutual entity (user and server) authentication as well as data origin authentication. The OffPAD can also support incremental authentication modalities, i.e. syntactic, semantic or cognitive authentication, as shown in Figure 4.

In the sections below is described how the OffPAD enables mutual user-server entity authentication as well as data authentication. Each authentication type is illustrated with a ceremony [2] which is simply a protocol where relevant actions by users and the context environment are included. The 3 ceremonies can be chained and seen as one general ceremony that provides all 3 types of authentication, starting with server authentication, followed by user authentication and finally data authentication. The novelty of our solutions is that it supports trusted interaction even in the presence of malware infected client platforms.

Server authentication supported by the OffPAD

Secure access to online services is typically implemented with mutual authentication, i.e. with user authentication on the application layer and server authentication on the transport layer. Since mutual authentication goes between the user and the server, we require server authentication by the user as [S → U] which most often is not satisfied in current implementations, and user authentication by the server as [U → S] which currently is satisfied in most implementations.

Despite strong cryptographic server authentication, the typical implementation of TLS in browsers only enforces syntactic server authentication, so that any server identity is accepted as long as the certificate is correctly validated. This is a serious vulnerability which is also the reason why phishing attacks often succeed even when TLS is being used for server authentication [20].

Because phishing works fine without server certificates, most phishing sites do not have server certificates. Phishing victims often do not know the difference between a http connection (without certificate) and a https connection (with certificate and TLS), so server certificates are probably seen by attackers as an unnecessary expense. However, there are phishing sites with certificates, and paradoxically, phishing site certificates are automatically validated by browsers.

Current browser implementations of TLS with certificates do not support semantic or cognitive server authentication, so using TLS with certificate does not offer any meaningful authentication. In order to provide cognitive server authentication, a *petname system* [21-23] must be used, as described below.

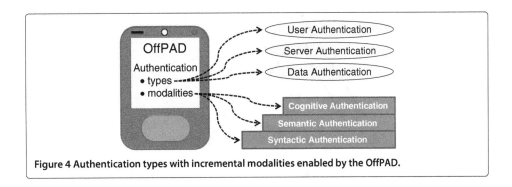

Figure 4 Authentication types with incremental modalities enabled by the OffPAD.

Reliable authentication of online entities require globally unique names that are understood by people. Domain names were designed to represent online identities of organisations, but domain names alone can be difficult to interpret.

Company names, trademarks and logos are typically used for recognising organisations in the real world, but would not be suitable for global online identification and authentication. This mismatch between names used in the online world and in the real world creates confusion about which unique domain name to expect when accessing online services. Without knowing which name to expect, authentication becomes meaningless.

Three fundamental desirable properties of names described by Bryce 'Zooko' Wilcox-O'Hearn [24] are to be global[e], unique[f] and memorable[g]. To be memorable a name has to pass the so-called *'moving bus test'* [25] which consists of testing whether an averagely alert person is able to correctly remember the name written on a moving bus for a definite amount of time, e.g. 10 minutes after the bus has passed. A name is unique if it is collision-free within the domain [23].

The triangle of Figure 5 where each of the three desirable properties of names are placed in one of the corners is commonly known as Zooko's triangle, and represents the basic foundation for the Petname Model [21,24].

Wilcox-O'Hearn claimed with supporting evidence that no name space can be designed where names generally have all three desirable properties simultaneously. A visual analogy of this idea is created by placing the three properties at the three corners of a triangle. In a triangle, the three corners are never connected by a single line, only pairs of corners are connected. The edges joining the corners then illustrate the possible properties that a name space can have. Wilcox-O'Hearn suggested to design name spaces of global and unique names (pointers), and name spaces of memorable and unique names (petnames).

The Petname Model consists of mapping a common name space of pointers to individual name spaces of petnames, which thereby combines all three desirable properties. A petname system is a system that implements the Petname Model. The OffPAD is ideal for hosting a petname system, so a simple petname system was implemented on the OffPAD represented by the prototype TazCard device.

In our implementation, the petname system on the OffPAD receives server certificates during the TLS handshake. In order to support cognitive server authentication, the server domain name (pointer) – received in a certificate – is mapped to a user-defined petname representing the SP, as illustrated in Figure 6. The server certificate is also validated in the

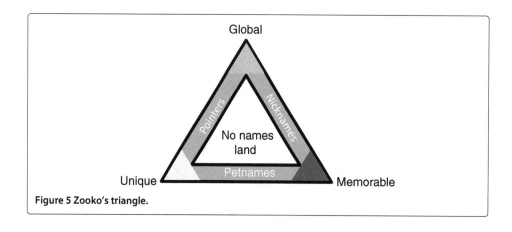

Figure 5 Zooko's triangle.

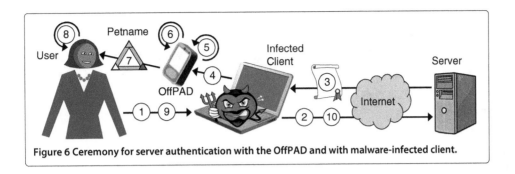

Figure 6 Ceremony for server authentication with the OffPAD and with malware-infected client.

traditional way, which provides syntactic server authentication. Strengthened authentication assurance can be obtained by having server certificates signed under DNSSEC, which would give a very high Server Authentication Assurance Level according to the server authentication framework proposed by Jøsang *et al.* [20].

The actions/messages of the ceremony of Figure 6 are described in Table 3.

The petname system combined with e.g. TLS enables manual trust evaluation by the user [21,26]. More specifically, a petname system in combination with TLS provides cognitive server authentication, which is precisely the security service needed to prevent phishing attacks.

If the user navigates to a web site where the petname system finds no match between its pointer (domain name) and a petname, the petname system should alert the user, or ask the user to add a new petname for the new service. Petname systems support cognitive authentication and protect users from falling victim to phishing attacks [21].

In a petname system, users create personal petnames to represent globally unique pointers for services that they use. When a specific service is accessed, the user recognises it by its petname, not by its pointer. A petname system makes it easy to manage the list of mappings between petnames and pointers, and automatically translates between pointers and petnames.

User authentication supported by the OffPAD

Online service users typically accumulate so many identities and related passwords that it becomes a usability challenge to manage them securely. In addition, since it is reasonable to assume that typical client platforms are infected by malware, storing and using

Table 3 Sequence of messages and actions for server authentication ceremony

Nr.	Message/action description
1.	User initiates secure TLS connection through client platform
2.	Client platform contacts server
3:	Server returns server certificate containing public key
4.	Server certificate is forwarded to OffPAD
5.	Server certificate is validated (syntactic server authentication)
6.	Server certificate is mapped to petname
7.	Petname is presented to user
8.	User performs cognitive server authentication
9.	User approves server authentication
10.	TLS connection established between client and server

credentials such as passwords on these platforms is a security risk. Passwords can be intercepted by Trojans either through keystroke logging, RAM-scraping, or by screenshots when shown on the screen in clear text. Even automatic log-in and identity management applications such as LastPass are not safe, as they release the clear text password to the web browser (or other application) during authentication, leaving it visible in memory for the Trojan to steal.

The OffPAD may be used to manage and authenticate a user to a system in a secure way. This would improve usability by providing a tool for identity management, and would also improve security in several respects. In a traditional scenario where the user types his password, or the password is decrypted by a password manager (e.g. LastPass), the password is exposed in the computer's memory and is vulnerable to attacks such as key logging or memory inspection. A solution for password authentication using an OffPAD is proposed by Klevjer *et al.* in [15], consisting of an extension to the original *HTTP Digest Access Authentication* scheme specified as a part of the HTTP standard in [27]. User credentials are stored in a hashed format on both the server and the OffPAD. When the user via the client requests a protected resource, the server responds with an authentication challenge, which on the client side is hashed with the user credentials and returned to the server. The server does the same challenge-response calculations locally, and compares the result and the response. If the two values match and the user corresponds to an authorized entity, the user is granted access to the resource. This can be done securely through an insecure channel, such as over HTTP, not requiring an extra connection to the server, just a browser plug-in or extension.

In this section, we describe a method for local user-side identity management based on the OffPAD, combined with an extension of the well-known HTTP Digest Access Authentication protocol. A brief overview of the existing HTTP Digest Access Authentication standard is provided next. We then describe our method of combining the OffPAD with extended HTTP Digest Access Authentication. The advantage of our method is that it totally prevents exposure of passwords on potentially vulnerable client platforms, and thereby represents secure local user-centric identity management solution. A proof-of-concept implementation of the method has been developed for the OffPAD prototype [28].

HTTP Digest Access Authentication (short: DAA) originates from the challenge-response authentication framework described in the original HTTP 1.0 specification [29]. It is a web standard for access control to a service or domain called *realm* by user authentication over HTTP. DAA was first defined in 1997 in RFC 2069 [30] and refurbished in RFC 2617 [27] in 1999. Its intended use is on the World Wide Web, but it is perfectly implementable for protection of local resources, or in any situation where application level access control is required[h].

The actions/messages of the ceremony of Figure 7 are described in Table 4.

Extended Digest Access Authentication (short: XDAA) represents an extension of traditional HTTP DAA in two respects. The actual IETF standard RFC 2617 is extended to allow more than just username and password as valid credential sets. The authentication process itself is also extended, physically, in that it is moved to another location. All client-side calculations done in the authentication phase are outsourced to the OffPAD.

Our XDAA is beneficial both for security and usability. By managing the user credentials on an external device, we get a local user-centric identity management system,

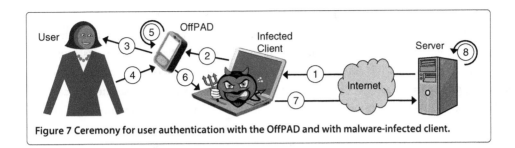

Figure 7 Ceremony for user authentication with the OffPAD and with malware-infected client.

so users are no longer required to remember their passwords. Moving the challenge-response calculations and handling of the values critical to authentication over to a mostly offline device, we reduce the risk of exposing these values. Moving the identity management over to such a device alleviates the cognitive and physical strain on the user during authentication, as well as removing the time penalty brought by user interaction in most situations[i].

In its simplest form (using the OffPAD and no further protection mechanisms), XDAA can be used with any HTTP server supporting original HTTP DAA without change to the server system. The immediate benefit is that the user's credentials themselves are never present. They are never shown on the screen, never exposed in any vulnerable state in the computer's memory and never transferred in clear text.

Data authentication supported by the OffPAD

Users generally rely on what they see on a computer display to read the output of transactions, to verify that they type correctly, and to ensure that the data being sent through online transactions is according to their intentions. In general, all this depends on the integrity of the computing platform to which the VDU (Visual Display Unit) is connected. Assuming that the computing platform is infected with malware it is *a priori* impossible to trust what is being displayed to be 100% correct [31-35].

The prospect that the computer display can lie to us is both frightening and real. This problem is amplified by the fact that we often read data from platforms that are not under our control, and that hackers have incentives for trying to manipulate the systems and the way data is displayed. For example, typical attacks against online banking consist of using a malicious Trojan on a client computer to send falsified transaction data to the bank server while displaying what the user expects to see.

In order to provide data authentication, some online banks offer SMS authorization of transactions, which consists of mirroring the received transaction data (destination

Table 4 Sequence of messages and actions for user authentication ceremony

Nr.	Message/action description
1.	Server sends http digest access authentication challenge to client
2.	Challenge from server is forwarded to OffPAD
3:	OffPAD presents user authentication request to user
4.	User approves authentication request
5.	OffPAD computes response to challenge from server
6.	Response is sent from OffPAD to client
7.	Client forwards response to server
8.	Server verifies response which completes user authentication

account and amount to be transferred) together with an authorization code by SMS to the user. After verifying the correctness of the transaction data, the user returns the authorization code via the browser to confirm that the integrity of the transmitted transaction data. In case of an attack, it is assumed that the user will notice when transaction data have been changed, so the attack can be stopped by canceling the transaction. This method can in theory provide strong data authentication, but it puts a relatively high cognitive load on the user for verifying the transaction data. In a study, it has been shown that about 30% of users fail to notice when transaction data in an SMS message have been changed, which means that 30% of attacks would succeed even in the presence of SMS authorisation [13]. The problem with SMS-authorisation is poor security usability, which fortunately can be solved with Lucidman as is explained below.

Figure 8 illustrates a simple ceremony for data origin authentication, i.e. to ensure that what is displayed on the VDU corresponds to what is being transmitted to other parties in online transactions. The method assumes that the user has an OffPAD with integrated camera, OCR (Optical Character Recognition) and communication functions. The user first captures a screenshot from the VDU with the OffPAD camera, then uses the OffPAD to recover the displayed data from the image through OCR, and finally to compute a MAC (Message Authentication Code) which is sent along with the original transaction data. The MAC enables the recipient server to authenticate the received original data.

The actions/messages of the ceremony are described in Table 5.

Even though it is assumed that the client platform is infected, it is easy to see that attackers will not be able to falsify the transaction data undetected. Falsified transaction data would produce a MAC mismatch, which would be discovered by the server in (8).

In order to successfully falsify data, the attacker would have to compromise both the client platform and the OffPAD simultaneously. Since the OffPAD is offline, it is assumed that the OffPAD will not be exposed to threats from the Internet. A more detailed threat analysis is provided in the next section.

Security analysis of the OffPAD

The OffPAD is considered as a trusted device, which means that it is assumed to provide the authentication services described in the sections above, more specifically 1) cognitive server authentication, 2) user authentication with never present cleartext passwords, and 3) cognitive data authentication. Should the OffPAD fail, then the mentioned authentication services would be invalidated. In this section we discuss possible threats against the OffPAD device and its integration into the security ceremonies described above. The discussed threats are summarized in Table 6.

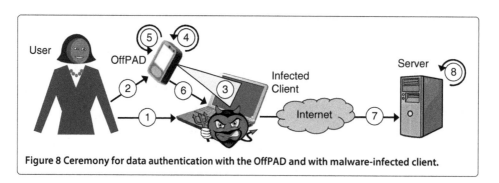

Figure 8 Ceremony for data authentication with the OffPAD and with malware-infected client.

Table 5 Sequence of messages and actions for data authentication ceremony

Nr.	Message/action description
1.	User types the transaction data in a browser window on the client computer
2.	User activates the OffPAD to take a snapshot of the browser window
3.	Snapshot is taken of the text displayed in the browser window on the VDU
4.	The OCR function recovers the transaction data from the snapshot
5.	MAC generation with the transaction data and the user-password as input
6.	OffPAD send the MAC to the client computer
7.	Client computer sends transaction data together with MAC to server
8.	Server verifies that the MAC corresponds to the received transaction data.

Unauthorized use of device

If an unauthorized person were able to use the functionality of the OffPAD device, the attacker might be able to activate the user authentication function as well as the data authentication function. This could have serious consequences, e.g. the masquerading as the user and executing fraudulent transactions. Furthermore, the attacker could breach the device integrity by making unauthorized modifications and configurations changes on the device, such as defining assigning existing petnames to fraudulent websites. In case the legitimate owner is unaware of the integrity breach and continues to use the OffPAD, the consequence could e.g. be that the owner is tricked to access fraudulent websites in the belief that they have been authenticated as legitimate websites by the petname system on the OffPAD.

To counter these threats, the OffPAD must authenticated its owner to unlock its functionality. User authentication must be based on owner credentials that can consist of PIN (something you know), on various biometrics modalities (something you are or do) such as fingerprint scan, face and iris recognition, touch and handling dynamics, or on something you have (physical token). Owner authentication and the design of owner credentials are outside the scope of this article. Suffice to say that it must be designed to provide adequate security assurance and usability.

Unauthorized use of the device can also be based on tampering. The OffPAD device must therefore be resistant to physical and electronic tampering, but these aspects are also considered to be out-of-scope.

Unauthorized use of unlocked device

If the owner unlocks the device and then leaves it unattended, it can be abused to access all protection realms to which the owner is authorized. The impact level of this abuse can be reduced by introducing a session timeout on the device. This way, an attacker has

Table 6 Threats against the OffPAD

Nr.	Threat name
1	Unauthorized use of device
2	Unauthorized use of unlocked device
3	Loss of owner credentials
4	Loss or destruction of device
5	Interception or modification of OffPAD communication
6	Data injection attacks
7	Ceremony protocol attacks

limited time to commit unauthorized actions. While he is also able to modify and delete identities on the device, there is no direct way for the attacker to recover the passwords on the device. Another prevention mechanism could be the use of continuous owner authentication through touch and handling dynamics.

Loss of owner credentials

By loss of owner credentials we mean that the owner is unable to use his or her credentials to activate the device, not that an attacker has gained control of the owner credentials. The owner can lose the ability to use credentials for various reasons, e.g. when forgetting the PIN or the fingers are damaged or too dirty to be recognized by the fingerprint scanner. In such situations there must exist a back-up procedure to unlock the device. This could e.g. be based on having separate primary and secondary owner credentials, where e.g. unlocking keys similarly to PUK (PIN Unlocking Key) for SIM cards, and/or on a physical key/token can represent secondary credentials to be used in case the primary credentials fail for some reason. The fundamental principle for secondary credentials is that they must provide equal or stronger security assurance than the primary owner credentials, but the usability might be inferior to that of the primary credentials. Other than these general comments, the topic of owner credentials recovery is outside the scope of this article.

Loss or destruction of device

Incidents of loss, theft or destruction of mobile devices occur relatively frequently, rendering the functions of the device unavailable. In such situations it is important that replacement devices can be obtained and configured relatively easily. For the OffPAD, this would require that a new OffPAD device can be configured with e.g. user passwords and petnames in an user friendly and secure manner. This requirement must be based on back-up procedures which e.g. to a storage device via a USB connection. The back-up data can be stored in cleartext format or in encrypted form, where both methods need to be studied and analysed further with regard to security assurance and usability. The design and analysis of back-up procedures are outside the scope of this article.

Interception or modification of OffPAD communication

As mentioned above the OffPAD must be able to communicate with client terminals e.g. trough a NFC radio link, or through a USB cable. This communication channel can be subject to passive interception or active modification, both of which represent a security and privacy threat. However this threat is relatively minor, as it is already assumed that the client platform is infected by malware. Thus, attacks against the communication channel would not cause significantly more damage than can already be caused by malware on the client platform. The only relevant aspect is that the possibility of attacking the communication channel represents a strengthening of threats that already exist. For example, in case the client platform is not infected by malware, an external third party could eavesdrop on the communication and thereby pose a threat to user privacy, but would be unable to attack authentication functions or the transactions themselves. The possibility of attacking the communication channel between the OffPAD and the client terminal requires physical proximity, which makes the attack difficult to execute in general and relatively easy to discover.

Data injection attacks

Data injection consists of sending malformed data to the OffPAD with the aim of causing harm to the OffPAD. Data injection could be generated by malware on the client computer with which the OffPAD communicates, or by malicious computers in physical proximity to the OffPAD. In case of software vulnerabilities on the OffPAD malformed data could damage the integrity of the OffPAD or cause data leakage, similarly to SQL injection attacks. It is therefore crucial that the format of received and transmitted data is well defined and validates, and that any malformed data can be properly handled and rejected. The data format will have XML at its core, but the detailed specification and the requirements for interpretation are outside the scope of this article.

Ceremony protocol attacks

Attacks can be directed at other elements of the security architectures than the OffPAD itself. The three proposed authentication ceremonies involve 4 entities and consists of up to 8 communication instances between those entities. A formal analysis if these ceremonies requires significant effort and is the subject of studies during the research activities of the OffPAD project started in 2014.

User experiment

A user experiment was conducted to assess whether cognitive server authentication with a petname system can improve users' resistance to phishing attacks, and to find out whether a petname system on an external device like the OffPAD is something that people would like to use. The experiment was conducted as part of a Master's project [36] at the University of Oslo.

Type of experiment

Data from user experiments can be collected qualitatively or quantitatively. Both methods have their advantages and disadvantages. Qualitative data gives insight, but can be challenging to analyse. Quantitative data can be subject to statistical analysis, but if taken out of context can often be misleading.

Several elements indicated that qualitative data would be best for our study. From a practical point of view we had to use one special computer with one specific connected device, which would make it difficult to let multiple participants undergo the experiment simultaneously to collect a sufficient amount of statistical data. The most important reason for collecting qualitative data was that it would give us more insight into the participants' thinking than statistical data could do.

For collecting qualitative data it is possible to use different types of methodologies [37], e.g. Conversation analysis, Analytic Induction, or Discourse Analysis. We did a simple case study combined with a usability experiment, where the user was observed while using the system, followed by an interview. Before doing the experiment we received the permission from the Data Protection Office for Research at the University of Oslo.

Selection of participants

While there is no agreed number of subjects in a qualitative study, Nielsen [38] states that a usability experiment only needs 5 subjects to spot the most relevant usability issues. The results can then be used to improve the prototype which in this way can be iteratively tested and improved in an economical way. Our purpose was not to iteratively improve our prototype, but simply to see whether cognitive server authentication as implemented in the prototype can give the intended positive security effect, as a proof of concept. Only a few participants would be needed to observe that effect. Using a high number of participants could be meaningful for validating the usability of the prototype when it is more finished and close to being introduced in a market.

The general consensus among experts is that the required number of participants depends on multiple factors [39]. Some of the factors to consider are the depth of the interview, what we want to get out of the study and the type of participants in the experiment. There is also some more tangible factors to take into account, like resources and time. When setting a number of participants the first factor we considered was the type of participants to invite. The target user group for an external device like the OffPAD consists of persons who regularly use services on the Internet where the goal of the experiment was to determine whether cognitive server authentication could provide increased security. With a prototype OffPAD available, the second goal was to find out if participants would be happy to use it. We concluded that six participants would be sufficient to get an indicative answer to these question.

The participants in this test were mainly students of informatics, but we chose to also include two students who did not have informatics as their field of study, to see if they would have other opinions than the rest. The results indicated that there was no clear difference.

Experiment set-up

The purpose of cognitive server authentication is to make it easy to detect fake websites. So for this experiment we created 4 fake sites to mimic 4 real websites. The subjects where asked to log in with a non existing account, because the petname system does not depend on having a user account on a specific website. Using real accounts would be problematic for three reasons. The first is that we would have to create accounts for non-existing users which would probably breach usage policies. Secondly, it was easier to implement a fake website with a page that says "Wrong user name or password" than to make a page that mimic the content served on the real site. Finally we did not want the users to enter their own user names and passwords for the real websites because it would make the subjects unwilling to participate. The fake sites consisted of a login-page and an account-refused page. The login-page of each of the fake sites were made to look almost exactly the same as that of the corresponding real websites. The domain names used are given in Table 7 below.

The real websites had domain names with .com as top level domain, whereas the corresponding fake sites had domain names with .ccm (the letter 'o' is replaced with the letter 'c') as top level domain. As .ccm does not exist as top level domain, the fake domains used

Table 7 Domain names for real and fake sites

Real domains	Fake domains
nb-no.facebook.com	nb-no.facebook.ccm
accounts.google.com	accounts.google.ccm
www.linkedin.com	www.linkedin.ccm
twitter.com	twitter.ccm

in this test were simply added to the host-file in Windows on the computer used for the experiment. This file is checked for a domain name to IP-address link before Windows asks the network's DNS-servers. These domain names pointed to a web server controlled by us.

All the real websites used TLS, but the fake websites did not. We considered whether to add server certificates for the fake sites, by generating a self-signed CA certificate and add it to the web browser repository. We concluded that it was not necessary, and that it would in fact be interesting to observe the participants' reaction to the lack of TLS for the fake sites.

Under the development of the fake sites and during the experiment Google Chrome was used as web browser. Most of the sites that we made copies of used JavaScripts to check if the domain name was the correct and redirect if not. So all of the images were saved locally and the JavaScripts removed. We made a change to the web server and the Chrome extension so that only this browser on this machine could open the phishing sites, thus making it impossible for anybody else to discover the phishing sites through the Internet.

Interview guide and questions

An interview guide was developed to introduce the participants to the experiment. The guide was based on Pathfinder International's guide to designing and conducting interviews [40]. The whole interview was conducted in Norwegian. A short summary in English is provided below.

The first part was an introduction to the experiment and interview. Where the subject was informed that the interview was audio recorded, where the recording would be kept confidential and the published results would not identify the subject. The subject was also informed that he or she was free to answer each question and could decide to terminate the interview at any time. It was important to respect the persons who offer their time for the experiment. The participants received a brief introduction to the petname system. Then the participant was presented with four obfuscated website links, and was asked to access each of the corresponding websites, log on with a given user name and password and add a petname for each website. The user name and password did not correspond to real accounts so the participant was simply given the message "Wrong user name and password" as expected. The participants were informed that a valid account was not a requirement for the petname system to work.

Then the participants were divided into two groups. The first group (hereafter refereed to as group A) did Exercise I first and then Exercise II, and the other group (refereed to as group B) did it in the opposite order.

After finishing these exercises, the participant was interviewed about their experience. The question are given below. The session concluded with an opportunity for the participant to add any last comments or remarks.

- **Exercise I, with OffPAD:** The participant sits down in front of the computer with a web browser running and the OffPAD connected. The participant is then invited to click on 4 different links in random order and to try to log on to the corresponding websites. One of the sites is fake, but it is different from the fake site of Exercise II. During this exercise the participants also uses the OffPAD connected to the computer.

- **Exercise II, without OffPAD:** The participant sits down in front of a computer with a web browser running. The participant is then invited to click on 4 different links in random order and to try to log on to the corresponding websites. One of the sites is fake, but it is different from the fake site of Exercise I. During this exercise the participant does not use the OffPAD.

Some of the questions were aimed at both checking if the participant has understood the petname system, and to see whether the petname system was easy to use. Then there were questions aimed at getting the participants' feelings and thoughts around their use of the petname system on the OffPAD. Finally there were questions aimed at determining the degree of awareness about possible phishing attacks with or without the petname system. We used the term 'OffPAD' in the questions to refer to the device they used, and the term 'petname system' when referring to the service it provided. The questions used in the experiment were the following:

1. While not using the OffPAD
    - Did all web sites work normally?
    - If you noticed anything unusual, what was it?
2. While using the OffPAD
    - Did all web sites work normally?
    - If you noticed anything unusual, what was it?
    - Would you have noticed the phishing site without the OffPAD?
    - If you think everything was normal, why did you not notice the warning on the OffPAD?
3. General questions to the experiment
    - How did your vigilance change after identifying the first phishing page?
    - How did your sense of security change when using the OffPAD?
    - Were you more or less aware during the experiment than usual?
    - How do you think the use of an OffPAD will impact your daily Internet use?
4. What would you think about using the Petname system...
    - if it was on your smart-phone?
    - if it was an own device?
    - if it was on a multi-purpose authentication device?
5. Normally when accessing and logging on to websites, how aware of phishing attacks are you?
6. How do you consider the possibility for phishing attacks against your person?
7. What do you think about the usability of the OffPAD prototype?
8. Is there something else you want to add?

Results

The experiment was conducted in the period 9 – 13 March 2013, and had six participants. Given the relatively low number of participants the statistics from the test are not representable for any group of people. However, their opinions and feedback about the system is valid. For some questions it is worth observing the number of participants who took one or the other stand, because it indicates whether it was a single point of view or if it reflected a more common opinion.

As a general observation, none of the participants reported any significant usability problems. Subject to the limited confidence provided by the small number of participants, it seems that the OffPAD prototype's user-friendliness is satisfactory.

Of the six persons we interviewed, only two did actually check the URL and discovered both the phishing sites before they used the user name and password. There was also one who saw some error in a graphical element, but when he or she checked it, he or she did not notice the change in the domain name.

None of the participants reacted to the missing TLS indicator in the web browser. All of the real pages used TLS, but none of fake ones did. A vigilant expert would maybe detect the phishing sites from the missing TLS. However, simply observing TLS on a website is no guarantee that the website is not a phishing site. We could very well have implemented the fake websites with certificates and TLS, and then even an expert would fail to detect the fake websites if he or she only used the presence of TLS as indicator.

In group B, which first did the exercise with the OffPAD, participants were generally more aware of possible attacks. This is because after detecting one phishing site they became more alert. It could be argued that the Hawthorne Effect [41] was at play, where a subject is more alert or efficient because they know they are being observed. However, this experiment was too small and simple to say anything about the possible influence of the Hawthorne Effect.

Without OffPAD

When not using the OffPAD and the petname system, four out of the six participants noticed the phishing site. One participant in group A said that he or she always checked the URL. In group B two of the participants said they detected the phishing site because they paid special attention to it during the experiment. Both claimed in their answers that they noticed something they thought was abnormal, but that that later turned out to be perfectly normal. The first person thought the URL was too long even if it was exactly the same length as the original, the other thought he read 'fakebook' in the URL even though the URL said 'facebook' as expected. The last participant in group B who noticed the phishing site without the OffPAD did so right away, he or she did also pinpoint the phishing site before trying to log into it in the exercise with the OffPAD.

With OffPAD

When using the OffPAD and the petname system, all participants detected the phishing site. The subjective feeling of security experienced with the OffPAD varied from indifference to a heighten sense of security with the OffPAD. Those who had an equal sense of security said the OffPAD did not add much to their own vigilance. The subjects who felt safer described the OffPAD as providing extra security protection when surfing the Internet. One of the important points mentioned by one of the subjects was that a petname system might make him or her more reckless on the Internet. This comment indicates that if the petname system is poorly implemented (e.g. not responding to GET-requests) it can give a false sens of security, making users an easier target for phishing attacks.

Feedback about the device

All the participants were negative to using an external device that only provided a petname system. Two participants mentioned that they would have considered it if it was in the size of a key chain. A third participant made the comment "Who should pay for this anyway?". It is a fair comment as such a device might be just as expensive as a simple smart phone.

Most of the participants were positive to a multi-purpose authentication device, as this would not require then to carry a separate device just for the petname system. One had an different approach to this, he or she said they would be more skeptical to a device with all of their credentials. "If it gets lost then you have more problems", referring to the case of theft where someone takes your device and manages to unlock it to access every service you are using.

The most preferable solution for all of the participants was to user their mobile phone in one way or another. One added "If it goes seamlessly, then I would use some time in the beginning to set it up. (...) As long as I only need to do define a petname for each website once".

Resistance to Phishing

Answers from the participants indicated that phishing sites are not considered to be a significant problem for them. This was because they either did not care or they did not believe they could not easily be tricked to access a phishing website since they mostly relied on their own bookmarks or typed the domain name themselves when logging in to a site.

There was one exception, where a participant considered phishing as a big threat. "You can lose much if you get phished". This person also mentioned indirectly to have been tricked by a phishing attack. This was also the person who discovered the phishing site before the petname system would do it. All participants considered themselves to be very unlikely targets of a directed spear-phishing attack, because they were only students without access to very sensitive information.

Usability of the prototype OffPAD

All of the participants was positive to the prototype, ranging from "It's quite alright" to "Surprisingly good". The size of the device was also mentioned here, where the participants typically commented that it has to be made smaller. The participants made positive remarks about its response time. One pointed out "It was intuitive and easy to use (...) for me it was no problems, but if you are not a technical person it might be a bit hard". It did not seem to be any problem to use the device for the two non-technical participants either.

Discussion and conclusion

It is challenging to provide trusted interactions between users and SPs in an environment where client platforms are infected by malware. Local user-centric identity management is a novel concept that provides a solution to this challenge, and is based on using an OffPAD which is an offline personal authentication device.

Complexity is the enemy of security, so the OffPAD should be simple and be limited in functionality. In contrast to smart phones or tablets that are designed to be open and have maximum connectivity and flexibility, the OffPAD should be a closed platform and have strictly controlled connectivity. These design principles are aimed at reducing the attack surface. The challenge is to offer adequate usability despite these constraints.

Communication between the client computer and the OffPAD requires drivers and software installed on the client computer. In case the client computer has been infected with malware the communication with the OffPAD could give attackers some information about the OffPAD, and potentially an opportunity to compromise the OffPAD itself. It is therefore important that the OffPAD enforces strictly controlled connectivity, e.g. by not having a direct connection to the Internet, and by enforcing time limits for connections to client computers or to other systems. The user should explicitly activate a connection, the OffPAD should clearly indicate when a connection is active, and should indicate when the connection ends. Typically, every connection should not last longer than one second at a time, just enough to exchange authentication information. If the communication takes much longer, the user is likely to leave the OffPAD connected to the client computer which would introduce new attack vectors.

The proposed ceremonies are designed to cross-check the processes of server authentication, user authentication and data authentication so that malware on the client platform can not break the integrity of these processes without detection. Malware could of course disrupt the processes and thereby cause a denial of service attack, but to protect against this form of attack is not within the scope of our proposed solutions.

Carrying an OffPAD as a separate device could represent a barrier for many people, so it is worth investigating whether the OffPAD could be integrated in a smart phone in a secure way. Modern mobile phones, or smart phones, are packed with advanced features and must be considered a 'general purpose computing platform'. This certainly provides great flexibility and support for many new business models, but it also opens up many new attack vectors. From 2010 to 2011 Juniper MTC reported a 155% increase in malware on mobile phones [42]. It should be noted that all the different mobile phone operating system manufacturers are trying to make their system more secure. At the same time, the market pressure enforces them to provide more connectivity and more flexibility into their devices, which necessarily also introduces new vulnerabilities. This makes a normal mobile phone unreliable for high security applications. A candidate smart phone is the 'TPH-One' produced by TazTag.

The integration of the OffPAD with a smart phone must basically be to implement within the same physical device two separate sub-systems, one being the OffPAD and the other the smart phone. Given the limited size of a smart phone, it would be practical to let both sub-systems share the I/O (input & Output) channels such as scree, microphone and loudspeaker.

However, a compromised smart phone could enable attackers to trick the user into believing that she is interacting with the OffPAD sub-system. It is therefore crucial that the user can be assured that she is interacting with one or the other sub-system, and not confuse the two sub-systems. To achieve this goal the user must be able to select each sub-system specifically, and the platform must clearly indicate which sub-system the user is interacting with at any time.

In this article we described local user-centric identity management as an architecture for providing robust authentication services of various types and modalities. In particular we have described the OffPAD as a personal device that supports mutual authentication between user and server, as well as authentication of data sent from the user to the server. These solutions can be integrated with many of the existing online security services and can provide trusted interaction even in environments where client systems are infected by malware.

The level of authentication assurance provided by our solutions can be compared the AAL (Authentication Assurance Levels) according to various frameworks for user authentication such as US EAG (Electronic Authentication Guideline) [43], the Norwegian FANR (Framework for Authentication and Non-Repudiation in Electronic Communication with and within the Public Sector) [44], the Australian NeAF (National e-Authentication Framework) [45], EU STORK (Secure Identity Across Borders Linked) [46], the Indian ePramaan Framework for e-Authentication [47], or ISO 29115 Entity authentication assurance framework [48]. According to these frameworks, our user authentication solution would be placed on AAL 3 (Authentication Assurance Level) on a scale from 1 to 4, where AAL 4 is the highest. However, our solutions could also support AAL 4 by implementing support for user certificates in the OffPAD. It can be mentioned that there are currently no frameworks for server authentication assurance levels, although it has been proposed [20,49].

Initial evaluations of the different authentication services have been carried out on the prototype OffPAD device. User experiments have already demonstrated that the OffPAD has the potential for good usability. Future work will focus on solutions for back-up and for updating software and the operating system on the OffPAD. Also to be investigated is whether the OffPAD system can be integrated as part of another device such as a smart phone, without compromising the security of the OffPAD. The goal is to find solutions that offer both strengthened security as well as increased usability, which thereby provides a robust basis for trusted interaction in online environments. Finally, it can be mentioned that research on local user-centric identity management continues in the OffPAD project during 2014-2016, supported by the *eurostars* research programme.

Endnotes
[a]Security Assertions Markup Language
[b]PKIX: Public-Key Infrastructure based in X.509 certificates [50]
[c]TLS: Transport Layer Security
[d]TazTag is a Lucidman project partner.
[e]Called *decentralized* in [24]
[f]Called *secure* in [24]
[g]Called *human-meaningful* in [24].
[h]The DAA challenge-response method is not restricted to HTTP.
[i]User interaction is necessary in situations where no identity or multiple identities are available for the user to authenticate with, the password is wrong, or another error appears.

Competing interests
The authors declare that they have no competing interests.

Authors' contributions
AJ edited the article and provided sections Introduction and Background and Related Work. KAV and AJ provided section Authentication Classes and Modalities, KAV, AJ and LM provided section OffPAD – The Offline Personal Authentication Device. AJ, CR, JD, KEH and PT contributed to section Local User-Centric IdentityManagement. HK and AJ provided section Security Analysis of the OffPAD. KAV provided section User Experiment, and all authors contributed to the Discussion and Conclusion. All authors read and approved the final manuscript.

Acknowledgements
The work reported in this article has been partially supported by eurostars project number E!8324 OffPAD, and by the Eureka project number 7161 LUCIDMAN.

Author details
[1]University of Oslo, Oslo, Norway. [2]ENSICAEN, Caen, France. [3]TazTag, Rennes, France. [4]Nets Norway AS, Oslo, Norway. [5]Domeneshop AS, Oslo, Norway. [6]CEV, Saint Lo, France. [7]Tellu, Asker, Norway. [8]Vallvi, Oslo, Norway.

References

1. PandaLabs (2012) PandaLabs Quarterly Report, Q2. http://press.pandasecurity.com/wp-content/uploads/2012/08/Quarterly-Report-PandaLabs-April-June-2012.pdf Accessed 2012-11-01
2. Ellison C (2007) Ceremony Design and Analysis. Cryptology ePrint Archive, Report 2007/399. http://eprint.iacr.org/2007/399
3. Stajano F (2011) Pico: No more passwords! In: Proceedings of the 19th International workshop security protocols. pp 49–81
4. Mannan M, van Oorschot PC (2011) Leveraging personal devices for stronger password authentication from untrusted computers. J Comput Secur 19(4):703–750
5. Laurie B, Singer A (2009) Choose the red pill and the blue pill: a position paper. In: Proceedings of the 2008 new wecurity paradigms workshop. ACM. pp 127–133
6. TCG (2014) Trusted platform module library specification, family "2.0", level 00, revision 01.16. Trusted Computing Group, Beaverton, Oregon, USA
7. Jøsang A (2012) Trust Extortion on the Internet. In: Proceedings of the 7th International workshop on security and trust management (STM 2011). Springer, Copenhagen
8. Jøsang A, AlFayyadh B, Grandison T, AlZomai M, McNamara J (2007) Security usability principles for vulnerability analysis and risk assessment. In: The proceedings of the annual computer security applications conference (ACSAC'07)
9. Jøsang A, Møllerud PM, Cheung E (2001) Web security: The emperors new Armour. In: The proceedings of the European conference on information systems (ECIS2001)
10. ITU (1991) Recommendation X.800, Security Architecture for Open Systems Interconnection for CCITT Applications. International Telecommunications Union (formerly known as the International Telegraph and Telephone Consultantive Committee), Geneva. (X.800 is a re-edition of IS7498-2)
11. Bodmer S (2012) SpyEye being kicked to the curb by its customers?. Research Note, Damballa Inc. http://www.damballa.com
12. Nayyar H (2010) Clash of the Titans: ZeuS v SpyEye. SANS Institute InfoSec Reading Room
13. AlZomai M, AlFayyadh B, Jøsang A, McCullag A (2008) An experimental investigation of the usability of transaction authorization in online bank security systems. In: The Proceedings of the Australasian information security conference (AISC2008)
14. Jøsang A, Pope S (2005) User-centric identity management. In: Clark A (ed). Proceedings of AusCERT 2005
15. Klevjer H, Jøsang A, Varmedal KA (2013) Extended HTTP digest access authentication. In: Proceedings of the 3rd IFIP WG 11.6 Working conference on policies & research in identity management (IFIP IDMAN 2013). Springer, London
16. Varmedal KA, Klevjer H, Hovlandsvåg J, Jøsang A, Vincent J, Miralabé L (2013) The OffPAD: requirements and usage. In: The 7th International conference on network and system security (NSS 2013)
17. Baloul M, Cherrier E, Rosenberger C (2012) Challenge-based speaker recognition for mobile authentication. In: IEEE Conference BIOSIG
18. Beton M, Marie V, Rosenberger C (2013) Biometric secret path for mobile user authentication: a preliminary study. In: International conference on mobile applications and security management (ICMASM)
19. Arkko J, Nikander P (2002) Weak authentication: how to authenticate unknown principals without trusted parties. In: Security Protocols Workshop. pp 5–19
20. Jøsang A, Varmedal KA, Rosenberger C, Kumar R (2012) Service provider authentication assurance. In: Proceedings of the 10th annual conference on privacy, security and trust (PST 2012)
21. Ferdous MS, Jøsang A (2013) Entity Authentication & Trust Validation in PKI using Petname Systems. In: Elçi A, et al. (eds). Theory and practice of cryptography solutions for secure information systems (CRYPSIS). IGI Global, Hershey, PA, USA
22. Ferdous MS, Jøsang A, Singh K, Borgaonkar R (2009) Security Usability of Petname Systems. In: Proceedings of the 14th Nordic workshop on secure IT systems (NordSec 2009)
23. Stiegler M (2005) Petname Systems. Technical Report HPL-2005-148, HP Laboratories Palo Alto. http://www.hpl.hp.com/techreports/2005/HPL-2005-148.pdf
24. Wilcox-O'Hearn BZ (2005) Names: Decentralized, secure, human-meaningful: Choose two. http://shoestringfoundation.org/~bauerm/names/distnames.html
25. Miller MS (2000) Lambda for Humans: The PetName Markup Language. Resources library for E, http://www.erights.org/elib/capability/pnml.html
26. Close T (2004) Trust Management for Humans. Waterken YURL, WaterkenInc. http://www.waterken.com/dev/YURL/Name/
27. Franks J, Hallam-Baker P, Hostetler J, Lawrence S, Leach P, Luotonen A, Sink E, Stewart L (1999) RFC 2617 – HTTP Authentication: Basic and Digest Access Authentication. IETF. http://www.ietf.org/rfc/rfc2617.txt
28. Klevjer H (2013) Requirements and Analysis of Extended HTTP Digest Access Authentication. Master's thesis, University of Oslo, Norway
29. Berners-Lee T, Fielding R, Frystyk H (1996) RFC 1945 – Hypertext Transfer Protocol – HTTP/1.0. IETF. http://www.ietf.org/rfc/rfc1945.txt
30. Franks J, Hallam-Baker P, Hostetler J, Leach P, Luotonen A, Sink E, Stewart L (1997) RFC 2069 – An Extension to HTTP : Digest Access Authentication. IETF. http://www.ietf.org/rfc/rfc2069.txt
31. Alzomai M, Alfayyadh B, Jøsang A (2010) Display security for online transactions. In: The 5th International conference for internet technology and secured transactions (ICITST-2010)
32. Jøsang A, Povey D, Ho A (2002) What you see is not always what you sign. In: Proceedings of the Australian UNIX and Open Systems Users Group Conference (AUUG2002)

33. Kain K, Smith SW, Asokanm R (2002) Digital signatures and electronic documents: a cautionary tale. In: Proceedings of IFIP conference on communications and multimedia security: advanced communications and multimedia security

34. Spalka A, Cremers AB, Langweg H (2001) The fairy tale of 'What You See Is What You Sign - Trojan Horse attacks on software for digital signatures. In: IFIP Working conference on security and control of IT in society-II (SCITS-II)

35. Weber A (1998) See What You Sign: Secure Implementations of Digital Signatures. In: Proceedings of the International Conference on Intelligence and Services in Networks (ISN 1998). pp 509–520

36. Varmedal KA (2013) Cognitive Entity Authentication with Petname Systems. Master's thesis, University of Oslo, Norway

37. Online QDA Project (2011) Methodologies. http://onlineqda.hud.ac.uk/methodologies.php (visited 13.03.2013)

38. Nielsen J (2000) Why you only need to test with 5 users. http://www.nngroup.com/articles/why-you-only-need-to-test-with-5-users/ (visited 25.02.2013)

39. Baker SE, Edwards R (2012) How many qualitative interviews is enough? Online. http://eprints.ncrm.ac.uk/2273/#.UF7md_-Mp-E.citeulike (visited 11.12.2013)

40. Boyce C, Neale P (2006) Conducting in Depth Interviews: A Guide for Designing and Conducting In-Depth Interviews for Evaluation Input. Pathfinder International. http://www.pathfind.org/site/DocServer/m_e_tool_series_indepth_interviews.pdf?docID=6301, (visited 11.12.2013)

41. McCarney R, Warner J, Iliffe S, van Haselen R, Griffin M, Fisher P (2007) The Hawthorne effect: a randomised, controlled trial. BMC Med Res Methodol 7(1):30

42. Juniper (2011) Juniper mobile threat report 2011. Technical report, Juniper Networks, Inc.

43. Burr WE, Dodson DF, Newton EM, Perlner RA, Polk WT, Gupta S, Nabbus EA (2013) Electronic Authentication Guideline – NIST Special Publication 800-63 Rev. 2. Technical report, National Institute of Standards and Technology

44. Ministry of Government Administration Reform M (2008) Framework for Authentication and Non-Repudiation in Electronic Communication with and within the Public Sector (in Norwegian: Rammeverk for autentisering og uavviselighet i elektronisk kommunikasjon med og i offentlig sektor). Technical report, Norwegian Gov.

45. Department of Finance and Deregulation (2009) National e-Authentication Framework (NeAF). Australian Government Information Management Office, Canberra

46. Hulsebosch B, Lenzini G, Eertink H (2009) Deliverable D2.3 - STORK Quality authenticator scheme. Technical report, STORK eID Consortium.)

47. Ministry of Communications and Information Technology (2012) e-Pramaan: Framework for e-Authentication, Government of India, Delhi

48. ISO (2013) ISO/IEC 29115:2013. Entity Authentication Assurance Framework. ISO, Geneva, Switzerland

49. Jøsang A (2014) Assurance requirements for mutual user and service provider authentication. In: 3rd International workshop on quantitative aspects in security assurance (QASA 2014)

50. ITU (1997) Recommendation X.509 V3, The Directory: Authentication Framework (also Known as ISO/IEC 9594-8). International Telecommunications Union, Telecommunication Standards Sector(ITU-T), Geneva

10

Detecting Sybil attacks in vehicular networks

Muhammad Al-Mutaz, Levi Malott[*] and Sriram Chellappan

*Correspondence: lmnn3@mst.edu
Department of Computer Science,
Missouri University of Science and
Technology, Rolla, MO (65401), USA

Abstract

A Sybil attack consists of an adversary assuming multiple identities to defeat the trust of an existing reputation system. When Sybil attacks are launched in vehicular networks, the mobility of vehicles increases the difficulty of identifying the malicious vehicle location. In this paper, a novel protocol for Sybil detection in vehicular networks is presented. Considering that vehicular networks are cyber-physical systems, the technique exploits well grounded results in the physical (i.e., transportation) domain to detect the Sybil attacks in the cyber domain. Compared to existing works that rely on additional cyber hardware support, or complex cryptographic primitives for Sybil detection, the protocol leverages the theory of *platoon dispersion* that models the physics of naturally occurring vehicle dispersion. Specifically, the proposed technique employs a certain number of roadside units that periodically collect reports from vehicles regarding their physical neighborhood. Leveraging from existing models of platoon dispersion, a protocol was designed to detect anomalously *close* neighborhoods that are reflective of Sybil attacks. To the best of the authors' knowledge, this paper is unique in integrating a well established theory in transportation engineering for detecting cyber space attacks in vehicular networks. The resulting protocol is simple, efficient, and robust in diverse attack environments.

Keywords: Vehicle-to-vehicle; Vehicle-to-infrastructure; Platoon dispersion; Sybil; Detection

Background and literature review

Introduction

Organizations in many countries today are investing in vehicular networks to leverage wireless networking support to improve state-of-the-art in road transportation. The US Federal Communications Commission (FCC) has allocated 75 MHz of spectrum in the 5.9 GHz band for Dedicated Short Range Communications, a set of protocols and standards for short to medium-range wireless communication for automotive use. Some recent vehicular networking efforts are the USDOT's Vehicle Infrastructure Integration (VII), which is a cooperative initiative between USDOT and automobile manufacturers, focusing on feasibility of deploying communications systems for safety and efficiency of road transportation systems. The ERTICO partnership is a multi-sector partnership pursuing development and deployment of Intelligent Transport Systems across Europe. Apart from these efforts, a variety of VANET test-beds have been set up in academia also for basic research and development of services.

This paper addresses a critical and emerging security problem in vehicular networks, namely detecting the presence of Sybil attacks. Sybil attacks are classified as an attack on the trust of a peer-to-peer system by an attacker assuming many pseudonymous identities. Using these identities, the attacker can gain a disproportionately large influence on system functionality. In vehicular networks, the presence of a Sybil attack can have negative consequences. For instance, in an application like road safety, consider a single malicious vehicle, V_M, assuming a large number of fake identities incorrectly reporting road conditions. Other benign vehicles will tend to believe such a message, since it appears to be coming from multiple vehicles, and may adjust their routes. In such a case V_M can potentially obtain exclusive access to the road, which it otherwise could not. A number of other applications like content exchange, intelligent traffic signalling, and ramp metering can all be compromised in the presence of Sybil attacks. Unlike static networks like the Internet, vehicular mobilities make Sybil detection very difficult with the added spatio-temporal constraints.

Related work

The problem of detection Sybil attacks in VANETs has been previously studied. In [1] and [2], the proposed solution detects Sybil attacks when vehicles may only hold one valid pseudonym at a time. When a pseudonym need to be refreshed, a new pseudonym is obtained from a trusted Road-Side Unit (RSU). The consequence of this approach is a possibly complex pseudonym allocation mechanism implemented by the RSU network. Another technique leverages directional antennas to identify the location/direction of message arrival [3]. A vehicle launching a Sybil attack will likely be detected as many messages will arrive from the location/direction. However, in dense networks, localization errors can lead to frequent false positives. This scheme may be compromised as a smart attacker may use directional antennas to mislead its neighbors about its direction.

In [4], heavy-weight cryptographic techniques are leveraged for detecting Sybil attacks in VANETs. Specifically, each vehicle is given a list of pseudonyms to protect their privacy during communication. However, the pseudonyms of each vehicle are designed in such a manner wherein they are all hashed to a common value. By calculating the hashed values at Road Side Units, a central server can determine whether or not certain pseudonyms came from the same pool. Sybil attacks are detected if many pseudonyms from the same pool are detected in a short interval of time. Unfortunately, the computational complexity of cryptographic protocols in this technique is quite high.

In [5], GPS and RSSI signal measurements are used for detecting Sybil nodes. The proposed scheme uses Vehicle-to-Vehicle (V2V) communications to confirm reported positions of vehicles by referencing the RSSI measurements. To correct inaccuracies arising from RSSI measurement, caused by vehicle mobility, traffic patterns and support from roadside base stations are used. Specifically, statistical algorithms are implemented to verify the signal strength distribution of a suspect vehicle over time to significantly reduce the detection rate. In [6], analysis is performed to quantify performance of Sybil detection under assumptions like transmission range, antenna model, signal strength etc. Unfortunately, the un-reliability of RSSI measurements limits the practical reliability of these techniques [7]. In [8], inability of multiple vehicles to exhibit close temporal and spatial correlations at multiple locations is exploited for Sybil defense. The idea is to have RSUs sign location and timestamp information for vehicles as they move. Upon detecting groups of vehicles having many similar locations with similar timestamps, a Sybil attack is detected. The overhead in this scheme though is quite high, especially in the case of urban networks. Significant cryptographic overhead is incurred as RSUs have to sign each received message.

We also would like to point out two other areas of work that are also closely related to our problem of Sybil attack detection in vehicular networks. The first area is secure localization in wireless networks like sensor and mobile ad hoc networks [9,10], wherein locations of nodes are determined in a secure manner. Our problem is similar, but orthogonal in the sense that we are attempting to verify integrity of relative location updates as vehicles move in the network. The other area we wish to highlight is the issue of detecting Sybil attacks and nodes in static networks like sensor, Internet scale, and social networks [11-14]. As can be observed, while the goal of these works are related to ours, the issue of vehicle mobility and unique mobility patterns of these nodes necessitates fundamentally new approaches for Sybil detection, which we attempt in this paper.

Contributions

Presented in this paper is an innovative protocol for Sybil detection in vehicular networks. Vehicular networks today are examples of cyber physical systems, where there is a clear integration of cyber and physical components. The premise of this paper starts with two simple questions: Can the natural physics of the underlying transportation domain be integrated with the Cyber domain in detecting Sybil attacks, and b) If so, can such an integration generate high quality solutions to detect Sybil attacks, while alleviating complexities (in the form of complex cryptography and additional hardware requirements) in the cyber domain. This papers yields a positive response to both questions.

The technique employs a certain number of road side units (RSUs) that periodically collect reports from communicating vehicles regarding this neighborhood. In the event of a vehicle performing Sybil attacks, the geographic proximity the Sybil identities will be long-term and repeating, while the geographical proximity of benign vehicles will short-term. To put it in terms of transportation engineering, Sybil identities will appear to *"platoon"* together, while identities of benign vehicles will eventually *"disperse"*. The dispersion of vehicles in roads occurs due to a combination of road conditions, vehicle dynamics and human factors. This theory has been extensively studied by transportation engineers in the last five decades in the form of a theory called *"platoon dispersion"* [15-18]. Integrating platoon dispersion models provide an alternative method for Sybil attack detection. To detect attacks, RSUs compare models of naturally occurring dispersion among benign vehicles with anomalously occurring platoons among Sybil nodes. Using a combination of both theoretical analysis and simulations, the simplicity, efficiency, practicality and quality of the protocol for Sybil detection in vehicular networks is demonstrated. To the best of the authors' knowledge, this paper is unique in proposing an inter-disciplinary approach for addressing cyber space attacks in emerging vehicular networks.

Paper organization

The rest of the paper is organized as follows. Section 'Platoon dispersion and its application to Sybil detection' presents a brief overview of platoon dispersion theory in transportation engineering, and its application for Sybil detection in vehicular networks. Section 'Research design and methodology' presents the formal attack model, problem statement, overall framework, and protocol for Sybil detection. Section 'Performance evaluations' will demonstrate the performance of the protocol, and the paper concludes in Section 'Conclusions'.

Platoon dispersion and its application to Sybil detection

Provided first is a brief overview of how models of dispersion among vehicles that naturally occur in roads have been studied by transportation engineers. Afterwards, a simplified example of how to use platoon dispersion theory for Sybil detection is presented. The discussions will help guide the proposed Sybil detection protocol discussed in the next section.

Platoon dispersion theory in transportation engineering

A platoon is a group of vehicles traveling in close proximity for some amount of time as shown in Figure 1. Ideally, consistent vehicle platooning is preferable and improves critical transportation parameters like signal optimization, congestion avoidance, improved road safety, and capacity [19-23][a]. Under normal traffic, vehicle platooning is short-term. Clearly, if all vehicles in an existing platoon are traveling at a constant speed, a platoon will never disperse. However, due to physical factors like road friction, vehicle characteristics and signalling, human factors, lane changes, and fatigue [24] cause platoons to disperse over time. The longer the travel time between points the greater dispersion, due to the difficulty of maintaining constant speed over longer time scales. This phenomena is called *platoon dispersion*, a simple illustration of which is shown in Figure 2.

Platoon dispersion has been well studied in transportation engineering [15-17,25-31], via two mathematical models. One is the (more popular) Robertson's geometric distribution model [16] and the other is the Pacey's normal distribution model [15]. Both models assume that road segment travel times follow some probability distribution. The Robertson platoon dispersion model follows a shifted geometric series, and has been implemented in traffic-simulation software like SCOOT [32], SATURN [33] and TRAFLO [34]. The basic of Robertson recursive platoon dispersion model takes the following form:

$$q'_t = R \cdot q_{t-T_{min}} + (1 - R) \cdot q'_{t-\delta t}.$$ (1)

Figure 1 An eight-car platoon. Real-life example of eight cars in a platoon configuration.

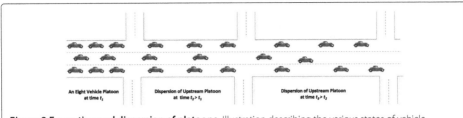

Figure 2 Formation and dispersion of platoons. Illustration describing the various states of vehicle platoons.

$$R = \frac{1}{1 + \alpha \beta T_{mean}}, \quad \text{where } 0 \leq R \leq 1. \tag{2}$$

A numerical procedure was developed for the Robertson model in [25] by rewriting Equation 1 as,

$$q'_t = \sum_{i=T_{min}}^{\infty} R \cdot (1 - R)^{i-T_{min}} \cdot q_{t-i}. \tag{3}$$

where,

q'_t: arrival flow at the downstream location at time t-T (veh/hr);

q_t: departure flow at the upstream location at time t (veh/hr);

δt: time step duration;

T_{min}:   minimum travel time on the roadway;

T_{mean}:   mean roadway travel time, measured in units of time steps.

$\alpha = \frac{1-\beta}{\beta}$:   dimensionless platoon dispersion factor depending on the level We are also investigating moreof friction along the roadway;

$\beta = \frac{2T_{mean}+1-\sqrt{1+4\sigma^2}}{2T_{mean}}$:   dimensionless travel-time factor;

R: smoothing factor governing dispersion, where $0 \leq R \leq 1$;

σ: the standard deviation of link travel time assuming individual vehicle speeds follow normal distribution and are unchanged.

As can be seen from Equations 1, 2, 3 and definitions of parameters, all we need to know are the speed deviations σ among vehicles, and the mean travel time T_a between the upstream and downstream locations. If both can be determined (which is quite straightforward to obtain), one could compute platoon dispersion factors α and β. These parameters subsequently can be used to compute the smoothing factor R, from which the degree of how an upstream platoon will disperse at the downstream location can be computed.

Figure 3 shows an illustration of *upstream* platooning and its *downstream* dispersion, wherein the shaded portion represents *similar* vehicle speeds that tend to platoon together, while non-shaded portion represents *varying* speeds of vehicles that *disperse* from the original platoon. A numerical example of dispersion based on the Robertson model [16-18] is shown in Figure 4. Each observation (i.e., downstream) point is one mile apart, and the minimum travel time between each point is one minute. For small speed deviations, the dispersion in expected number of vehicles reaching the observation point

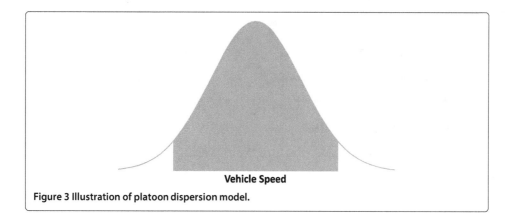

Figure 3 Illustration of platoon dispersion model.

is less than the case where the speed deviation increases. This leads to platoon sizes decreasing, progressively, as vehicles travel from one observation point to another.

An illustrative example of Sybil detection using platoon dispersion

Consider a case where there are 50 vehicles in an upstream platoon. Let each vehicle have a unique identity given by $\{V_1, V_2, \ldots, V_{50}\}$. Vehicle V_{50} is malicious and possesses 50 fake identities $\{\bar{V}_1, \bar{V}_2, \ldots, \bar{V}_{50}\}$. When all vehicle communicate with each other (including V_{50} with all of its identities to launch a Sybil attack), the up-stream platoon will appear to have 100 vehicles. With prior knowledge of road characteristics and (either currently sampled or prior estimates of) vehicle speeds, the dispersion parameters and the expected degree of dispersion at downstream can be computed. Say the smoothing factor is $R = 20\%$. If the Sybil, V_{50}, is part of the downstream platoon (recall shaded area in Figure 3), the number of identities actually seen in the downstream platoon is $n_d = 0.20 \times 50$ (benign vehicle identities) + 50 Sybil identities = 60 identities. If the Sybil vehicle falls outside of the downstream platoon (recall the non-shaded area in Figure 3), then the number of identities actually seen in the downstream platoon is $n_d = 0.20 \times 50 = 10$ identities.

It is easy to see that abnormalities in the physical domain will manifest in the form of abnormal platooning (and ensuing dispersion) under Sybil identities in cyber space. If all

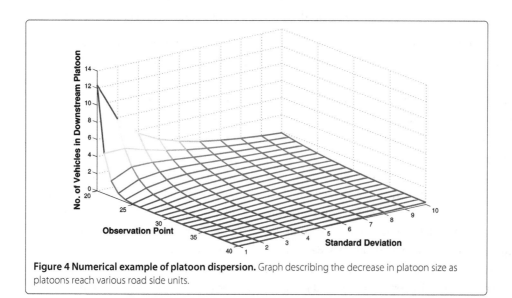

Figure 4 Numerical example of platoon dispersion. Graph describing the decrease in platoon size as platoons reach various road side units.

the identities upstream (i.e. 100 of them) are benign, the number of vehicle identities in the downstream platoon is expected to be $n_d = 0.20 \times 100 = 20$. Sufficient abnormalities in platoon dispersion that are straightforward to determine leading to a natural, elegant, and simple technique to detect Sybil attacks. To the best of the authors' knowledge, such a technique has not been attempted yet, and is formalized and elaborated in the next section.

Research design and methodology

In the previous section, a basic theory of platoon dispersion was illustrated, and how in principle can be leveraged for detecting Sybil attacks in vehicular networks. In this section, the protocol for detecting Sybil attacks via leveraging from platoon dispersion is presented. Several practical challenges in the actual design and implementation of the proposed protocol are addressed afterwards.

Vehicular network model

It is assumed that a certain number of Road Side Units (RSUs) are deployed in the vehicular network. The RSUs can communicate with each other and vehicles on the road. Communication is achieved through a 2-way radio, such as a DSRC (Dedicated Short Range Communications), to send and receive messages to other vehicles and RSUs. Each Vehicle V_x also has a unique identity that can identify it in the network. The identity for each V_x also acts as a unique public key P_x used for message encryption. Each vehicle maintains a secure private key for decryption of messages. Since energy is not a constraint, asymmetric encryption is feasible in vehicular networks [35]. Note that message confidentiality and privacy are not emphasized in this paper. It is assumed that some system exists for protecting confidentiality. If privacy is desired, techniques have been proposed for utilizing temporal pseudonyms that expire after a certain time [36], or using local coordination among vehicles and aggregating responses before forwarding messages. Such techniques do preserve vehicle privacy, and their usage will not affect the proposed protocol. Furthermore, a Central Coordination Authority (CCA) is involved in coordination among all RSUs, along with any key and pseudonym distribution among vehicles. The CCA and RSUs are assumed to be trusted.

For the proposed protocol, RSUs must have some prior information about vehicles and speed distributions along road segments. Such knowledge is reasonable and practical. In many countries across the world, including the US, efforts are being made to estimate vehicle densities and speed distributions for traffic management purposes. This is acheived using a variety of modern equipment like road side sensors, traffic light cameras and remote sensing imagery [37-40]. More discussion on this assumption and the accuracy of estimates are detailed in the next subsection during the description of the proposed protocol.

Simple attack model and problem definition

The attack model provides contextual information and elaborates the roles of the various agents. The attacker intends to subvert the integrity of peer vehicle communications by launching Sybil attacks. The attack has captured a certain number of legitimate identities (or keys) belonging to other vehicles. Such an attack model is practical, powerful, and has not been considered yet in related literature [1-6]. For example, a malicious parent could easily steal identities of multiple members of their family that have identities already provisioned. Clearly with more sharing of vehicles today (e.g., rental cars and car pools), the feasibility of skimming attacks in vehicles (or in related hardware) to steal identities is even more practical. With multiple legitimate identities in hand, the potency of an attacker is much higher. The mobile nature of vehicular networks makes detection of such identity thefts quite difficult in practice. It is assumed that the attacker will utilize all its Sybil identities to attack the network in an attempt subvert the network integrity. Note that in this paper, we consider for simplicity one attacker in the network. The protocols we propose can be directly applied to multiple (but non-colluding) attackers. Analyzing and enhancing protocols for thwarting colluding attackers is part of future work[b].

Given the attack model, the formal problem statement is to rapidly detect the presence of Sybil attacks in a vehicular network.

Protocol 1 Protocol Executed by Each Vehicle V_x

1: **Each Vehicle V_x Executes the Following Steps when traveling between RSUs**
2:   **For** every Vehicle V_y communicating with V_x
3:     Store V_y
4:   **End For**

5: **Each Vehicle V_x Executes the Following Steps when in range of RSU**
6:   Forward Stored Vehicle Identities to RSU

Methods
Proposed technique for Sybil detection in vehicular networks
Overview

In Section Platoon dispersion and its application to Sybil detection, the basic overview of platoon dispersion and how it can be leveraged in principle for Sybil detection was presented. Unfortunately, there is one critical challenge to overcome before practical Sybil attack detection via leveraging platoon dispersion. Recall from Section 'Platoon dispersion theory in transportation engineering' that existing models for platoon dispersion assume that vehicle speeds from an upstream point to a downstream point are unchanged. These speeds are then used to derive σ (which is used to derive Smoothing Factor R in Equation 2), that subsequently determines dispersion phenomena. Anomalies in the dispersion phenomena naturally provide an ideal foundation for detecting Sybil attacks *in theory*. However, in practice, vehicle do not travel with constant speed and speed can vary widely between vehicles. This is solved by using measurement samples from peer vehicles and incorporating these data to determine platooning anomalies. A high level of confidence of detecting Sybil attacks is possible through this method.

Protocols description and analysis
Protocols 1 and 2 executed by vehicles and RSUs, respectively, illustrate the proposed technique for Sybil detection. As demonstrated in Protocol 1, each Vehicle V_x will store the identities of all vehicles with which it has communicated when traveling between RSUs. These identities are forwarded to an RSU when the vehicle is in range. Upon a vehicle transmitting its internally stored list of other communicating vehicles, the list may be

---

Protocol 2 Protocol Executed by Each Downstream RSU R_d

1: **Inputs:**

Definition of Platoon; Mean (μ_N^*) and Standard Deviation (σ_N^*) of Travel Times for N Vehicles in Upstream Platoon at R_u traveling to R_d based on Historical Information;

CDF of Platoon Dispersion $\left(F_R(r) = \int_0^r \frac{1}{\sigma_N^*\sqrt{2\pi}} e^{-\frac{1}{2}\left(\frac{\sqrt{\frac{1-x}{x^2}}-\mu_N^*}{\sigma_N^*}\right)}\right) dx$; Confidence Interval of Sybil Detection (ϵ);

2: **Upon Receiving Vehicle Ids (Y_u) of a Platoon from Upstream RSU R_u**

3: Denote N as Number of Received Identities

4: Wait for Minimum Travel Time (T_{min}) between Location of R_u and Current Location

5: Receive Identities from every Forwarding Vehicle

6: Denote Y_d as Number of Vehicles Currently Platooning

7: Set m as Platoon Ratio $(m = \frac{Y_d}{Y_u})$

8: Compute CDF of m vehicles in current platoon as $F_R(r = m) = \int_0^m \frac{1}{\sigma_N^*\sqrt{2\pi}} e^{-\frac{1}{2}\left(\frac{\sqrt{\frac{1-m}{m^2}}-\mu_N^*}{\sigma_N^*}\right)} dx$

9: **If** $\frac{\epsilon}{2} < F_R(r = m) < 1 - \frac{\epsilon}{2}$

10: Flag No Sybil Attacks

11: **Else**

12: Flag the Detection of Sybil Attack

13: **End If**

14: Forward Current Platoon to Downstream RSU

---

deleted. Additionally, vehicles do not have to disclose their location for the protocol to work.

Protocol 2 presents the steps executed by a downstream RSU R_d for Sybil detection. The inputs to the protocol are as follows. First, the Central Coordination Authority defines what constitutes a platoon. One simple way to define a platoon is to say all vehicles currently within the communication range of an RSU is a platoon. Alternate definitions can also exist depending on traffic models and does not change the protocol or its execution. Second, R_d will have prior models of vehicle densities and speed distributions from historical information. Such information can be obtained from a number of traffic management organizations. These organizations regularly collect information on vehicle volumes, densities, and speeds along road segments to improve congestion control, signalling, accident management, and other traffic attributes. A number of recent studies also propose innovative and accurate approaches to obtain such information including deployment of road side sensors and remote sensing imagery to obtain such information [37-40].

From such information, each RSU can derive the mean (μ_N^*) and standard deviation (σ_N^*) of vehicle travel time based on the number of vehicles N traveling from upstream. Note that even if such information may be historical and may not reflect existing trends, it is always possible to obtain samples in real-time from current traffic to build accurate more profiles. Recall from Equation 2, that the smoothing factor R governing platoon dispersion is given by $R = \frac{\sqrt{1+\sigma^2}-1}{2\sigma^2}$, where σ is the standard deviation of link travel time assuming individual vehicle speeds follow normal distribution and are unchanged. To obtain σ, Equation 2 can be rewritten as $\sigma = \sqrt{\frac{1-R}{R^2}}$. In practice vehicle speeds and link travel times on roads between RSUs fluctuate. Assuming the link travel times of each vehicle follows normal distribution [41,42] with parameters μ_N^*, σ_N^*, and N vehicles in an upstream platoon, the probability density function (pdf) of σ is

$$f_\sigma(x) = \frac{1}{\sigma_N^* \sqrt{2\pi}} e^{-\frac{1}{2}\left(\frac{x-\mu_N^*}{\sigma_N^*}\right)} \tag{4}$$

Consequentially, the probability density function (pdf) for the smoothing factor R as

$f_R(r) = \frac{1}{\sigma_N^* \sqrt{2\pi}} e^{-\frac{1}{2}\left(\frac{\sqrt{\frac{1-r}{r^2}}-\mu_N^*}{\sigma_N^*}\right)}$. The Cumulative Distribution Function (CDF) is then given by

$$F_R(r) = \int_0^r \frac{1}{\sigma_N^* \sqrt{2\pi}} e^{-\frac{1}{2}\left(\frac{\sqrt{\frac{1-r}{r^2}}-\mu_N^*}{\sigma_N^*}\right)} d_x. \tag{5}$$

The final input to the protocol is the confidence interval (ϵ) of Sybil Detection, that is predetermined by the Central Coordination Authority.

Once R_d obtains the number of vehicles n_d departing from R_u, it waits for T_{min}, the minimum travel time on the link. R_u starts receiving messages from vehicles regarding identities they had communicated with. Based on times of messages received, R_d determines the number of vehicles in the current platoon as Z. It then computes the platoon ratio as $m = \frac{Z}{Y}$ and $F_R(r = m)$ from the CDF of the smoothing factor. There are two cases of interest here. When the Sybil attacker is part of an upstream platoon and part of the downstream platoon, the number of vehicles Y_d in the downstream platoon will be abnormally large as the Sybil identities will not disperse. In the second case, the Sybil vehicle is not in the downstream platoon, causing the number of vehicles Y_d in the downstream platoon will be abnormally less. This is due to large number of Sybil identities being dispersed. In the first case, $F_R(r = m)$ will assume a large value as the platoon size will show little relative change, and in the latter case $F_R(r = m)$ will assume a much smaller value as the relative change in platoon size is high. This is captured in Step 9 of Protocol 2, where abnormal platoons in both cases are checked to indicate a Sybil attack.

Results and discussion

Only a limited number of numerically obtained parameters are used in the execution of the protocol. The critical parameters are μ_N^*, σ_N^* and ϵ. When μ_N^* is low, dispersion is low. This means that the likelihood of vehicles platooning together is higher, hence lowering the chances of detecting Sybil identities. On the other hand, σ_N^* denotes the standard deviation or error in the estimation of link arrival time. If σ_N^* is low, then the error in estimation of link arrival time is better, yielding a steeper CDF, which improves detection accuracy. The parameter ϵ determines the degree of confidence in detection. Finally, all of these parameters are integral to the attacker strength in terms of number of Sybil nodes during detection. Next, the impacts of these parameters on the performance of the protocol are detailed.

Performance evaluations

In this section, the performance evaluation of our protocol to detect Sybil attacks in vehicular networks are reported. Section 'Preliminaries' presents preliminaries, while Section 'Analysis and simulation results' illustrates performance data.

Preliminaries

The simulations were performed on Simulation of Urban Mobility (SUMO), which is an open source traffic simulation package [43]. SUMO allows importing custom maps, user-defined vehicle trips, and detailed simulation output for every vehicle. A map consisting of 10 intersections by 10 intersections was constructed to simulate a typical inner-city topology. The distance between each intersection 400 ft or approximately 122 m. This gives a block of 400 ft × 400 ft. The map was then populated with varying number of vehicles generated with random source/destination pairs with the trip defined as the shortest route between the source and destination. The simulator provides a high degree of configurability for the protocol analysis while providing reports in easy-to-process formats. Additionally, the simulator provides fine-grain data as information for every vehicle for every second is saved. We wish to point out that the grid based topology we employ is widely used for simulation purposes and hence we adopted it in this paper. Extending our simulations to more complex and realistic topologies is part of future work.

A normal distribution with the current case parameters were used to randomly assign start and maximum speeds for vehicles. The simulator then creates a simulation report after completion. The output file includes every vehicle's speed, position, current road, position on road, and other data. Then these logs files were parsed to create individual files for every vehicle containing the timestep, vehicle speed, current position, and current road at that timestep.

The same data was used to create an output file containing the time a vehicle encountered a RSU and the speed of that vehicle. Note that RSUs were placed at each intersection. The simulator was utilized to learn μ_N^* and σ_N^* ^{c} for various values of number of vehicles N from 10 to 1000. Unless otherwise stated, the confidence internal was $\epsilon = 0.05$, and all vehicles within a 0.5 mile range were considered as part of a platoon. All results were averaged over 50 iterations, with a $\mu = 35$ mph. Due to space limitations, only simulation data are reported and discussed. However, it should be noted that the analysis data agrees well with simulations results.

Analysis and simulation results

A road with a length of 10 miles was implemented for this study to allow for sufficient dispersion among vehicles. T_{min} and the average of σ^* (denoted as σ) are determined from simulation data, as shown in Figure 5. Then they were substituted in Equation 3 to determine the expected number of vehicles in the downstream platoon. As the number of vehicles increase, the trend remains the same. This sufficiently demonstrates the fidelity of the simulation environment in conducting further investigations. The trend

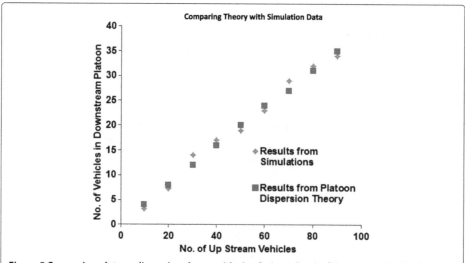

Figure 5 Comparing platoon dispersion theory with simulations. Graph of the expected results from the platoon dispersion model along with the simulation calculated results.

also remains for road segments of different lengths, which are not reported due to space limitations.

Figure 6 illustrates the basic features of our protocol, when the number of vehicles in upstream platoon $n_u = 50$. The Y-axis denotes the detection time, or number of RSUs traversed before a detection of Sybil detection is made. In this case, σ^* is constant and fixed as 1.0. When μ^* increases, Sybil attacks are detected faster. This high value of μ^* causes increased dispersion which increases the chances of detecting anomalous platoons. Also, varying the percentage of Sybil attackers varies the detection time. When the percentage of Sybil attackers increase, anomalous platoons are easier to detect, quickening the detection time.

Figure 7 illustrates the trend of false negatives in the protocol. The number of vehicles in upstream platoon is still set as $n_u = 50$, and $\sigma^* = 1.0$. As μ^* increases, the false negatives decreases. Again, the high value of μ^* increases dispersion and the chances of detecting anomalous platoons correctly which lowers false negatives. Interestingly, the false negatives rate decreases as the percentage of Sybil attackers increase. As more Sybil attackers

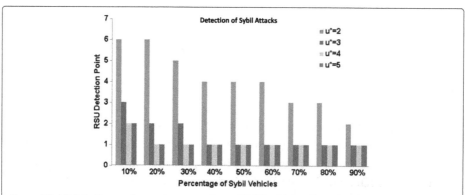

Figure 6 Sybil detection under varying percentage of Sybil vehicles. Chart characterizing at which road side unit Sybil nodes are detected against the percentage of vehicles classified as Sybil nodes.

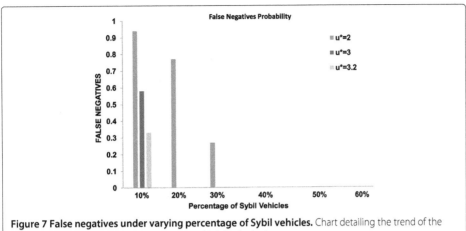

Figure 7 False negatives under varying percentage of Sybil vehicles. Chart detailing the trend of the number of false negatives as the percentage of Sybil vehicles increases.

leads to increased chances of detecting anomalous dispersion. For the case of Sybil attackers reaching 40% and above, the false negatives completely disappear, demonstrating that the protocol is robust against increasing degree of Sybil attacks.

In Figure 8, the trend of how increasing number of vehicles affects detection performance when the percentage of Sybil vehicles is 10% is shown. The observed trend is straightforward to interpret. When the number of vehicles decrease, σ^* increases. This causes increased platoon dispersion, thus accelerating the detection rate. When the number of vehicles increases, roads become congested and degree of dispersion decreases, causing an increased duration of Sybil detection.

In Figure 9, the trade-off between false negatives and false positives when $N = 50$, $\mu^* = 2$ and $\sigma^* = 0.4$ is shown. As we can see when the percentage of Sybil vehicles is low, the protocol yields excellent performance in terms of false positives and false negatives. Though, with increasing attack intensity the performance degrades. The false positive rate is decided by the parameter ϵ, which is user specified. When ϵ is low, the false positive rate is low and the false negative rate is higher, and vice versa. However, this is also sensitive to the number of Sybil vehicles. How to address this trade-off in practical settings is the topic of future research. One plan is to integrate long term predictions from RSUs

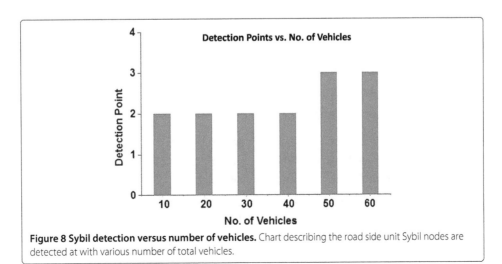

Figure 8 Sybil detection versus number of vehicles. Chart describing the road side unit Sybil nodes are detected at with various number of total vehicles.

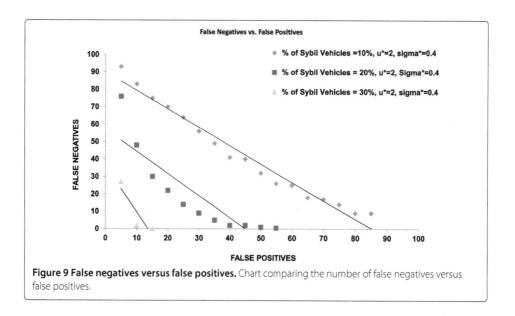

Figure 9 False negatives versus false positives. Chart comparing the number of false negatives versus false positives.

leveraging platoon dispersion with short term prediction models using distributed computation among local vehicles. Also, adapting the protocol to changing road conditions under traffic dynamics is also part of future research.

Advanced attack model

The previous results and discussions have pertained to a simple attack model where the Sybil vehicles broadcast all stored pseudonyms during an attack. Once an RSU network attempts to identify a Sybil attack, the Sybil vehicles may change their message distribution algorithms to avoid detection. The following scenarios describes alternate attack methods a Sybil vehicle can implement to avoid detection. To determine the robustness of the proposed protocol, the results of the protocol against different Sybil attack schemes are presented.

Normal dispersion attack efficiency scenario

The main objective of the attacker is to maintain the efficiency of an attack. Attack efficiency is defined as ratio of Sybil pseudonyms to benign pseudonyms. In other words, the attack efficiency can be defined as

$$e = |V_s|/|V_b| \cdot 100\%, \text{ where}$$

$e = $ the attack efficiency

$V_s = $ set of Sybil pseudonyms

$V_b = $ set of benign pseudonyms

The attacker wants to maintain a high efficiency in order to masquerade Sybil pseudonyms as benign pseudonyms. For this to become possible, the attacker must have a priori road information. Say, the attack releases a subset of V_s, called $V_{s,1}$, at an upstream RSU. At the downstream RSU, the attack can release a subset of $V_{s,1}$ such that it appears the platoon dispersed under normal circumstances. The number of pseudonyms to "disperse" can be derived from the a priori road information and platoon dispersion theory.

Normal dispersion attack efficiency results

There are some practical limitations to this attack scenario, which the our protocol to detect Sybil attacks exploits. In order to have an effective attack, V_s (set of Sybil identities) must be large compared to V_b (set of benign identities) otherwise the Sybil attack will have little influence on the benign vehicles. Using the previous example of Sybil nodes incorrectly reporting road conditions, if exactly 50% of the pseudonyms were Sybil and reporting false information while the other 50% (benign pseudonyms) are reporting true information. No decision could be made on what information to believe. Therefore, an attacker needs more than 50% Sybil pseudonyms to launch an effective attack.

The attack efficiency, e, is held constant as both the Sybil and benign pseudonyms are dispersing at the exact same rate, as shown in Figure 10. This effect leads to an exhaustion point for the Sybil pseudonyms, where there are no more available pseudonyms to use. The attacker cannot reuse previous pseudonyms for some time interval as that would trigger an attack detection. Essentialy, reuse of previously dispersed pseudonyms leads anomalous behavior and is caught by the protocol. Figure 11 shows at which RSU the attacker has completely exhausted all available pseudonyms. At that point, the attacker must cease to launch an attack for some time or risk being detected.

Comparing the results of Figures 6, 7, 8, 9, 10 and 11, for the 10% and 20% Sybil pseudonyms cases, the attacker actually exhausts all available pseudonyms before the protocol could even detect an attack. The 30% to 60% cases show pseudonym exhaustion near the same point of detection, under the simple attack scheme. The highest percent Sybil pseudonym cases, 70% to 90% show a significant increase of attack duration before exhaustion. Under the simple attack method, these cases could be identified within 1 RSU. With the normal dispersion efficiency attack, the pseudonym exhaustion does not occur until the 6th RSU. This may seem as a favorable scheme for the attacker, but even the best case of the simple attack method resulting in Sybil attack detection at the same RSU. The

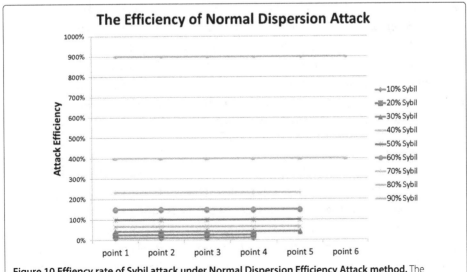

Figure 10 Effiency rate of Sybil attack under Normal Dispersion Efficiency Attack method. The efficiency rates of Sybil attacks under this method are held constant due to some pseudonyms being "dispersed" as the attacker moves. Benign vehicles disperse at the same rate leading to the constant efficiency.

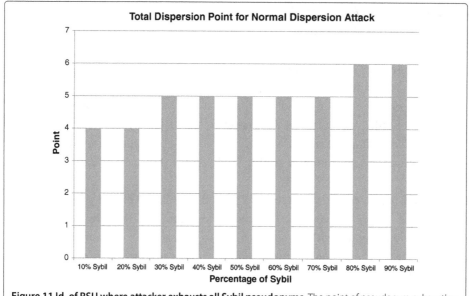

Figure 11 Id. of RSU where attacker exhausts all Sybil pseudonyms. The point of pseudonym exhaustion under the Normal Dispersion Efficiency Attack scheme. As the percentage of Sybil pseudonyms increase, the longer it takes for that set to exhaust. In the worst case, all pseudonyms are used by the 6th RSU, showing comparable performance to the simple attack.

result of this simulation demonstrates the robustness of the protocol to multiple attack methods.

Minimum efficiency attack scenario

Similar to the Normal Dispersion Efficiency Attack, the Minimum Efficiency Attack (MEA) attempts to reduce the number of Sybil pseudonyms used while maintaining an influential attack on a vehicular network. The MEA reduces the number of pseudonyms used by computing the minimum number needed to gain an influence. The attack measures the number of vehicles neighboring platoon to obtain N_p. In order to influence the platoon, the attacker needs to use $N_p + 1$ pseudonyms at a minimum. This allows the attacker to launch a new attack once it knows the attack will be detected. For example under the 80% Sybil case and 100 vehicles, the attacker knows that $N_p = 20$. The attacker will then launch 21 of its 80 Sybil pseudonyms to start an advantageous attack. Knowing the detection scheme, the attacker also knows that this attack will be detected by the fifth RSU. Consequentially, the attacker retires the previous pseudonyms and launches a new attack with 21 of the remaining 59 pseudonyms available. This process continues until all of the attackers Sybil pseudonyms have been exhausted.

Minimum efficiency attack results

As the platoon travels, benign vehicles will disperse but the attack will maintain the original pseudonym number of $N_p + 1$. Under this scheme, the attack efficiency of every case becomes over 100% efficient, as shown in Figure 12. This is ideal for an attacker that cannot obtain many pseudonyms from the network. Even the lowest Sybil percentage case (10%) increases to over 100% attack efficiency. This type is practical and ideal for attackers with very few Sybil pseudonyms. Some cases do not reach the high level of efficiency as in Normal Dispersion Efficiency attacks, but those cases have an increased duration before pseudonym exhaustion.

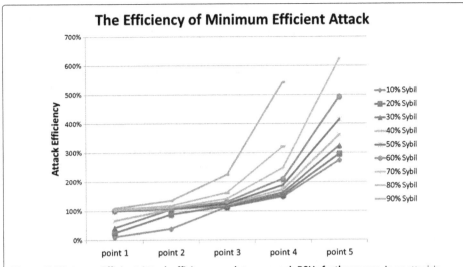

Figure 12 Minimum Efficient Attack efficiency as platoons reach RSUs further away. As an attack is launched, the attacker determines the minimum number of Sybil pseudonyms necessary to gain an advantage in the platoon. As the platoon disperses, the attacker increases its efficiency while minimizing the number of Sybil pseudonyms needed.

For the cases of less than or equal to 50% Sybil pseudonyms, the attacker cannot launch an effective attack. Each of these cases can only launch one attack and are detected at the sixth RSU, as shown in Figure 13. So even though those cases reach an attack efficiency of over 100%, it is short-term as another attack cannot be launch. The efficiency immediately drops to below 100% after the fifth RSU when the attacker attempts to launch another attack. The cause of this drop is the number of Sybil pseudonyms remaining is less than the number of vehicles in the platoon.

When the Sybil pseudonym percentage reaches 60%, detection time increases dramatically. The attacker knows when an attack will be detected, can retire the current Sybil

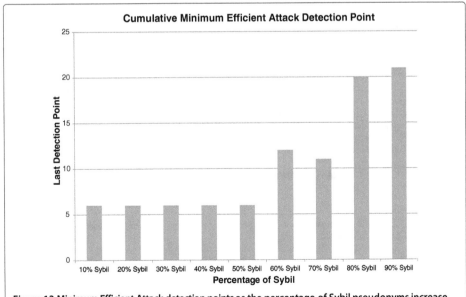

Figure 13 Minimum Efficient Attack detection points as the percentage of Sybil pseudonyms increase. As the number of Sybil pseudonyms increase, the detection point of an attack increases. In each case, multiple attacks may be launched so the last detection points are shown.

pseudonyms, and use fresh pseudonyms from V_s. This action is equivalent to launching another attack even though the motive may be the same. For example, in the 60% case the attacker can launch two undetectable attacks until the number of Sybil pseudonyms is less than the platoon size. At this point, the attacker uses the remaining pseudonyms to launch a final attack. This attack will be detected in a few RSUs. The summation of total RSUs traversed before the final detection is shown in Figure 13. The high-percent-Sybil cases show an apparent defeat in the proposed protocol. This attack scheme could be countered with the addition of mechanism to detect additions of many vehicle pseudonyms. It should be noted, though, obtaining such a high percent of Sybil pseudonyms could be a difficult task in real life.

Conclusions

In this paper, a novel protocol for defending against Sybil attacks in vehicular networks is presented. The novelty comes from the fusion of physical phenomena and the cyber domain to detect Sybil attacks. The combination of physical and cyber environments makes the protocol effective, practical, efficient, and simple. Additionally, this paper presents advanced attack methods where the attacker knows the detection scheme and has a priori road information. The protocol shows similar performance for Normal Dispersion Efficiency Attack model, while the Minimum Efficiency Attack model may remain undetected at high Sybil percentages. Future work involves integration of machine learning algorithms with platoon dispersion and wireless communication support to not only detect the presence of Sybil attacks, but identifying which are the Sybil nodes. Advanced collusion attacks to validate our protocol performance are also under investigation.

Endnotes

[a] In a recent 2011 study, platooning was exploited for content management in vehicular networks [44].

[b] The issue of detecting attacks where identities are selectively used (in which case attack potency is lowered) is part of future work.

[c] The subscript N in μ_N^* and σ_N^* is dropped in this section for ease of readability.

Competing interests
The authors declare that they have no competing interests.

Authors' contributions
MAM adapted the platoon dispersion Model to vehicular networks. He also conducted the theoretical analysis and also led the design of the proposed protocol. LM led all aspects of simulation studies, and results. He also conducted related work on Sybil attacks. SC defined the problem, and participated in the theoretical analysis. He also led the discussions on interpretations of the results and paper writing. All authors read and approved the final manuscript.

References
1. Parno B, Perrig A (2005) Challenges in securing vehicular networks. In: Workshop on Hot Topics in Networks (HotNets-IV). ACM, College Park, Maryland, pp 1–6
2. Studer A, Shi E, Bai F, Perrig A (2009) Tacking together efficient authentication, revocation, and privacy in vanets. In: IEEE Sensor, Mesh and Ad Hoc Communications and Networks (SECON). IEEE, Rome, Italy, pp 1–9
3. Golle P, Greene D, Staddon J (2004) Detecting and correcting malicious data in vanets. In: Proceedings of the 1st ACM international workshop on vehicular ad hoc networks. ACM, Philadelphia, PA, USA, pp 29–37
4. Zhou T, Choudhury RR, Ning P, Chakrabarty K (2011) P2dap sybil attacks detection in vehicular ad hoc networks. IEEE J Sel Area Comm 29(3): 582–594
5. Xiao B, Yu B, Gao C (2006) Detection and localization of sybil nodes in vanets. In: Proceedings of the 2006 workshop on dependability issues in wireless ad hoc networks and sensor networks. ACM, Los Angeles, CA, USA, pp 1–8

6. Guette G, Ducourthial B (2007) On the sybil attack detection in vanet. In: IEEE inernational conference on Mobile Adhoc and Sensor Systems (MASS). IEEE, Pisa, Italy, pp 1–6
7. Parameswaran AT, Husain MI, Upadhyaya S (2009) Is rssi a reliable parameter in sensor localization algorithms: an experimental study. In: Field Failure Data Analysis Workshop (F2DA09). IEEE, Niagara Falls, NY, USA
8. Park S, Aslam B, Turgut D, Zou CC (2009) Defense against sybil attack in vehicular ad hoc network based on roadside unit support. In: IEEE Military Communications Conference (MILCOM). IEEE, Boston, Massachusetts, pp 1–7
9. Capkun S, Hubaux J-P (2005) Secure positioning of wireless devices with application to sensor networks. In: IEEE INFOCOM. IEEE, Miami, FL, USA, pp 1917–1928
10. Jadliwala M, Zhong S, Upadhyaya S, Qiao C, Hubaux J-P (2010) Secure distance-based localization in the presence of cheating beacon nodes. IEEE Trans Mobile Comput 9(6): 810–823
11. Newsome J, Shi E, Song D, Perrig A (2004) The sybil attack in sensor networks: analysis & defenses. In: Proceedings of the 3rd international symposium on information processing in sensor networks. ACM, Berkeley, CA, USA, pp 259–268
12. Douceur J (2002) The sybil attack. Peer-to-peer Systems. Lecture Notes in Computer Science 2429: 251–260
13. Kurve A, Kesidis G (2011) Sybil detection via distributed sparse cut monitoring. In: 2011 IEEE International Conference on Communications (ICC). IEEE, Kyoto, Japan, pp 1–6
14. Yu H, Kaminsky M, Gibbons PB, Flaxman A (2006) Sybilguard: defending against sybil attacks via social networks. ACM SIGCOMM Comput Commun Rev 36(4): 267–278
15. Pacey G (1956) The progress of a bunch of vehicles released from a traffic signal. RN/2665/GMP, Transport and Road Research Laboratory, Growthorne, UK. Research note No. Rn/2665/GMP. Road Research Laboratory, London
16. Robertson D (1969) Transyt-a traffic network study tool. rrl report lr 253. London: TRRL
17. Yu L (2000) Calibration of platoon dispersion parameters on the basis of link travel time statistics. Trans Res Rec: J Trans Res Board 1727(-1): 89–94
18. Rakha H, Farzaneh M (2006) Issues and Solutions to Macroscopic Traffic Dispersion Modeling, pp 555-564
19. Robinson T, Chan E, Coelingh E (2010) Operating platoons on public motorways: an introduction to The SARTRE platooning programme: 1–11. World Congress on Intelligent Transport Systems
20. SARTRE-Consortium The SARTRE Project. http://www.sartre-project.eu/en/Sidor/default.aspx accessed 10 October 2012
21. Varaiya P (1993) Smart cars on smart roads: problems of control. IEEE Trans Automatic Control 38(2): 195–207
22. Frankel J, Alvarez L, Horowitz R, Li P (1994) Robust platoon maneuvers for avhs 10. Manuscript, Berkeley, November
23. Tongue BH, Yang Y, White MT (1991) Platoon collision dynamics and emergency maneuvering i: Reduced order modeling of a platoon for dynamical analysis
24. Van Winsum W (1999) The human element in car following models. Trans Res Part F: Traffic Psychol Behav 2(4): 207–211
25. Seddon P (1972) Another look at platoon dispersion: 3. the recurrence relationship. Traffic Eng Contr 13(10): 442–444
26. Salter RJ, Hounsell NB (1996) Highway traffic analysis and design. Palgrave Macmillan
27. Denney RWJr (1989) Traffic platoon dispersion modeling. J Transport Eng 115: 193
28. El-Reedy T, Ashworth R (1978) Platoon dispersion along a major road in sheffield. Traffic Eng Contr 19: 186–189
29. Abbas M, Bullock G, Rhodes A (2001) Comparative study of theoretical, simulation, and field platoon data. Traffic Eng Contr 42(7): 232–236
30. Liu HX, Bhimireddy S (2009) Evaluation of integrated platoon-priority and advance warning flasher system at high-speed intersections. Trans Res Rec: J Trans Res Board 2128(-1): 121–131
31. Li J, Wang H, Chen QY, Ni D (2010) Traffic viscosity due to speed variation: modeling and implications. Math Comput Model
32. Hunt P, Robertson D, Bretherton R, Winton R (1981) Scoot-a traffic responsive method of coordinating signals. Technical report
33. Hall M, Van Vliet D, Willumsen L (1980) Saturn-a simulation-assignment model for the evaluation of traffic management schemes. Traffic Eng Contr 21(4): 168–176
34. Lieberman EB, Andrews B (1980) Traflo: a new tool to evaluate transportation system management strategies. Transport Res Rec 772
35. Wasef A, Lu R, Lin X, Shen X (2010) Complementing public key infrastructure to secure vehicular ad hoc networks [security and privacy in emerging wireless networks]. IEEE Wireless Comm 17(5): 22–28
36. Gerlach M, Guttler F (2007) Privacy in vanets using changing pseudonyms-ideal and real. In: IEEE Vehicular Technology Conference (VTC), pp 2521–2525
37. Tan Q, Wei Q, Yang S, Wang J (2009) Evaluation of urban road vehicle detection from high resolution remote sensing imagery using object-oriented method. In: Urban Remote Sensing Event, pp 1–6
38. Grant C, Gillis B, Guensler R (2000) Collection of vehicle activity data by video detection for use in transportation planning. J Intell Transport Syst 5(4): 343–361
39. Oh S, Ritchie SG, Oh C (2002) Real-time traffic measurement from single loop inductive signatures. Trans Res Record: J Trans Res Board 1804(-1): 98–106
40. Haoui A, Kavaler R, Varaiya P (2008) Wireless magnetic sensors for traffic surveillance. Transport Res C Emerg Tech 16(3): 294–306
41. Roess RP, Prassas ES, McShane WR (2004) Traffic engineering. Pearson/Prentice Hall
42. Yousefi S, Altman E, El-Azouzi R, Fathy M (2008) Analytical model for connectivity in vehicular ad hoc networks. IEEE Trans Veh Tech 57(6): 3341–3356
43. Krajzewicz D, Hertkorn G, Rossel C, Wagner P (2002) Sumo (simulation of urban mobility) In: Proc. of the 4th middle east symposium on simulation and modelling, pp 183–187
44. Zhang Y, Cao G (2011) V-pada: Vehicle-platoon aware data access in vanets. IEEE Trans Veh Tech 99: 1–1

11

Efficient private multi-party computations of trust in the presence of curious and malicious users

Shlomi Dolev[1]*, Niv Gilboa[2] and Marina Kopeetsky[3]*

*Correspondence:
dolev@cs.bgu.ac.il;
marinako@sce.ac.il
[1]Department of Computer Science,
Ben-Gurion University of the Negev,
Beer-Sheva 84105, Israel
[3]Department of Software
Engineering, Sami-Shamoon
College of Engineering, Beer-Sheva
84100, Israel
Full list of author information is
available at the end of the article

Abstract

Schemes for multi-party trust computation are presented. The schemes do not make use of a Trusted Authority. The schemes are more efficient than previous schemes in terms of the number of messages exchanged, which is proportional to the number of participants rather than to its square. We note that in our schemes the length of each message may be larger than the message length typically found in previously published schemes. The calculation of a trust, in a specific user by a group of community members starts following a request by an initiator. The trust computation is provided in a completely distributed manner, where each user calculates its trust value privately and independently. Given a community C and its members (users) $U_1, \ldots, U_n$, we present computationally secure schemes for trust computation. The first scheme, Accumulated Protocol AP computes the average trust attributed to a specific user, U_t following a trust evaluation request initiated by a user U_n. The exact trust values of each queried user are not disclosed to U_n. The next scheme, Weighted Accumulated Protocol WAP generates the average weighted trust in a specific user U_t taking into consideration the unrevealed trust that U_n has in each user participating in the trust evaluation process. The Public Key Encryption Protocol $PKEP$ outputs a set of the exact trust values given by the users without linking the user that contributed a specific trust value to the trust this user contributed. The obtained vector of trust values assists in removing outliers. Given the set of trust values, the outliers that provide extremely low or high trust values can be removed from the trust evaluation process. We extend our schemes to the case when the initiator, U_n, can be compromised by the adversary, and we introduce the Multiple Private Keys and the Weighted protocols ($MPKP$ and $MPWP$) for computing average unweighted and weighted trust, respectively. Moreover, the Commutative Encryption Based Protocol ($CEBP$) extends the $PKEBP$ in this case. The computation of all our algorithms requires the transmission of $O(n)$ (possibly large) messages.

Keywords: Private trust computations; Multi-party computations; Anonymity

Our contribution

The purpose of this paper is to introduce new schemes for decentralized reputation systems. These schemes do not make use of a Trusted Authority to compute the trust in a particular user that is attributed by a community of users. Our objective is to compute trust while preserving user privacy.

We present new efficient schemes for calculating the trust in a specific user by a group of community members upon the request of an initiator. The trust computation is provided in a completely distributed manner, where each user calculates its trust value privately. The user privacy is preserved in a computationally secure manner. The notions of privacy and privately computed trust, are determined in the sense that given an output average trust in a certain user, it is computationally infeasible to reveal the exact trust values in this user, given by community users. We assume a community of users $C = \{U_1, U_2, \ldots, U_n\}$. Let U_n be an initiator. The goal of U_n is to get an assessment of the trust in a certain user, U_t by a group consisting of $U_1, U_2, \ldots, U_{n-1}$ users from C. The AP calculates the average trust (or the sum of trust levels) in the user U_t (Section 'Accumulated protocol AP'). The AP protocol is based on a computationally secure homomorphic cryptosystem, e.g., the Paillier cryptosystem [1], which provides a homomorphic encryption of the secure trust levels $T_1, \ldots, T_{n-1}$ calculated by each user $U_1, U_2, \ldots, U_{n-1}$ from C. The AP satisfies the features of the Additive Reputation System [2] and does not take into consideration $U_n's$ subjective trust values in the queried users $U_1, U_2, \ldots, U_{n-1}$. A decentralized reputation system is defined as additive/non additive [2] if feedback collection, combination, and propagation are implemented in a decentralized way, and if a combination of feedbacks provided by agents is calculated in an additive/non additive manner, respectively. The WAP carries out a non additive trust computation (Section 'Weighted accumulated protocol WAP'). It outputs the weighted average trust which is based on the trust given by the initiator U_n in each C member participating in the feedback. The WAP is an enhanced version of the AP protocol. The AP and WAP protocols cope with a curious adversary and are restricted to the case of an uncompromised initiator, U_n. The $MPKP$ and $MPWP$ protocols, introduced in Section 'Multiple Private Keys Protocol $MPKP$', use additional communication to relax the condition that the initiator U_n is uncompromised and provide average unweighted and weighted privately computed trust, respectively.

Compared with the recent results in [2] and [3], our schemes have several advantages.

The Private Trust scheme is resistant against either curious or semi-malicious users
The AP and WAP protocols preserve user privacy in a computationally secure manner. Our protocols cope with any number of curious but honest adversarial users. Moreover, the $PKEBP$ (Section 'Protocols for removal of outliers') is resistant against semi-malicious users that return false trust values. The $PKEBP$ supports the removal of outliers. The general case, when the initiator, U_n, can be compromised by the adversary, is addressed by the $MPKP$, $MPWP$ and $CEBP$ (Sections 'Protocols for removal of outliers' and 'Multiple Private Keys Protocol $MPKP$') protocols. Unlike our model, [2] suggests protocols that are resistant against curious agents who only try to collude in order to reveal private trust information. Moreover, the reputation computation in some of the algorithms in [3] contains a random parameter that reveals information about the reputation range of the queried users.

Low communicational overhead The proposed schemes require only $O(n)$ size messages to be sent, while the protocols of [2] and [3] require $O(n^3)$ communication messages.

No limitations on the number of curious users The computational security of the proposed schemes does not depend on the number of curious users in the community. Moreover, privacy is preserved regardless of the size of the coalition of curious users. Note that the number of the curious users should be no greater than half of the community users in the model presented in [2].

Background and literature review

The use of homomorphic cryptosystems in general Multiparty Computation (MPC) models is presented in [4]. In [4] it is demonstrated that, given keys for any sufficiently efficient homomorphic cryptosystem, general MPC protocols for n players can be devised such that they are secure against an active adversary who corrupts any minority group of the players. The problem stated and solved in [4] is as follows: given the encryptions of two numbers, say a and b (where each player knows only its input), compute securely an encryption of $c = ab$. The correctness of the result is verified. The total number of bits sent is $O(nkC)$, where k is a security parameter and C is the size of a Boolean circuit computing the function that should be securely evaluated. An earlier scheme proposed in [5] with the same complexity was only secure for passive adversaries. Earlier protocols had complexity that was at least quadratic in n. Threshold homomorphic encryption is used to achieve the linear communication complexity in [4]. The schemes proposed in [4,6], and [7] are based on public key infrastructure and use Zero Knowledge proofs (ZKP) as building blocks. When compared to [4,6], and [7] our schemes privately compute the average unweighted (additive) and weighted (non additive) characteristics, respectively, without using relatively hard-to-implement techniques such as ZKP.

Independently, (though slightly later than [8,9]), linear communication MPC was presented in [10]. A perfectly secure MPC protocol with linear communication complexity was proposed in [11]. Our model presented herein, (with a semi-honest but curious adversary) copes with at most $\frac{n}{2} - 1$ compromised users that supply arbitrary trust values, while [11] copes (in an information theoretic manner) with up to $\frac{n}{3}$ compromised users (even totally malicious users) with a similar communication overhead, $O(n^3 \cdot ln^3)$. Here, l denotes the total message length.

Following [8,9], privacy preserving protocols were investigated in [12] and [13]. Protocols for efficient multi-party sum computation (in the semi-honest adversarial model) are proposed in [12] and [13]. The derived protocols are augmented (by applying Zero Knowledge Proofs of plaintext equality and set membership) to handle malicious adversary. The simulation results demonstrate the efficiency of the designed methods. Compared with our results, the most powerful and efficient StR protocol of [12] and [13] is based on a completely connected network topology where each network user is directly connected to all other users. In addition, the schemes of [12] and [13] can be applied in the Additive Reputation Systems, while our schemes are designed also for the Non-Additive Reputation System.

Homomorphic ElGamal encryption is used in [6] as part of a scheme for multi-party private web search with untrusted partners (users). The scheme is based on multi-party computation that protects the privacy of the users with regards to the web search engine and any number of dishonest internal users. The number of sent messages is linear in the number of users (each of the n users sends $4n - 4$ messages). In order to obtain a secure permutation (of N elements), switches of the Optimized Arbitrary Size Benes network (OAS-Benes) are distributed among a group of n users, and the honest users control at least a large function $S(N)$ of the switches of the OAS-Benes. The proposed MPC protocol is based on the homomorphic threshold n-out of-n ElGamal encryption. Nevertheless, unlike our model, a MPC protocol is based on the computationally expensive honest-verifier ZKP protocol, and the Benez permutation network.

The efficient scheme for the secure two-party computation for "asymmetric settings" in which one of the devices (smart card, mobile device, etc.) is strictly computationally weaker than the other, is introduced in [7]. The workload for one of the parties is minimized in the presented scheme. The proposed protocol satisfies one-round complexity (i.e., a single message is sent in each direction assuming trusted setup).The proposed protocol performs only two-party secure computations, while the number of participants is not bounded in our schemes. Moreover, computationally expensive, Non Interactive Zero-Knowledge Proof techniques, and "extractable hash functions" are used in the scheme of [7].

A number of systematic approaches and corresponding architectures for creating reliable trust and reputation systems have been recently proposed in [14-18]. The main scope of these papers is the definitions of variety of settings for decentralized trust and reputation systems. A probabilistic approach for constructing computational models of trust and reputation, is presented in [17], where trust and reputation are studied in the scope of various social and scientific disciplines.

The computation models for the reputation systems of [16] support user anonymity by generating a pseudonym for any user, therefore, concealing user identity. In contrast to [16], the main challenge of our approach is to preserve the user anonymity in the computation process of the trust.

One of the common problems stated and discussed in [18] is that most existing reputation systems lack the ability to differentiate dishonest from honest feedback and, therefore, are vulnerable to malicious cooperations of users (peers in P2P systems) who provide dishonest feedback. The dishonest feedback is effectively filtered out in [18] by introducing the factor of feedback similarity between a user (pair) in the collusive group, and a user (peer) outside the group. We propose a different approach for the removal of dishonest users (outliers) by estimating the range of the correct trust values [19].

Two other works that are related to our scheme appear in [2] and [3]. In [2] several privacy and anonymity preserving protocols are suggested for an Additive Reputation System.

The authors state that supporting perfect privacy in decentralized reputation systems is impossible. Nevertheless, they present alternative probabilistic schemes for preserving privacy. A probabilistic "witness selection" method is proposed in [2] in order to reduce the risk of selecting dishonest witnesses. Two schemes are proposed. The first scheme is very efficient in terms of communication overhead, but this scheme is vulnerable to collusion of even two witnesses. The second scheme is more resistant toward curious users, but still is vulnerable to collusion. It is based on a secret splitting scheme. This scheme provides a secure protocol based on the verifiable secret sharing scheme [20] derived from Shamir's secret sharing scheme [21]. The number of dishonest users is heavily restricted and must be no more than $\frac{n}{2}$, where n is the number of contributing users. The communication overhead of this scheme is rather high and requires $O(n^3)$ messages.

An enhanced model for reputation computation that extends the results of [2] is introduced in [3]. The main enhancement of [2] is that a non additive (weighted) trust and reputation can be computed privately. Three algorithms for computing non additive reputation are proposed in [3]. The algorithms have various degrees of privacy and different levels of protection against adversarial users. These schemes are computationally secure regardless of the number of dishonest users.

The paper [22] (published later than [8,9]), proposes the distributed *Malicious-k-shares* protocol, which extends the results of [2] and [3] in the sense that a high majority of users (agents) can find k, $k << n$ sufficiently trustworthy agents in a set of $n - 1$ users-feedback providers. This protocol is based on homomorphic encryption and Non-Interactive Zero-Knowledge proofs. The *Malicious k-shares protocol* is applicable in the Additive Reputation System only, while our schemes privately compute also the weighted trust. The techniques, used for removal of outliers, is based on Non-Zero Knowledge Proofs of set-membership and plain-text equality, while the proof preserves that a certain share lies in the correct interval. The proposed protocol requires the exchange of $O(n + \log N)$ messages (where n and N are the number of users in the protocol and environment, respectively), while we use a more computationally effective techniques for removal of outliers exchanging only $O(n)$ messages.

We propose new efficient trust computation schemes that can replace any of the above schemes. Our schemes enable the initiator to compute unweighted (additive) and weighted (non additive) trust with low communication complexity of $O(n)$ (large) messages.

Table 1 summarizes the approaches proposed in this paper, computations that they perform, resistance to the different types of attacks and the crypto building blocks that are used.

This paper extends the schemes of [9] by introducing the *MPKP* and *MPWP* protocols that compute average unweighted and weighted trust in the general case, even when the initiator U_n can be compromised by the adversary. The proofs of correctness of the proposed protocols extend the presentations of [9] and [8].

Paper organization

The formal system description appears in Section 'Research design and methodology'. The computationally resistant (against curious but honest adversary) private trust protocol, *AP*, is introduced in Section 'Results and discussion' (Subsection "Accumulated protocol *AP*"). The enhanced version of *AP*, *WAP*, is presented in Section 'Results and discussion' (Subsection "Weighted accumulated protocol WAP"). The (resistant against semi-malicious users) *PKEBP* and *CEBP* and the scheme for removing outliers are presented in Section 'Results and discussion' (Subsection "Protocols for removal of outliers"). The generalized *MPKP* protocol and the weighted *MPWP* protocol are introduced in Section 'Results and discussion' (Subsection "Multiple Private Keys Protocol *MPKP*"). Conclusions appear in Section 'Conclusions'.

Research design and methodology

The purpose of this paper is to generate new schemes for private trust computation within a community. The contribution of our work is as follows: (a) the trust computation is

Table 1 Summary of the Presented Approaches

Protocol	Computation	Adversarial model	Crypto building blocks
AP	Average trust	Honest but curious	Homomorphic (of Paillier)
WAP	Weighted average trust	Honest but curious	Homomorphic (of Paillier)
PKEBP	Vector of exact trust; removal of outliers	Semi-malicious (restricted)	Any public key encryption
CEBP	Vector of exact trust; removal outliers	Semi-malicious (non restricted)	Commutative (Polhig-Hellman), ElGamal

performed in a completely distributed manner without involving a Trusted Authority. (b) the trust in a particular user within the community is computed privately. The privacy of trust values, held by the community users is preserved subject to standard cryptographic assumptions, when the adversary is computationally bounded. (c) The proposed protocols are resistant to a curious but honest poly-bounded k-listening adversary, Ad [23]. Such an adversary Ad may do the following: Ad may trace all the network links in the system and Ad may compromise up to k users, $k < n$. We require that an adversary Ad, compromising an intermediate node can only learn the node's trust values and an adversary Ad, compromising the initiator U_n can learn the output of the protocol, namely the average trust. We distinguish between two categories of adversaries: honest but curious adversaries, and semi-malicious adversaries [2]. An honest but curious k-listening adversary follows the protocol by providing correct input. Nevertheless, it might try to learn trust values in different ways, including collusion with, at most, k compromised users. While an honest but curious adversary does not try to modify the correct output of the protocol, a semi-malicious adversary may provide dishonest input in order to bias the average trust value.

Let $C = U_1, \ldots, U_n$ be a community of users such that each pair of users is connected via an authenticated channel. Assume that the purpose of a user U_n from C is to get the unweighted T_t^{avr} or weighted average trust wT_t^{avr} in a specific user, U_t, evaluated by the community of users. Denote by T^i, $i = 1 .. n$, the trust of user U_i in U_t, and by $T_t^{avr} = \frac{\sum_{i=1}^{n} T^i}{n}$ and $wT_t^{avr} = 1/10 \sum_{i=1}^{n} w_i T^i$ the unweighted and weighted average trust in U_t, respectively. Here $w_i = 1, 2, \ldots, 10$ is the subjective trust of the initiator U_n in U_i in the form of an integer that facilitates our secure computation. In the subsequent work we always assume that w_i is an integer in this range. Denote by M_t the message sent by U_n to the first member of the community, C.

Our definitions of computational indistinguishability, simulation and private computation follow the definitions of [24]. Informally speaking, two probability ensembles are *computationally indistinguishable* if no polynomial time, probabilistic algorithm can decide with non-negligible probability if a given input is drawn from the first or the second ensemble. A distributed protocol computes a function f *privately* if an adversary cannot obtain any information on the input and output of other parties, beyond what is implicit in the adversary's own input and output. The way to prove that a protocol is private is to show that there exists a polynomial time, probabilistic *simulator* that receives as input the same input and output as an adversary and generates a string that is computationally indistinguishable from the whole view of the adversary, including every message that the adversary received in the protocol. Intuitively, the existence of a simulator implies that the adversary learns nothing from the execution of the protocol except its input and output.

Methods

The main tool we use in our schemes is public-key, homomorphic encryption. In such an encryption scheme there is a modulus, M, and an efficiently computable function ϕ that maps a pair of encrypted values $(E_K(x), E_K(y))$, where $0 \leq x, y < M$, to a single encrypted element $\phi(E_K(x), E_K(y)) = E_K(x+y \bmod M)$. In many homomorphic encryption systems the function ϕ is multiplication modulo some integer N. Given a natural number, c, and an encryption, $E_K(x)$, it is possible to compute $E_K(c \cdot x \bmod M)$, without knowing the private key. Set $\beta = E_K(1)$ and let the binary representation of c be $c = c_k c_{k-1} \ldots c_0$. Go over the bits $c_k, \ldots, c_0$ in descending order. If $c_j = 0$, set $\beta = \phi(\beta, \beta)$ and if $c_j = 1$, set $\beta = \phi(\phi(\beta, \beta), E_K(x))$. If ϕ is modular multiplication, this algorithm is identical to standard modular exponentiation.

There are quite a few examples of homomorphic encryption schemes known in the cryptographic literature, including [1,25-28]. There are also systems that allow both addition and multiplication of two encrypted plaintexts, e.g., [29] where only a single multiplication is possible for a pair of ciphertexts, and [30]. All of these examples of homomorphic cryptosystems are currently assumed to be semantically secure [26].

Results and discussion

Accumulated protocol AP

The AP protocol may be based on any homomorphic encryption scheme such that the modulus N satisfies $N > \sum_{i=1}^{n} T_i$. We illustrate the protocol by using the semantically secure Paillier cryptosystem [1]. This cryptosystem possesses a homomorphic property and is based on the Decisional Composite Residuosity assumption. Let p and q be large prime numbers, and $N = pq$. Let g be some element of $Z_{N^2}^*$. Note that the base, g, should be chosen properly by checking whether $gcd(L(g^\lambda mod \ N^2), N) = 1$, where $\lambda = lcm(p - 1, q - 1)$, and the L function is defined as $L(u) = \frac{u-1}{N}$. The public key is the (N, g) pair, while the (p, q) pair is the secret private key. The ciphertext, c, for the plaintext message $m < N$ is generated by the sender as $c = g^m r^N \ mod \ N^2$, where $r < N$ is a randomly chosen number. The decryption is performed as $m = \frac{L(c^\lambda \ mod \ N^2)}{L(g^\lambda \ mod \ N^2)} \ mod \ N$ at the destination. Our schemes are based on the homomorphic property of the Paillier cryptosystem. Namely, the multiplication of two encrypted plaintexts m_1 and m_2 is decrypted as the sum $m_1 + m_2 \ mod \ N$ of the plaintexts. Thus, $E(m_1) \cdot E(m_2) \equiv E(m_1 + m_2 \ mod \ m) \ mod \ N^2$ and $E(m_1)^{m_2} \equiv E(m_1 \cdot m_2 \ mod \ N) \ mod \ N^2$. The AP protocol is described in Algorithm 1.

Algorithm 1 Accumulated Protocol.

1: AP **Initialization :**
2:    U_n sets $A = 1$ and $M_t = A$
3:    U_n sends M_t to U_1
4: AP **Execution :**
5:    *for* $i = 1 \ldots n - 1$
6:        $A = A \cdot E(T_i) \ mod \ N^2$
7:        $M_t = A$
8:        U_i sends M_t to U_{i+1}
9:    *end for*
10:   Upon M_t receipt at U_n
11:   $S_t = D(M_t) = \sum_{i=1}^{n-1} T_i$
12:   $T_t^{avr} = \frac{S_t}{n-1}$

Assume that the initiator, U_n, has generated a pair of its public and private keys as described above, and it has shared its public key with each community user. Then, U_n initializes to 1 the single entry trust message M_t and sends it to the first U_1 user (lines 1–3). Upon receiving the message, M_t, each node, U_i, encrypts its trust in U_t as $E(T_i) = g^{T_i} r_i^N \ mod \ N^2$. Here, T_i is a secret $U_i's$ trust level in U_t and r_i is a randomly generated number. The $U_i's$ output is accumulated in the accumulated variable A multiplying its current value by the new encrypted $U_i - th$ trust $E(T_i)$ from the $i - th$ entry as $A = A \cdot (E(T_i))$. Then U_i sends the updated M_t message to the next user, U_{i+1}. This procedure is repeated until all trust values are accumulated in A (lines 4–9). The final M_t message received by the initiator, U_n is $M_t = A = \prod_{i=1}^{n} E(T_i) \bmod N^2$. As a result, the U_n user decrypts the value accumulated in the M message as the sum of trusts $S_t = D(M_t) = \sum_{i=1}^{n} T_i$. Thus, the average trust is $T_t^{avr} = \frac{S_t}{n-1}$ (Algorithm 1, lines 10–12). Proposition 1 proves that AP is a computationally private protocol to compute the trust of a community in U_t.

Proposition 1. Assume that an honest but curious adversary corrupts at most k users out of a community of n users, $k < n$. Then, AP privately computes T^{avr}, the average trust in user U_t.

Proof. In order to prove the proposition, we have to prove that for every adversary there exists a simulator that given only the adversary's input and output, generates a string that is computationally indistinguishable from the adversary's view in AP. Let $I = \{U_{i_1}, U_{i_2}, \ldots, U_{i_k}\}$ denote the set of users that the adversary controls. Let $view_I^{AP}(X_I, 1^n)$ denote the combined view of all users in I. $view_I^{AP}$ includes the input, $X_I = \{T_{i_1}, \ldots, T_{i_k}\}$, of all users in I, and a sequence of messages $E(\sum_{j=1}^{i_1} T_j), \ldots, E(\sum_{j=1}^{i_k} T_j)$ received by users in I. A simulator cannot generate the exact sequence $E(\sum_{j=1}^{i_1} T_j), \ldots, E(\sum_{j=1}^{i_k} T_j)$, since it does not have the input of uncorrupted users. Instead, the simulator chooses a random value α_j for any user $U_j \notin I$, from the distribution of trust values, D. The simulator denotes $\alpha_{i_1} = T_{i_1}, \ldots, \alpha_{i_k} = T_{i_k}$ and computes $E(\alpha_j)$ for $j = 1, \ldots, n-1$. The simulator now computes: $\prod_{j=1}^{i_1} E(\alpha_j) \equiv E(\sum_{j=1}^{i_1} \alpha_j) \bmod N^2, \ldots, \prod_{j=1}^{i_k} E(\alpha_j) \equiv E(\sum_{j=1}^{i_k} \alpha_j) \bmod N^2$. Hence, a simulator replaces $E(\sum_{j=1}^{i_k} T_j)$ by $E(\sum_{j=1}^{i_k} \alpha_j)$.

Assume, in contradiction, that there exists an algorithm DIS that distinguishes between the encryption of partial sums $E(\sum_{j=1}^{i_1} T_j), \cdots E(\sum_{j=1}^{i_k} T_j)$ of the correct trust values and the values $E(\sum_{j=1}^{i_1} \alpha_j), \cdots E(\sum_{j=1}^{i_k} \alpha_j)$ randomly produced by a simulator. We construct an algorithm, B, that distinguishes between the two sequences $E(T_1), \cdots E(T_{n-1})$ and $E(\alpha_1), \cdots, E(\alpha_k)$, contradicting the semantic security property of E. The input to algorithm B is a sequence of values $E(x_1), \cdots E(x_{n-1})$ and it attempts to determine whether the values $x_1, \ldots, x_{n-1}$ are equal to the values $T_1, \ldots, T_{n-1}$ that the users provide, or is a sequence of random values chosen from the distribution D. The algorithm B computes for every $\ell = 1, \ldots, k$

$$\prod_{j=1}^{i_\ell} E(x_j) \equiv E\left(\sum_{j=1}^{i_\ell} x_j\right) \bmod N^2,$$

and provides the encryption of partial sums $E(\sum_{j=1}^{i_1} x_j), \ldots E(\sum_{j=1}^{i_k} x_j)$ as input to DIS. B returns as output the same output as DIS. Since the input of DIS is $E(\sum_{j=1}^{i_1} T_j), \ldots E(\sum_{j=1}^{i_k} T_j)$ if and only if the input of B is $E(T_1), \ldots E(T_{n-1})$, we find that B distinguishes between its two possible input distributions with the same probability that DIS distinguishes between its input distributions. $\square$

AP uses $O(n)$ messages each of length $O(n)$.

Weighted accumulated protocol WAP

The Weighted Accumulated WAP protocol, in addition to the AP protocol, generates the weighted average trust in a specific user, U_t, by the users in the community. The WAP protocol is based on an anonymous communications protocol proposed in [31] and on the homomorphic cryptosystem, e.g., Paillier cryptosystem [1]. It is described in Algorithm 2.

Algorithm 2 Weighted Accumulated Protocol WAP.

1: **WAP Initialization:**
2:     U_n generates $TV = [E(w_1) .. E(w_{n-1})]$
3:     U_n sets $A = 1$ and $M_t = (TV, A)$
4: **WAP execution:**
5:     U_n sends M_t to U_1
6:     *for* $i = 1 \ldots n-1$
7:         $A = AE(w_i)^{T_i} E(\bar{0}) \bmod (N^2)$
8:         Delete $TV[i]$
9:         U_i sends M_t to U_{i+1}
10:    *end for*
11: **Upon M_t reception at U_n:**
12:    $S_t = D(A) = \sum_{i=1}^{n} w_i T_i$
13:    $wT_t^{avr} = \frac{1}{10} \frac{S_t}{n-1}$

The initiator, U_n, generates $n-1$ weights $w_1, \ldots, w_{n-1}$. Each w_i value reflects the $U_n's$ subjective trust level in user U_i. U_n initializes the accumulated variable, A, to 1, encrypts each w_i value by means of, e.g., the Paillier cryptosystem [1] as $E(w_i) = g^{w_i} h^{r_{n,i}} (mod\ N^2)$, composes a Trust Vector $TV = [E(w_1) .. E(w_{n-1})]$ and sends the message $M_t = (TV, A)$ to U_1. Here, as in the AP case, p, q are large prime numbers which compose the Paillier cryptosystem, $N = (p-1)(q-1)$, and g and h are properly chosen parameters of the Paillier cryptosystem. $r_{n,i}$ is a random degree of h chosen by U_n for each U_i from C. Note that the AP protocol is a private case of the WAP protocol where all weights w_i are equal to 1.

As in the AP case, the M_t message is received by the community users in the prescribed order. Each U_i user encrypts its weighted trust in U_t as $E(T_i) = E(w_i)^{T_i} E(\bar{0})$ and accumulates it in the accumulated variable A (lines 6–10). Note that multiplying by the random encryption of zero $E(\bar{0})$ ensures semantic security of the WAP protocol since the user's output cannot be distinguished from a simulated random string. As a result, the initiator, U_n, receives the M_t message and decrypts the value accumulated in A as the weighted sum of trust $S_t = D(A) = \sum_{i=1}^{n-1} w_i T_i$. Therefore, the average trust is equal to $wT_t^{avr} = 1/10 \sum_{i=1}^{n} w_i T^i$. Proposition 2 proves the privacy of the weighted average trust wT_t^{avr} in the U_t user by the community users in a computationally secure manner.

Proposition 2. Assume that an honest but curious adversary corrupts at most k users out of a community of n users, $k < n$. Then, WAP privately computes wT^{avr}, the average weighted trust in user U_t.

Proof. The proof is similar to the proof of Proposition 1. View of adversary includes the input of compromised users $T_{i_1}, \ldots, T_{i_k}$, trust vector TV, and the accumulated variable, A. Each compromised user U_{i_j} from I receives $TV = [E(w_{i_j}), E(w_{i_{j+1}}) \ldots, E(w_n)]$ and $A = \prod_{i=1}^{i_j} E(w_i)^{T_i} E(\bar{0})$.

A simulator for the adversary simulates $view_I^{WAP}$ as follows. The simulator input $T_{i_1}, \ldots, T_{i_k}$ is the same as the input of the compromised users. A simulator chooses at random $v_1, \ldots, v_n$ according to a distribution, W, of weights, and $\widetilde{T}_1, \ldots, \widetilde{T}_n$ according to a distribution, D, of trust values. Here $\widetilde{T}_{i_1} = T_{i_1}, \ldots, \widetilde{T}_{i_k} = T_{i_k}$. Due to the semantic security of the homomorphic cryptosystem, the encrypted random values $E(v_1), \ldots, E(v_n)$ are indistinguishable from the encrypted correct weights $E(w_{i_1}), \ldots, E(w_{i_n})$.

The randomization of any $U_i - th$ user output is performed by multiplying its secret $w_i^{T_i}$ by the random encryption of a zero string $E(\bar{0})$. Given $E(w)$, the two values $E(w)^T$ and $E(u)$, where u is chosen at random from the distribution of wT, can be distinguished since T is chosen from a small domain of trust values. Given $E(w)$, the values $E(w)^T E(\bar{0})$ are distributed identically to an encryption $E(w)^T = E(wT \mod N)$. Based on the semantic security of the homomorphic cryptosystem, $E(u)$ and $E(wT)$ cannot be distinguished even given $E(w)$. $\qquad\square$

WAP uses $O(n)$ messages each of length $O(n)$.

Protocols for removal of outliers

The protocols for outliers removal are introduced in this section. The Public Key Encryption Based Protocol $PKEBP$ produces a vector of the exact trust values. As a result, the initiator, U_n, can evaluate the correct trust range by removing the outliers that provide extremely high or low trust feedback. $PKEBP$ preserves user privacy in a case where the adversary cannot corrupt the initiator and several users at the same time.

The generalized Commutative Encryption Based Protocol ($CEBP$) relaxes this limitation and privately computes the exact trust values contributed by each community user, even in the case when an adversary can corrupt the initiator and several users at the same time.

Public Key Encryption Based Protocol PKEBP

Denote the encryption algorithm used in this scheme by E and the decryption algorithm by D. U_n generates a pair (k, s) of public-private keys. Then U_n publishes its decryption public key k, while the private decryption key s is kept secret.

The Public Key Encryption Based Protocol $PKEBP$ is performed in two rounds (Algorithm 3, Figure 1). At the initialization stage U_n initializes the $n - 1$-entry vector $TV[1 .. n - 1]$ and sends it to the community of users in the prescribed order in the $M_t = (TV[1 .. n - 1])$ message (Algorithm 3, lines 1–2 and Figure 1, Round 1).

Algorithm 3 Vector Protocol $PKEBP$.

1: **Initialization:**
2:     U_n initializes $TV =! [1 .. n - 1]$
3: **Round 1:**
4:     U_n sends $M_t = TV[1 .. n - 1]$ to C
5:     FOR $i = 1 \ldots (n - 1)$
6:         $TV[i] = E(T_i)$
7:     END FOR
8: **Round 2:**
9:     FOR $i = 1 \ldots (n - 1)$
10:         $random\ \pi : swap(TV[i], TV[i_j])$
11:     END FOR
12: **Upon $M_t = (TV[1 .. n - 1])$ reception at U_n:**
13:     $D(M) = [T_1, .. T_{n-1}]$

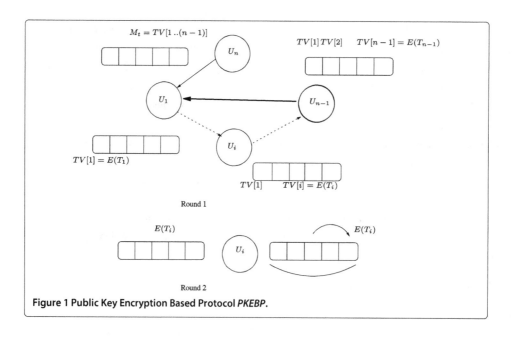

$M_t = TV[1..(n-1)]$

$TV[1]\, TV[2] \quad TV[n-1] = E(T_{n-1})$

U_n

U_1

U_{n-1}

U_i

$TV[1] = E(T_1)$

$TV[1] \qquad TV[i] = E(T_i)$

Round 1

$E(T_i)$ $\qquad\qquad\qquad\qquad\qquad\qquad E(T_i)$

U_i

Round 2

Figure 1 Public Key Encryption Based Protocol *PKEBP*.

In the first round, on reception of M_t each user, U_i, encrypts its trust, T_i, by k in the corresponding $TV[i]'s$ entry as $E(T_i)$, and sends the updated message M_t to the next user (Algorithm 3, lines 3–7).

The second round of the *PKEBP* protocol is performed when the updated $TV[1..n-1]$ vector returns from U_{n-1} to the user U_1 (see Algorithm 3, lines 8–11 and Figure 1, Round 2). Note that the TV vector does not visit the initiator U_n after execution of the first round. Each user, U_i, performs a random permutation of its $i-th$ entry with a randomly chosen $i_j - th$ entry during the second round. After that, the newly updated M_t vector-message is sent to the next U_{i+1} user (Algorithm 3, lines 8–11).

The result of round 1 is a sequence of encrypted elements $(E(T_1), \ldots, E(T_{n-1}))$ while the result of round 2 is a sequence $TV[1..n-1] = (E(T_1^*), \ldots, E(T_{n-1}^*))$. The multi-set $T_1, \ldots, T_{n-1}$ is identical to the multi-set $T_1^*, \ldots, T_{n-1}^*$. The sequence $T_1, \ldots, T_{n-1}$ is permuted to $T_1^*, \ldots, T_{n-1}^*$ by a permutation π, which is computed in a distributed manner by all community members (Algorithm 3, line 10). Thus, by applying the decryption procedure, all encrypted trust values $T_1, \ldots, T_{n-1}$ are revealed (Algorithm 3, lines 12–13). Moreover, the random permutation π performed at the second round preserves the unlinkability of user identities.

Proposition 3 proves the privacy of the *PKEBP* protocol.

Proposition 3. *PKEBP* performs computationally secure computation of exact private trust values assuming that an adversary cannot corrupt the initiator and several users at the same time.

Proof sketch. Case 1: $U_n \notin I$. We argue that *PKEBP* is private by showing that an adversary that controls a set of compromised users does not learn any information on the trust values of other users. We achieve that by showing a *simulator* that, given the input of compromised users, can simulate the messages that these users receive as part of the protocol. Therefore, protocol messages do not give users in I any information on users outside of I. Assume that the set I of compromised users includes k members $I = \{U_{i_1}, \ldots, U_{i_k}\}$, while the uncompromised users are $U_{i_{k+1}}, \ldots, U_{i_n}$. The view of users in I includes the input of compromised users $T_{i_1}, \ldots, T_{i_k}$ and trust vectors TV. Each compromised user U_{i_j} from I receives the TV vector with partially permuted entries.

A simulator for the adversary simulates this view as follows. The simulator input is the same as the input of compromised users and it contains the trust values of the compromised users $T_{i_1}, \ldots, T_{i_k}$ and the set of their permuted indexes $i_{j1}, \ldots i_{jk}$. The simulator chooses a random value, α_{i_ℓ}, for any user $U_\ell \notin I$ from the distribution D of trust values. The simulator sets $\alpha_\ell = T_\ell$ and computes $E(\alpha_j)$ for $\ell = k+1, \ldots, n$. Due to the semantic security of the homomorphic cryptosystem [24,32], the simulator cannot distinguish between the encryption of the correct trust values and the encryption of simulated random variables, $E(\alpha_j)$, of uncompromised users, U_j, chosen from the distribution, D, of trust values.

Case 2: $\{U_n\} = I$. In this case, the view of U_n consists of the TV with the randomly permuted entries. TV includes the sequence of the randomly permuted exact trust values, decrypted by the secret key, s. We prove the privacy of $PKEBP$ by showing a simulator that, given a $PKEBP$ output sequence $T_{i_1}, \ldots, T_{i_{n-1}}$ of the exact trust values, can simulate the TV as U_n receives it as a part of the protocol. A simulator for the compromised U_n simulates this view as follows. The simulator input is the multi-set $T_1, \ldots, T_n$ of the exact trust values that have been decrypted by $U_n's$ public key, s. The simulator chooses a random permutation and permutes the received values. Due to the random permutation, π, performed by each community user, the simulator cannot distinguish between the simulated sequence $T_{j1}, \ldots, T_{j_{n-1}}$ and the correct output of the $PKEBP$.

As a result, given a multi-set of the exact trust values, U_n cannot link these values to the users that contributed them. □

$PKEBP$ uses $O(n)$ messages each of length $O(n)$.

Generating the average trust level in the presence of semi-malicious users is based on the algorithm suggested in [19]. Let us define by U, the multi-set of non corrupted users which provide correct feedback, and by V, the multi-set of all users participating in the trust computation process. According to [19] the following requirement must be satisfied in our model: $|V - U| \leq J$ and $|V| \geq 2J$ for a certain J value. Then the range of the correct trust values, $range(U)$, contains the subset $reduce^J(V)$ of V. Here $reduce^J(V)$ is received from the V multi-set of all (correct and extremely low/high) trust values, by deleting the J smallest and J largest values, respectively.

If an adversary can corrupt the initiator and several users at the same time, a different protocol is required. The generalized Commutative Encryption Based Protocol $CEBP$ is presented in the next subsection.

Commutative Encryption Based Protocol CEBP

The $CEBP$ we propose, uses *commutative encryption* as a building block. An encryption scheme is commutative if a ciphertext that is encrypted by several keys can be decrypted regardless of the order of decryption keys. Formally, denote the encryption algorithm by E and the decryption algorithm by D. The encryption scheme is commutative if for every plaintext message m and every two keys k_1, k_2 if $c = E_{k_1}(E_{k_2}(m))$

then $m = D_{k_1}(D_{k_2}(c))$ (note that for any encryption scheme $m = D_{k_2}(D_{k_1}(c))$. One possible candidate for a commutative encryption scheme is the Pohlig-Hellman scheme [33].

The basic idea of *CEBP* is for each user to encrypt all the trust values and then decrypt and permute them at the same time so that an adversary cannot associate decrypted trust values with the users that published their encryption. The *CEBP* protocol is executed in three rounds (Algorithm 4). Each round passes sequentially from the first user U_n to the last U_{n-1}.

Algorithm 4 Commutative Encryption Based Protocol *CEBP*.

1: **Round 1:**

2:   U_n chooses parameters for El-Gamal encryption p, q, g, k_n.

3:   U_n initializes an empty vector $TV[1, \ldots, n-1]$.

4:   U_n sends $p, q, g, g^{k_n} \bmod p$ and $TV[1, \ldots, n-1]$ to U_1.

5:   FOR $i = 1, \ldots, n-1$

6:   U_i chooses four Pohlig-Hellman key pairs $(a_i^1, b_i^1), (a_i^2, b_i^2), (\alpha_i^1, \beta_i^1), (\alpha_i^2, \beta_i^2)$.

7:   U_i sets $TV[i] = \left(g^{k_i a_i^1} \bmod p, (T_i g^{k_i k_n})^{\alpha_i^1} \bmod p \right)$.

8:   U_i sends p, q, g, k_n and $TV[1, \ldots, n-1]$ to U_{i+1}.

9:   END FOR

10: **Round 2:**

11:   U_n sends $TV[1, \ldots, n-1]$ to U_1.

12:   FOR $i = 1, \ldots, n-1$

13:   FOR $j = 1, \ldots, n-1, j \neq i$

14:   U_i sets $TV[j, 1] = (TV[j])^{\alpha_i^1 a_i^1} \bmod p$.

15:   U_i sets $TV[j, 2] = (TV[j])^{\alpha_i^2 a_i^2} \bmod p$.

16:   END FOR

17:   U_i sets $TV[i, 1] = (TV[j])^{\alpha_i^1} \bmod p$.

18:   U_i sets $TV[j, 2] = (TV[j])^{\alpha_i^2} \bmod p$.

19:   U_i sends $TV[1, \ldots, n-1]$ to U_{i+1}.

20:   END FOR

21: **Round 3:**

22:   U_n sends $TV[1, \ldots, n-1]$ to U_1.

23:   FOR $i = 1, \ldots, n-1$

24:   FOR $j = 1, \ldots, n-1$

25:   U_i sets $TV[j, 1] = (TV[j])^{\beta_i^1 b_i^1} \bmod p$.

26:   U_i sets $TV[j, 2] = (TV[j])^{\beta_i^2 b \sum_i^2} \bmod p$.

27:   U_i randomly permutes the $n-1$ elements of TV.

28:   END FOR

29:   U_i sends $TV[1, \ldots, n-1]$ to U_{i+1}.

30:   END FOR

31: **Epilogue:**

32:   U_n decrypts $TV[1, \ldots, n-1]$, thus obtaining the multi-set of trust values.

The first round begins with the initiator, U_n choosing and publishing a public key. Every other user selects a symmetric key for a commutative encryption scheme. All the users encrypt their trust values both with their keys and with the public key of U_n. Encryption with the initiator's public key prevents an adversary that does not control the initiator, U_n, from obtaining the multi-set of trust values. After the first round, for every $i = 1, \ldots, n-1$, the i-th entry in the trust vector, TV, includes the trust value of U_i encrypted by both the public key of U_n and the symmetric key of U_i.

In the second round each user encrypts all entries in TV entries in such a way that at the end of the second round the i-th entry is the trust value of U_i encrypted by the keys of $U_1, U_2, \ldots, U_n$. Finally, in the third round, for every $i = 1, \ldots, n - 1$, U_i decrypts every entry using its own symmetric key and randomly permutes the entries of TV. At the end of round 3 the trust vector contains all the trust values, encrypted by the public key of U_n and permuted. By decrypting all the entries in TV, U_n obtains the vector of all trust values.

We use El-Gamal encryption [34] as the initiator's public key scheme. The symmetric scheme for users $U_1, \ldots, U_{n-1}$ is Pohlig-Hellman. Both the Pohlig-Hellman and the El-Gamal schemes are implemented over the same group, which is defined as follows. Let p be a large prime, such that $p - 1$ has a large prime factor, q. Let $g \in \mathbb{Z}_p^*$ be an element of order q in $\mathbb{Z}_p^*$. In a Pohlig-Hellman scheme, the key is a pair $a, b \in \mathbb{Z}_{p-1}^*$ such that $ab \equiv 1 \bmod (p-1)$. A plaintext $m \in \mathbb{Z}_p$ is encrypted by $c \equiv m^a \bmod p$ and a ciphertext is decrypted by $m \equiv c^b \bmod p$. In an El-Gamal scheme, the private key is $a \in \{0, \ldots, q-1\}$, the public key is $g^a \bmod p$ and a plaintext $m \in \mathbb{Z}_p$ is encrypted by the pair $(g^b \bmod p, g^{ab} \cdot m \bmod p)$. We refer to the two parts of an El-Gamal encryption as two *components*.

By using Pohlig-Hellman and El-Gamal encryption schemes over the same group we ensure that the security of $CEBP$ can be reduced to the hardness of the Decisional Diffie-Hellman (DDH) problem [35]. The DDH problem is to distinguish between the two ensembles $(g^x \bmod p, g^y \bmod p, g^z \bmod p)$ and $(g^x \bmod p, g^y \bmod p, g^{xy} \bmod p)$. The hardness assumption of DDH is that no probabilistic, polynomial time algorithm can distinguish between these two probability ensembles with non-negligible probability.

The details of the protocol follow.

The initiator begins round 1 (lines 1–9) by choosing parameters for El-Gamal encryption and distributes its public key $g^{k_n} \bmod p$. Every other user U_i ($i = 1, \ldots, n - 1$) chooses four random and independent pairs of Pohlig-Hellman keys (a_i^1, b_i^1), (a_i^2, b_i^2), (α_i^1, β_i^1), (α_i^2, β_i^2). U_i uses the El-Gamal public key to encrypt its trust value, T_i. The result is $(g^{k_i} \bmod p, T_i g^{k_i k_n} \bmod p)$, where U_i chooses k_i randomly in the range $0, \ldots, q - 1$. U_i proceeds to encrypt the El-Gamal encryption of T_i with its Pohlig-Hellman keys. Each of the two components of the El-Gamal encryption is encrypted by one distinct Pohlig-Hellman key. The result is

$$\left(g^{k_i a_i^1} \bmod p, \; (T_i g^{k_i k_n})^{a_i^2} \bmod p \right).$$

U_i completes the round by publishing this value in $TV[i]$. We think of $TV[i]$ as having two components, $TV[i, 1]$ and $TV[i, 2]$. U_i stores $g^{k_i a_i^1} \bmod p$ in $TV[i, 1]$ and stores $(T_i g^{k_i k_n})^{a_i^2} \bmod p$ in $TV[i, 2]$.

In round 2, every user, U_i, $i = 1, \ldots, n - 1$ makes sure that every entry in $TV[]$ is encrypted with all four of its Pohlig-Hellman encryption keys (where two of the keys are used to encrypt the left component and two are used to encrypt the right component). Thus, U_i encrypts $TV[i]$ with α_i^1 and α_i^2 and encrypts $TV[j]$ for any $j \neq i$ with a_i^1, a_i^2, α_i^1 and α_i^2. After the second round the entry $TV[i]$ holds the value:

$$\left(g^{k_i \cdot \alpha_1^1 a_1^1 \cdots \alpha_{n-1}^1 a_{n-1}^1} \bmod p, \; (T_i g^{k_i k_n})^{\alpha_1^2 a_1^2 \cdots \alpha_{n-1}^2 a_{n-1}^2} \bmod p\right).$$

In round 3, the users both decrypt and permute all the values. Each user decrypts all values using both its pairs of Pohlig-Hellman keys (lines 20–27) and then randomly permutes the resulting vector of values. Due to the commutative property of the scheme, the initiator, U_n, holds all the trust values at the end of round 3. However, the random permutation each user applies to the encrypted values in round 3 ensures that even if only a pair of users is not compromised, the decrypted trust values are randomly permuted in relation to their associated users.

Proposition 4. Assume that the DDH problem is hard and assume that an honest but curious adversary corrupts at most k users out of a community of n users, $k \leq n$. If the trust values of all the users are in the sub-group generated by g, then, *CEBP* privately computes the set of all trust values of community users.

Proof sketch. If the adversary controls at least $n - 1$ users, including the initiator, then the protocol is trivially private, since the output reveals the exact trust values of every user, and thus any protocol does not add information. If the adversary does not control the initiator then the protocol is private because all trust values are encrypted by the initiator's public key throughout the protocol. Since the El-Gamal encryption scheme is semantically secure, given the hardness of DDH problem, it is easy to argue privacy.

Therefore, the most interesting case is when $k \leq n - 2$ and the adversary controls the initiator. To prove privacy we define a simulator that is given the adversary's input and output (which includes the set of trust values) and simulates the adversary's view of protocol messages.

Each message in our protocol consists of the trust vector TV. Each entry in this vector is a pair of elements in $\mathbb{Z}_p^*$. Thus, the whole view of the adversary can be written as $e_1, \ldots, e_m$, where $e_i \in \mathbb{Z}_p^*$ for every $i = 1, \ldots, m$. The value of m is at most $O(n^2)$ because the number of elements in TV is $2(n - 1)$ and the adversary receives a message with TV in it at most $n - 2$ times for each of the three rounds.

Note that each element e_i is obtained by raising g to a power η_i that depends on the input and random coin tosses of each participant. The simulator generates a simulated view $f_1, \ldots, f_m$ as follows. If η_i is determined by the input and coin tosses of the adversary, then the simulator who has access to this input and coin tosses sets $f_i = e_i$. However, if η_i is generated at least partially by an uncorrupted node then the simulator independently chooses a random element $\zeta_i \in \{0, \ldots, q - 1\}$ and sets $f_i = g^{\zeta_i}$.

To prove that the simulator's view is computationally indistinguishable from the real-world view, we construct a series of hybrid ensembles $H_0, \ldots, H_m$, such that H_0 is the real world view $e_1, \ldots, e_m$ and for every $i = 1, \ldots, m$ we define $H_i \stackrel{\triangle}{=} f_1, \ldots, f_i, e_{i+1}, \ldots, f_m$. Essentially, H_m is the view of the simulator.

We can show that for every i, if H_i can be computationally distinguished from H_{i+1} then the DDH assumption is false. Since we assume that DDH is a hard problem we have that

H_i and H_{i+1} are computationally indistinguishable and since m is of polynomial size in n, we have that H_0 is indistinguishable from H_m, completing the proof.   □

The protocol requires $O(n)$ messages, each of length $O(n)$ and the computation complexity for each participant in the scheme is $O(n)$.

Multiple Private Keys Protocol *MPKP*

The *AP* and *WAP* protocols introduced in the previous sections carry out private trust computation assuming that the initiator U_n is not compromised and does not share its private key with other users. In the rest of this work assume that any community user, including U_n, may be compromised by a poly-bounded k-listening curious adversary.

The generalized Multiple Private Keys Protocol *MPKP* copes with this problem and outputs the average trust. The idea of the *MPKP* protocol is as follows. During the initialization stage the U_n user initializes all entries of trust vector, *TV*, and accumulated vector, *AV*, to 1, sets the accumulated variable A to 1, and sends the $M_t = (TV, AV, A)$ message to the first community user U_1 as in the previous protocols. During the first round of the *MPKP* protocol execution each user, U_i, randomly fragments its secret trust, T_i, to a sum of $n - 1$ shares, encrypts the corresponding share by the public key of each U_j, $j = 1 .. n - 1$ user and accumulates its encrypted shares (multiplying each of them with the corresponding entries) in the accumulated vector, *AV*. After execution of the first round, the updated *AV* vector does not return to the initiator U_n. The *AV* vector visits each community user, while each U_i opens the $i - th$ entry (that is encrypted by $U_i - th$ public key) revealing a sum of decrypted shares, encrypts this sum by the public key of the initiator U_n, accumulates this sum in the accumulated variable ,A, and deletes the $i - th$ entry of the *AV* vector.

A detailed description of the *MPKP* protocol follows. Assume that each community user, U_i, $i = 1 .. n - 1$ generates its personal pair (P_i^+, P_i^-) of private and public keys. Denote by E_i and D_i the encryption and decryption algorithms produced by U_i. The private key, P_i^+, is kept secret, while the public key, P_i^-, is shared with all other users $U_1, \ldots, U_{i-1}, U_{i+1} \ldots U_n$. As in the previous schemes, the cryptosystem must be homomorphic. An additional requirement is that the homomorphism modulus, m, must be identical for all users. One possibility is to use the Benaloh cryptosystem [28,36] for which many different key pairs are possible for every homomorphism modulus. The system works as follows. Select two large primes, p, q, such that: $N \overset{\triangle}{=} pq$, $m | p - 1$, $\gcd(m, (p-1)/m) = 1$ and $\gcd(m, q - 1) = 1$, which implies that m is odd. The density of such primes along appropriate arithmetic sequences is large enough to ensure efficient generation of multiple p, q (see [36] for details). Select $y \in \mathbb{Z}_N^*$ such that $y^{\phi(N)/m} \not\equiv 1 \bmod N$. The public key is (N, y), and encryption of $M \in \mathbb{Z}_m$ is performed by choosing a random $u \in \mathbb{Z}_m^*$ and sending $y^M u^m \bmod N$. In order to decrypt, the holder of the secret key computes at a preprocessing stage $T_M \overset{\triangle}{=} y^{M\phi(N)/m} \bmod N$ for every $M \in \mathbb{Z}_m$. It should be noted that m is small enough such that m exponentiations can be performed. Decryption of z is performed by computing $z^{\phi(N)/n} \bmod N$ and finding the unique T_M to which it is equal.

The *MPKP* is performed in two rounds (Algorithm 5). The initialization procedure is shown in lines 1–4. The first round is the accumulation round, where all users share their secret trust T_i values with other users. Upon reception of a message, M_t, each user, U_i, proceeds as follows: (a) U_i chooses $r_1^i, \ldots, r_{n-1}^i$ uniformly at random such that $T_i = \sum_{j=1}^{n-1} r_j^i$; (b) U_i encrypts each r_j^i, $j = 1 .. n - 1$ by the public key P_j^- of the U_j user and multiplies it by the current value stored in $j - th$ entry of AV. As a result, the output AV vector contains the accumulated product $\prod_{k=1}^{n-1} E_j(r_j^k)$ in each $j - th$ entry (lines 5–12).

Algorithm 5 Multiple Private Keys Protocol MPKP.

1: **MPKP Initialization:**
2:    U_n generates $TV = [1 .. 1]$
3:    U_n sets $AV = [1 .. 1], A = 1$ and $M_t = (TV, AV, A)$
4:    U_n sends M_t to U_1
5: **Round 1:**
6:    *for* $i = 1 \ldots (n - 1)$
7:      $T_i = \sum_{j=1}^{n-1} r_j^i$
8:      *for* $j = 1 \ldots (n - 1)$
9:        $AV[j] = AV[j] E_j(r_j^i)$
10:     *end for*
11:     U_i sends M_t to U_{i+1}
12:   *end for*
13: **Round 2:**
14:   *for* $i = 1 \ldots (n - 1)$
15:     $D_i(AV[i]) = \sum_{j=1}^{n-1} r_i^j$
16:     $A = A E_n(\sum_{j=1}^{n-1} r_i^j)$
17:     Delete $AV[i]$
18:   *end for*
19: **Upon** $M_t = (A)$ **reception at** U_n:
20:   $A = \prod_{i=1}^{n-1} E_n(\sum_{j=1}^{n-1} r_i^j)$
21:   $S_t = D_n(A)$
22:   $T_t^{avr} = \frac{S_t}{n-1}$

In the second round, on reception of message M_t, each user, U_i, decrypts the M_t message and decrypts the corresponding $i - th$ entry by its private key, P_i^+, computes the $\sum_{j=1}^{n-1} r_i^j$ sum, encrypts it by the $U_n's$ public key, P_n^-, as $E_n(\sum_{j=1}^{n-1} r_i^j)$, accumulates this sum in the accumulated variable, A, deletes the $i - th$ entry and sends the updated TV vector to the next U_{i+1} user. Note that the partial sum $\sum_{j=1}^{n-1} r_i^j$ that U_i decrypts reveals no information about correct trust values. As a result of the second round the initiator U_n receives $A = \prod_{i=1}^{n-1} E_n(\sum_{j=1}^{n-1} r_i^j)$ (lines 13–19). U_n decrypts $\prod_{j=1}^{n-1} E_n(r_i^j)$, and computes the sum of trusts as $S_t = \sum_{i=1}^{n-1} \sum_{j=1}^{n-1} r_i^j$. Actually, the average trust T^{avr} is equal to $\frac{S_t}{n}$ (lines 20–22). Proposition 4 states the privacy of the MPKP protocol. The communication complexity of the MPKP protocol is $O(n)$ messages, each of length $O(n)$.

Proposition 5. *MPKP performs computationally secure computation of the exact private trust values in the Additive Reputation System. No restriction is imposed on the initiator U_n.*

The last introduced protocol is the *MPWP* for the weighted average trust wT_t^{avr} computation. The idea of the *MPWP* is as follows. During the initialization stage the U_n user generates a vector, TV, such that each $i - th$ entry contains the $U_i - th$ weight w_i encrypted by the $U_n - th$ public key. U_n sends TV and a $(n-1) \times (n-1)$ matrix, SM, with all entries initialized to 1 to the first community user, U_1, as in the previous protocols. During the first round of the $MPWP$ execution each U_i computes its encrypted weight in the power of its secret trust $E_n(w_i)^{Ti}$, multiplies it by a randomly chosen number (bias) z_i, and accumulates the product in the accumulated entry (by multiplying the entry by the obtained result). In addition, U_i fragments its bias, z_i, into $n - 1$ shares, encrypts each $j - th$ share by the public key of U_j, and inserts it in the $j - th$ location of $i - th$ matrix row. At the end of the first round U_n decrypts the total biased weighted trust. The total random bias is removed during the second round of the $MPWP$ execution when each U_j decrypts the entries of $j - th$ matrix column, encrypts the sum of these values by the public key of the initiator, accumulates it in an accumulation variable, A, and deletes the $j - th$ column.

The details follow. The initiator, U_n, starts the first round by generating the encryption of the $n - 1$ entries trust vector, $TV = [E_n(w_1) .. E_n(w_{n-1})]$. Note, that each weight w_i is encrypted by the $U_n - th$ public key, P_n^-. In addition, U_n initializes to 1 each entry of the $(n-1) \times (n-1)$ matrix of shares SM. The M_t^w message sent by U_n to the community users is $M = (TV, SM)$. Upon the TV vector reception each U_i user proceeds as follows: (a) U_i computes $E_n(w_i)^{Ti} \cdot z_i$. Here z_i is a randomly generated by U_i number that provides the secret bias. (b) U_i accumulates its encrypted weighted trust in the accumulated variable A by setting $A = A \cdot E_n(w_i)^{Ti} \cdot z_i$. After that, the $i - th$ entry of TV is deleted. (c) U_i shares z_i in the $i - th$ row of the SM shares matrix as $SM[i] [] = [E_1(z_i^1) .. E_{n-1}(z_i^{n-1})]$. At the end of the first round U_n receives the $TV[]$ entry that is equal to the biased product $BT = \prod_{j=1}^{n} E_n(w_i)^{Ti} z_i$, encrypted by its public key, and the updated shares matrix SM while $SM[i] [j] = E_j(z_i^j)$. Actually, the decryption procedure applied on the $TV[]$ vector outputs the decrypted sum $D(TV[]) = \sum_{i=1}^{n-1} w_i T_i + \sum_{i=1}^{n-1} z_i$. A second round is performed in order to subtract the random bias $\sum_{i=1}^{n-1} z_i$ from the correct weighted average trust wT^{avr}. The second round of the $MPWP$ is identical to the corresponding round of the $MPKP$. Upon reception of the SM matrix each user, U_i, decrypts the corresponding $i - th$ column $E_i(z_1^i) E_i(z_2^i) \ldots E_i(z_{n-1}^i)$, encrypted by all community users by $U_i - th$ public key, P_i^-. Each U_i, $i = 1 .. n - 1$ computes the sum of the partial shares $PSS_i = \sum_{j=1}^{n-1} z_j^i$, encrypts it by the $U_n - th$ public key, P_n^-, and accumulates it in the accumulated variable A. After that, $i - th$ $SM's$ column $SM[] [i]$ is deleted. As a result of the second round, the initiator, U_n, receives the accumulated variable, $A = \prod_{i=1}^{n-1} E_i(PSS_i)$. The encrypted bias, BT, is decrypted as $D(A) = \sum_{i=1}^{n-1} \sum_{j=1}^{n-1} z_j^i$.

Finally, the weighted average trust wT^{avr} is equal to $wT^{avr} = TV - A$. The private trust computation carried out by the $MPKP$ and the $MPWP$ protocols is preserved in the computationally secure manner due to the following reasons:

(a)   Each community user, U_i, fragments its trust, T_i, randomly into $n - 1$ shares (Algorithm 5, lines 6–8).

(b)   Each r_i^j encrypted by U_i by the $U_j - th$ public key, P_j^-, shared with each $U_j, j = 1, \ldots, n - 1$ user and accumulated in the TV vector, reveals no information about the exact T_i value to U_j (lines 9–14).

(c)   The decryption performed by each $U_i, i = 1, \ldots, n - 1$ by its private key, P_i^+, at the second round, outputs the sum of the partial shares, $D_i(TV[i]) = \sum_{j=1}^{n-1} r_j^i$ of all community users. In essence, the $\sum_{j=1}^{n-1} r_j^i$ value reveals no information about the secret trust values $T_1, \ldots, T_{i-1}, T_{i+1}, \ldots, T_{n-1}$.

(d)   The encryption $E_n(\sum_{j=1}^{n-1} r_j^i)$ of the partial shares sum performed by each U_i with the initiator U_n public key P_n^- and accumulated in A, can be decrypted by U_n only.

(e)   Assume a coalition $U_{j_i}, \ldots, U_{j_{i+k-1}}$ of at most $k < n$ curious adversarial users, possibly including the initiator U_n. Then the exact trust values revealed by the coalition, are the coalition members trust only. The privacy of the uncorrupted users is preserved by the homomorphic encryption scheme which generates for each user its secret private key, and by the random fragmentation of the secret trust.

In *MPWP*, $O(n)$ messages of length $O(n^2)$ are sent.

Conclusions

We derived a number of schemes for the private computation of trust in a given user by a community of users. Trust computation is performed in a fully distributed manner without involving a Trusted Authority. The proposed *AP* and *WAP* protocols are computationally secure, under the assumption of an uncompromised initiator, U_n. The *AP* and *WAP* protocols compute the average unweighted and weighted trust, respectively. The generalized *MPKP* and *MPWP* protocols relax the assumption that U_n is non-compromised. They carry out the private unweighted and weighted trust computation, respectively, without limitations imposed on U_n. The number of messages sent in the proposed protocols is $O(n)$ (large) messages.

The *PKEBP* and *CEBP* for the removal of outliers are presented as well. The protocols, introduced and analyzed in this paper, may be efficiently applied in the fully distributed environment without any trusted authority. Compared with other models, our schemes privately compute trust values with low communication overhead of $O(n)$ (large) messages in the simplified ring network topology. The schemes may be applied to complete topology systems when all network users are connected by direct links. The schemes may be attractive in the case when sending the linear number ($O(n)$) of large messages is better than sending a substantially larger number ($O(n^3)$) of possibly smaller messages. Moreover, the outliers removal (performed by the *CEBP* protocol) may be efficiently performed by the computationally restricted users when there are no resources for generating computationally expensive Interactive and Non Interactive Zero Knowledge Proofs. The schemes proposed in this paper are not restricted to trust computation. They may be extended to other models that compute privately sensitive information with only $O(n)$ messages.

In a case where the trust is represented by several values rather then a single value, one can apply our techniques to each such value independently.

Competing interests
The authors declare that they have no competing interests.

Authors' contributions
All authors read and approved the final manuscript.

Acknowledgments
Supported by Deutsche Telekom Laboratories at Ben-Gurion University of the Negev, Israel, Rita Altura Trust Chair in Computer Sciences, ICT Programme of the European Union under contract number FP7-215270 (FRONTS), Lynne and William Frankel Center for Computer Sciences, and the internal research program of the Sami Shamoon College of Engineering. The paper is a full version of two extended abstracts each describing a different part of the results [8,9].

Author details

[1]Department of Computer Science, Ben-Gurion University of the Negev, Beer-Sheva 84105, Israel. [2]Department of Communication Systems Engineering, Ben-Gurion University of the Negev, Beer-Sheva 84105, Israel. [3]Department of Software Engineering, Sami-Shamoon College of Engineering, Beer-Sheva 84100, Israel.

References

1. Paillier P (1999) Public-key cryptosystems based on composite degree residuosity classes. Advances in cryptology, EUROCRYPT 99. Springer Berlin Heidelberg, pp 223–238
2. Pavlov E, Rosenschein JS, Topol Z (2004) Supporting privacy in decentralized additive reputation systems. Trust Management, Springer Berlin Heidelberg, pp 108–119
3. Gudes E, Gal-Oz N (2009) A grubshtein: methods for computing trust and reputation while preserving privacy. Proceedings of 23rd Annual IFIP WG 11.3 Working Conference on Data and Applications Security, Springer Berlin Heidelberg, pp 291–298
4. Cramer R, Damgard IB, Buus Nielsen J (2001) Multiparty computation from threshold homomorphic encryption. In: EUROCRYPT '01: proceedings of the international conference on the theory and application of cryptographic techniques. Springer, Berlin Heidelberg, pp 280–299
5. Franklin M, Haber S (1996) Joint encryption and message-efficient secure computation. J Cryptology 9(4):217–232
6. Romero-Tris C, Castella-Roca J, Viejo A (2012) Multi-party private web search with untrusted partners. Security and Privacy in Communication Networks, Springer Berlin Heidelberg. pp. 261-280. In: Rajarajan M, et al., Proceedings of SecureComm 2011, pp 261–280
7. Damgard I, Faust S, Hazay C (2012) Secure two-party computation with low communication. In: Cramer R (ed) TCC 2012, LNCS 7194, pp 54–74
8. Dolev S, Gilboa N, Kopeetsky M (2010) Computing trust privately in the presence of curious and malicious users. In: Proceedings of the international symposium on stochastic models in reliability engineering, life sciences and operations management. Sami Shamoon College of Engineering, Beer-Sheva, Israel
9. Dolev S, Gilboa N, Kopeetsky M (2010) Computing multi-party trust privately in $O(n)$ time units sending one (possibly large) message at a time. In: Proceedings of 25-th Symposium On Applied Computing (SAC 2010), Sierre, Switzerland, pp 1460-1465
10. Asharov G, Jain A, Tromer E, Vaikuntanathan N, Wichs D (2012) Multiparty computation with low communication, computation and interaction via threshold FHE In: Proceedings of the EUROCRYPT 2012, pp 483–501. 2012
11. Beerliova-Trubmiova Z, Hirt M (2008) Perfectly-secure mpc with linear communication complexity. TCC2008, LNCS 4948: 213–230
12. Dimitriou T, Michalas A (2012) Multi-party trust computation in decentralized environment. In: Proceedings of the 5-th, IFIP international conference on New Technologies, Mobility and Security (NTMS 2012), Istanbul, Turkey
13. Dimitriou T, Michalas A (2013) Multi-party trust computation in decentralized environments in the presence of malicious adversaries. Ad Hoc Netw J. Elsevier, http://dx.doi.org/10.1016/j.adhoc.2013.04.013
14. Bachrach Y, Parnes A, Procaccia AD, Rosenschein JS (2009) Gossip-based aggregation of trust in decentralized reputation systems. Autonomous Agents, Multi-Agent Syst 19(2):153–172
15. Huynh TD, Jennings NR, Shadbolt NR (2004) An integrated trust and reputation model for open multi-agent systems. In: Proceedings of 16th European Conference on Artificial Intelligence, Spain, pp 18-22
16. Kinateder M, Rothermel K (2003) Architecture and algorithms for a distributed reputation system. Trust, Management, Vol. 2692, pp 1-16. Springer Berlin Heidelberg
17. Mui L, Mohtashemi M, Halberstadt A (2002) A computational model of trust and reputation. System Sciences, 2002. HICSS. Proceedings of the 35th Annual Hawaii International Conference on. IEEE/pp 1435–1439
18. Xiong L, Liu L (2004) PeerTrust: supporting reputation-based trust for peer-to-peer electronic communities. IEEE Trans. Knowl Data, Eng 16(7):843–857
19. Dolev D, Lynch NA, Pinter SS, Stark EW, Weihl WE (1986) Reaching approximate agreement in the presence of faults. J ACM 33(3):499–516
20. Pedersen TP (1991) Non-interactive and information theoretic secure verifiable secret sharing. Advances in Cryptology CRYPTO 91,. Springer Berlin Heidelberg, pp 129-140
21. Shamir A (1979) How to share a secret. Commun ACM 11(22):612–613
22. Hasan O, Brunie L, Bertino E, Shang N (2013) A decentralized privacy preserving reputation protocol for the malicious adversarial model. Inf Forensics Secur J 8(6):1-14
23. Dolev S, Ostrovsky R (2000) Xor-trees for efficient anonymous multicast and reception. ACM Trans Inf Syst Secur 3(2):63–84
24. Goldreich O (2000) Foundations of cryptography: volume 1, basic tools. Cambridge University Press, New York
25. Naccache D, Stern J (1998) A new public key cryptosystem based on higher residues. Proceedings of the 5th, ACM Conference on Computer and Communications Security, pp 59–66
26. Goldwasser S, Micali S (2004) Probabilistic encryption. J Comput Sci Contr Syst 28:108–119
27. Okamoto T, Uchiyama S (1998) A new public-key cryptosystem as secure as factoring. EUROCRYPT 1998: 308–318
28. Benaloh J (1994) Dense probabilistic encryption. In: Proceedings of the workshop on selected areas of cryptography. Kingston, pp 120–128
29. Boneh D, Goh E-J, Nissim K (2005) Evaluating 2-DNF formulas on ciphertexts. Theory of cryptography TCC, Springer Berlin Heidelberg, pp 325–341
30. Gentry C (2009) Fully homomorphic encryption using ideal lattices. In: Proceedings of the forty-first annual ACM symposium on Theory of computing STOC. ACM, New York, NY, USA, pp 169–178
31. Beimel A, Dolev S (2003) Buses for anonymous message delivery. J Cryptology 16(1):25–39

32. Goldreich O (2004) Foundations of cryptography: volume 2, basic applications. Cambridge University Press, New York
33. Pohlig SC, Hellman ME, (1978) An improved algorithm for computing logarithms in GF(p) and its cryptographic significance. IEEE Trans. Inf. Theory 24(1):106–110
34. El Gamal T (1985) A public key cryptosystem and a signature scheme based on discrete logarithms. In: Proceedings of CRYPTO 84 on Advances in cryptology. Springer-Verlag New York, Inc, New York, NY, USA, pp 10–18
35. Boneh D (1998) The decision Diffie-Hellman problem. In: Proceedings of Algorithmic Number Theory, Third International Symposium, ANTS-III., pp 48–63
36. Benaloh J (1987) Verifiable secret-ballot elections. Ph.D. thesis. Yale University

Permissions

The contributors of this book come from diverse backgrounds, making this book a truly international effort. This book will bring forth new frontiers with its revolutionizing research information and detailed analysis of the nascent developments around the world.

We would like to thank all the contributing authors for lending their expertise to make the book truly unique. They have played a crucial role in the development of this book. Without their invaluable contributions this book wouldn't have been possible. They have made vital efforts to compile up to date information on the varied aspects of this subject to make this book a valuable addition to the collection of many professionals and students.

This book was conceptualized with the vision of imparting up-to-date information and advanced data in this field. To ensure the same, a matchless editorial board was set up. Every individual on the board went through rigorous rounds of assessment to prove their worth. After which they invested a large part of their time researching and compiling the most relevant data for our readers.

The editorial board has been involved in producing this book since its inception. They have spent rigorous hours researching and exploring the diverse topics which have resulted in the successful publishing of this book. They have passed on their knowledge of decades through this book. To expedite this challenging task, the publisher supported the team at every step. A small team of assistant editors was also appointed to further simplify the editing procedure and attain best results for the readers.

Apart from the editorial board, the designing team has also invested a significant amount of their time in understanding the subject and creating the most relevant covers. They scrutinized every image to scout for the most suitable representation of the subject and create an appropriate cover for the book.

The publishing team has been an ardent support to the editorial, designing and production team. Their endless efforts to recruit the best for this project, has resulted in the accomplishment of this book. They are a veteran in the field of academics and their pool of knowledge is as vast as their experience in printing. Their expertise and guidance has proved useful at every step. Their uncompromising quality standards have made this book an exceptional effort. Their encouragement from time to time has been an inspiration for everyone.

The publisher and the editorial board hope that this book will prove to be a valuable piece of knowledge for researchers, students, practitioners and scholars across the globe.

List of Contributors

Davide Ceolin
The Network Institute, VU University Amsterdam, de Boelelaan, 1081a, 1081HV Amsterdam, The Netherlands

Archana Nottamkandath
The Network Institute, VU University Amsterdam, de Boelelaan, 1081a, 1081HV Amsterdam, The Netherlands

Wan Fokkink
The Network Institute, VU University Amsterdam, de Boelelaan, 1081a, 1081HV Amsterdam, The Netherlands

Robin Cohen
David R. Cheriton School of Computer Science, University of Waterloo, Waterloo, Canada

Jie Zhang
School of Computer Engineering, Nanyang Technological University, Singapore, Singapore

John Finnson
David R. Cheriton School of Computer Science, University of Waterloo, Waterloo, Canada

Thomas Tran
School of Electrical Engineering and Computer Science, University of Ottawa, Ottawa, Canada

Umar F Minhas
David R. Cheriton School of Computer Science, University of Waterloo, Waterloo, Canada

Michael Wißner
Human Centered Mutimedia, Augsburg University, Universitätsstr. 6a 86159, Augsburg, Germany

Stephan Hammer
Human Centered Mutimedia, Augsburg University, Universitätsstr. 6a 86159, Augsburg, Germany

Ekatarina Kurdyukova
Human Centered Mutimedia, Augsburg University, Universitätsstr. 6a 86159, Augsburg, Germany

Elisabeth André
Human Centered Mutimedia, Augsburg University, Universitätsstr. 6a 86159, Augsburg, Germany

Johannes Sänger
University of Regensburg, Universitätsstraße 31, 93053 Regensburg, Germany

Christian Richthammer
University of Regensburg, Universitätsstraße 31, 93053 Regensburg, Germany

Günther Pernul
University of Regensburg, Universitätsstraße 31, 93053 Regensburg, Germany

Jason RC Nurse
Cyber Security Centre, Department of Computer Science, University of Oxford, Oxford, UK

Ioannis Agrafiotis
Cyber Security Centre, Department of Computer Science, University of Oxford, Oxford, UK

Michael Goldsmith
Cyber Security Centre, Department of Computer Science, University of Oxford, Oxford, UK

Sadie Creese
Cyber Security Centre, Department of Computer Science, University of Oxford, Oxford, UK

Koen Lamberts
Department of Psychology, University of York, York, UK

Abdullah M Aref
School of Electrical Engineering and Computer Science (EECS), University of Ottawa, 800 King Edward Ave. Ottawa, Ontario, K1N 6N5, Canada

Thomas T Tran
School of Electrical Engineering and Computer Science (EECS), University of Ottawa, 800 King Edward Ave. Ottawa, Ontario, K1N 6N5, Canada

Heather Crawford
Department of Computer Sciences and Cybersecurity, Florida Institute of Technology, 150 W. University Blvd., Melbourne, FL 32901, USA

Karen Renaud
School of Computing Science, University of Glasgow, Sir Alwyn Williams Building, Lilybank Gardens, Glasgow G12 8QQ, UK

Kewen Wu
Department of Computer Science, University of Saskatchewan, Saskatoon, Canada

Zeinab Noorian
Department of Computer Science, University of Saskatchewan, Saskatoon, Canada

Julita Vassileva
Department of Computer Science, University of Saskatchewan, Saskatoon, Canada

Ifeoma Adaji
Department of Computer Science, University of Saskatchewan, Saskatoon, Canada

Audun Jøsang
University of Oslo, Oslo, Norway

Christophe Rosenberger
ENSICAEN, Caen, France

Laurent Miralabé
TazTag, Rennes, France

Henning Klevjer
Nets Norway AS, Oslo, Norway

Kent A Varmedal
Domeneshop AS, Oslo, Norway

Jérôme Daveau
CEV, Saint Lo, France

Knut Eilif Husa
Tellu, Asker, Norway

Petter Taugbøl
Vallvi, Oslo, Norway

Muhammad Al-Mutaz
Department of Computer Science, Missouri University of Science and Technology, Rolla, MO (65401), USA

Levi Malott
Department of Computer Science, Missouri University of Science and Technology, Rolla, MO (65401), USA

Sriram Chellappan
Department of Computer Science, Missouri University of Science and Technology, Rolla, MO (65401), USA

Shlomi Dolev
Department of Computer Science, Ben-Gurion University of the Negev, Beer-Sheva 84105, Israel

Niv Gilboa
Department of Communication Systems Engineering, Ben-Gurion University of the Negev, Beer-Sheva 84105, Israel

Marina Kopeetsky
Department of Software Engineering, Sami-Shamoon College of Engineering, Beer-Sheva 84100, Israel

CPSIA information can be obtained
at www.ICGtesting.com
Printed in the USA
LVHW061550040323
740933LV00006B/346